THE VIEW
FROM WITHIN

Published in the UK by Imprint Academic
PO Box 1, Thorverton EX5 5YX, UK

Published in the USA by Imprint Academic
Philosophy Documentation Center, Bowling Green State University
Bowling Green, OH 43403-0189, USA

ISBN 0 907845 25 8 (paperback)

ISSN 1355 8250 (*Journal of Consciousness Studies*, **6**, 2-3, 1999)

British Library Cataloguing in Publication Data
A catalogue record for this book is available from the British Library

The publishers would like to thank the Institute of Noetic Sciences
for their generous sponsorship of this project.

ALS OF INTEREST FROM IMPRINT ACADEMIC

Full details on: www.imprint-academic.com

Series Editor:
Professor J.A. Goguen, Computer Science, UCSD

Thomas Metzinger, ed.,
Conscious Experience

Shaun Gallagher and Jonathan Shear, ed.,
Models of the Self

Joseph A. Goguen, ed.,
Art and the Brain

Benjamin Libet, Anthony Freeman and J.K.B. Sutherland, ed.,
The Volitional Brain: Towards a neuroscience of free will

Rafael E. Núñez and Walter J. Freeman, ed.,
Reclaiming Cognition: The primacy of action, intention and emotion

Leonard D. Katz, ed.,
Evolutionary Origins of Morality: Cross-disciplinary perspectives

Nicholas Humphrey,
How to Solve the Mind–Body Problem

THE VIEW FROM WITHIN

First-person approaches to the
study of consciousness

edited by
Francisco J. Varela
and
Jonathan Shear

IMPRINT ACADEMIC

Contents

Francisco J. Varela and Jonathan Shear

First-person Methodologies: What, Why, How?

I: Inside–Outside: The Misleading Divide

By first-person events we mean the lived *experience* associated with cognitive and mental events. Sometimes terms such as 'phenomenal consciousness' and even 'qualia' are also used, but it is natural to speak of 'conscious experience' or simply 'experience'. These terms imply here that the process being studied (vision, pain, memory, imagination, etc.) appears as relevant and manifest *for* a 'self' or 'subject' that can provide an account; they have a 'subjective' side.

In contrast, third-person descriptions concern the descriptive experiences associated with the study of other natural phenomena. Although there are always human agents in science who provide and produce descriptions, the contents of such descriptions (i.e. of biochemical reactions, black holes or synaptic voltages) are not clearly or immediately linked to the human agents who come up with them. Their defining characteristics refer to properties of world events without a direct manifestation in the experiential-mental sphere; they can only be linked to this sphere indirectly (via the actual laboratory life, the modes of scientific communication and so on). Such 'objective' descriptions do have a subjective-social dimension, but this dimension is hidden within the social practices of science. The ostensive, direct reference is to the 'objective', the 'outside', the content of current science that we have today concerning various natural phenomena, such as physics and biology.

Now, recent history and philosophy of science often suggests that this apparent objectivity cannot be characterized as dealing with things-out-there, as independent of mental contents-in-here. Science is permeated by the procedural and social regulations that go under the name of scientific *method*, that permits the constitution of a corpus of shared knowledge about natural objects. The linchpin of this constitution is public verification and validation according to complex human exchanges. What we take to be objective is what can be turned from individual accounts into a body of regulated knowledge. This body of knowledge is inescapably in part subjective, since it depends on individual observation and experience, and partly objective, since it is constrained and regulated by the empirical, natural phenomena.

This brief reminder that the subjective is already implicit in the objective highlights how the received distinction between objective and subjective as an absolute

Journal of Consciousness Studies, **6**, No. 2–3, 1999, pp. 1–14

demarcation between inside and outside, needs to be closely scrutinized. *Mutatis mutandis*, dealing with subjective phenomena is not the same as dealing with purely *private* experiences, as is often assumed. The subjective is intrinsically open to inter-subjective validation, if only we avail ourselves of a method and procedure for doing so. One central purpose of this first-person methodologies Special Issue is, precisely, to survey some major current approaches that attempt to provide the basis for a *science of consciousness which includes first-person, subjective experience as an explicit and active component.*

II: First and Third: The Necessary Circulation

Setting the question as we just did, the next point to raise is what is the status of first-person accounts? In some basic sense, the answer cannot be given *a priori*, and it can only unfold from actually exploring this realm of phenomena, as is the case in the contributions presented herein. However let us state at the outset some thorny issues, in order to avoid some recurrent misunderstandings.

First, exploring first-person accounts is not the same as claiming that first-person accounts have some kind of *privileged* access to experience. No presumption of anything incorrigible, final, easy or apodictic about subjective phenomena needs to be made here, and to assume otherwise is to confuse the immediate character of the givenness of subjective phenomena with their mode of *constitution* and *evaluation*. Much wasted ink could have been saved by distinguishing the irreducibility of first-person descriptions from their epistemic status.

Second, a crucial point in this Special Issue has been to underline the need to overcome the 'just-take-a-look' attitude in regards to experience. The apparent familiarity we have with subjective life must give way in favour of the careful examination of what it is that we can and cannot have access to, and how this distinction is not rigid but variable. It is here that methodology appears as crucial: without a sustained examination we actually do not produce phenomenal descriptions that are rich and subtly interconnected enough in comparison to third-person accounts. The main question is: How do you actually *do* it? Is there evidence that it *can* be done? If so, with what *results*?

Third, it would be futile to stay with first-person descriptions in isolation. We need to harmonize and constrain them by building the appropriate *links* with third-person studies. In other words we are not concerned with yet another debate about the philosophical controversies surrounding the first-person/third-person split, (a large body of literature notwithstanding). To make this possible we seek methodologies that can provide an open link to objective, empirically based description. (This often implies an intermediate mediation, a second-person position, as we shall discuss below.) The overall results should be to move towards an integrated or global perspective on mind where neither experience nor external mechanisms have the final word. The global perspective requires therefore the explicit establishment of *mutual constraints*, a reciprocal influence and determination (Varela, 1996). In brief our stance in regards to first-person methodologies is this: don't leave home without it, but do not forget to bring along third-person accounts as well.

This down-to-earth *pragmatic* approach gives the tone to the contributions that follow. On the whole, what emerges from this material is that, in spite of all kinds of received ideas, repeated unreflectingly in recent literature of philosophy of mind and cognitive science, first-person methods are available and *can* be fruitfully brought to bear on a science of consciousness. The proof of the pudding is not in *a priori* arguments, but in actually pointing to explicit examples of practical knowledge, in case studies.

III: The Notion of Phenomenal Data

The notion of phenomenal data can provide a common first-person/third-person ground for the methodological questions just raised, and therefore a brief discussion of it is in order here, given its key role in this Special Issue. A large body of modern literature addresses the 'explanatory gap' between computational and phenomeno-logical mind,[1] to use Jackendoff's terminology (1987). The latter is variously phrased, as we already said, in terms of subjectivity, consciousness, or experience. It is important to examine these different concepts and see how they relate to the more basic one of *phenomenal data* (Roy *et al.*, 1998).

In spite of the variety of terminology being used, a consensus seems to have emerged that Thomas Nagel's expression 'what it is like to be' succeeds in capturing well what is at stake. Clearly 'what it is like to be' a bat or a human being refers to how things (everything) looks when being a bat or a human being. In other words this is just another way of talking about what philosophers have called phenomenality since the Presocratics. A phenomenon, in the most original sense of the word, is an appear-ance and therefore something relational. It is what something is for something else; it is a *being for* by opposition to a being in itself independently of its apprehension by another entity.

Phenomenality certainly is a crucial fact for the domain of living beings. It would for instance surely seem to be the case that an organism with a sonar system like the bat does not perceive what an organism equipped with a visual system like man can perceive: the external world presumably looks very different to both. Similarly, although to a lesser extent, the experience of two individuals belonging to the same species can be expected to differ. Accordingly, it is fair to say that — as advocates of the explanatory gap argument complain — cognitive science often appears to be a theory of mind that leaves phenomenality or subjectivity out, either because it does not attempt to account for it or because it fails to account for it adequately.

These notions need further refinement, however, to really capture the point at stake. And this is where the notion of consciousness needs to step in. The progress of cognitive science (as well as the development of psychoanalysis) has made familiar the idea that something might happen for a subject, and in that sense be subjective, but nevertheless not be accessible to this subject. We naturally describe such a case by saying that the subject is not conscious of the phenomenon in question. A distinction must therefore be introduced between conscious and non-conscious phenomena, or again between conscious and sub-personal subjectivity. The notion of consciousness

---

[1] We are using in this article a three-fold distinction between phenomenal, phenomenological and Phenomenology. The first, a broad and general term used in both third- and first-person discussion, refers to whatever is available for examination. It is defined in this section. 'Phenomenological' has been used repeatedly in a general sense to designate conscious experience and subjectivity (e.g. by R. Jackendoff, in his pioneering work, and by some of the contributors to this special issue).This broad use of the word is linked to the previous one, and is to be sharply distinguished from work based on the philosophical tradition of Phenomenology, where a 'phenomenological' description is necessarily based on 'reduction' as presented in the papers in Section II of this issue.

itself is clearly meant primarily to designate the fact that the subject knows about, is informed about, or in other words is aware of, the phenomenon.

It might be tempting to conflate the two concepts of phenomenal data and conscious subjectivity. But the notion of non-conscious or subpersonal phenomena argues against that move: there are, for example, numerous instances where we perceive phenomena pre-reflectively without being consciously aware of them, but where a 'gesture' or method of examination will clarify or even bring these pre-reflexive phenomena to the fore. What is being objected to here is the naive assumption that the demarcation line between the strictly subpersonal and the conscious is fixed.

It surely has not escaped the reader that this entire Issue is based on the conclusion (assumption) that lived experience is irreducible, that is, that phenomenal data cannot be reduced or derived from the third-person perspective. We are, of course, well aware that the issue is far from consensual,[2] and it would be superficial to try and settle it here. However, it is only fair to give the reader the three main bases on which the assumption of irreducibility of experience is cast.

First, to accept experience as a domain to be explored is to accept the evidence that life and mind includes that first-person dimension which is a trademark of our on-going existence. To deprive our scientific examination of this phenomenal realm amounts to either amputating human life of its most intimate domains, or else denying science explanatory access to it. In both cases the move is unsatisfactory.

Second, subjective experience refers to the level of the *user* of one's own cognitions, of intentions and doings, in everyday practices. I know that my movements are the products of coordinated series of muscle contractions. However, the activity of moving my hand operates on the emergent scale of motor plans that appear to me as motor *intentions* as an active agent-user, not the muscle tones that can only be seen from a third-person position. This practical dimension is what makes interaction with third-person accounts possible in the first place (and not an abstract armchair description so familiar in philosophy of mind).

Third, experience in human practices is the privileged entry point for *change* mediated by professional interventions of all kinds, such as education and learning, sports training, and psychotherapy. In all these domains there is abundant evidence not only that the realm of experience is essential for human activity and life involving the use of one's own mind, but that the experiential domain can be explored, as we see in transformations mediated by specific practices and human interactions in prescribed settings (training course, sports coaching, psychotherapeutic sessions). Again, we need to put into question the assumption that the demarcation line between the strictly subpersonal and conscious are fixed and given once and forever. First-person methodologies include as a fundamental dimension the claim that this is a movable line, and much can be done with the intermediate zone. Exploring the pre-reflexive represents a rich and largely unexplored source of information and data with dramatic consequences.

---

[2] For a recent survey of arguments pro and con, see Shear (1997).

IV: What the Reader Will Find in this Special Issue

Having covered the basic ground, it is now time to make a brief guided tour of the material presented in this Special Issue. We have retained three extant methodological traditions, which give rise to three sections:

- *Section I:* the *introspective* approach, derived from scientific psychology;
- *Section II:* the method of *phenomenological reduction*, derived from the philosophical tradition of Phenomenology and phenomenological psychology;
- *Section III:* the pragmatics of *meditation practices* derived from the Buddhist and Vedic traditions.

The opening article in Section I by Pierre Vermersch sets the tone for the entire enterprise. He traces the early history of the disciplined use of introspection in psychology back to the origins of scientific psychology, and the much maligned schools of Introspectionism linked to the names of Wundt and Titchener, among others. Vermersch's point is clear: when we go back to see what they actually did (instead of relying on secondary sources) we can hardly fault these researchers for their spirit of innovation, methodological rigour, or wealth of empirical observations. The question remains: why is it that they did not give rise to a whole tradition of work linking eventually to contemporary cognitive science? The answer is bound to be complex, but one of the key points Vermersch notes is that those researchers were tricked by the apparent simplicity of the task, which obscures the necessary subtle know-how, including the important role of mediation.

Claire Peugeot takes up where Vermersch leaves off, exploring a specific example that shows in detail how the difficulties appear, and what kind of methods can be fostered to overcome them. She has chosen to address a thorny but important issue: intuitive experience. The results she presents are a testimony that careful introspective methods are an essential component to explore the experiential.

Finally, in this Section we give voice to a more hands-on account of bodywork by Carl Ginsburg, where introspection plays a role, not as a research tool, but in the area of applied disciplines such as education, therapy, management and so on. In fact, it is these areas that embody the richest sources of practical knowledge about human experience articulated over the past half century. Ginsburg brings in some of the key elements of the how and the why of a client's interest in working with his/her lived experience in the tradition of somatic transformation initiated by Moshe Feldenkrais.

Section II is based on the most important western school of thinking where experience and consciousness is at the very heart: Phenomenology as inaugurated by Edmund Husserl at the turn of the century and elaborated in various directions since. The main purpose of Natalie Depraz's opening paper, however, is to expose the basis of the method that inaugurates phenomenology, phenomenological reduction. To the extent that reduction is linked to introspective gesture and that phenomenology is concerned with experiential content, the intercrossing between this philosophical tradition and introspective psychology is evident. Depraz shows how reduction is a practice that is oriented to the needs of philosophical analysis and yet interleaves with (phenomenological) psychology. The main difference between introspective psychology and phenomenology is one of intent. The psychologist is motivated by research, seeks protocols and objects that can be isolated in the laboratory, and also to establish empirical results that can be linked to neural correlates. The phenomenologist is interested in the same mental content in order to explore their broader meaning and place in ordinary human areas such as temporality, intersubjectivity and language.

From this perspective Francisco Varela tries to address the experience of present time consciousness in human temporality, with an eye for its bridges to natural science. What is central in this contribution is whether the phenomenal description can help us both validate and constrain the empirical correlates that are available with the modern tools of cognitive neuroscience and dynamical systems theory.

The work of William James is justly cited as a source for much of the revival of interest in the psychology of consciousness; it provides an introspectionism or phenomenology of its own kind. Andrew Bailey's contribution brings to light how this Jamesian approach to the first-person is manifest in his studies on inner time as 'transitional parts' of the stream of consciousness. The links and discrepancies with other methods highlighted in this special issue have yet to be drawn more precisely.

The contribution by Jean Naudin and his colleagues addresses analogous issues in the realm of human communication in psychiatry. Their point is that in particular the schizophrenic experience induces a form of reduction that the physician must work with in order to enter into his or her role as a therapist. Here is another case of human practices rather than research where first-person methods seem important.

In Section III Alan Wallace presents an account of the pragmatics of a fundamental practice in the Buddhist tradition, mindfulness sitting practice (samatha) and its gradual unfolding into its 'natural' state devoid of habitual conceptualizations (mahamudra). We can completely put aside in this Special Issue the motivation and values underlying such Buddhist practice and traditions. The point is to emphasize that for their own reasons the Buddhist traditions have accumulated a vast amount of expertise in training the mind and cultivating its ability for reflection and introspection. It has done so over centuries, and expressed some of its observation in terms that are not too far removed from either introspective psychology or phenomenological psychology (according to whom we read). It would be a great mistake of western chauvinism to deny such observations as data and their potential validity. The attempt to integrate Eastern meditation practices and their results into Western culture, however, raises serious problems of interpretation and empirical validation.

Jonathan Shear's and Ronald Jevning's contribution addresses precisely this issue. In it they examine reports of 'pure consciousness' experiences associated with Transcendental Meditation (TM) and Zen Buddhist meditation procedures in terms of cross-cultural, cross-tradition congruencies of the verbal reports, and of laboratory examination of their physiological correlates.

V: The Notion of a Method

We can at this point begin to see for all these traditions what a method is. At this first stage of approximation we can say that there are at least two main dimensions that need to be present in order for a method to count as such:

(1) Providing a clear *procedure* for accessing some phenomenal domain.
(2) Providing a clear means for an *expression and validation* within a community of observers who have familiarity with procedures as in (1).

Keeping in mind that the distinction between experiencing (following a procedure), and validation (following a regulated intersubjective exchange) is not an absolute one, the material presented can be outlined thus:

	Method	*Procedure*	*Validation*
1	Introspection	Attention during a defined task	Verbal accounts, mediated
2	Phenomenology	Reduction-suspension	Descriptive invariants
3	Meditation: Samatha; Mahamudra; Zen; TM	Sustained attention; uncontrived awareness; suspension of mental activity	Traditional accounts, scientific accounts

We should of course add that this table is only a cross-section of current knowledge, and there should be no hesitation to evaluate the methods' relative strengths and weakness. Tentatively we would at present evaluate them thus:

	Evaluation of procedure	*Evaluation of validation*
1	Medium, needs improvement	Medium, good use of protocols
2	Medium, needs improvement	Medium, some useful examples
3	Good, detailed methods	Historically rich, sometimes relies too much on inside accounts, some good scientific protocols, more needed

In short, our overall conclusion is that enough useful results are already at hand to make a case that such first-person methods are not a chimera.

VI: Sketch of a Common Structure[3]

Content and mental act

Implicit in our presentation so far is that all these methods can be legitimately brought into register to the extent that they do have some core structures in common. It is now time to try and provide some pointers for such commonalities.

Let us consider the situation of a subject in an experimental situation, requested to perform an explicit task. During the accomplishment of this task the person experiences something, and following Vermersch (this issue), we shall call that its lived content, L1, a reference for what will follow. In the context of the task, the subject (with or without mediation) is then required to examine (describe, analyse, and/or become aware of, attend to) L1. For this to happen, within a short time L1 will then become part of the content of a new experience: examining one's own mentation, a new content, L2, which is a product of the act of noticing one's own mentation, and L2 will typically have additional new content characterized by the particular manner of access to L1. Notice that for the pair L1–L2 to appear, there is necessarily a redirec-

---

[3] This section borrows very significantly from a forthcoming book that Francisco Varela has written in collaboration with Natalie Depraz and Pierre Vermersch. Many thanks to both of them for allowing some of these ideas to be presented in this Introduction (Depraz *et al.*, forthcoming).

tion of thought, a suspension, an interruption of the natural attitude which normally does not stop to access its own contents.[4]

The core element appearing in this layering, which is common to all first-person methods, is the clear distinction between the *content* of a mental act (for instance I am requested to picture my house) and the *process* through which such content appears (how do I come up with the image being requested). Not keeping this fundamental distinction in view is a source of much confusion. To be sure, the methods listed above show some differences. The first two types involve a focused attention to content, oriented towards gaining some knowledge or insight. Thus the successful learning of a method is here always concomitant to internalizing such doubling from L1 to L2 with ease. Methods of the third and fourth type are more subtle. In early stages of mindfulness (samatha) training, the role of attention to immediate mental content is crucial. But as the practice unfolds, one can relax the initial effort, and content as such becomes less central than the quality of conscious presence itself, as emphasized in the Mahamudra-Dzogchen techniques.The Vedic TM tradition, Dzogchen and Zen Buddhism, and some practices in Vajrayana Buddhism, are from the outset unconcerned with content (above and beyond what is needed for the method itself to be performed). Here the aim is to develop the method until it annihilates itself, yielding states of 'pure' (contentless) consciousness.

It should be noted that the methods represented here often yield first-person accounts that seem flat and poor. This is one of the recurrent complaints of those who criticize first-person accounts, and they are not wrong. What is missing here is the continuation of the process that involves a shift from the natural attitude where L2 is aimed at directly. This, in turn, mobilizes a second phase that makes it clear that from the initial suspension a new initially void field is progressively filled with new phenomenal data. It is the stage of discovery, or experiential filling-in, and this requires a sustained discipline to accomplish. The apparent facility for access to one's experience is what is misleading: the filling-in made possible by suspension has its own developmental time which needs cultivation and to be borne patiently. All methods (and individual practitioners), however, have their own developmental time, which can vary greatly.

Second-person
The establishment of a method then requires the creation of means to go beyond these difficulties. Again each tradition has come up with different means, and they vary substantially. All of them, however, share a common discovery, namely, that in any case the progress in becoming familiar with a particular method requires mediation. By mediation we mean here another person(s) who provides a curious intermediate position between first and second position, whence the name *second-person* position. A mediator is eccentric to the lived experience L1 but nevertheless takes a position of one who has been there to some degree, and thus provides hints and further training.

[4] Even less common is the possibility of going to yet a third step, where L2 becomes the object of an experience, L3, the introspection of introspection. Contrary to a first impression this is not infinite regress: since all this is happening in a brief period of time, the levels of examination stop there, since experience shows clearly that L2 is already an effort, and for L3 to appear one needs a highly trained sustained attention!

The second-person position is given prominence in all the traditions invoked in this Special Issue, with the exception of the natural sciences where it appears only when the social process of learning is analysed, and a researcher seeks the mediation of a more experienced tutor to improve and progress his skill as a scientist. Although it is standard practice to accord importance to the lineage of the training a scientist has followed, attention to such second-person mediation disappears by the time an article is published in a scientific journal.

In brief, then, the three positions (first-, second-, third-) are structured not so much in regards to what content they address, but in the *manner in which* they appear — inserted in the network of social exchanges. It is the particular roles social agents take in each case that determines their belonging to one or the other position, with gradations. We are therefore not concerned with a dual opposition between the private and the public, or the objective and the subjective. We are, however, very much concerned with questions of interpreting the results of first-person investigations as valid data, and here the matter of how the three positions relate is of crucial importance. Figuratively, then, the situation can be depicted as this:

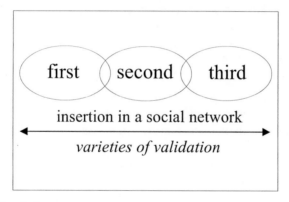

Expression and validation

It is precisely because validation hinges on the manner the intersubjective network is constituted, that these positions are, by necessity, marked by gradations. Or, in other words, the three-fold distinction of positions is, to some degree, a descriptive convenience. It seems, in fact, that each one of them is in turn layered as a function of the *emphasis* one puts in accomplishing a particular mode of validation. Let us re-examine the three positions again at this light.

The third-person, taken as the standard observer of scientific discourse, emphasizes to the extreme the apparent dualism between the internal and the objectively external, and is the basis for scientific reductionism in all its forms. The cognitive sciences represent an intrinsic challenge to this 'pure' form of objective science, however, since the topic under study directly implies the social agents themselves. It is thus a singularity of sorts, one that is completely absent in all other domains of the natural sciences. Nevertheless, to the extent that its scientific content is strongly focused on biochemical and neural operations, the question of persons (first-, second-, third-) does not become pressing. For in human studies, like those of other animals, behaviour (including verbal behaviour) is an integral part of the relevant data that can be studied in the frame of classical recording and measurement without necessarily being taken as expressions of mental life.

The imputation of a mental correlate to such verbal or behavioural phenomena is another matter, however, and behaviourism based its research programme on making just this distinction between behaviour and subjectivity. In practice most cognitive neuroscientists make this into a principled distinction, and assume, in a more or less explicit manner, that such behaviour comes from a cognitive subject or agent, without elaborating further. Thus although such practices are squarely within the norm of third-person accounts, they already insinuate the other's position and concerns, in a way that studying cells and crystals does not. This is why we single out cognitive science as implying a layering within the third-person stance that edges towards a second-person position.

From a second-person position, what appeared merely as overt external behaviour is now taken explicitly as traces or manifestation of mental life, and furthermore as the only lead into what such mental life is. Recently Daniel Dennett (1991) has formulated just this position in what he aptly calls *hetero*phenomenology, which he depicts as the position of an anthropologist studying a remote culture. For an anthropologist the mere collection of tapes, pictures and inscriptions does not constitute an answer to his quest. He must obtain inferentially models of mental (cultural) life from these, using an intentional stance. In other words:

> We must treat the noise-emitter as an agent, indeed a rational agent, who harbors beliefs and desires and other mental states that exhibit intentionality or 'aboutness' and how actions can be explained on the basis of those mental states (Dennett, 1991, p. 76).

But the heterophenomenologist does not indulge in taking his sources at face value, simply subscribing to their own interpretation. The anthropologist does not here become a member of the tribe. The reason this stance falls into second-person position is that although strictly using external traces, the heterophenomenologist is nevertheless present as a situated individual, who has to generate intentional interpretations of the data. None of this is needed when validation leaves out entirely any form of intentional stance, as the neural and behavioural scientist does when studying animals, and can do when studying humans.

The temptation to become part of the tribe is just where the next change of emphasis takes us, namely, to the full second-person position. Here, in the second-person position, one gives up explicitly his/her detachments to become identified with the kind of understanding and internal coherence of his source. In fact, that is how he sees his role: as an empathic resonator with experiences that are familiar to him and which find in himself a resonant chord. This empathic position is still partly heterophenomenological, since a modicum of critical distance and of critical evaluation is necessary, but the intention is entirely other: to meet on the same ground, as members of the same kind. Examples of this position abound in the traditions that we have examined in the sphere of human practices. The position here is not that of a neutral anthropologist; it is rather one of a coach or a midwife. His/her trade is grounded on a sensitivity to the subtle indices of his interlocutor's phrasing, bodily language and expressiveness, seeking for indices (more or less explicit) which are inroads into the common experiential ground, as we shall elaborate below. Such encounters would not be possible without the mediator being steeped in the domain of experiences under examination, as nothing can replace that first-hand knowledge. This, then, is a radically different style of validation from the others we have discussed so far.

This empathic second-person stance can also be seen from the experiencer point of view, as it were. This position now concerns the subject himself progressing through a working session, with the possibility of seeking a validation through his actions and expressions. This call for intersubjective validation is not obligatory in every case. But the converse is: there is no possibility of first-person methodology in our sense of the term without at some point assuming the position of direct experience that seeks validation. Otherwise the process then becomes purely private or even solipsistic. We do not deny that such an alternative is possible for human beings — even to the extreme of complete self-imagined worlds that from the vantage point of a social network appear as delusions, and are treated as such. But all such questions aside, passage into a position open to second-person mediation is clearly necessary at some point to come within the scope of our methodological quest.

Common traits

In brief then we have seen that the first-person methods as presented here share some fundamental common traits or stages:

- *Basic attitude:* They require a moment of suspension and redirection moving from content to mental process.
- *Phenomenal filling-in:* They require a specific training to pursue the initial suspension into a more full content, and the role of mediation or second-person is important here.
- *Expression and intersubjective validation:* In all cases, the process of expression and validation will require explicit accounts amenable to intersubjective feedback.

We can also conclude that first-person methodologies are not quick-and-easy. They require a sustained dedication and interactive framing before significant phenomenal data can be made accessible and validatable. Finally the role of mediation is a unique aspect of these methods, one that has received little attention so far.

VII: Degrees of Blindness

The above discussion allows us now to evaluate more precisely the situation of first-person methodologies in the cognitive science world at large. In the current debate about a science of consciousness, there are a number of authors who explicitly leave out any concern with first-person data, and by implication cannot be taken into account here. What is interesting is to take a glance at those who do, and characterize them by what can be called their degrees of blindness to the role and importance of working with first-person methods.

Our view is that the field of consciousness studies and cognitive neuroscience has been far too much under the influence of one particular style of philosophy of mind, cut off from other traditions that have made their speciality the methodical exploration of human experience. Thus it is not surprising that (with notable exceptions) we end up in recurrent repetition of the same kinds of arguments. Perhaps this move is nowhere more limpid than in reading the war of words between David Chalmers and John Searle, recently featured in the *New York Review of Books* (Searle, 1997). Here we have two philosophers who uphold, in their own ways, the need to incorporate the subjective or experiential dimension as irreducible. But this adherence to the pertinence of first-person experience is not followed with methodological advances. Not surprisingly, Chalmers and Searle then manage to accuse each other of being completely wrong on just about every important issue. This is a sign that we need to turn to other ways of advancing, with new sources and new tools.

Let is now turn to the notion of 'degrees of blindness' to the usefulness of working with first-person methods. The most basic degree, of course, is represented by those who are sensitive to first-person experience, but want to approach it exclusively by third-person means. This is a position shared by a large majority of cognitive neuroscientists, and is well articulated by Dennett in his notion of heterophenomenology.

A second, more refined blindness is represented by those who claim that first-person accounts should be involved, but who then stop at the announcement, and propose nothing explicit one can work with. This is most commonly seen in the Anglo-American philosophy of mind, where the problem of consciousness is often assimilated with that of 'qualia' for some particular features of mental states. Consider, for example, Searle (1992), who argues for the irreducibility of first-person ontology. Yet when it comes to the study of subjectivity he proposes nothing more than a quick dismissal of introspection. He wants us to accept that 'the irreducibility of consciousness is merely a consequence of the pragmatics of our definitional practices' (p. 122), and therefore, although the irreducibility of consciousness is a 'straightforward argument' it 'has no deep consequences' (p. 118). In fact,

> The very fact of subjectivity, which we were trying to observe, makes such an observation impossible. Why? Because where conscious subjectivity is concerned, there is no distinction between the observed and the thing observed. . . . Any introspection I have of my own conscious state is itself that conscious state (p. 97).

The mental thus does not have any sound manner to investigate itself, and we are left with a logical conclusion, but in a pragmatic and methodological limbo.[5] This is not unlike the limbo in Ray Jackendoff's views, where in his own manner he also claims the irreducibility of consciousness, but when it comes to method is tellingly silent. He does claim that insights into experience act as constraints for a computational theory of mind, but follows with no methodological recommendations except 'the hope that the disagreements about phenomenology can be settled in an atmosphere of mutual trust' (Jackendoff, 1987, p. 275).

At a third level of inclusiveness a few have been slightly more constructive. Chalmers, for example, maintains that '[a phenomenological] approach must be absolutely central to an adequate science of consciousness'(Chalmers, 1997, p. 36), and takes seriously the idea that both eastern and western sorts of methodologies may prove useful. But his own work so far does not appear to go beyond this positive general suggestion to the methodologies themselves. Owen Flanagan's notion of reflective equilibrium combines third-person and phenomenological account in some 'natural method', linking phenomenological, psychological and neural data (Flanagan, 1994, p. 11). We can all concur and follow some of his examples (on split hearing, or bi-stable perception). But this case-by-case analysis is hardly the equiva-

---

[5] Surely, however, the contents of mental states can be examined, and theories about them accepted and/or rejected. Indeed, cognitive-developmental studies show that children have to learn which of their experiences are properly to be taken to be of the objective world and which only of their minds (and even adults on occasion make mistakes here). This makes it apparent that there is a sense of 'observation' which is prior to and independent of the subjective/objective split, that, on Searle's account, supposedly makes subjective observation impossible (cf. Shear, 1996).

lent of a full-blown methodology which Flanagan does not advance. Bernard Baars is substantially more explicit in introducing a method he calls 'contrastive phenomenology': 'The key is to compare two active brain processes that are similar in most ways but differ in respect to consciousness' (Baars, 1997a, p. 21). This is certainly a very basic procedure implicitly followed in most empirical studies published today dealing with neural correlates of conscious processes such as attention and imagery. Although this is an important step forward in methodology, when working with contrasting conditions there are still a host of subjective phenomenal data to be explored, as Peugeot's contribution to this Special Issue makes clear. This is precisely why the methods discussed in this Special Issue, if nothing else, provide evidence that there is a lot more to looking into one's experience than meets the eye, if one makes use of a method that consistently suspends habitual thoughts and judgments.[6]

In conclusion, this rapid sketch of degrees of blindness shows that there is still a long road to go in introducing first-person methodologies into cognitive science with a full citizenship. There are some signs that this is slowly beginning to happen.[7]

VIII: Can Experience Be Explored? An Objection From the Start

Our pragmatic orientation is likely to leave some readers feeling cold. The sceptical reader will want to raise what is perhaps the most fundamental objection to the avenue of inquiry proposed here. This objection can be formulated thus: How do you know that by exploring experience with a method you are not, in fact, deforming or even creating what you experience? Experience being what it is, what is the possible meaning of examination? We may call this an 'excavation fallacy' or, philosophically, the *hermeneutical* objection, that goes to the heart of our project here. In another form it can also be found as the *deconstruction* objection, based on post-modern philosophical analysis (mostly derived from J. Derrida). The emphasis here is on the claim that there is no such thing as 'deeper' layers of experience, since any account is 'always already' (toujours déjà) enfolded in language; hence a new account can only be that: an inflexion of linguistic practices.

Our answer to the excavation/deconstruction fallacy is first to admit that there is, indeed, a significant problem, and that no *a priori* argument or methodological contortion will dissipate it *per se*. It seems inevitable that any method will be part and parcel of the kinds of entities and properties found in the domain of observation at hand. As stated in Section I (above), the experiential and social dimension in science is often hidden, but never entirely absent. This is quite visible in the most consecrated forms of natural science, as recent scholarship has made abundantly clear (cf. the recent studies by Shapin and Shaeffer [1994] on Boyle's air pump).

---

[6] Even for a writer like Baars this needed further development still evokes resistance. In discussing a precis of his book one of us raised this very point but Baars did not appreciate (Varela, 1997). In his rejoinder he says: 'The whole array of methods is still reducible to "are you conscious right now of this word in front of your eyes".There is no need to complicate that' (Baars, 1997b, p. 357). However there is indeed a great deal of complexity that is not readily available in fist-person data. That's where the need for refined methods comes in.

[7] One should note here the outstanding pioneering work of Eugene Gendlin, whose contribution deserves to be better known (Gendlin, 1972/1997). For a recent collection of comparative methodologies see Velmans (in press).

Indeed no methodological approach to experience is neutral, it inevitably introduces an interpretative framework into its gathering of phenomenal data. To the extent that this is so, the hermeneutical dimension of the process is inescapable: every examination is an interpretation, and all interpretation reveals and hides away at the same time. But it does not follow from this that a disciplined approach to experience creates nothing but artifacts, or a 'deformed' version of the way experience 'really' is.

To be sure, the exploration of experience will suffer along with all other methodical investigations from cultural expectations and instrumental bias, but there is no evidence that the phenomenal data gathered are not equally constrained by the proper reality of conscious contents. Thus whatever descriptions we can produce through first-person methods are not pure, solid 'facts' but potentially valid intersubjective items of knowledge, quasi-objects of a mental sort. No more, no less.

Furthermore, human experience is not a fixed, predelineated domain. Instead, it is changing, changeable and fluid. If one undergoes a disciplined training in musical performance, the newly acquired skills of distinction of sounds, of sensitivity to musical phrasing and ensemble playing, are undeniable. But this means that experience is explored and modified with such disciplined procedures in non-arbitrary ways. Indeed, to speak of experience as being standard, raw, or pure generally makes no sense. All we have is experience at its own level of examination, and depending on the kinds of effort and methods brought into play. It moves and changes, and its exploration is already part of human life, albeit generally with other objectives than understanding experience itself.

We thus want to position ourselves in a middle ground with respect to the hermeneutical objection. On the one hand we wish to explore to the utmost the tools available for first-person accounts. On the other hand we do not claim that such an access is method-free or natural in any privileged sense. This mixture is yet another manifestation of the pragmatic spirit of the work featured in this Special Issue. Time will tell if this orientation bears the fruits that are expected. Nothing is gained by refusing the entire enterprise because of some *a priori* argument.

References

Baars, B.J. (1997a), *In the Theater of Consciousness* (New York: Oxford University Press).
Baars, B.J. (1997b), 'Reply to commentators', *Journal of Consciousness Studies*, 4 (4), pp. 347–64.
Chalmers, D.J. (1997), 'Moving forward on the problem of consciousness', *JCS*, 4 (1), pp. 3–46.
Dennett, D.C. (1991), *Consciousness Explained* (New York: Little, Brown).
Depraz, N., Varela, F. and Vermersch, P. (forthcoming), *On Becoming Aware: Steps to a Phenomenological Pragmatics*.
Flanagan, O. (1994), *Consciousness Reconsidered* (Cambridge, MA: MIT Press).
Gendlin, E. (1972/1997), *Experiencing and the Creation of Meaning* (Evanston, IL: Northwestern University Press).
Jackendoff, R. (1987), *Consciousness and the Computational Mind* (Cambridge, MA: MIT Press).
Roy, J.M. Petitot, J., Pachoud, B and Varela, F.J. (1998), 'Beyond the gap. An introduction to naturalizing phenomenology', in: *Naturalizing Phenomenology: Issues in Contemporary Phenomenology and Cognitive Science*, ed. Petitot *et al.* (Stanford University Press).
Searle, J.R. (1992), *The Rediscovery of the Mind* (Cambridge, MA: MIT Press).
Searle, J.R. (1997), *The Mystery of Consciousness* (New York: New York Review of Books).
Shapin, S. and Shaeffer, S. (1994), *Leviathan and the Air Pump* (Princeton, NJ: Princeton Univ. Press).
Shear, J. (1996), 'The hard problem: Closing the empirical gap', *JCS*, 3 (1), pp. 54–68.
Shear, J. (ed. 1997), *Explaining Consciousness: The Hard Problem* (Cambridge, MA: MIT Press).
Varela, F.J. (1996), 'Neurophenomenology', *Journal of Consciousness Studies*, 3 (4), pp. 330–49.
Varela, F.J. (1997), 'Metaphor to mechanism; natural to disciplined', *JCS*, 4 (4), pp. 344–6.
Velmans, M. (ed. forthcoming), *Investigating Phenomenal Consciousness: New Methodologies and Maps* (Amsterdam: Benjamins).

Part 1

Introspection

Pierre Vermersch

Introspection As Practice

How can one gain access to subjective experience and regulate this mode of access?
How can one develop the necessary competence to know that such access has genuinely been obtained and to establish a reliable methodology which can be transmitted
and used to train researchers in a precise and deliberate fashion? Phenomenology, as a
global idea, gives us a clue and indicates the requisite epistemology, but does not
seem to provide the know-how, nor does it specify the practice, since the philosophers
who established and developed it (Husserl, Fink, Patocka, Merleau-Ponty . . .) did not
succeed in specifying this practice, while many of those who are indebted to the
method today seem to be more concerned with the study of historical texts than with
anything like a phenomenological practice. Psychology has a long and established
tradition of suspicion, and even of dismissal, of anything which stems from the first-
person point of view. A tradition of attentive presence offers us numerous hints as to
the conditions under which attention can be stabilized in such a way as to make possible an apprehension of subjective experience (cf. Varela *et al.*,1991; Wallace, this
issue) but the employment of such a method requires a long apprenticeship and runs
the risk of limiting the selection to a few well-trained subjects. In such a context, one
may well ask whether it even makes sense to take up again the question of introspection. Unless we look at this from the opposite angle: psychology began with introspection and a first reversal was accomplished by leaving introspection behind and
adopting that third-person approach, which was badly needed at the time but which in
turn gave way to a second reversal which consisted in once again according a place to
the first-person point of view. Only, on account of the prohibition to which it has been
subjected, first-person methodology has not been able to develop and so to progress
in a normal way.

In this article I am not going to try and define introspection. I am going to try to
state as precisely as possible how the practice of introspection can be improved, starting from the principle that there exists a disjunction between the logic of action and of
conceptualization and the practice of introspection does not require that one should

Correspondence: Pierre Vermersch, CNRS, GREX, Place de la Mairie, 43300 Saint-Eble, France.
E-mail : pvermers@es-conseil.fr

Journal of Consciousness Studies, **6**, No. 2–3, 1999, pp. 17–42

already be in possession of an exhaustive scientific knowledge bearing upon it. (Just suppose that before studying cognition, you were required to define it or that you were required to have a complete knowledge of perception before being permitted to read a set of instructions). To make matters worse, innumerable commentators upon what passes for introspection do not seem to have practised it and have certainly never contributed anything to its development. My aim is therefore to bring to light a procedure for progressive improvement in the practice of introspection when it is employed in a programme of research.

I would like to have been able to proceed directly to the clarification of the practice of introspection. But before getting there it will be necessary to first go back over the history of the development of introspection from the beginning of this century and to cut a way through the undergrowth represented by all the criticisms that have been directed at its very possibility. As a result of my many years of exposure to the literature on introspection I sometimes get the impression of being overwhelmed by the negative implications of all the critical objections, to the point of almost forgetting the practical efficacy of introspection.

Do we have to take the time to criticize the critics of introspection?

In the course of the two centuries over which the list of these critics never ceases to get longer, have there ever been any which have been conclusive? By trying too hard to denigrate introspection the critics themselves become suspect. After all, if any one of these criticisms were conclusive, the rest would become unnecessary! By forcing matters a little one might conclude that any such discussion would be a waste of time. Why bother to justify the method, to demonstrate the irrelevance of these criticisms because none of them is in principle capable of being conclusive, and on this point I am in agreement with Howe: 'Thus it has been suggested that if there is an argument against the use of introspection, it has yet to be found.' (Howe, 1991a, p. 25.) Why? Essentially, because these criticisms, which have hardly changed in two centuries, all adopt the same purely negative approach: impossibility, uselessness, impracticality, an approach intended to cast doubt either upon the act or the object. Trying to prove the absence or the impossibility of something is not a very well founded epistemological enterprise, to say the least. If a claim can be rejected by simply furnishing a counter example, it becomes very difficult to rule out the possibility of finding counter examples in any field of empirical enquiry.

Only the ability to master the totality of the available possibilities (now and for ever, or else it would only by a provisional sentence) would give one the right to deny the possibility of a certain type of result or of a particular event. The research strategy which consists in trying to prove the impossibility of something is a waste of time. In general, it seems much more profitable to investigate 'under what conditions . . . ?' 'within what limits . . .?' Unless of course the arguments which inspire the attempt to demonstrate the impossibility of something are based on lines of reasoning quite different from the scientific, which does indeed seem to recur frequently with the 'opponents' of the examination of subjective experience and the use of introspection.

Let us take account of two of the oldest and most tenacious of these criticisms, since they both stem from Auguste Comte, founder of positivism.

The first denies the very possibility of introspection on the grounds that it calls for a duplication of the subject, who cannot at one and the same time be both on the balcony and in the street. 'The thinking individual cannot split himself in two, one part of which would think while the other would watch the former thinking. The organ observed and the organ observing being, in this case, identical, how could any such act of observation take place? This supposedly psychological method is therefore radically faulty in principle' (Comte, 1830, Lesson 1, p. 34). In the first place this criticism, based as it is upon a material representation of cognitive activities stemming from Gall's phrenology, could be discarded as having simply failed to take account of the evidence. However, at another level, this question of a self-duplication can be taken up again not as being impossible but as posing certain difficulties with regard to characterizing and modelling reflective activity which, as its very appellation reminds us, tends to trap us conceptually in the metaphor of reflection, in the representation of consciousness as self-duplicating.

The second criticism claims that introspection is unusable in research because it modifies the object which it is directed toward. Both Janet and Binet sought to get past this difficulty by invoking retrospection. This solution creates a new problem of its own, that of the reliability of memory and the necessity of establishing the nature of the link between what is described from the past and what is lived at the very moment it is being recalled and described. In other words, this solution only succeeds in dodging the difficulty by replacing observation in the present by observation bearing upon the 'presentification' of past lived experience. But over and beyond this response, the most remarkable fact is that one would have to be informed about such an eventual change in viewpoint even to be in a position to develop this criticism; and how would one be in a position to do so if not by making use of introspection? It alone is able to determine that there has been a modification, what kind of modification there has been, and how great the modification has been. For knowing about my internal state of mind, as also attesting to any transformation in it, presupposes in every instance the bringing into play of a first-person point of view! So either the criticism of the results of introspection remains radical but also valueless since it disqualifies itself, or else it points in the direction of a good question (and not as devastating a question as might have been hoped for) and then it simply underlines the need for introspection as the condition of any assessment of its effects. The influence of observation on what is observed is a major epistemological problem, but it is a problem which extends throughout the sciences. For it is obvious that the idea of an observer who had somehow succeeded in situating himself outside the system he is engaged in studying is an epistemological fiction.

From an empirical standpoint, there is certainly a methodological advantage to be gained by moving from a first-person point of view, where researcher and observer coincide, to a second-person point of view, where the basic data is drawn from persons other than the researcher and can be multiplied in the context either of experience or of observation. Henceforward, the criticisms can be reversed, the impact of internal observation, if it is correctly set up, being eventually supplemented by information on the degree of stability of states, of acts, as well as of the contents aimed at in introspection (Piaget, 1968, p. 186).

These last two critical examples have been introduced to show that, in principle, there is no real obstacle to using introspection. It only remains to consider the use that is actually made of it in programmes of research.

I: The Evidence from the Early Years of Psychology

It is impossible to do justice to the emergence of psychology at the beginning of the nineteenth century without first considering that its subject matter did not fall under the aegis of common sense but intrinsically demanded a much more sophisticated approach. The use made of 'introspection', of 'internal sense' and of 'apperception' has to be judged in this context. The life of consciousness, of thought, of imagination and of affective life was no longer to be studied in a purely speculative way, in the manner of philosophy, but on the basis of observation in the perspective of the natural sciences.

This point of view was upheld from the very beginnings of psychology, for example by Maine de Biran (1807), generally recognized to have been the first author who could be identified as a psychologist (Voutsinas, 1964; Moore, 1970) and who not merely drew attention to interior events but also made use of internal sense. He adopted the first-person point of view, which meant not only that what was to be taken into account was what appeared to the consciousness of the one living it, but also that the research was restricted to the only person capable of observing it.

For all that, the strategy should not be regarded as naive, even if it cannot be controlled intersubjectively. For example, Maine de Biran is well aware of the facilitating role that effort can play in the observation of intellectual activities. He studied the experience of reading and showed how, at the very moment in which we are aware that we have failed to understand a passage and in which consequently we reread it (Montebello, 1994), we can observe our awareness of our own acts of thought on the occasion of our attempt to correct them. This initial insistence upon introspection is to be found again, considerably modified, with several founding figures of the psychology of the nineteenth century, such as Brentano (1874), Wundt (1874), or in the celebrated declaration of William James in 1890, who described psychology as follows: 'Introspective observation is what we have to rely on first and foremost and always'. An echo of this sentiment can be found in a statement by Binet (1894): introspection is 'the act by means of which we perceive directly what takes place in us, our thoughts, our memories, our emotions.' And in 1903: 'The new movement which has been launched for some years now and to which I, along with several of my students, have contributed as much as I can . . . consists in according a larger place to introspection.' From this time on it is in order to make fun of the 'old introspective psychology which asks us (its representatives) if by chance and by a barely concealed regression, we are not going to take over from the old school philosophers like Cousin (therefore harking back to the 1830s), those methods of auto-contemplation which have been the subject of so much ribaldry'and to show in what respects 'the experimental study of the higher forms of mentality can be carried out with sufficient precision and control to have scientific value' (Binet, 1903).

The primacy accorded initially to introspective methodology may appear very naive today. But what is truly naive is to think it so. One has to realize that this introspection was already the result of a difficult initiative, demanding a reflexive conversion, a first *epochè*,[1] in other words, the utilization of a phenomenological reduction. This first step was anything but simple. There is nothing naive about the suspension of the natural attitude which gets us involved in the perceptual spectacle, with a view,

---

[1] See the article by Depraz in this Special Issue on phenomenological terminology.

for example, to grasping its actual unfolding. Acquiring a practical mastery of the reduction presents real problems at this very time for researchers and students.

Moreover, these authors did not allow themselves to be limited by one single method. All those whom I have cited, even the oldest of them, were very knowledgeable about the physiology of their time and about its connection with the psychic. They were also well informed about the need for indirect methods to study children, the sick, animals, in short, those who did not have access to speech.

II: Methodological Improvements — The beginning of the Twentieth Century

The beginning of the twentieth century is the great period for the mobilization of the methodology of introspection, which will now be presented as scientific and entitled 'systematic introspection', 'experimental introspection'. It is employed with great intellectual enthusiasm in the context of a rigorously scientific experimental psychology of complex intellectual activities.

Three centres[2] dominate the field: in Paris, Binet and his students; in the United States, at Cornell University, we find Titchener[3] who was trained by Wundt (whose work he translated into English) and then there is the group of German researchers who go by the name of the Wurtzburg school and who, under the direction of Külpe (former student of Wundt who broke with his teacher) published intensively in the decade starting 1901.[4]

The determination to establish a rigorous methodological framework capable of upholding the scientific character of the research is evident in the manner in which this research is presented. In effect, the transformation since the start of the nineteenth century is best described in terms of the passage from an exclusively first-person point of view, where researcher and subject were not clearly distinguished, to a 'second-person' point of view where descriptions of subjective experience are gathered from a selection drawn from several persons.

This is the start of a process by which the gathering of data has become independent of the person of the researcher. When the researcher makes reference to his own experience (which happens frequently in the Titchener school), his experience (specifically labelled as being his own) remains just one among other inputs.

The subjective experience in question is now much better defined. Contrary to the initial research bearing on the experience of effort (but not on any specific occurrence of this experience) or the investigation of the flow of consciousness in general, specific tasks are now proposed, tasks which circumscribe, both with regard to time and the object, the experience under examination. This orientation towards the realization of definite tasks represents a real revolution, a revolution which enables this research to be supported by what is now known as the experimental set-up and control tech-

---

[2] But there has never been an author who has mastered all three fields and the historical articles are always incomplete. Sartre is probably the most complete but he only deals with the imagination.

[3] There exists a very detailed bibliography relating to Titchener and his principal students: Jacobson, Okabe, Clarke, etc. in Leahey (1987).

[4] In addition to original publication in the German, one can find a detailed presentation of the world of this school in French in Burloud (1927a); in English in Titchener (1909) as well as in the remarkable critical work by Humphrey (1951 but drafted in 1934). A book made up of articles translated by J.M. & G. Mandler (1964) and which contains first hand texts should also be mentioned: *Thinking from Association to Gestalt*.

niques. The tasks are the same for everyone and they take place under identical conditions (we still don't have all the systematic refinements which will be strictly enforced thirty years later) and in accordance with precise instructions. In addition, the definition of these tasks will lead researchers to introduce independent variables by taking account of the reaction between one task and another, a relation which, with regard to the analysis of the results, will make it possible to draw inferences concerning the disparity of the success rate as between tasks and as between subjects. The researchers pay close attention to the methodological problems bearing upon the description itself (Titchener in particular had a lot to say about this, cf. the synthesis produced by English [1921], but Mandler and Mandler [1964] are also highly critical of abuses), the need to be as impersonal as possible in the use of descriptive terms, the need to distinguish between the description of the subjective experience itself as opposed to the reality evoked or any second order commentary (Titchener, 1912a). The need to break the description down into smaller units to facilitate formulation is already beginning to be felt (Watt, 1905). But one is still very far from an exact awareness of what is required by a description and by the non inductive guidance made possible by a proper interviewing technique. A part of the difficulty raised by description and by the problems associated with attention to subjective experience is surmounted by working with subjects who are trained in this kind of experience, which however raises its own potential objections: this very training may render them less suitable as subjects, since they may already be sympathetic to the hypothesis of their observer.

This latter question is one which keeps turning up: is expertise even desirable? If yes, then who is supposed to have developed it? The person who is the subject, making possible better access to and description of subjective experience, and/or the researcher, thereby improving his (the researcher's) ability to guide and to follow the subject (in a non-inductive manner) in the latter's attempt to accede to and to describe his or her experience?

Let us take one piece of research in particular in order to understand how these different improvements are put into place: for example Watt's research of 1905. He decided to study directed recollection for which he created a set of six tasks. I do not intend to go into the formulation of his hypotheses or the internal coherence of the theoretical frameworks of his time but simply to examine the form of the experiment.

> On the one hand we have a list of key words, on the other hand, six instructions: find a concept which stands in a relation of super or sub-ordination, in a relation of whole to part or of part to whole, in a relation of coordination of part to part. One is therefore faced with a variety of task which make comparisons possible. What has been developed since is the possibility of establishing a list of words with imagist etc connotations which, with regard to a particular verbal material, make it possible to know in advance, and with reference to a given population, how to master their inductive value from the standpoint of familiarity etc.
>
> The key words are for the most nouns never exceeding three syllables. I was not able to locate the description of the instructions in the strict sense nor the device by means of which the key word was presented but from the instructions it is clear that the word was presented in writing.
>
> The sample is homogeneous, composed entirely of professors and doctors of philosophy. The group is six in number, but for each subject there are fifteen series of tests, undertaken on average at a rate of two per day, each of which is devoted to one of the tasks in question (it might have been possible to adopt a procedure which would have

controlled the ordering of the experiment more satisfactorily) with the result that, in all, several thousand items of elementary information are made available.

For each item (induced) the researcher is in possession both of the actual performance (the induced response) and of the possibility of classifying it with regard to its respect for, and its success in, following the instructions, as well as in regard to the way in which it establishes the relation between the key word and the induced response. On the other hand, the time taken to record a response, that is, the time between the presentation of the key word and the reply, is registered. Finally, the researcher also makes a transcript of the verbal description of the experience as lived out by the subject in the course of accomplishing his task. This description is split up into four moments which the subject was invited to describe separately: 1) the preparation, 2) the period prior to the presentation of the key word, 3) the appearance of the key word, 4) the search for the word induced by the key word and the reply itself. Three series of independent data are thereby obtained for each item of the test (the response to the instructions, the period required for working out the response, and the description of the process of working out a response offered after the event) and data as rich as this also allows for further possibilities of analysis and inference. It seems to me that we have here all the ingredients needed for a scientific research which respects the rules of experimental method (Watt, 1905).

This data was gathered in 1902 and published in 1905. We find here an experimental plan, a control of the experimental set-up, a collection of independent though complementary data. It would therefore not be on the score of its methodology that this procedure could be criticised! In fact, very often discussion bearing upon the interpretation of the data has been amalgamated with criticism regarding the way in which it was gathered by reducing both to introspective data alone.

What I have sought to underline in spelling out this example in some detail is the fact that, from the beginning of this century, the methodological criteria for research based on introspection had become 'standardized' with regard to the requirements of experimental method. We could take other examples from the research done by the Wurzburg school (e.g. Meyer and Orth, 1901) or that done by Binet (1903) or, again, by such students of Titchener as Hayes (1906), Nakashima (1909), Geissler (1909), Pyle (1909), Okabe (1910), Clarke (1911) or Jacobson (1911), who largely took over from him.

If one wants to criticise this research it will not be in the name of some confused assortment of complaints leading one to believe that they were not very rigorous, that a century ago researchers only worked in a very approximative way and that this explains why the results have always been 'judged' unreliable (but who has bothered to read carefully the research protocols of this period?). Of course, there remains the temptation to admit that they did indeed have a rigorous experimental method (in spite of the fact that they relied on introspective data!) On the contrary, what remained problematic for the Wurzburg school was that the data did not agree with the hypotheses formulated at the outset, leaving the researchers confronting an interpretive problem of major proportions which led them in a direction which varied radically from their expectations. This aroused an enormous scientific debate, Wundt (1907) severely criticising the experiments conducted at Wurzburg in the name of an exaggeratedly purist methodology, Titchener (1909; 1913) criticizing the interpretation of the results by the Wurzburg school, and having his own results criticized in turn. I simply want to emphasize that the debate was directed toward the problem of contradictory interpretations: can there be anything like thinking without an evocative content (that is, without accompanying images — provided one does not assimilate the term 'image' to a purely visual representation — neglecting all the other sensorial modalities? The work of the Wurzburg school all pointed in the direction of the possibility of a non-evocative form of thinking (without denying, however, the evocative associations of all kinds present in their results). Titchener's theory (1909), backed up by his own data and that of many of his students, claimed that all mental activity was accompanied by sensorial representations. But he distinguished between representations relating to the content of the thought and those accompanying the execution of a mental act. However, not only does this distinction seem to have been lost on the critics (at all times), the very notion of a representation accompanying the act and not the content has never been understood. What Boring (1953) emphasizes (and we will get back to this later) is probably a clear indication of the lack of understanding of data proceeding from introspection. In fact, the general topic of the relation between figurative and operative activity (as Piaget was wont to say), between representation and cognitive activity, remains a problem to this day, a problem which has certainly been complicated by numerous new theories and new original data but which still has not been completely cleared up. If one had to reject any research which led to apparently contradictory results one would have to expel from the province of scientific research some of its most precious discoveries!

Our view runs counter to the general opinion regarding the feeble, inadequate and unreliable character of this research. The problem was not the methodology but the fact that the data bore directly upon a major problem for which the emerging scientific psychology of the day was not yet prepared. The data was not too weak, methodologically speaking, but too 'strong' for the theoretical and epistemological framework at the disposal of the researchers. They were unable to do much more than take up a position for or against associationism.[5] Their expectations were so strong and so evident that the apparently contradictory results which they obtained could not be integrated at that time.

This work coincides with the birth of a long tradition of research which continues to this day and which consists in studying cognitive functioning from a problem-solving angle. The point of departure is the decision to study 'the higher functions', in opposition to the partisans of a study of elementary acts (cf. the opposition Wundt encounters from his former student Külpe, who is with the Wurzburg school from the very start), and to seek to define tasks and problems, a wholly new approach for the day, with a view to studying intellectual functioning with reference to goal directed and productive activity (the subject has to get a result, propose a reply), all of which makes it possible to establish a relation between what the subject does, what he says he has done, and the properties of his final response or even of intermediary responses when observable traces of such responses are available.

III: Across the Century — Neutrality, Rejection, Incomprehension

As a methodology, introspection is now going to be regularly justified and defended, for example by Burloud (1927a,b; 1938) and the manuals and tracts of the period generally take a very cautious view. They tolerate this procedure but only on condition

---

[5] Bakan (1954) even suggests that the brutal disappearance of the Wurzburg school is linked to the incapacity of this group to make sense of new data incompatible with their initial hypotheses.

that it is not used exclusively. In the conclusion of Dumas' famous treatise on psychology the editor expresses this point of view quite well:

> We don't need to insist upon the importance and the need for introspective psychology. Even though reflex psychology claims to be able to dispense with introspection, no one is under any doubt that every other form of psychology would be impossible without introspection. One can criticise the significance of introspective method, point out its difficulties, express reservations about the type of certainty which is claimed for it, prove that it deforms the very mechanisms it seeks to determine, even when it does not cook them up to simplify the explanations and to confirm preconceived ideas etc., but when all these criticisms have been assembled one is still obliged to recognise that none of them is decisive and that the difficulties to which our attention is drawn simply require that we take certain precautions. (Dumas, 1924.)

Nevertheless, the role officially accorded to introspection is on the wane. One of the last but most remarkable of the attempts to employ introspection is that of a philosopher, Sartre (1940), who employs it precisely with a view to answering questions concerning the relation of thought and imagery in one of the earliest attempts on the part of the young philosopher to establish a phenomenological psychology. In so doing he succeeds in bringing out the delicacy and the significance of analyses in the first-person with respect to his own cognitive activity but neither makes use of a second-person point of view nor acknowledges the constraints of experimental method.

It is also worth our while to quote some remarks by Guillaume in his manual of psychology dating from 1932, to the extent that he is able to point out in a dispassionate way the complementarity of introspective methods and the collection of observable evidence with reference to a simple example:

> [Pages 11–12 of a paragraph entitled 'Introspection and language' in the first chapter: 'The Aim and Methods of Psychology'.]

> Learn the table of numerals shown here in such a way as to know it by heart.

12	8	9
4	21	6
7	15	11

> On careful observation, some will perhaps find that, in reciting this table, they in a certain manner, read it off an imaginary table and so make use of a visual representation. Others will let themselves be guided by an auditory recollection as if they were reproducing a melody that had just heard. The first have a simultaneous image of the whole in which each figure has its place; the second listen inwardly to a succession of syllables. What can we learn from these descriptions drawn from introspection? The results do not seem to be essentially different from those that an objective method can furnish. If we now require of those who have learnt the table of numbers not to observe and describe themselves but to reproduce the lines either vertically or horizontally, . . . These variations are extremely difficult for those who learn by hearing who are really only able to write the numbers down in the order in which they were learnt. Those who are capable of evoking a visual table have much less difficulty. . . . These examples show that the subjective method is not so very different from the objective, to the extent that the fruitlessness of the former is enhanced by being tied down to verbal expression and that it is really just a matter of alternative approaches to the same science. We shall see that both of these methods have

contributed to the development of psychology. If the purely objective technique tends to prevail in animal, infant and pathological psychology, the two procedures are employed concurrently throughout the greater part of normal human psychology. One should never fail to make use of introspection in order to clarify an experience; for it has its part to play in making sense of the objective results and will often make it possible to dispense with laborious control techniques.

This example shows that there should not be any antagonism between different approaches; it shows the limits which the 'objective' method confronts in discovering how the subject goes about things. In fact complementary requirements can bring to light the use of different modes of encoding information (simultaneous/successive), but it does not make it clear, for instance, whether the successive approach stems from a verbalization of the reading of the numbers or whether it is a matter of placing each number in the line of a particular path; whether the verbalization of the reading of the numbers makes use of a counting system, relies upon a rhyming scheme or not, etc. A comparison between these two approaches also shows that an interpretation of the objective data is impossible with reference to the content of subjective experience. Finally, this study seems to me to be exemplary, in the sense that neither of the two methods is capable of yielding the meaning of the data, that by themselves they are not capable of providing a theoretical framework for interpreting the data.

Introspection disappears behind verbalization

Studies of problem solving are now going to multiply rapidly and provide the paradigm for the study of cognition. At the same time, references to introspection are going to disappear. Discussions of method take priority over the accumulation of verbalizations, that is, over the results of introspection. Verbalization takes the place of any taking account of the introspective act which might promote an awareness of the experience and, from 1934, with Claparède, we find a procedure destined to become well known, the procedure of 'thinking aloud'.

Introspection seems to have disappeared. Only the results of introspection, that is verbalizations, are brought to light. For the latter are public, objectifiable; they issue from a piece of behaviour so everything is satisfactory, is scientific, even if one has lost an essential part of what takes place with the subject when one asks him to describe how he has proceeded. Along the same lines, innumerable questionnaires are going to be developed, questionnaires which ask intimate questions of the subject without being in the least concerned with the way in which the subject goes about answering them. Is there only one way to do this? As Boring points out (1953), introspection is still there under another name: verbalization. The most remarkable case, one which constitutes a point of reference for an entire generation of cognitive psychologists, is that of Ericsson and Simon, whose book *Protocol Analysis* (1984) enjoyed a great success. Strategically, the authors have to defend themselves against the criticism of practising introspection. They have to show that it is possible to use verbalizations descriptive of the subject without, for all that, relapsing into a 'non scientific' introspection. They will even go so far as to cite Watson, to establish that it is 'scientifically correct' to collect data of this kind. On the basis of innumerable experimental results, they will argue that simultaneous verbalization of the activity taking place does not modify the process under investigation and that the contemporaneous character of this putting into words eliminates most of the risks of deformation, of forgetting, of rationalisation, which an aposteriori verbalization might bring with it. While talking of verbal encoding, of simultaneous verbalizations, they manage to forget that, in order to produce these verbalizations, the subject has to have access to something even to be in a position to describe his mental acts, the contents of his representations, and that, in consequence, he certainly does make use of a particular cognitive act.

This deliberate restriction of the methodology to concomitant verbalizations alone, without taking into account the subjective act which is responsible for producing them, for nourishing them, also makes it possible to confine oneself to an extremely impoverished subjectivity. A simple opening instruction to 'say aloud' is enough; no need for relational dimensions, for genuine maintenance techniques ensuring an element of mediation in the course of the introspective process, which is however certainly present. This way of concealing introspection under verbalizations alone is a way of tolerating the employment of introspection without having to compromise oneself by taking account of it, and so constitutes an indirect testimony to the impossibility of dispensing with the point of view of the subject. But the most important consequence of this taboo placed upon introspection has been fifty years without any development or improvement in this methodology.

If it held any interest, we would know about it . . . this data is unusable
Nothing illustrates more convincingly the calling in question of a methodology of the first-person than the history of these programmes of research.

One gets the impression that they were brutally expelled from the university scene. One is entitled to think that however forceful the criticism of behaviourism or other modish approaches, if there had been something interesting in the world based on the methodology of introspection, it would have been pursued, even if only discreetly, on account of its results if nothing else. To the extent that it seems to have produced no enduring results,[6] perhaps one should simply continue to do without it! The argument appears convincing. It gives us reason to question the interest in pursuing the matter further at the risk of finding oneself in the uncomfortable situation of trying to be in the right where everyone else, and not just the negligible quantities, seem to have been in the wrong in the eyes of history.

To start off with, one might look for historical explanations for this lack of continuity. First of all, the three schools disappeared with their founders: Külpe takes off from Berlin in 1909 and dies in 1915 and no more work comes out of Wurzburg; Titchener dies in 1927 (Leahay, 1987) without leaving a successor; Binet (1857–1911), famous for the diversity of his interests (Avanzini, 1974), was already devoting himself to other work, in particular to his scale for the rating of intelligence. Still, this work was at least initially connected with the research of Burloud (1927a,b; 1938), and then with that of de la Garanderie (1969; 1989), a pupil of Burloud, who produced a number of works destined for pedagogical use. To this it has to be added that the disappearance of introspection coincides with troubled times in European history, which

---

[6] Cf. Fraisse (1963) who, at the time, was the Frenchman most deeply involved in the scientific and institutional defence of experimental psychology, and wrote in a basic manual for students in psychology: 'Titchener, a student of Wundt, who, in the course of the 35 years of his teaching at Cornell, came to represent in America a psychology systematically founded upon introspection, only makes clear — through the vacuity of his immense opus — the basic errors of this psychology' (p. 20).

caused numerous lines of research to be interrupted. Also, all work was stopped by the 1914–18 war, and it is not until 1921 that a link with the past is re- established with further publications. And the same holds of the rise of fascism: the emigration of German psychology, silence on the part of Italian and Russian psychology, then the rupture caused by the second world war.

But this historical background still seems insufficient to account for the virtual disappearance of introspection. Why did it not make a come-back in the 1950s? I believe that the real problem is the meaning accorded to the descriptive data accessible to introspection. The criticism no longer bears upon the method of collecting data but on the significance of the data collected, on their functionality.

Hence, introspection is supposed to be useless because the mechanisms and essential properties of cognitive functioning do not stem from subjective experience but are sub-personal. This offers a way of interpreting the results obtained by the Wurzburg school relative to the evidence for imageless thinking. What is essential to the functioning of thought is not accessible to consciousness, does not bring with it any describable phenomenal evidence. In other words, don't ask the subject for something about which he cannot know anything. As a matter of fact, the hypothesis is not unreasonable. Many of the facts studied by psychologists can only be brought to light by means of special equipment or by statistical inference. What is wrong about this line of reasoning is that it moves from the premise that there are facts which are inaccessible to consciousness to the conclusion that even what is accessible to consciousness is uninteresting or non-scientific, and this *a priori*, which is not only absurd but wholly unjustified. However the question which now remains open is that of the meaning and function of those psychological elements which arise from a properly phenomenological consciousness, that is, those which the subject can experience.

This is one of the most crucial criticisms directed at the world of Titchener by Boring (1953, p. 174). The latter quotes in particular an anecdote in which Baird,[7] a student of Titchener, attempted to demonstrate the process of introspective questioning at the 1913 APA Congress, and in which he describes the general reaction as a failure to appreciate the interest in descriptions which are perceived as '. . . a dull taxonomic account of sensory events which, since they suggest almost no functional value for the organism, are peculiarly uninteresting to the American scientific temper.' In particular, during the undertaking reference was made to kinaesthetic sensations which no one knew what to do with. Whereas a visual image can support a piece of reasoning, can be described in terms of the properties of the task, the presence of kinaesthetic sensations does not seem to have any interest with regard to the functions of the mind. It is precisely this sensorial dimension which attracts the most complete incomprehension. The cognitive psychology of the beginning of this century hoped to come to terms with cognitive functioning as a prolongation of sensualism by means of conscious images which were supposed to accompany all thought and runs up against an imageless dimension of thinking, its operative dimension (in Piaget's sense), its finalized dimension. The study of problem solving seeks logical laws connecting phases of reasoning structured by the content of the reasoning process. In this

---

[7] Also the author of a manual of introspective methodology which it would be interesting to revive (referred to by English, 1921, p. 404).

framework, the sensorial dimension of thought, initially rejected as an outdated hypothesis is then later totally forgotten in the programmes of research.

In fact, it will be practitioners (teachers, re-educators, speech therapists, trainers, etc.) who are going to make sense of it, who are going to take account of the sensorial modality in which a content of thought, a mental act, is experienced as being used. These practices are numberless,[8] the articles and works devoted to it not bearing any relation to what has been developed in the course of fifty years of apparent neglect of introspection. The implications of this development are so important that they ought to be developed in their own right. For the gathering of information stemming from subjective experience and making use of introspection (without the latter ever being the explicit theme) bring to light an entire set of cognitive properties, linked to the subject's own use of cognition (primarily in a pre-reflective way). How do I provide myself with an image, how do I organize information in my representation, what are my criteria for the recognition of an identification? Obviously, a great deal of third-person research is to be found relating to all these points, but what these practices reveal is that there is a disjunction between what the subject knows how to do with his cognition in a practical way and the deeper laws which objectify the properties of the practice. That to which one can have access through the description of subjective experience appears secondary or less central, but one could also say that it is a question of the handle of cognition. To be sure, the blade is what is essential but it cannot be used without the handle. Or rather, the way in which the handle is used describes the reality of the subjective practice of cognitive activity. This remarkable fact is consistent with the fact that the data which stems from introspection proves to be more directly relevant to occupations which form, re-educate, look after, improve the activities in question.

What makes sense of the information stemming from introspection is to be found in practices, in as much as it is the latter which bring to light their functionality, their relevance. From the other side, the practices of psychotherapists, of re-educators, of trainers employ know-how which is built up in a pragmatic fashion on the basis of the professional practice itself and aside from the university programmes of research in cognitive science which seem to have been left behind.[9]

In the first place, introspection seems, to the researchers of the beginning of the century, to be the only viable methodological approach; but then it was only retained at best as an auxiliary procedure or only employed on condition that no mention should be made of it and that reference should simply be made to its product in the form of verbalization. It seems to me that subjective experience is now taken account of in such a way as to open up a new programme which is no longer to be thought of as simply complementary to research in the third-person but also as establishing a level of analysis which could be supported by a phenomenological psychology.

---

[8] Cf. the work of de la Garanderie in France, Gendling's experiments with 'focusing', the techniques developed by Bandler, Grinder, Andreas, Dilts and known by the generic name of neuro-linguistic programming, Gallway's techniques for athletic training etc.

[9] For instance, the work on sensorial sub-modalities, the basic date for which one finds in Titchener, and the highly sophisticated intervention techniques developed by Bandler and MacDonald (1988). It is amusing to note that 80 years after the death of Titchener, it is again in the USA that one finds a new interest in the sensorial dimension of subjective experience developed both to a high degree of refinement and in the context of an unparalleled pragmatism.

IV: Improving Introspection?

Have we improved the methodology of introspection since Maine de Biran? If none
of the criticisms which have been formulated have proved decisive then how could
the practice of introspection be improved?

   We can try to reply to these questions by envisaging introspection successively:

- as the source of empirical data,
- as an epistemological, ethical and practical question,
- as an act.

Introspection as a source of empirical data

As a source of empirical data, introspection furnishes descriptive verbalization in the
second-person of what can appear to the subject, within the limits of what has already
been brought to conscious awareness or of what could be brought to conscious awareness. In this respect introspection presents no greater problem than any other source
of data or, what comes down to the same thing, just as great a problem. No more than
with any other source of data, no claim is made on behalf of these verbalizations being
true *a priori*. The fact that it is the subject who verbalizes his own experience does not
render it any more certain *a priori*. Just as much as any other source of data, introspective data has to be subject to critical evaluation and, more particularly, inserted into a
framework of research which makes it possible for it to be correlated with other sets
of data obtained independently (traces, observable data, time). The play of experimental variables as well as the sampling choice will play their usual role whether this
be on the plane of experience or upon that of observation (Vermersch, 1993). There is
nothing new about this point of view. One finds it regularly expressed by authors who
do not understand the relentless criticism to which introspection has been subject
(Radford, 1974, for example). Piaget, in his polemical work of 1968 which targets
philosophical psychology, has this to say:

> On the other hand the problem of introspection remains over and it is on this point that we
> touch upon the essential difference between scientific psychology and philosophy. . .
> (p. 168).

> Even if it uses introspection, scientific psychology looks for controls, which means that
> we are not talking about objectivism, since consciousness is involved, but of objectivity
> (p. 192).

Besides, with scientifically minded psychologists, this point of view had already been
adopted from the beginning of the twentieth century, as I tried to show above with reference to the world of the Wurzburg school, of Binet, of Titchener and his students.
Improvement has been confused with the general evolution of research methodology,
even if we are still waiting for ways of dealing with the data of verbalization which
would facilitate its exploitation (Ericsson and Simon, 1984).

Introspection as an epistemological question

If psychology certainly enjoys the dubious privilege of working with a double faced
object, since it is one of those disciplines which has the subject as its object of study,
the question of drawing the line between the first-person point of view and a third-
person point of view which relies upon traces and upon observable evidence remains
unresolved, even if, in the first place, it proved simpler to set it aside (what Piaget

calls a type beta regulation which consists in trying to maintain an equilibrium by ignoring the source of perturbation). The effort to ignore first-person data has meant that we are very far from having developed the competence and experimental experience needed to develop a rigorous methodology in the light of which researchers might have been formed. Now that psychology is certain of its status as a science in its own right, perhaps it might be possible to stop being frightened of introspection and to start shoring up the phenomenological point of view with a view to bringing it into relation with other sources of evidence. It seems rather obvious that, for example, the ever more refined data which is proceeding from neuro-imagery calls for more precise coordination with the description of subjective experience which the tasks and instructions are supposed to induce. As long as the comparisons relate to highly contrasting situations (visual perception versus visual imaging for example) averaging out allows one to obtain results where the residual variation can be set aside. But the whole history of research shows that, sooner or later, one has to refine the qualitative typology of the data furnished by the subject, if only tentatively, in order to be in a better position to integrate the inter- and intra- individual sources of variation (Marquer, 1995).

Over and above the epistemological aspect, several authors underline the ethical motive involved in taking account of subjective experience (Varela *et al.*, 1991; Howe, 1991a,b). How much longer can we afford to remain blind to this dimension? Are we not under some sort of obligation to add a truly scientific dimension to subjectivity? For my part, I would want to add that what is also at stake is the need to coordinate the innumerable practices which make use of first-person data (teaching, remedial action, re-education, training, coaching, therapy, etc.) with the present scientific vacuum which surrounds all those aspects of cognitive functioning which can only be apprehended at a phenomenological level.

Introspection as act

But these two points of view have done nothing more than clear the ground. If I were to stop here, I would be stuck in the position — unchanged from the beginning of the century — of one who talks around the topic of introspection without ever tackling it as concrete praxis, that is to say, as a psychological act effectively put into operation by an individual subject. Here too however, it is necessary to distinguish different aspects of the problem, the first concerning introspection as reflexive activity, the second touching upon the verbalization which follows thereupon.

(1) Introspection and reflecting activity

What does it mean to treat introspection as an act? We first have to get past a piece of specious reasoning. As if the very use of the word 'act' exhausted all that could be said about it, one first encounters an obstacle well known now in teaching and in psychology, the implicit character of the procedural dimension. Describing an act structure requires that one describes its temporal unfolding at different levels of density: the linkage between subordinate goals, the succession of stages and, at the heart of each stage, elementary actions seen both as acts to be accomplished and as information-gathering acts, then the micro operations, etc. (Vermersch, 1994).

But in order to work with such a description it is not only necessary to practise introspection (it is certainly necessary to refer to lived experience) but, in addition, it is necessary to take account of the act itself as a subjective experience or, in other words, to proceed in the direction of an introspection of the act of introspection, which had never been done before by psychologists practising introspection. Titchener alone (1912b) posed a question with regard to the description of the practice of introspection — without giving any very satisfactory response.

> Experimental introspection, we have said, is a procedure that can be formulated; the introspecting psychologist can tell what he does and how he does it (p. 500).

For after having reviewed the publications put out by the Wurzburg school, then his own and those of his students, he admits that his conclusions are meagre:

> it is evident that this account is meagre; it is evident too that it contains an unsifted mixture of fact and theory, of exposition and evaluation (*ibid.*, p. 506).

and a little further on:

> one gets the impression, indeed, that the experimenters, or at least the earlier of them, took the introspective method for granted: they were setting a straightforward task, which the trained observer was competent to perform (*ibid.*, p. 507).

In the final analysis the harvest proves disappointing, a fact whose significance he tries to reduce by pleading the novelty of this step and the need for improvement but which leaves entirely unanswered the question concerning the nature of introspective practice. In all the literature bearing on introspection I have not been able to find a position more clearly and lucidly expressed than that offered by Titchener. However, what he did not see in this article is that he was only exploiting second hand information. In all his citations the only thing that is taken account of is the third-person discourse of experimenters. No reference is to be found to first-person descriptions bearing on the practice of introspection. What is missing is a recognition of what has to be done to bring to fruition a first-person study of the act of introspection, that is, to use as an instrument what one hoped to study by bringing into play a supplementary stage which philosophers call 'meta-reflection'.

Let us try to clarify the framework which might allow us to throw light upon the act of introspection.

Consider the diagram below: at time t1 the subject carries out a task. He lives through something and this lived experience constitutes an initial point of reference (L1) with reference to what follows. In the context of his research work, the subject, alone or with a mediator, tries to describe his lived experience L1. In the course of

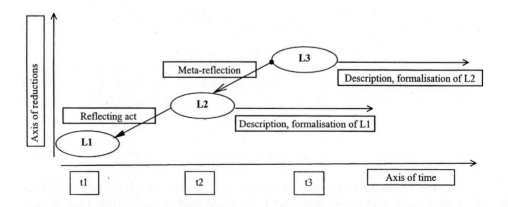

doing this he lives through another lived experience L2, which enables him to gain access to L1 and to describe what he thereby becomes conscious of.

Let us note in passing that this movement directed retrospectively at L1 requires a first reduction in the phenomenological sense of that word, so a mode of givenness which transforms the act which I accomplish in a natural and transparent way (give me the image of a word for which I look for the spelling for instance) into an object for my attention. In order for there to be a givenness of the act by means of which I bring to mind the visual image of a word, there has first to be a break in the way things are given.

Now, in order to know in what the act of introspection consists, my attention has to be directed at L2, and the focus of the problem has been shifted. For in order to know how I gain access to L1 with a view to becoming conscious of it and describing it (which is the whole point of carrying through L2), I have to bring about a new reduction/mode of givenness which, in a later time t3 is directed at the act of introspection carried out at L2. The content of L2 is the past lived experience L1, while the content of L3 is the past accomplishment of that I did in L2. There has to have been an act of the kind which has come about in L2 in order for L3 to be carried through. In other words, one must first have practised introspection (in time L2) in order to make of it an object of study and so to practise an introspection of an introspection. This had quite simply never been done in the context of scientific research!

To get a better idea of the practice of introspection one certainly has to practise it (which seems to have escaped the attention of numerous commentators). Three elements have to be taken account of: the time of meta-reflection, the description of the act, the originality of the reflective activity.

Access to the time in which the introspection is practised (L2) and its description are the essential condition for a comprehension of its realization.

But just as essential is the use of the *act category*. For this is the condition without which it becomes impossible to dissociate, in the description, between the content of the activity (in other words the theme, for example, the word whose image I am looking for), and the act by means of which this image is given. The absence of this distinction between content and act seems to me to lie at the root of many of the difficulties experienced by psychologists at the start of this century, restricting them to descriptions in terms of the mental state or the image and neglecting the temporal unfolding which guides the organisation of any precise description of an activity.[10]

With the distinction between the different lived experiences L1, L2, L3, and that distinguishing content and act, we have only succeeded in bringing to light the framework necessary for grasping introspection as the effectuation of an act; but the act itself still has to be described.

In trying to do this,[11] the first result one obtains is a feeling of poverty, of indigence, of the platitudinous character of the description which comes at the very beginning. What is easy to describe (though still at a global and highly synthetic level) is the content of the act, what it relates to. On the other hand, apprehension of the temporal un-

---

[10] In France however, an utterly unknown author, E. Augier (1934) fully appreciated the question.

[11] I make reference here to the experiential work undertaken by research groups in Paris, on the one hand, in the context of a research group devoted to elucidation (www.es-conseil.fr/GREX), on the other hand in the seminar on practical phenomenology organized in collaboration with N. Depraz and F. Varela.

folding is gappy and highly limited. In retrospect, Titchener's complaints about the meagre harvest regarding the practice of introspection seem to be justified and Lyons (1986; 1991) seems to be right when, in attempting to reproduce the research of one of Titchener's students, Okabe (1910), he concludes that the experiment came to an end before it had even started since the students had nothing to describe. In truth, this initial poverty is only the typical symptom of reflecting activity, that is, of a cognitive activity undertaken with a view to developing conscious awareness, therefore, to relate to something which has not yet become the object of conscious awareness. In the second place,[12] a more or less durable vacuum is experienced. By contrast to rapidly developed reflected activity (the content has already been brought to consciousness, at worst it is momentarily pre-conscious) reflecting activity is a constituting activity, it creates new data on the representational plane (if one follows here the principle underlying Piaget's model of becoming conscious, which begins with a stage of reflectivity) and this creation takes time. The principal obstacle is that the subject who relies upon what he can have access to most easily and most rapidly, that is, reflected consciousness, is then convinced that he knows that he knows nothing or at best a few banal generalities. The practice of introspection, therefore of reflecting activity, shows that the 'filling in' takes place by stages and in accordance with a rhythm which is different from that of reflected activity and that certain conditions are necessary: suspension of the familiar activity making way for a momentary vacuum so that a new fulfilment can be effectuated, access to the lived experience which serves as a point of reference in line with a genuine presentification of the past situation (whose criterion is the presence of sensorial impressions resulting from the reliving of the experience). It lies outside the confines of this article to enter into a detailed description of this reflecting activity,[13] but what seems to me both essential and novel is to have brought to light an initial difficulty surrounding any attempt to carry out an act of intentional introspection (aimed at producing a detailed description), a difficulty which has not been seen, still less studied, but which can now be surmounted.

In order to improve introspection we have to invent ways of getting past the difficulty connected with the means of access. Two ways forward are possible, both of which presuppose mediation as also an apprenticeship, followed by the period needed to develop practical expertise. But this expertise can be developed either by the subject himself in the course of his own self-observation or by the mediator responsible for conducting the interview.

1. This expertise can be acquired by the one practising the introspection. This was the path adopted from the beginning of the century by Wundt and Titchener, both of whom insisted (although in a very different way) on the need to form 'observers', to subject them to a long training until they had become reliable in regard to what they described. Hence, this expertise was not verified with reference to the practice of gaining access to subjective experience (the meta-reflective dimension) but with reference to the calibration of the results obtained by verbalization. A completely different way of proceeding is operative in the formation of a meditator who learns to stabilize his attention and to distinguish objects of observation which did not stand

---

[12] In talking about the first place, I had in mind the possibility of directing attention to the act rather than the content, which corresponds to a first reduction/givenness.

[13] This work has been brought to fruition, in the context of a collaboration with Natalie Depraz and Francisco Varela, in the book *On Becoming Aware,* which is going to appear soon.

out at first in and through an accompanied practice. The main difference with psychologists was the latter were not themselves very competent and were quite incapable of giving advice on the development of the practice itself, while contemplative practices have enjoyed centuries of training and have developed sophisticated teaching skills. Unfortunately, this solution requires a lot of training time and so only a limited number of students can be prepared for research in this way. It also brings with it the disadvantage of limiting the sample still further in the case of specialized activities (for instance, if I have to combine this sampling criterion with the learning of scores by pianists). By contrast, for certain research themes it might be necessary to count on the expertise of such subjects to the extent that they would be the only ones capable of gaining access to certain objects of research, for example, those of short duration or which require high levels of discrimination.

2. It is also worth thinking about second-person methodology based upon a mediator whose aim is to help in the unfolding of the internal act making possible access to the lived experience which features as the point of reference and then to guide the process of verbalization. In this case, the expertise relative to the act of introspection is borne primarily by the one who accompanies the process and indeed makes up one of the dimensions of an interviewing technique. This is what I have chosen to develop by clarifying interview techniques (Vermersch, 1994). My source of inspiration has been contemporary psychotherapeutic practices which regularly make use of introspection to gain access to traumatic events by reliving them. But the past does not have to have been traumatic in order to be presentified. Nor does one have to be a therapist, or even to be in a psychotherapeutic situation, to guide someone towards the reliving of a past moment! The advantage of this solution is that it is not necessary to require in advance that the subject possesses any personal expertise[14] with regard to introspection and so one can easily gather second-person data with a view to extending the sample or, as we are wont to do in our present research, with a view to taking account of all the subjects belonging to the population in question. However, not every observable object can be rendered accessible in this way. To gain access to objects of very short duration or whose observation requires a high level of discrimination an interview may not offer the requisite mediation.

It seems to me that both these two paths, that of mediation and that of expertise relative to gaining access to subjective experience have to be retained and employed in a complementary manner, depending of course upon the particular programme of research.

The work of meta-reflection shows that the development of introspection presupposes the controlled employment of reflecting activity as the condition of conscious apprehension of lived experience which otherwise remains largely pre-reflective. In other words there is a field of potential information which does not simply bear upon first-person facts relating to subjective experience but, in addition, the greater part of this data is only accessible in the context of a consciousness which is retrospectively directed. Indeed, this is the real meaning of reflecting activity. Most of the research has been guided by the idea that it was enough to ask the subject for a description in order to obtain one or at least to put certain questions to him in order to have his answers. Simply adopting this approach is enough to see that things don't work like this.

---

[14] But of course this situation of guidance is itself highly formative.

If the subject wants to be able to produce a description he first has to presentify the lived experience which serves as the point of reference and to suspend his usual way of doing things in order that what previously only existed 'in act' (therefore in a pre-reflective way) now appears as object. This is the difficulty, or even the condition, which makes mediation or an apprenticeship necessary.

(2) Introspection and verbalization

But the reflecting activity which characterizes introspection in its way of relation to pre-reflective lived experience is of interest for our research only to the extent that it creates data, only that is, to the extent that the subject verbalizes[15] what appears to him. Since verbalization is not the whole of introspection but only one facet of it, the quality of this verbalization is what matters, that is, its precision (the density of the description), its completeness relation to a particular object of research, its character as a description — which should minimise the element of interpretation.

To set out deliberately to obtain verbalizations meeting these qualities only seems to me to be possible on condition that mediation is employed, that is, an interview technique. This decision is not at all obvious. With regard to the collection of verbalization data relative to the study of problem solving, for example, the use of an expert interviewing technique has hardly ever been envisaged. The intersubjective exchange can be summed up as a matter of finishing verbalization instructions and of offering encouragement (Ericsson and Simon, 1984). This choice had already been discussed at the beginning of the century but since the very concept of an interview technique did not exist then it finished up as a debate about the interest of posing questions of formulating follow-up strategies. Titchener (1912c, p. 506) came down strongly against such procedures, so the Wurzburg school researchers were divided on this issue. The great fear, and a perfectly relevant one, was and still is that of inducing the content of the replies by the formulation of question and so to run the risk eliminating spontaneous expression or prompting the replies. However, some progress has been made in interviewing techniques since the 1900s. Innumerable therapeutic techniques have been devoted to promoting careful attention of what is said, to improving the prompts, a technical progress which seems to have entirely ignored by cognitive research. It is possible to pose closed questions or to pose questions in the form of alternatives which bring, by their very formulation, more information than they are supposed to be gathering. Much is gained by replacing the questions: 'Did you begin by looking at the drawing?' or 'Did you look at the drawing or did you read the instructions?' with the question : 'What did you begin with?' The latter formulation is at one and the same time both open (it makes no suggestion as to what has taken place) and structurally focused, since it directs attention to a relatively well-defined and identifiable moment (the beginning) unlike a question such as: 'what do you think of what you have done' which is also open but oriented more towards the production of a judgment or a commentary than towards a descriptive verbalization of the lived experience. This is not the place to enter into the detail of all the techniques allowing one to produce questions which are both precise and which do no induce

---

[15] I am simplifying matters because not only do we have to take account of the discursive dimension which I emphasize but also the larger expressive dimension which covers all modes of symbolisation: drawing, dancing, modelling, all of which can be employed.

specific responses, nor to review all the theoretical grids allowing one to gather what is implicit in what is said with a view to pressing for information which one sees has not yet been formulated. But a more adequate exploitation of introspection depends on techniques such as these, which I have presented elsewhere (Vermersch, 1993).

I am very much in favour of apprenticeship and the use of interviewing techniques. What are my arguments?

- *The subject expresses more than his project requires him to communicate.*
This claim already seems to me to require a witness who collects and notes indications which are non verbal, para-verbal and epi-verbal. A video recorder could provide all this information. But it is not the camera which, having recorded some gesture accompanying the verbal expression, is going to draw the attention of the subject to this gesture which expresses more or something other than, the words used and so prompts further clarification. The subject itself is not capable of exploiting these signals since he is not conscious of them. To be sure we must not fantasize the existence of an observer capable of knowing everything the other is trying to say, but simply that of a companion attentive to what is being expressed across what is said and who utilizes these signals to redirect the subject with a view to getting him to explain what he expresses but does not formulate.

- *The subject verbalizes less by himself than he would have done with a mediator.*
This second claim might appear to be in contradiction with the first. But this is not the case inasmuch as it does not bear on the same issue. In the first case, the subject provides — in non-conscious fashion — more information than he thinks he has given and the presence of an interviewer makes it possible to prompt him with regard to what has been shown but not named, in the second case, and with reference to what the subject intends to formulate, it is possible to carry him along further than he is capable of going by himself. And this for several reasons:

~ As soon as there is a need for delay, for an inhibition of the most immediate modes of response, the presence of a mediator facilitates the necessary suspension. In fact, putting something into words is done in accordance with the rhythm of what is disclosed, so preferable slowly, and external guidance can help the subject to take the time to become open to the appropriate form of expression. Gaining access to subjective events of short duration or the descriptive dismantling of intermediary stages requires a slowing down, a temporal dilation of the moment which has just been lived, which can be facilitated by a guidance which transfers the attentions of the observer to the specifics of what he has just lived through rather than to the regulation of his mode of access. The interviewer can help to regulate the moments when the reflected knowledge takes over from the reflecting process (a little like in drawing when I draw a rectangular table because I know it is rectangular even when what I see is trapezoid). Staying with the articulation in words of what appears is a delicate matter and demands that one maintain a meta position with respect to what one verbalizes. It can be done by oneself but not without a long apprenticeship and training.

~ The search for a precise description, its scheduling, are activities which are superimposed upon the simple fact of saying. This multiplies the risks that certain aspects remain implicit. The presence of someone capable of detecting the implications helps in the production of a more precise and complete description. Paying attention to the fragmentation of the description (Vermersch, 1994) immediately alerts one to the global character of what is named and so makes it possible to follow the matter up by asking for a break-down of what is described.

~ The subject can also be induced to say more if left to himself than if he is prompted by questions which lead him to turn his attention to aspects of his lived experience for which he lacks the categories needed to make it possible for him to be aware of them. But again this guidance requires structuring.

It is not difficult to find arguments in favour of utilizing the mediation of an interviewer but the limitations of the mediator himself may well present a problem. On the one hand, becoming an expert interviewer takes a long time and a lot of training is needed to master the techniques and to deploy them in the course of the exchange. On the other hand, whatever the level of his detachment the mediator is still bound by the limits of his culture, his preconceptions, his implicit blinkers, his unconscious projections. And it would be vain to suppose that it is even possible to throw off all these limitations. This affirmation can only bring us back to the double necessity of intersubjective regulation and of cross-referencing verbalization data against alternative sets of data such as traces or observable evidence.

Introspection and description

Let us suppose that we have succeeded in perfecting this reflecting activity. Let us suppose that the process of verbalization goes off well thanks to an effective, precise and reliable interview technique. Even so a fresh stratum of problems still awaits us, linked to the fact that verbalization produces descriptive data.

On the one hand, this implies that first-person descriptive data are insufficient in themselves to generate a complete research, they are not sufficient in themselves to deliver causal explanations and must necessarily be integrated into a larger programme which takes in other data. Titchener certainly saw this difficulty (1912) even if his own work did not go very far towards solving it.

But on the other hand, this only serves to emphasize the fact that we cannot restrict introspection to descriptions and, therefore, to ask the subject for something other than descriptions is to leave the field of introspection and to move in the direction of representations, towards naive theories of the subject. The goal of introspection is to gather factual descriptions, not to expect the subject to become knowledgeable about his own subjective experience. In consequence, it seems completely out of order to ask the subject for explanations of what he did or to expect him to understand the causes of his behaviour (Nisbett and Wilson, 1977). For we are now asking him for inferences, for theories, and not for a description of what happened to him from his own particular standpoint. It is important not to confuse research into the views held by the subject, his spontaneous representations, his explanations of the world and his cognitive functioning, on the one hand, and testimony regarding what happened in a particular moment of his lived experience, that is, experience lived out within the limits of what can be brought to conscious awareness and what he is capable of expressing, on the other. By the same token, the object of research, as it presents itself to the researcher who inadequately undertakes research into a causal connection or the evidence for a particular mechanism, must not be confused with the object as it presents itself in the lived experience of subjects and with regard to which therefore the subject can only describe what he has lived through.

However, it is obvious that one is not in control of what the subject is going to verbalize, even if one accompanies his activity in an expert manner and precisely because one is interested in descriptions one does not, in the treatment of the data, give the same weight to description that one gives to commentary, judgment or the spontaneous expression of theories. But one might well ask whether this precaution is not pointless to the extent that any expression in a natural language, even if it is intentionally descriptive, is upheld by a horizon of interpretations of which the subject is not conscious? This is a powerful objection and one that cannot be evaded. But perhaps one can relativize its effects by relating them to different frames of reference:

(1) Even while an interview is going on one can easily construct a scale separating descriptive language (relative to our culture at this time) from what immediately appears as an interpretation, an abusive generalization or the expression of a judgment rather than a fact. On this basis, it becomes possible to push towards a verbalization which furnishes the more factual descriptive elements contained in a process of nomination or in an excessively global action verb. Contrary to Titchener's techniques aimed at training students to verbalize only highly refined and basic descriptions, it is possible to collect every type of verbalization and to make use of them as the point of departure for more appropriate descriptions.
(2) The gathering of second-person data makes it possible to compare the variety of responses due to individual differences and so to bring to light the presuppositions of a particular description, and the result is the same when one compares one's own data with that obtained by other teams.
(3) Finally, and to varying degrees, each passing year makes it possible to go back over the data previously registered and to take account of the presuppositions inherent in the viewpoints of that era.

The emphasis placed upon verbalizations and the need for an interview technique underscore the intersubjective framework of second-person research at the very moment in which access to lived experience (reflecting act) is sought and in which descriptive verbalizations of this experience is obtained. Cognitive psychology seems to have wanted to conceal the fact that this intersubjective dimension, linked to the mediation needed to accompany the subject in his effort to gain access to his own subjective experience and to thematize it, requires that the researcher should be trained not only in the 'techniques' but also in developing the kind of personal relation without which the techniques cannot be used effectively. Introspection requires that the 'subject' of cognitive psychology be treated as a person and that, in consequence, the researcher should also be trained at this more personal level.

Conclusion

What I have tried to do is to justify introspection as a practice, to take account of successive improvement in the procedure and even to propose a certain number myself. In attempting to do this I have had to ignore a great many problems, a great many authors. I have tried to lay out the general lines of a regulated methodology, one which can certainly be improved but only on condition that it is actually employed.

Introspection is difficult; it is a technique; it demands an apprenticeship, requires the progressive development of a genuine expertise. And worst of all, the technical

side of introspection is concealed; it can be overlooked on account of the apparent
ease with which it is possible to obtain at least some information about our states, our
thoughts, our emotions, a facility which proves fallacious just as soon as one attempts
to provide true descriptions and to gain access to subjective experience in a stable and
precise fashion. But just as looking at a garden does not of itself give one the ability to
be a gardener or a botanist, so to be in familiar contact with our own states does not
give us the competence of a phenomenologist or a psychologist. Piaget (1953,
pp. 282–6) was remarkably accurate when he pointed out that knowledge of the 'internal' world is not given to us in a way essentially different from that of the world of
objects. In both cases there is a construction on the basis of the interaction between
the subject and the world, between the subject and himself.

The first improvement in the use of introspection has been to pass from the first-
person point of view in which subject and observer cannot be distinguished to a
second-person point of view where several subjects distinct from the researcher are
studied. Today, I would add the rider that the researcher ought to have an in-depth personal experience of the practice of introspection, that he should have a real familiarity
with the structure of his subjective experience relative to his object of research and in
such a way as to be able to control his implicit projections upon the experience of others. This 'rite of passage' imposes an obligation to work on verbalizations and, even
more obviously, poses questions concerning techniques relative to their production,
to their collection, to the ways in which one can help in developing these verbalizations which I think about, personally, in terms of interviewing techniques. The second
improvement has been to control the framework, in other words, to define a task, to
specify the instructions, to standardize the transitions, to gather complementary and
independent traces. The third stage seems to me to rest on the development of the dimension of 'meta-reflection', by applying introspection with a view to improving our
understanding of it. This is what we are presently working at. The line of thought we
are presently pursuing[16] is that of learning to appreciate the originality and the importance of reflecting activity. Introspection is based upon this reflecting activity, but so
is the phenomenological reduction as well as the intuitive acts analysed by C. Peugeot
(in this volume). On the one hand, this result is a way of showing how examining attentively the practice by means of which one gains access to subjective experience
leads one to an important question with regard to consciousness envisaged as an explicit becoming conscious 'of'. On the other hand, this reflecting activity brings to
light another field of data. For we can no longer allow ourselves to be confined within
the dichotomy of sub-personal and phenomenological consciousness. Rather we must
be open to the possibility of interposing between these two a whole host of non-
conscious information (and not even at the level of reflected consciousness) but information which can nevertheless be brought to full conscious awareness. Becoming
conscious and becoming capable of verbalization presupposes a procedure, a suspension of one's habitual attitudes, a modification of the quest for information, a semantic suspension whereby the process of putting into words is subordinated[17] to that of
being open to experience. In short, a process of guidance which is something other

---

[16] See footnote 13 above.

[17] cf. Piguet's (1975) idea regarding semantic reversal.

than a set of instructions. After all, subjective experience is certainly a fact of personal life. Perhaps we need a more refined theory and practice of intersubjectivity?

References

Augier, E. (1934), *Mécanismes et conscience* (Paris: Alcan).
Avanzini, G. (1974), *A. Binet: écrits psychologiques et pédagogiques* (Toulouse: Privat).
Bakan, D. (1954), 'A reconsideration of the problem of introspection', *Psychological Bulletin*, **51**, pp. 105–18.
Bandler, R. And MacDonald, W. (1988), *An Insider's Guide to Sub-modalities* (Cupertino: Meta Publications).
Binet, A. (1894), *Introduction à la psychologie expérimentale* (Paris: Alcan).
Binet, A. (1903), *L'étude expérimentale de l'intelligence* (Paris: Costes).
Biran, Maine de (1932/1807), *Essai sur les fondements de la psychologie et sur ses rapports avec l'étude de la nature*, Tome VIII et IX (Paris: Alcan).
Bode, H. B. (1913), 'The method of introspection', *Journal of Philosophy*, **10**.
Boring, E.G. (1938), 'Titchener on meaning', *Psychological Review*, **45**, pp. 92–5.
Boring, E.G. (1953), 'A history of introspection', *Psychological Bulletin*, **50** (3), pp. 169–89.
Brentano, F. (1944/1874), *Psychologie du point de vue empirique* (Paris: Aubier).
Burloud, A. (1927a), *La pensée d'après les recherches expérimentales de Watt, Messer, Bühler* (Paris: Alcan).
Burloud, A. (1927b), *La pensée conceptuelle* (Paris: Alcan).
Burloud, A.(1938), *Principes d'une psychologie des tendances* (Paris: Alcan).
Claparède, E. (1934), 'Genèse de l'hypothèse', *Archives de Psychologie*, **25** (93/94), pp. 1–155.
Clarke, H.M. (1911), 'Conscious attitudes', *American Journal of Psychology*, **22**, pp. 214–49.
Comte, A. (1830/1975), *Philosophie première. Cours de philosophie positive*, Leçons 1 à 45 (Paris: Hermann).
Dumas, G. (1924), *Traité de psychologie*, deux tomes (Paris: Alcan).
English, H.B. (1921), 'In aid of introspection', *American Journal of Psychology*, **32**, pp. 404–14.
Ericsson, K.A. and Simon, H.A. (1984/1993), *Protocol Analysis, Verbal Protocols as Data* (Cambridge, MA: MIT Press).
Ericsson, K.A. and Crutcher, RJ, (1991), 'Introspection and verbal reports on cognitive processes — Two approaches to the study of thinking : a response to Howe', *New Ideas in Psychology*, **9** (3), pp. 57–71.
Fraisse, P. (1963), 'L'évolution de la psychologie expérimentale', in *Traité de Psychologie expérimentale*, tome I, by P. Fraisse & J. Piaget (Paris: PUF).
Garanderie, A. de la (1969), '*Schématisme et thématisme' Le dynamisme des structures inconscientes dans la psychologie d'A. Burloud* (Louvain: Nauvelaert).
Garanderie, A. de la (1989), *Défense et illustration de l'introspection* (Paris: Centurion).
Geissler, L.R. (1909), 'The measurement of attention', *American Journal of Psychology*, **20**, pp. 437–529.
Guillaume, P. (1932), *Manuel de psychologie* (Paris: PUF).
Hayes, S.P. (1906), 'A study of the affective qualities', *American Journal of Psychology*, **17**, pp. 358–93.
Howe, R.B.K. (1991a), 'Introspection a reassessment', *New Ideas in Psychology*, **9** (1), pp. 25–44.
Howe, R.B.K. (1991b), 'Reassessing Introspection : a reply to Natsoulas, Lyons, and Ericsson and Crutcher', *New Ideas in Psychology*, **9** (3), pp. 383–94.
Humphrey, G. (1951), *Thinking: An Introduction to Its Experimental Psychology* (London: Methuen).
Jacobson, E. (1911), 'On meaning and understanding', *American Journal of Psychology*, **22**, pp. 553–77.
James, W. (1890), *The Principles of Psychology*, 2 vol. (London: Macmillan).
Leahey, T.H. (1987), *A History of Psychology* (Englewood Cliffs, NJ: Prentice-Hall).
Lennon, P. (1989), 'Introspection and intentionality in advanced second-language acquisition', *Language Learning*, **39**, pp. 375–96.
Lyons, W.E. (1986) *The Disappearance of Introspection* (Cambridge, MA: MIT Press).
Lyons, W.E. (1991), 'Introspection — A two-level or one-level account ? : a response to Howe', *New Ideas in Psychology*, **9** (3), pp. 51–5.

Mandler, J.M. and Mandler, G. (1964), *Thinking from Association to Gestalt* (New York: John Wiley & Sons).

Marquer, J. (1995), 'Variabilité intra et interindividuelles dans les stratégies cognitives : l'exemple du traitement des couples de lettres', in *Universel et différentiel en psychologie*, ed. J. Lautrey (Paris: PUF).

Mayer, A. and Orth J. (1901), 'Zur qualitativen Untersuchung der Association', *Zeitschrift für Psychologie*, **26**, pp. 1–13.

Montebello, P. (1994), *La décomposition de la pensée* (Grenoble: Million).

Moore, F.C.T. (1970), *The Psychology of Maine de Biran* (Oxford: Clarendon Press).

Nakashima, T. (1909), 'Contributions to the study of the affective processes', *American Journal of Psychology*, **20**, pp. 157–93.

Nisbett, R.E. and Wilson, T.D. (1977), 'Telling more than we can know: verbal reports on mental processes', *Psychological Review*, **84** (3), pp. 231–59.

Okabe, T. (1910), 'An experimental study of belief', *American Journal of Psychology*, **21**, pp. 563–96.

Piaget, J. (1950), *Introduction à l'épistémologie génétique*, tome III (Paris: PUF).

Piaget, J. (1968), *Sagesse et illusion de la philosophie* (Paris: PUF).

Piguet, J-C. (1975), *La connaissance de l'individuel et la logique du réalisme* (Neuchâtel: A la Baconnière).

Pyle, W.H. (1909), 'An experimental study of expectation', *American Journal of Psychology*, **20**, pp. 530–69.

Radford, J. (1974), 'Reflections on introspection', *American Psychologist*, **29**, pp. 245–50.

Sartre, J-P. (1940), *L'imaginaire* (Paris: Gallimard).

Titchener, E.B. (1909), *Lectures on the Experimental Psychology of Thought Processes* (New York: Macmillan).

Titchener, E.B. (1912a), 'Description vs statement of meaning', *American Journal of Psychology*, **23**, pp. 165–82.

Titchener, E.B. (1912b), 'Prolegomena to a study of introspection', *American Journal of Psychology*, **23**, pp. 427–48.

Titchener, E.B. (1912c), 'The schema of introspection', *American Journal of Psychology*, **23**, pp. 485–508.

Titchener, E.B. (1913), 'The method of examination', *American Journal of Psychology*, **24**, pp. 429–40.

Varela, F.J., Thompson, E. and Rosch, E. (1991), *The Embodied Mind* (Cambridge, MA: MIT Press).

Vermersch, P. (1993), 'Pensée privée et représentation pour l'action', in *Représentations pour l'action*, ed. A. Weill, P. Rabardel and D. Dubois (Toulouse: Octarès).

Vermersch, P. (1994), *L'entretien d'explicitation* (Paris: ESF).

Voutsinas, D. (1964), *La psychologie de Maine de Biran* (Paris: SIPE).

Watt, H.J. (1905), 'Experimentelle Beiträge zu einer Theorie des Denkens', *Archiv für die gesamte psychologie*, **4**, pp. 289–436.

Wundt, W. (1904/1874), *Principles of Physiological Psychology* (New York: Macmillan).

Wundt, W. (1907), 'Uber Ausfrageexperiments und über die Methoden zur Psychologie des Denkens', *Psychologische Studien*, **3**, pp. 301–60.

Claire Petitmengin-Peugeot

The Intuitive Experience

Throughout the history of human thought and in every field of knowledge intuition has played an essential role. It is therefore very surprising that so few studies have been dedicated to the study of the subjective experience which is associated with it.

For example, the history of the sciences from Archimedes to Ampère, Gauss, Kékulé, Pasteur, Poincaré, Hadamard, Heisenberg . . .[1] is full of testimonies of scientists telling about how a new idea came to them in a sudden, unexpected manner, without any discursive activity. A lot of attention has been paid to the content of these intuitions, and a considerable amount of energy spent on exploring their consequences. However, even though a discovery has had important repercussions in our daily lives, very little attention has been paid to the experience itself, what the scientist was living through at the very moment of the intuitive breakthrough: 'the art of knowing has remained unspecifiable at the very heart of science' (Polanyi, 1962, p. 55). Astonishingly enough, this 'forgetting' of the intuitive experience also affects philosophy. Yet there are very few philosophic systems that do not work with the notion of intuition. From Plato's intuition of Idea, to Descartes' intuition of simple natures, to Hegelian and Husserlian intuition, 'intuition represents the ideal of all knowledge, the ideal of understanding of being in general' (Heidegger, 1993, p. 167.) Nevertheless, compared to the volumes and volumes consecrated to the definition of the concept of intuition, to the description of the content of philosophic intuitions, and to the theoretical exploration of their consequences, how many pages have been written on the intuitive experience itself? Far from being 'our most intimate and our most personal experience' (Schelling, 1856, p. 87), is not the philosopher's intuition just an intellectual act, an experience in thought, a project of an experience? Is not the philosopher's intuition nothing more than a certain familiarity with a play of language, as Wittgenstein suggested (notably in 1968, sections 109 ff.)?

The intuitive experience is not studied for itself, neither in the field of artistic creation, nor in the field of psychotherapy, nor in that of managerial decision-making, not even in daily life, where intuition often appears although in a more subtle form. When

Correspondence: Claire Petitmengin-Peugeot, Institut National des Télécommunications, 9 rue Charles Fourier, 91011 Evry, France.   Email: claire.peugeot@int-evry.fr

---

[1] We should add to this list, which is very long, the testimony of contemporary scientists, for example, mathematicians like Laurent Shwartz, Alain Connes, etc.

Journal of Consciousness Studies, **6**, No. 2–3, 1999, pp.43–77

studies on intuition are not just limited to the recording of anecdotes, their objective is usually to prove the existence of the intuitive phenomenon, or to identify popular beliefs about intuition, or even to evaluate the intuitive capacities of a given population, but not to describe the actual subjective experience associated with the intuition.

Why evade the subject? Can we explain this through the weight of rationalism, which, considering knowledge as an analytical, deductive process, can only ignore intuition, or bring it down to the level of an unconscious inference, which is the same as denying the phenomenon? Can it be explained through the weight of positivism, which, only considering objective phenomena as objects of science, rejects the study of the subjective experience? This attitude would partially explain why scientific research has not yet developed a method which would make this kind of study possible. Above and beyond positivist prejudices, we know that the largely 'pre-thought' character of actual subjective experiences renders it extremely difficult to elaborate a method which would enable one to become aware of it and to describe it.

But it seems to us that a supplementary reason, specific to intuition, could explain the absence of studies of the intuitive experience: these studies have perhaps been discouraged by a confusion about the different meanings of the character of 'immediacy' which defines intuitive knowledge.

'Immediate' knowledge is first of all direct knowledge, which cannot be reached through an intermediary reasoning process. It is not understood progressively, at the end of a deductive process consisting of the accumulation of middle terms. On the contrary, the appearance of an intuition contains a character of discontinuity: it surges forth with a leap, unexpectedly, out of our control. The testimonies generally focus on this moment of surging forth, which could explain the absence of descriptions of the intuitive experience: for, if it is possible to describe a process unfolding over time, how can you describe an unpredictable surging? Moreover, in the most famous accounts of intuitive experiences, this first dimension of immediacy (discontinuity in the intuitive experience) is often assimilated with a discontinuity of appearance:[2] the content of the intuition appears all of a sudden, complete. There again, there is no room for a genetic description of the intuition.

Now it seems, on the one hand, that the assimilation of these two types of discontinuity is unjustified because instantaneity is not the most common mode of appearance of intuition: it appears most often in a progressive manner, in the form of a slow ripening; which renders a genetic description possible.

On the other hand, does the direct character of an intuition eliminate all possibility of description? For, if there is no method to produce the intuition, are there not 'training' circumstances that make it possible to prepare an interior disposition which allows the intuition to appear? Without being the direct result, the reward of the mediation, is not the unpredictable surging forth of the intuition encouraged by a propitious conditioning? And could not this preparation, this interior moving forward, become the object of a description?

Moreover the philosophers of intuition agree on the existence of a pre-intuitive gesture: Platonic conversion, Cartesian doubt, phenomenological reduction, etc., are all such gestures making it possible to carry out an unlearning process, a break in our usual manner of looking at the world, thus liberating an interior space for intuition to

---

[2] We take our formulation in these terms of this distinction from Judith Schlanger in: *Les concepts scientifiques. Invention et pouvoir*, p. 67.

spring forth. But once again, philosophers remain very cautious concerning the experiential characteristics of this gesture, which initiated their search for wisdom .

Our research comes as the result of our surprise at the silence surrounding the intuitive experience, though it seems to be at the heart of human experience. We wanted to go a little further into the description of the intuitive experience, to attempt the adventure of the psycho-phenomenology of intuition. Specifically, we wanted to verify to what degree intuition is an experience which mobilizes our whole being, not only its intellectual dimension but also its sensorial, emotional dimension.

To do this, we carried out a series of interviews, adopting a special method of exploration which we will describe in the first section: how to have access to the pre-thought-out aspects of the intuitive experience, how to clarify them, how to analyse and compare the descriptions we have obtained.

To our surprise, we saw a generic structure of the intuitive experience emerge from this work of description and analysis. This structure is made up of an established succession of very precise interior gestures with a surprising regularity from one experience to another and from one subject to another. In our second section we will present the most significant aspects of this generic experiential structure.

In a third section we will bring up a number of considerations and questions resulting from this phenomenological description.

I: METHODOLOGY

The method that we have employed to carry out a phenomenological description of the intuitive experience is broken down into three stages:

- gathering descriptions of intuitive experiences,
- analysis and modelling of the descriptions,
- comparing the established models.

1. GATHERING DESCRIPTIONS

The difficulty of obtaining descriptions of the intuitive experience comes essentially from the fact that the gestures which prepare and follow the emergence of an intuition belong to that dimension of experience which is not a part of thought-out consciousness. According to Pierre Vermersch's development of this idea in the explicitation session, supported by Piaget's theory of awareness, we do not need to know what we did in order to succeed in carrying out a physical or mental action. A successful action can even be accompanied by an erroneous representation of its unfolding. Our know-how, 'remarkably efficient, though not knowing itself' (Piaget, 1974a, p. 275), is, in large part, made up of 'pre-thought'.

This part of our knowledge, which is non-conscious — and which is not explainable as an unconscious repression in the Freudian sense — seems to be present even at the centre of our most abstract activities, those most conceptualized, those most lacking in affectivity.

It is the depth of this 'personal knowledge' (Polanyi, 1962) that makes the difference between the expert and the beginner, who is satisfied just in applying the rules, even if there is an element of pre-thought gesture at every degree of expertise.

For a person to be able to describe his experience, he must become conscious of this pre-thought knowledge. And this awareness necessitates a reversal, a break with his habitual attitude, which consists of acting without knowing how he does it, without knowing what he knows. This reversal is far from being trivial. It is sometimes triggered off under the pressure of an obstacle, of a failure. The explicitation session is a technique which enables us to provoke this awareness during an interview, through the mediation of the interviewer.

1.1 The Explicitation Session

It is a matter of clarifying the pre-thought 'lived' experience of an action, that is, of bringing the subject to the point where he describes what he really does, and not what he thinks or imagines he does. The process of explicitation unfolds in three stages:

- bringing the subject to the point of living, or reliving, the action or experience to be explored,
- helping him to operate a 'thinking-through' of his experience, that is, to pass his know-how from the level of action to the level of representation,
- enabling him to put into words, to clarify, this represented experience.

1.1.1 Accessing the experience

One of the strong ideas that supports the explicitation session is that the lived-out experience can only be singular. In other terms, access to pre-thought can be brought about only by exploring a precise experience, precisely situated in time and in space. One cannot live an experience 'in general'. What would then be described would not be an experience but rather the abstract impoverished representation of an experience, in which the implicit aspects would be lost. There are two possible processes of access to this singular experience:

Reliving a past experience
In this case, the interviewer guides the subject towards a position of 'embodied'[3] speech in order to help him evoke a particular experience from the past, in such a way that the subject 'relives' the past situation, with all the sensorial and emotional dimensions that it includes, and to the point that the past situation becomes more present for the subject than does the situation of being interviewed.[4] This position of speech is in opposition to a position of 'abstract' speech, in which a subject expresses himself more from his knowledge than from his experience.

To guide a subject towards the concrete evocation of his experience, different techniques are used; the main one consists of helping the subject to rediscover, in a very precise manner, the images, sensations, sounds . . . that are associated with his experience, until he feels that he is reliving it.[5]

A certain number of indications enable the interviewer to verify if the subject is really reliving an experience: in particular, letting go of eye contact, unfocusing — that is, the fact that the subject drops eye contact with the interviewer and looks off

---

[3] Used in the signification that F. Varela, E. Rosch and E. Thompson give this term in *The Embodied Mind* (1991) to describe the deep-rooting of thought in the corporeal experience.

[4]   In the technique of the explicitation session, this particular state of consciousness is called 'a state of evocation'.

[5] The theoretic model which supports the interview of explicitation on this point is the model of 'affective memory', or 'concrete memory', developed by G. Gusdorf in *Mémoire et Personne* (1951).

into empty space, off into the horizon. Using the present tense instead of the past can also be an indication.

Living the experience 'in the present'

In this case, the subject describes the experience as he is living it out. Access to this experience is therefore much easier because it is being lived out here and now. But even in this case access to the pre-thought is not trivial. For even while he is living the experience, the subject is rarely completely present in it. Whether the experience is being lived while being experienced or is 'relived', the subject interviewed often escapes to a position of abstract language, that is, instead of precisely describing the singular experience that he is living through, he slides towards making comments, judgments about the experience or about the intuitive experience in general. The interviewer's mediation will help him to stay within the limits of his own experience.

1.1.2 Access to pre-thought

The procedure used to facilitate access to pre-thought aims at provoking a reversal of the subject's attention to his internal process, and a slowing down of the 'film' of his experience. The slowing down can be obtained by directly asking the subject to slow down his rhythm of speech, to take his time.

When we are talking about a past experience, another procedure to bring about both a reversal of the attention and a slowing down consists of formulating questions which the subject cannot answer without recalling the past experience: for example questions concerning the context of the evocation.

An important slowing down of the rhythm of speech, often broken by moments of silence, is the sign that the subject is not reciting ready-to-use knowledge but is becoming aware of aspects of his experience which until then were pre-thought.

1.1.3 Putting into words

The form of questioning in explicitation encourages the description of the experience; this privileges the 'hows' to the exclusion of the 'whys', which would veer the subject off course towards a position of abstract speech. In order to avoid infiltrating his own presuppositions the interviewer uses a language 'empty of content', also called 'Ericksonian' language.[6] Referring to the subject's experience without naming its content, this language allows him to clarify his own experience without inducing the content of the responses nor of influencing the choice of words.

The principle of this form of questioning is to get the subject started again each time indications of implicit information come up, such as:

- non-verbal indications such as the direction of the gaze, which indicates the sensorial register of where the subject is, or gestures which accompany speech (or are substituted for) in a non-conscious manner and indicate a pre-thought corporeal knowledge. As intuition is a mode of knowledge deeply anchored in the body (and we will see this), we have often encountered this kind of gesture during the interviews.
- verbal indications as generalizations, nominalizations.[7]

---

[6] Referring to the American psychotherapist Milton Erickson whose technique Pierre Vermersch has adapted. See Bandler and Grinder (1975).

[7] This questioning of explicitation is inspired by the 'Meta-model' of Neuro-Linguistic Programming, a tool which is presented, in particular, in Grinder and Bandler (1976).

Here are a few typical extracts from the interviews we carried out, which illustrate both the directive (the interviewer guides the subject towards the exploration of certain aspects of his experience) and the neutral character of this form of questioning:

Explicitation of state:

> J: I feel that it's time to visualize my interior landscape.
> C: How do you know that it's time?
> J: Because I have this sensation of calmness.
> C: What's this sensation like, where do you feel it?
> (. . .)

Explicitation of act:

> J: I am concentrating.
> C: How do you concentrate?
> J: I am listening to what is happening inside me.
> C: How do you listen? If you wanted to teach me how to do it, what would you tell me?
> J: First, I'm going to place my consciousness much more towards the back of the skull.
> C: How do you place your consciousness at the back of the skull?
> (. . .)

We noticed that it was difficult, if not impossible, for several of the subjects to live out (or to relive) an intuitive experience and simultaneously to put it into words. Thus the interview acts as a succession of periods of time in which the person silently relives an aspect of the experience, and of periods in which he/she describes the corresponding experience while he/she retains an interior 'trace'. Once this trace has weakened, he has to re-immerse into the experience in order to revive the memory of it and to continue putting it into words.

1.1.4 Intuitive experiences described by using the explicitation session

Twenty-four interviews were carried out, all of which are about knowledge that came about without the intermediary either of a deductive mechanism nor through the habitual senses. This intuitive knowledge can be classified according to its object, which, depending on each case, is:

- the physical, emotional, or mental state of another person (11 intuitions),
- an event distanced in space or in the future (6),
- the behaviour to follow in a given situation (3),
- the solution to a personal question or an abstract problem (4).

The described interviews can also be classified according to the setting in which they took place: therapeutic, scientific, artistic, or daily life. We interviewed:

- Eight psychotherapists belonging to different schools of therapy,[8] either about intuitions concerning the interior state or the life of their patients, or about intuitions that came up in their private lives. Several of these intuitions were explored as they were being experienced.
- Two scientists: one doing research in the 'Economic Studies' department of a big bank, about his intuitive strategy for detecting mistakes in a research report;

---

[8] Psychoanalysis, Bio-energy, Rebirth, S. Grof Holotropic Breathing, Orthobionomy, P.N.L, Vittoz Method.

the second one an astrophysicist, about the sudden intuition he had had on the 'logical structure of quantum mechanics'.

- Two artists: a photographer and a painter, about moments of creative intuition.
- Twelve interviews were carried out about intuitions occurring in 'daily life' (for example: long distance perception of a fire, of the death of someone close, premonition of an accident, intuitive behaviour adopted during a hopeless situation).

1.2 Analysis of Texts

To gather information for the description of the intuitive experience, we also turned to autobiographical testimonies of certain authors who went beyond the exploration of singular intuitive experiences to a stage of elaboration and transmission of knowledge on this mode of cognition and the means to access it. In this way we gathered and analysed the meta-cognition of:

- the psychoanalyst Theodor Reik (1948), in his work *Listening with the third ear: the inner experience of a psychoanalyst.*
- Barbara McClintock, Nobel prize in biology, who devoted her life to the study of 'jumping genes' in corn cells, in Evelyn Fox Keller's biography (1983): *A feeling for the organism: the life and work of Barbara McClintock.*

Through an analysis of the writings of certain authors, notably philosophers (Aristotle, Descartes, Husserl), it was also possible for us to bring certain aspects of their intuitive experiences to light, even if they did not give explicit descriptions. The metaphors used, the choice of words, reveal, at the very limits of their language, something of the private experience (not necessarily conscious), underlining their theories.

2. ANALYSIS AND MODELLING OF THE DESCRIPTIONS

The objective is to extract the structure of different experiences from a rather considerable volume of information, in a form that enables us to compare them in their smallest details.

The transcription of each interview, and of each text containing a meta-cognition, was analysed and modelled in the following way.

2.1 Reduction of the Text to the Descriptive Aspects of the Experience

After having transcribed the interview, the first task consists of selecting the parts of the text which supply the effective description of the experience of an intuition, and of eliminating those which concern other levels of description:[9]

- description of the context, the circumstances of the intuition: useful in understanding the unfolding of the experience, this does not give information on the lived experience of the intuition ('at the moment I put my foot on the step of the bus, the idea came to me').
- commentaries, judgments, beliefs, about the experience in question or the intuitive experience 'in general' for the subject ('the solution often appeared to me at the moment of sudden awakening').

---

[9] In the explicitation session, these levels correspond to the 'system of information surrounding the action' (Vermersch, 1994, pp. 43 ff).

- beliefs, opinions about intuition in general ('women are more intuitive than men').
- theoretical knowledge about intuition ('intuition is a function of the right side of the brain'), or explanations of the phenomenon ('intuition is an unconscious inference').

None of this information tells us about the experience itself, that is, about the possible actions that the subject carries out to encourage the appearance of an intuition, about their links in series, or the interior state which is associated with them.

For example, in the following extracts, commentaries and beliefs about intuition (in italics), are interspersed with the description of actions and states:

> I get comfortably into my feet, and when I exhale, I push the idea upwards, I push towards the middle, I push downwards, I create a bubble. I am in my arms which push, I am in my arms which rise up and create the bubble. I am completely in the feeling. I don't have any images. *Even though when I explain something I always give an image. Therefore I think that I am very visual, but actually, with Vittoz, I have learned a lot about how to just be in the sensation.* (Monique, 195)

> I breathe, I try to find this axis which is destabilized, I say to myself 'don't be afraid', I reassure myself. *Because I am often afraid of this somatization which often comes,* I therefore need to reassure myself at that moment. *It's funny because you always associate intuition with something serious, negative, painful, that happens or will happen, even when it can also be an intuition about something positive, pleasant, and wonderful to live, you see.* (Vanessa, 58)

We also set aside the content of the intuition. The content, like the context, can be useful to understand what kind of experience it is, but contains no information on the subjective living out associated with this experience. That is why we were able to interview a scientist for two hours about his sudden intuition of 'the logical structure of quantum mechanics', while ignoring almost everything about the content of this intuition, and concentrating only on the form of its appearance.

Only the description of the acts carried out by the subject and the description of his state during the experience are retained.

2.2 Elaboration of a Model of the Experience

From the description we have thus reduced to its experiential dimension, we now need to extract a 'model' of the experience, that is, a structured and synthetic representation which enables us:

- to understand the unfolding of and the principal dimensions of the experience,
- to compare it with other experiences.

The construction of this model takes place in three steps (steps 2 and 3 can take place concurrently):

(1) Identification of the interior gestures which make up the experience
(2) Construction of a diachronic model of the experience
(3) Construction of a synchronic model of the experience

2.2.1 Identification of the interior gestures that make up the experience

This step consists of identifying in the description of the experience, the principal gestures that it is made up of. Each gesture is defined by a unique preoccupation which generally corresponds to the realization of an objective, for example: reaching a state of interior availability, entering into contact with another person . . .

When the gestures are not explicitly formulated, it is possible to identify them indirectly, by spotting in the description the actions which are carried out in order to trigger off their realization, or to verify that the objective has been reached. These actions of triggering off and of verifying constitute the main points of the hinging of the experience, and enable us to fragment the description.[10] In the intuitive experience the objective of a gesture is often to obtain a particular interior state. So the actions of verifying correspond to the gathering of interior information which make it possible to ensure that the desired state has been reached. This taking of information corresponds to the most implicit aspects of the experience.

Let us take as an example one of the experiences described by Judee. In the transcription of the interview we spotted key sentences which describe some actions of triggering off and of verifying, on which hinges the description of this experience.

1. *Beginning of the description: change of manner of breathing*

   First I begin to breathe in a connected manner, there is no stopping between breathing in and breathing out, so that there is a sense of continuity in the breathing, and it's a breathing that is calming, and when I breathe like that . . . (9)[11]

   [Description of the procedures to reach 'the intuitive state']

   Verification that the intuitive state is reached:

   When I am in my intuitive state, I have images that correspond, and these images are a verification for me: am I sufficiently in my state or not, and if I feel that it is still loaded, at that moment I go a little further, I take my time to get more inside. (59)

   There, I've been ready to do something with my intuition, for the last few minutes. (67)

2. *Decision to extend her interior vision:*

   And there, I extend my interior vision, I come like with these kinds of threads . . . (119)

   [Description of the procedures to extend her consciousness]

3. *Beginning of interior listening*

   And at that moment I wait, I have nothing to do, I'm in a kind of availability, of expectation, and also a kind of curiosity, a lucidity. . . . I am present. . . . It's a listening, but it's especially being free, available, in my interior seeing. (129)

   [Description of interior listening]

4. *Appearance of the intuition*

   Almost immediately, after a little waiting . . . there's an image which is distilled . . . and then I look at this image. . . . The image that I get, it's . . . (133)

   [Description of the intuitive 'reading']

   Verification that the story is finished:

   Up to a given moment, I arrive at the end of the story, I arrive at the end of . . . images. And at that moment, I feel inside me that it's all right, that it's wrapped up, I have nothing more

---

[10] This modelling was developed by Miller *et al.* (1960) with the name of Model TOTE, that is, Test-Operation-Test-Exit. It is based on the hypothesis that physical or mental behaviour aim at carrying out a certain objective with the help of defined procedures. However, we will see that the intuitive experience does not totally fit this model.

[11] Numbers in parentheses refer to the numbering of the sentences of the interviews.

to say . . . on my side, because I have done my job, I have done what I've been asked to do. (143)

5. *Decision to disconnect:*

So I am going to consciously empty out my body, bring me to an empty state . . . interiorly, to find again this state where my intuition is there, but I don't do anything with it. (95)

[Description of the procedures to return to the interior state]

End of the description

These key sentences constitute the hinging points of the description of Judee. They enable us to reorganize this description around five preoccupations or objectives which correspond to certain distinctive interior gestures:

1) reaching the intuitive state,
2) extending one's consciousness towards another,
3) listening, waiting in a state of receptivity,
4) welcoming the images and sensations that come,
5) returning to the intuitive state.

We will now group together the parts of the text which describe each of the gestures, and which were sometimes overlapped.

2.2.2 Construction of a diachronic model of the experience

The diachronic model represents the temporal structure of the experience. It is constructed at different levels of detail: the level of the phases, the level of the operations, and the level of the elementary actions.

The level of the phases

At the level of the phases, the diachronic model displays the train of interior gestures (sequence, parallelism), located in the preceding step.

Let us take the example of Judee again: the five preoccupations which we have identified correspond to five successive phases of the experience; we represent their linking and hinge in the following diachronic model:

Phase 1 ———————————————————————— **Phase 2** ————

1.1 Procedures to reach the intuitive state	**1.2 Intuitive state**	**1.3 Verification that the state is reached**	**2. Procedures to extend her consciousness**
		No —> 1.1	
		Yes —> 2	

Phase 3 ———— **Phase 4** ———————————————— **Phase 5** ————

3. Interior listening, waiting, availability	**4.1 'Intuitive reading'**	**4.2 Verification that the story is finished**	**5. Procedures to return to the intuitive state**
		No —> 4.1	
		Yes —> 5	

Re-scheduling of the description

In order to simplify this presentation, and to illustrate steps 1 and 2, we have chosen an interview in which the description follows quite closely the chronological order of the experience. But for most of the experiences, an additional step of re-scheduling is necessary.

Indeed, the awareness of the pre-thought of the experience rarely follows the chronological order of its unfolding. Several flashbacks — guided by the inter- viewer's questions — are generally necessary so that the most unconscious aspects can be brought to consciousness and be described. This implies therefore that the modeller carries out an additional operation of re-scheduling of the parts of the text which describe the different gestures, before constructing the diachronic model.

The level of the operations

Each phase is then represented with more details in the form of a train of operations. For example, phase 1 of the preceding model is broken down in the following manner:

1.1	1.2	1.3	1.4	1.5
Corporeal procedures	**Visualization of a natural landscape**	**Ascending itinerary of consciousness in the body**	**Emptying out**	**Test of the intuitive state**
Postural alignment				Verification of the emotional and energetic state of the body through interior vision
Closing of the eyelids				
Connected breathing from the stomach				
Displacement of the consciousness towards the back of the skull				**OK —> phase 2** **Not OK —> 1.3**

The level of elementary actions

Each operation of the model can still be described at the level of a more refined aggregation, through a train of elementary actions, which are represented by:

1) the sensorial modalities that are associated to them,
2) possibly a short extract of the text, which we call a 'descriptive trait'.

Here, for example, is the detailed model of a psychoanalytical intuition of Reik, constructed from the following passage:

> (…) Without the slightest hesitation and in a reproachful voice I said, 'But why did you not tell me that you had had an abortion ?' I had said it without an inkling of what I would say and why I would say it. It felt as if, not I, but something in me had said that. The patient jumped up and looked at me as if I were a ghost.

> (…) When I look back on the session, what was it that happened in me ? At first there was silence in me as in the patient; then suspense, a waiting for something to come; her words echoed in me; a new suspense; a new resounding of her words, and then all blank and dark for a second, out of which came the knowledge, nay, the certainty, that she had had an

abortion, that she thought with grief of the baby for which she had longed and which she had to give up. I did not give a damn about logic and what I had learned in the books. I did not think of any psychoanalytic theory. I simply said what had spoken inside me against and contrary to all logic, and I was right. (p. 264)

1. —>	2. —>	3. —>	4. —>	5. —>
Ai	**Ae:Ki**	**Ae:Ki**	**Vi+Ki+Ai+Di**	**Des**
'At first there was silence in me;'	'Then suspense, a waiting for something to come; her words echoed in me;'	'A new suspense; a new resounding of her words,'	'and then all blank and dark for a second . . .'	'Without the slightest hesitation . . . I said . . .'

Notation used to represent the train of elementary actions[12]

—>	succession
+	simultaneity
A/B	comparison, test
A:B	synesthesia[13]
A	absence or stopping of A[14]
(A)	optional
>A	decrease
<A	increase

Notation used to represent the sensorial modalities

V	visual
A	auditory
K	kinaesthetic
O	olfactory
G	gustatory
D	digital (words)

e	external
i	internal
e/i[15]	

+	pleasant
–	unpleasant
r	remembered
c	constructed
s	spontaneous[16]

2.2.3 Construction of a synchronic model

Each gesture of the experience is not only described by a diachronic model, but also by a synchronic model, which represents the experience in other dimensions than its temporal dimension. While the diachronic model represents the 'film' of the experience (the linking of the phases), the synchronic model corresponds, in a way, to an 'image by image pause'.

It is constructed through a succession of operations of abstraction, using the parts of the text describing the same gesture. It is made up of *descriptive traits* and of *experiential categories*, bound by relations of classification and of aggregation[17] (see box). A descriptive trait is a direct quotation from the text, which represents a unit of meaning. An experiential category corresponds to:

---

[12] The notation comes from N.L.P. See Dilts (1994).

[13] Overlapping of two sensorial modalities, or the transformation of one modality into another. For example, Ae:Vi: to see the form of a sound, or Vi:Ki: image transforming into sensation.

[14] For example Di : absence of interior dialogue.

[15] We introduced this notation to describe certain sensations, especially kinaesthetic, for which it is difficult to determine if it is an internal or an external sensation, for the subject's perception of the limits of his body are modified.

[16] For example : Vr = visual memory, Vc = constructed image (a voluntary vizualisation of something : 'imaginary'), Vs = spontaneously appeared image ('imaginal').

[17] We adopt the definition and the formalism which are given of these relations of abstraction in semantic networks, a technique used in the fields of artificial intelligence and the design of information systems to model static or structural aspects of a system. See Sowa (1984) and Smith and Smith (1977).

- either a regrouping of descriptive traits of close meaning into a more abstract category, through an operation of classification/instantiation,
- or a regrouping of experiential categories into a category which has a higher level of abstraction, through an operation of aggregation/disaggregation.

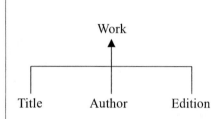

Aggregation is the mechanism of abstraction which makes it possible to consider a relation between objects as an object of a higher level, by neglecting certain details of the relation. The opposite mechanism is disaggregation.

Formalism:

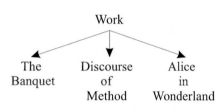

Classification is the mechanism of abstraction which makes it possible to go from a set of events to the description of a class of objects, by neglecting the details which differentiate the events. The opposite mechanism is instantiation.

Formalism:

The construction of a model is ascending when we go from a text to progressively extract experiential categories, using operations of classification or of aggregation; descending when we go from already known categories to structure the description, using the opposite operations.

Let us take the example of the ascending construction of a synchronic model. After having identified a 'listening gesture' in Amel's description of his intuitive experience, we take out the relevant descriptive traits:

'I go into the interior of myself.' (114)
'I'm listening to what goes on inside of me.' (122)
'Listen to yourself, listen to yourself on the inside. There's going to be a place in your body where something is going to be manifested.' (124)

'I place my hands, and then it's as if it didn't depend on me.' (148)
'It's going to come or it isn't going to come, but I can't do anything about it.' (150)

'I am there, I wait for it to come (the feeling), generally at the level of my hands.' (108)
'When I go behind, it's not that (the hands) but that (the solar plexus) which feels. It's a part of me which feels.' (114)

We decided to regroup these descriptive traits into three experiential categories: 'internal attention', 'involuntary attention' and 'kinaesthetic listening'; their aggregation represents Amel's structural listening gesture. The graphic representation of this structure follows:

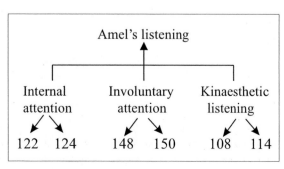

The association of the diachronic model and the synchronic model constitute the specific model of a given experience.

3. COMPARING THE MODELS

The comparison of the specific models is carried out through the construction of generic models; this corresponds to two different levels of genericity:

(1) The generic model of the intuitive experience of a person, constructed by bringing together the different specific models carried out for this person.

This intermediary level of the model is not done for all of the people interviewed, because we were not able to explore more than one experience for some of them.

(2) The model of the 'intuitive experience', constructed by bringing together the generic models of different people.

At each level of genericity the construction of the generic model takes place in two steps:

(1) Construction of a generic synchronic model
(2) Construction of a generic diachronic model

3.1 Construction of Generic Synchronic Models

Each generic synchronic model represents the generic structure of one of the gestures which makes up the intuitive experience. It is made up of experiential categories that are more abstract than those of specific models.

For each generic gesture, a generic synchronic model is constructed from specific synchronic models through the intermediary of two mechanisms of abstraction: aggregation (already used for the construction of specific models) and generalization (see box).

> Generalization is the mechanism of abstraction which allows us to extract the description of a more general object, from the description of several objects of distinct classes, by making obvious the properties that are shared by the specialized objects and by neglecting the details with differentiate them. The opposite mechanism is specialization.
>
> Formalism:
>
> Work
> ↗   ↖
> Novel   Essay

Here is an example of a generic synchronic model, made from two listening gestures in which we spotted proximity of objective and of structure:

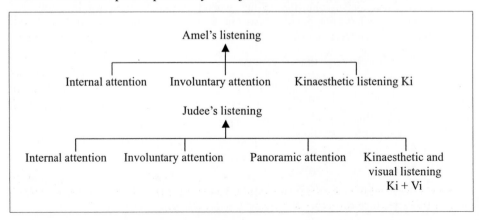

We aggregate the descriptive categories of attention encountered in the specific models into a more abstract category: 'attention mode'.

We regroup the sensorial modalities encountered in the specific models into a more abstract category: 'sensorial modalities of listening', by using a relation of generalization. The graphic representation of this generic structure of listening is the following:[18]

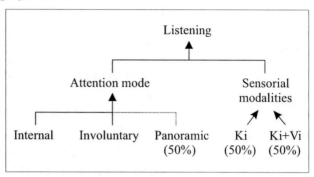

Each of the above specific models is a specialization of this generic model.

3.2 Construction of Generic Diachronic Models

The generic diachronic models are constructed at different levels of detail (phase, operation, elementary action), by bringing about either the union or the intersection of specific diachronic models.

We used the construction by intersection of specific diachronic models to spot the diachronic structures shared by different people at each level of detail.

Let us take as an example the two following diachronic models (level of phases):

(1) Judee

Phase 1 ——— Phase 2 ——— Phase 3 ——— Phase 4 ——— Phase 5 ——-

| Procedures to reach the intuitive state | Procedures to extend consciousness | Interior listening | 'Intuitive reading' | Procedures to return to an intuitive state |

(2) Reik

Phase 1 ——— Phase 2 ——— Phase 3 ——— Phase 4 ——— Phase 5 ———

| Interruption of discursive thinking | Gesture of the introjection of the patient | Listening to the patient + interior listening | Psychoanalytic insight | Interpretation |

The structuring of these gestures as carried out in the generic synchronic models allows us to recognize certain gestures of these two models as the specializations of the same generic gestures. For example, the listening gestures of Judee and of Reik are the specializations of the same generic gesture. Judee's procedures to extend consciousness and Reik's introjection are the specializations of the same generic gesture of 'connection'. Judee's 'reading' and Reik's 'insight' are the specializations of the same gesture of 'intuition'. Bringing these together allows us to obtain the dynamic structure below, by constructing the intersection of the two models. This generic structure is found in a large number of the interviews:

Gesture to reach the intuitive state —> Connection —> Listening —> Intuition

---

[18] The relation of aggregation is represented by a dotted line when the corresponding category (here the panoramic characteristic) does not appear in all the specific models. The percentages indicated in parentheses represent the frequency of appearance of the category.

4. SYNTHESIS OF THE METHOD

The diagram below summarizes the method explained in this section.

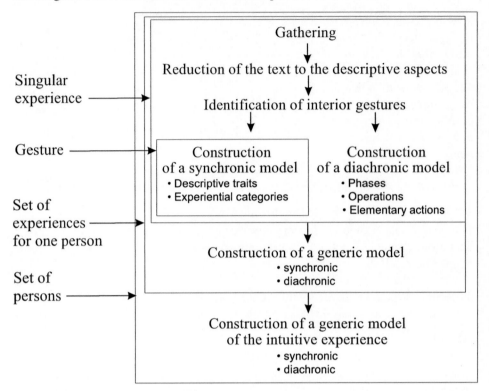

Iterative Characteristic of the Process:

To construct the model of the first interviews we used an 'ascending' technique, which consists of progressively abstracting experiential categories and generic gestures from texts. When generic structures began to emerge we used rather a 'descending' technique, which consists of questioning these texts from structures that have already been identified: does the experience studied contain a listening gesture ? One of connection?

The fact that a generic structure allowed us to understand and to model an interview rapidly constituted for us, each time, a verification of the validity of this structure.

The appearance of generic structures not only influenced the modelling of the following interviews, but also enabled us to perfect the way we conducted these interviews. For example, the appearance of a generic gesture of 'connection' allowed us to guide the next subjects interviewed towards the exploration of this phase, which was perhaps also present in them, in a pre-thought stage.

Each new interview also enabled us to discover new structures, which did not correspond to any already identified structure, and which progressively enriched the generic model.

The method of modelling, which has been described as an ascendant sequential process to simplify it, is therefore in reality a successive iteration process, which can be represented in the following manner:

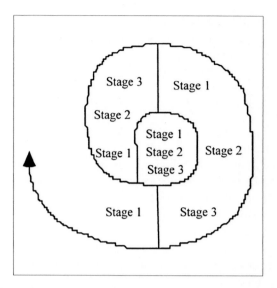

In following this iterative method, we have progressively constituted:

- a set of diachronic structures of the intuitive experience,
- a vast semantic network which links the concrete description of the singular experiences to a synchronic model of the intuitive experience.

In the following section, we will present certain particularly significant aspects of these results.

II: RESULTS

Out of this modelling and comparison of different descriptions emerged a generic structure of the intuitive experience, which is made up of a succession of very precise interior gestures. Four of them can be found in a large number of the explored experiences:

- the gesture of letting go, of deep-rooting, of interior self-collecting, and of the slowing down of the mental activity, which makes it possible to reach a particular state of consciousness, the 'intuitive state' (described in 22 interviews).

For several of the people interviewed, access to this calm state is made easier through some preliminary work of interior clarification, a work of deep transformation carried out thanks to daily practicing, which is integrated into a long term process.

- The gesture of connection, which makes it possible to enter into contact with the object of the intuitive knowledge (a human being, an abstract problem, a situation...) (described 14 times).
- The gesture of listening, with an attention that is at the same time panoramic and very discriminating, focused on the subtle signs announcing the intuition (described 13 times).
- The intuition itself, of which certain of the subjects have acquired (or acquire during the interview) a sufficiently discriminating consciousness to point out three distinct moments: the moment preceding the intuition, the intuition, the moment following the intuition.

The similarity of these interior gestures in different experiences is striking; they are often described with the same words even, independently of the kind of intuition.

Eight other gestures appear in only a few descriptions. Their absence in the other descriptions can be explained by the fact that either they were not the object of a clarification because they stayed at a pre-thought state, or the gestures in question effectively present no reason for existing in certain particular cases of intuition.

- The gesture of maintaining, which makes it possible to remain in the intuitive state (5 times)
- The gesture of anchoring, which makes it possible to rediscover the intuitive state more easily by associating a sensorial stimulus to it (once).
- The process of disconnecting (once).
- The process of getting out of the intuitive state, of getting back to the usual mode of functioning (4 times).
- The gesture of protection, found only in certain cases of intuition: when the object or the person one has come into contact with carries an energy that could be harmful (twice).
- The process of distinguishing intuition/projection, which makes it possible to distinguish a real intuition from a projected desire or fear thanks to subtle interior criteria (3 times).
- The process of interpreting the content of the intuition when it is not sufficiently explicit (1 time).
- The process of translating the content of the intuition into a communicable form: words, drawing, scientific hypothesis… (6 times).

In the following pages we will present the generic synchronic model of the first four phases of the intuitive experience, that is, the main experiential categories identified for these phases, illustrated by a few examples of descriptive traits.

Synchronic Model of the Intuitive Experience

1. PHASE OF LETTING GO

This is a phase of returning to the centre, of medi-tation in the original meaning of the word. While keeping its unpredictable character as far as its content and moment of appearance are concerned, the intuition seems to have, as a condition, a particular interior state, which can be obtained thanks to specific interior gestures. First we will describe these gestures, then the characteristics of the interior state obtained.

1.1 Gestures of Letting Go

The purpose of these gestures is to introduce a break with the usual manner, 'natural' manner, of relating to the world: they make it possible to shift the attention from the flood of representations of the past and of the future towards the singular concrete situation that is being lived through here and now.

On the one hand, these are procedures that can be used in a deliberate way starting from the modification of either the relation to the body or the relation to mental activity; on the other hand, they are gestures that do not seem to be able to be voluntarily provoked.

1.1.1 Modification of the relation to the body

The goal is to 'go down' inside the body, to shift the interior gravity center from the head to the body. We have identified four main gestures most often carried out conjointly:

(1) Change of posture: this means adopting a defined, vertical, tonic and stable posture.

(2) Gesture of reunification, of an interior gathering and realignment, brought about thanks to a special attention being paid to the corporeal axis and to the movement of breathing.

> When I begin, I get into what I call the 'one', I do the 'one'. I breathe in, and that makes like a kind of current that goes all through my body. That is doing the 'one'. (Monique, 8)

This movement of reunification and thickening of the body can be encouraged by dancing to certain music, particularly repetitive rhythms and the base vibrations of drums.

(3) Transformation of breathing: it goes down, way down, becomes abdominal. And it slows down, almost to the point of stopping. Muriel describes this sensation of 'breathlessness' in precisely this way:

> When my breathing stops, it's as if there were something in my stomach which was swinging softly, a little swing, back and forth, back and forth, like that, in an empty space, without anything, and there at that moment… I think that I have a sensation that goes up along the spine, like that, which opens up a little bit like a flower here, and often I catch just another little breath in the bottom of my stomach just at that moment. (Muriel, 84)

(4) Shifting consciousness to the back of the skull. Five of the people interviewed described an interior gesture designed to deepen the consciousness of corporeal sensations, and consisting of 'going to the back'. Judee describes this gesture as the sliding of consciousness towards the back of the skull, induced by adjusting the posture very subtly towards the back of the body.

> When I'm going to enter into my intuitive mode, I'm going to place my consciousness much more towards the back of the skull. It's linked to the posture, I have to be very straight, and it's linked too, to the way I fit into my hips. It's somehow linked to the spinal column, I bend a little bit to the back, there's a kind of spinal alignment that sets in. It's a way for the head and the back of the neck to be in relation to the shoulders and the back. I think it's a kind of sliding. I slide to the back. The whole body is involved with this adjustment. It's minute, very subtle. (Judee, 19)

1.1.2. Modification of mental activity

At the same time that these corporeal procedures are being employed, sometimes the subjects use processes that aim at inducing an interior state which is calm and spacious, by slowing down the mental activity.

Visualizing

For example Judee visualizes a natural landscape to get back into herself, a 'sanctuary' where she settles in to meditate. Monique uses the following exercise to eliminate parasitic thoughts:

> You mentally write: 1, 2, 3, 4, 5 on a black board. You see them, you write them, you feel them while writing. And you begin to erase them. You mentally say: ' I erase the 5, the 1,

2, 3, 4 are left. I erase the 4, the 1, 2, 3, are left... I erase the 1 and there's only the board left.' (Monique, 169)

Prayer
Two of the people we interviewed also use prayer to have access to an interior intuitive state.

1.1.3. Non-voluntary gestures

Renunciation
Three of the people described an interior movement of renunciation, of abandoning, that they cannot bring about, but which happens at the moment of an important psychological shock: moral suffering, illness or a serious accident, grief. When the person 'hits bottom', in the deepest instance of pain or fear, there comes a moment when he stops fighting, accepts dying. And curiously enough at this moment there opens up inside a space of calm and trust which allows for a much more attentive listening to his own interior sensations, and of another way of connecting to life as it surges forth from instant to instant.

> I hit bottom. At that moment I stopped holding on to things; I accepted impermanence, death. It was a passage towards death. Then I was in an interior state where I was no longer fighting; I let myself be carried along with the flow.' (Vanessa)

Passage from wakefulness to sleep
For three people the intuition came when they were in an intermediate state between wakefulness and sleep. Access to this state requires a gesture of letting go which is both physical and mental. But it is not brought about deliberately in order to induce an intuitive state.

1.1.4. Absence of conscious gestures
In three cases we were not able to bring out a gesture leading to the intuitive state. As these people were not in the group of psychotherapists, they apparently could not get in touch with their own interior movements as easily as the other group. For that reason it is not impossible that they did carry out a pre-intuitive gesture, that the interview could not bring to consciousness.

1.2   Internal State
The 'intuitive' state induced by a movement of letting go is characterized by a transformation of the perception of the body and of the mental activity.

1.2.1. Perception of body and space
Most of the people interviewed described a feeling of profound well-being, where a feeling of unity and a feeling of opening up were indissolubly linked.

Feeling of unity
It is the sensation of being unified, gathered together, whole. Two of the people interviewed perceived an interior 'column'. A very strong feeling of presence, of really being there, accompanied this sensation of unity. A sensation of being deeply-rooted, of strength and energy is felt in the hips and the legs.

Sensation of opening up

It is a sensation of interior space and fluidity, associated with a sensation of expanding. Indeed, the perception of the limits between the interior space and the body becomes more indistinct, and even disappears:

> As if I were much bigger than my body, no longer certain of where the body stopped. (Henry)
>
> An absence of limits between the space and the body. (Annette)

This sensation of expansion is particularly present concerning the head:

> An open cone at the top of the head. (Alain, 30)
>
> A balloon where the head should be. (Francis, 48)
>
> The head swollen up. (Chea Hoeng, 109)
>
> As if the skull were no longer there. (Judee, 59)

It is sometimes accompanied by a sensation of light in the head:

> A light that you cannot see but that you know is there. (Alain)

Simultaneously, the space is perceived as denser, more vibrant, full of a light 'that you don't see', of a sound 'that you don't hear'.

> A kind of light that's in the space. A sound that you don't hear, a space that fills the ears which gives the impression of a sound. (Alain, 120)

1.2.2 Mental activity

In the intuitive state, the flow of thought and discursive activity calm down to give place to an interior silence:

> The mind begins functioning more slowly, and sometimes stops. There are segments of silence which last a certain period of time. (Alain, 90)
>
> Speaking, I don't even know if that exists. There is no language, there's nothing, in that state. (Sylvia, 83)

For some people, and especially for the two scientists that we interviewed, it was not a question of a stopping of the mental activity but of a transformation, which abandoned the abstract discursive mode for an imaged, kinaesthetic mode anchored in the corporeal experience:

> I see the results like a coating with holes and bumps in it. I am in the film. It's more a corporeal impression of being swung. I move in the coating. I feel myself go down, come up. And then I have the impression that the coating collapses. (Christophe, 5)

1.2.3 State between wakefulness and sleep

For three people, the explored intuition occurred during an intermediary state between wakefulness and sleep. It was either at the precise moment of falling asleep or in the moments preceding waking up, or in the first moments after waking up.[19] These states of consciousness present certain characteristics common to the intuitive state, such as the absence of mental activity and the dissolution of the limits usually perceived between the body and the exterior space.

---

[19] Numerous famous scientific intuitions occurred during such states of consciousness, during a moment of exhaustion of rational thinking (e.g. Kékulé). How can we not remember Descartes' dream ?

1.3 Verification and Maintenance in the State

Certain people possess interior criteria which allow them to verify if the intuitive state has been reached. Some also employ criteria to 'test' the state (for example verify the corporeal alignment) in order to bring about the needed adjustments to maintain it (for example rectifying the posture and becoming conscious of breathing again).

2. PHASE OF CONNECTION

Once the intuitive state has been reached, fourteen of the people that we interviewed carry through an interior gesture of connection to enter into and to stay in contact with the object they propose to explore. The gesture of connection is defined by its object, its distance, its source, its sensorial modalities, and the process used.

2.1 Object

This can be:

- a physical object,
- a person (even oneself); in this case the connection is made either at the level of the physical body or at the level of the emotional or mental state,
- a personal question, a scientific problem, a literary or artistic project . . .

Several people interviewed use particular processes to connect with an abstract object of this kind.

In the following paragraphs we will describe the connection with a person, essentially through descriptions of psychotherapeutic intuitions.

2.2 Distance

This is a question of direct contact or getting nearer, consisting of laying one's hands on the person, or in approaching them, or of connection from a distance: in this case the person whom we connect with can be present or absent, sometimes even very far away.

2.3 Source

The zone of the body which is the source of the connection can be the hand, the heart, the stomach, or the spinal column. For Judee, the connection is made at the level of the head in order to see, of the stomach in order to feel:

> I'm conscious only of these two places that I extend. It's either for seeing, and that's done by the head, or it's for feeling, and feeling — it's through the stomach. And that, that's interesting for me, because my heart, I stay here. I don't need to involve my heart, my chest, to be successful in this story. (Judee, 155)

2.4 Sensorial Modalities

Even outside direct contact the connection seems to be essentially kinaesthetic in nature, even if the terms used to describe it are borrowed from different sensorial registers.

Visual register: beam, channel of light, network of rays, threads of energy...

> It's as if I were linked to the patient from center to center, it's a ray. (Alain,112)

> It's a channel of light. And a channel of light with a force. Of energy. Of luminous energy. (Sylvie, 27)

Kinaesthetic register: 'energetic hands' or vibration, breathing, gentle rocking:

> An unconscious vibration in time with the instinctive rhythm of the other. (Reik, 1948 p. 329)

Auditory register: echo, resonance, harmony

> I wait for something like a little — an echo that would come to meet my whole body. (Alain, 52)

2.5 Processes

For most of the people interviewed the gesture of connection is brought about unconsciously and became conscious during the interview.

> This process has none of the characteristics of conscious activity. It takes place wholly in areas that are not accessible to our thought-efforts and it is almost unthinking. (Reik, 1948, p. 275)

Some people however bring about this act consciously and deliberately:

> It's as if I had a layer of skin, of flesh, something that opens through my intention, my decision. It's like that — that I go into the experience of fusion consciously, that I go into the interior reality of the other and that I feel him. (Judee, 99)

Different processes of connection are used:

Introjection

For five of the people interviewed, the connection consists of 'welcoming' or bringing the other into oneself, into the interior space freed during the preceding phase:

> I have the impression that it is the other who comes into my space. Open yourself up and leave the space to the other. (Alain, 124)

> I open up my stomach and I go into the atmosphere of the other, I'm going to bring a part of this atmosphere into me so that I can feel it in my stomach. (Judee, 141)

For Reik, it is a question of a process of 'introjection' of the patient by the psycho-analyst:

> We can attain to psychological comprehension of another's unconscious only if it is seized upon by our own, at least for a moment, just as if it were a part of ourselves — it is a part of ourselves. (Reik, 1948, p. 464)

Extension, absorption

For three people interviewed the connection consists of extending oneself into the other until one is absorbed in the other:

> I open up, I open myself up, and it's as if hands… energetic, which are going to touch, which are going to feel all over. (Judee, 99)

Getting into resonance

For three people, it is a question or harmonizing with the rhythm of the other, of synchronizing with the vibration, the 'music' emitted by the other.

> The analyst can vibrate unconsciously in the rhythm of the other person's impulse. (Reik, 1948, p. 468)

> It is as if all of a sudden we were breathing together. As if, for a given moment, rhythmically we were one and the same person. (Sylvia, 148)

Some of the interviewees use interior criteria which allow them to verify that the connection has been carried out:

Just there I go into another register, another rhythmic level... inside. First, there's just me, and then all of a sudden, there are two of us inside. And when we reach this harmony, we've arrived. (Sylvia, 185)

Once the connection is established, it seems to become more real than the subjects that it links together, to be accompanied by the effacing of the limits of the internal world:

What really exists, rather than the other person and me, is this channel. (Sylvie, 41)

We're no longer anything except one shared breathing. (Sylvia, 169)

3. LISTENING PHASE

After this phase of letting go, the subject finds himself in a state of interior calm and presence which enables him to listen very closely to his own sensations. This interior gesture of listening is characterized by its sensorial modalities and the kind of attention that it puts into play.

3.1 Sensorial Modalities

Most of the people that we interviewed seemed to privilege a particular listening mode. Some of them are more attentive to their interior images. One of them has an exceptionally refined ear for listening, capable of hearing vibrations emitted by animate and inanimate beings, normally inaccessible to the human ear. The majority of the people interviewed have more or less developed listening to their internal kinaesthetic sensations.

I pick the vibrations with my hand. (Monique, 2)

For some people, intuitive listening seems to involve all the senses at the same time, or rather an indifferentiation of the senses. That seems to be the case with Reik's 'third ear' which involves:

The visual:

Elusive psychical nuances and shades (p. 315)

The auditory:

He who has the sharpest ear for what his own thoughts whisper to him (p. 271)

Inner voices (p. 269)

Almost imperceptible undertones (p. 315)

The kinaesthetic:

These unconscious feelers . . . are not there to grasp, but to touch. (p. 145)

His yarn was good but there were little imperfections in it, slight unevennesses not apparent to the eye but perceptible to testing hands that glide slowly and carefully over the fabric. (p. 194)

Vague impressions (p. 270)

A seismograph reacting to a faint subterranean variation. (p. 480)

For some of the subjects interviewed the body zone which is perceived as the center of attention has moved from the head to another part of the body:

It's as if my thought center . . . as if I no longer thought with the head, that I thought with my stomach. I listen with my stomach. (Sylvia, 165)

3.2 Attention Mode

Intuitive listening is characterized by a special mode of attention: internal, peripheral, and involuntary.

Internal attention

The attention that characterizes intuitive listening is above all turned inward to the internal processes. It is a question of listening to the repercussion of the sensations, the thoughts of the other inside oneself:

> I focus on myself in order to receive the echo of the other. (Alain, 86)

External attention

However, it is sometimes the perception of an exterior event, sometimes a tiny detail, that will spark off the intuitive awareness, through a coincidence which makes us think of the phenomenon of synchronicity. In this way, Reik has the intuition that his patient has had a miscarriage at the very moment that she remarks to him that one of the books on the library shelves is upside down.

Remember however that for certain subjects, at the end of their phases of letting go and of connection, the limits between the interior and the exterior worlds become hazy, vague, which renders this distinction of internal and external attention of little pertinence.

Panoramic attention, not focused on any special object

Unlike focused attention which is concentrated on a particular psychic content, narrow and rigid, the attention which characterizes intuitive listening is non-selective, peripheral, 'floating', it covers vast territory.

> That which will kindle the lightning must for a long time be a cloud. (Reik, 1948, quoting Nietzsche, p. 117)

> I stay conscious of everything that happens inside me without holding on to anything, simply with a presence and a lucidity about everything that is happening. (Judee, 75)

This attention however is very attuned, sensitive to the slightest detail:

> More attuned and wider perceptions. I feel myself in a very focused state of consciousness, very, very present in the moment. (. . .) I have the impression of being a little bit like a funnel, a very long funnel with a very small opening, a little bit like a laser beam, which is at the same time there, very present, and at the same time I'm conscious of everything that is happening around me. (Francis, 28).

This form of attention seems to correspond to 'lateral' thinking which characterizes the research strategy of numerous scientists, and which consists of thinking 'aside', in a more vast framework than the narrow context of the problem itself.

Involuntary attention, not directed towards any specific goal

Intuitive listening is characterized by the absence of any precise intention, of research of a defined goal. On the contrary it is being 'open' enough to let the unexpected come.

It is relaxed, detached, light. It does not involve any effort. It is a peaceful waiting, patient, which is not expecting anything in particular.

> I lay my hands down and I wait; it's as if it didn't depend on me. The huss [sensation] is going to come or isn't going to come, but I can't do anything about it. (Amel, 150)

> What's needed is putting your hand, then you wait. And then little by little things are described in your hand. If you have an idea of what you are going to feel or want to feel, you don't feel anything, or just false things. (Monique, 77)

Intuitive listening corresponds to a state of receptivity, which consists not of looking for and grasping at, but of letting it come and welcoming it.

> To see in receiving, isn't casting your gaze towards something, projecting it, holding it out, but really it's letting the thing imprint itself in you. You are completely passive, and you let the color, the landscape, come to you. You aren't going to look for it, you're going to gather it in. You're there and you receive it. (Monique, 4)

This receptive gazing enables us to find the sensation in all its immediacy and fresh-ness:

> When you look in this way, there's no filter in your head. It's more alive. Things are much more alive, more real. (Monique, 158)

Listening in a receptive way is not trying to recognize the sensations, to identify them immediately, and to pull out some information at all costs:

> The aim of 'poised' attention cannot be instantaneous understanding, immediate placing among things known. (Reik, 1948, p. 165)

It is a question of having a sufficiently attuned ear to listen to one's own sensations, one's own fledgling thoughts which 'walk on dove's feet'[20], before conceptualizing anything:

> I suggest that the seeker forget what he has learned, neglect what he has heard and read, and listen to his own response. (Reik, 1948, p. 303)

4. INTUITION

The descriptions of certain of our subjects whose consciousness of their intuitive functioning was particularly attuned has led us to discern three distinct moments in the appearing of an intuition: the moment immediately preceding the intuition, the emerging of the intuition, and the moments which follow this emerging.

4.1 The Moment Just Preceding the Intuition

The moment which immediately precedes the emergence of the intuition is often characterized by an 'empty passage' ('passage à vide'), a moment of confusion, obscurity, silence.

> With me the emergence from the deeper or obscurer planes of thought is preceded for the fraction of a second by a sense of alienation, a rapidly passing feeling of absent-mindedness, even a kind of foggy sensation (…) a moment of eclipse, (...) of 'absence' in the French meaning, (…) a passing chaotic situation. (Reik, 1948, p. 192)[21]
>
> Then all blank and dark for a second. (Reik,1948, p. 244)

In several of the intuitions that we have described, this moment of emptiness corre-sponds to the moment when the person is falling asleep or just emerging from sleep.

4.2 Intuition

Unlike the other phases of the intuitive experience, the moment of the appearance of the intuition does not include a description of the act. The arrival of the intuition is not an action, but a process that cannot be forced. However, it is possible to describe:

- the sensorial form of the intuition,
- the reaction of the subject to its contents,

---

[20] According to Nietszche's formula.

[21] Reik compares this moment of confusion to the one that immediately precedes understanding a joke.

- the internal state of the subject at the moment of its appearance,
- the threshold of the awareness of the sensation.

4.2.1 Sensorial form of the intuition

The intuition can surge forth as an image, a kinaesthetic feeling, a sound or a word, or even a taste or an odour, most of the time in several simultaneous or successive sensorial forms.[22]

Image

Most often this means internal images, more rarely visual hallucinations:

> I take my bowl, and all of a sudden there comes out of the bowl . . . I can't say it otherwise, at that distance, a photo. A kind of face in black and white, a dark fellow with a black pullover, a black and white photo. (Sylvia, 8)

Feeling

In the descriptions that we have collected we distinguish two kinds of feeling.

(1) Sensations which reflect the interior state of the other person. For example, during a Vittoz therapy session, Monique 'takes on the vibrations' of the patient, that is she verifies the evolution of his interior state thanks to very subtle sensations that she feels in her hand. These vibrations are perceptible when she puts her hand on the patient's forehead, but a well trained hand can feel them at a distance of several meters. Monique, for example, can discern a state of tension in her patient:

> In general, when there is tension it's like champagne, you see, it goes ding ding… it stings in my hand; that's tension when something is happening that isn't true to a relaxed state. (Monique, 3)

Judee captures the interior atmosphere of the other person in her stomach:

> I have sensations that are her/his sensations, I spot them in my body. (Judee, 83)

(2) Sensations that forebode the imminence of an event or of a thought, are therefore in the category of internal signals.

Sound

Antoine hears habitually inaudible sounds that are emitted by vegetable and animal beings and vary according to their state.

Word

The intuition takes on the form of words, either heard (usually interiorly) by the person, or pronounced out loud. For example, Reik received a patient without knowing that she had just had an abortion:

> Without the slightest hesitation and in a reproachful voice I said, 'But why did you not tell me that you had had an abortion ?' I had said it without an inkling of what I would say and why I would say it. It felt as if, not I, but something in me had said that. (Reik, 1948, p. 264)

Taste, smell

Sylvia had the same kind of intuition about a patient:

> I had a taste in the mouth. It was strong, it was as if someone had put blood under my nose and in my mouth. It didn't leave me. (Sylvia, 93)

---

[22] The scientific intuitions that have been described to us have also emerged in a visual and/or kinaesthetic sensorial form.

Several sensorial modalities

Most of the time the intuition appears in a synesthetic form, that is in the form of a simultaneity or a fading of sensations. Thus Muriel, while she was on vacation in the south of France, had the sudden intuition that her Parisian apartment was threatened by fire (which she later verified). This intuition was simultaneously manifested in the form of an image, a feeling and an interior voice.

Image of my apartment

> Suddenly I thought of my apartment, and when I thought of my apartment, I immediately saw it in reality, I saw the inside of my home… I saw it as it was at that very moment. (4)

Sensation of compression

> And at the same time that I saw this image, I had an unpleasant sensation, a little worrying (…) My throat tightened. And at a point in my solar plexus, here, a feeling of… not queasiness, but something that isn't normal, something that upset, a warning … something is happening. (Muriel, 52)

'I have the impression that it is very hot'

> I very quickly said something to myself, something that was linked to the heat. I said to myself 'I have the impression that it is very hot, really too hot, in Paris'. (48)

'Thoughts without words'

When she enormously slowed down the interior 'film' of her sensations, Muriel had the impression that at its very beginning the intuition appeared as a direct, global understanding, later differentiated into sensations and into distinct words.

4.2.2 Reactions to the content of the intuition

A feeling of certitude

The emergence of the intuition into consciousness is often accompanied by a feeling of obviousness, of certitude.

> I really *feel* when I can be serious about this intuition. I know it. I am absolutely sure. I don't talk about it, I don't need to discuss with anyone about it, I am simply *certain* that I have the solution. (Barbara McClintock, in Fox Keller, 1983, p. 139)

For psychotherapists, this feeling of certitude is often shared by the patient:

> A patient *does not believe t*hat an analytic interpretation is true. He *knows it.* (Reik, p. 267)

A feeling of coherence, of meaning

There is a feeling of coherence, of meaning added to this feeling of certitude. Not just an abstract meaning, but a living meaning, endowed with depth, thickness, density, rhythm, colour … an incarnate sense, of which the corresponding concept is only the skeleton. This is no simple acquisition of information or of knowledge, but rather an experience which touches being in its totality.

4.2.3 Internal state at the moment of the intuition

Even if it is possible to prepare, to encourage the appearing of an intuition, this appearance always retains a capricious, unpredictable character; it escapes all control. All of the subjects — this is an invariable characteristic of the intuitive experience — notice a state of passivity at the moment when the intuition springs forth. 'It

escapes from me', 'It happens to me', 'It doesn't depend on me', 'It's given to me'...
this kind of statement is found in all the descriptions.

This feeling of passivity can be partially explained by the absence of mental activity at the moment when the intuition appears. Recourse to concepts and rules, or learned knowledge, all form of memory like all form of premeditation, are excluded.

This feeling of an absence of control is linked to a transformation of the feeling of individual identity. The sensation of the floating of the limits of the ego felt in the preceding phases is accentuated: at the moment of the intuition, the sensation of being an 'ego' distinct from the world vacillates and even dissolves:

> You forget yourself. (Alain, 86)

> I no longer exist. (Sylvie, 5)

> You forget who you are. You lose consciousness of yourself. I am no longer there. (Barbara McClintock, in Fox Keller, 1983 , p. 155)

Paradoxically, at the same time the person feels that he has found his wholeness, that he has become unified, body and spirit, in harmony with his inner being.

> Body, emotion, spirit, all of a sudden it's as if these three were linked, indissolubly linked. In a kind of lightning state. (Muriel, 121)

She feels deeply in correspondence, in harmony with her surroundings. She has the feeling of being wholly herself, in the right place.

> I feel more myself than I have ever been. (Judee, 159)

> I feel that at that very moment I am the right person in the right place to be doing that thing. (Catherine, 50)

All of the subjects interviewed have the impression of living something very important, even when the intuitions have an innocuous content. They feel completely mobilized, captivated by the experience:

> The huss is a thing that gets hold of you in your totality. A little bit like a music that takes hold of you completely. . . . It's a little bit like a thing of life or death. (Amel)

They feel that they enter into contact with something essential for a few instants.

> I have the impression that when I go down into my center, God is waiting for me there. (Monique, 204)

For some of them this experience brings on a sensation of astonishment, amazement — of being struck — or of fear:

> I was afraid. I had the feeling that I was in contact with something I could not understand, that we cannot play with that. (Sylvie, 43)

For a lot of them it is a very moving experience, which brought tears when they told about it during the interview:

> One of the first vibrations that I felt was so beautiful in my hand that I had two big tears that flowed. (Monique, 42)

4.2.4 Threshold of awareness

The intuition does not always emerge in a precise, complete, immediately understandable form. Most often it first caresses the consciousness as a hazy image, a vague sensation, diffuse, a line of interior force.

The threshold of awareness of the sensations varies considerably from one person to another, and essentially depends on the degree of practice in pre-intuitive gestures. The more a person practices bringing on the calm inside and listening, with the special mode of attention which characterizes intuitive listening, the more precocious will be his awareness, the more subtle will be the sensations perceived.

According to the people with the most experience, of those we interviewed, intuitive sensations are always present; the only variable is the attention we bring to them.

> The day that I realized that I felt in a different way, I became aware of it suddenly, but it was already there. It was obvious. Because I had probably been living it for years, it seemed obvious to me; I knew how it functioned. (Antoine, 42)

It even seems that intuitive sensations can influence our behaviour before they reach the threshold of awareness.

4.3 Moments Immediately Following the Intuition

At the moment the intuition emerges into consciousness, several interior attitudes are possible:

(1) Chase away, repress the sensation:

> Little pieces of thought that I don't really let get in, that I don't let develop. (Annette)

The sensation sometimes continues to develop outside consciousness and reappears only when it has been transformed into a violent indisposition or a disease.

(2) Grasp the sensation, either by immediately weighing it down with emotions or interior commentaries that will disturb listening:

> At the moment I hear something, immediately after comes an emotion and with the emotion a verbalization. And this verbalization disturbs me in listening to the information of the intuition. (Muriel, 137)

or by immediately seeking to give it a defined outline, to recognize it , to understand it, to interpret it, all of which have the effect of fixing it, of stopping it.

(3) Silently welcoming this sensation, this burgeoning thought, confidently and patiently letting it ripen, take form, by itself. One of the scientists describes the process of maturation of his idea in this way:

> It is in a way *contemplating* one's *own* development of this idea. (Roland, 18)

Several persons use precise strategies to translate their feeling into a communicable form, without fixing the feeling or cutting it off. For example, in order to do an 'intuitive reading': first let the received image, which reflects the interior state of the other, become stable, become 'distilled'. Then enter into contact with the constantly moving 'atmosphere' of the image, without forcing anything, until this atmosphere becomes recognized and one can associate a precise formulation to it. Communicate this formulation to the other person; if the words are right, this will have the effect of the developing of the image. And so forth until the end of the reading.

Some of the subjects interviewed use interior criteria which enable them to verify that the maturing process of the intuition has come to its conclusion.

4.4 Intuitive Behaviour

For several of the people that we interviewed there have been times when this receptive attitude which characterizes the intuitive state continues beyond just a few moments to become a behavior, a mode of being intuitive. In desperate circumstances they stop struggling and bring an intense attention to the situation in such a way that the situation spurts out from moment to moment; they enter into resonance with it, letting themselves be carried by it, adopting the right behavior that will save them.

III: REMARKS

Confronting the results obtained with other testimonies, and with other studies[23] that have been carried out on the themes of scientific invention, of artistic creativity and of psychoanalytic insight for example, would enable us to confirm them and to make them more precise. Comparing them with different traditions of meditation would also be enlightening. But that is not the purpose of the present article ; these comparative studies will be carried out in another article. In the following pages we will simply list the difficulties and questions that we encountered in our attempt to clarify and model the intuitive experience.

1. DIFFICULTIES OF EXPLICITATION

1.1 Use of the Explicitation Session

At first we found the technique of the explicitation session difficult to master; it took a certain amount of time before we gathered real descriptions of intuitive experiences. We were surprised to see how difficult it was for the interviewer to maintain the interviewee within the limits of his own experience, how much one needed both firmness and gentleness to guide the other person on the fine line of here and now . When the subject stopped fleeing to abstract levels and let himself live, or relive in the present , a singular intuition, he frequently began by stating: 'I'm not doing anything' or 'I don't know what I'm doing'. Nevertheless, although the interview starts out with such a discouraging affirmation, the form of questioning of explicitation often enables the subject to describe the different gestures and states which make up his experience with unexpected precision; little by little during the interview he becomes aware of these gestures and states, sometimes with great astonishment. When the subject 'lets go', gives up his representations, beliefs, and judgements about intuition, and begins speaking slowly, from this place inside himself where he is in contact with his lived experience, the words he says seemed to us each time extremely precious, in their smallest details.

1.2 Correlation Between Degree of Awareness and Intuitive Expertise

However we did notice a certain variation from one person to another in the difficulty of adopting a position of embodied speech and of becoming aware of the pre-thought experience.

Most often, it is those people who have most worked on their intuition — generally psychotherapists or those practicing meditation — who have the highest degree of awareness of their intuitive experience, and who access most easily, during the interview, what remains of pre-thought. Contrary to appearances, this preceding sentence is not tautology: for the general rule says that the more a person is an expert in his field the more his know-how becomes personal, incorporate, distant from easily transmissible knowledge in the form of concepts and rules, and the more the portion of pre-thought is important.[24] If we had carried out research on the processes of mem-

---

[23] For example, the sudies in experimental psychology gathered by Sternberg and Davidson (1994), or in the field of psychoanalysis the works of De M'uzan (1977) and Anzieu (1981).

[24] This is in particular the theory of Hubert Dreyfus in chapter 1 of *Mind over Machine* (1986), entitled 'Five Steps from Novice to Expert'.

orization, we probably would not have noticed the same correlation between level of expertise and ease of explicitation.

This correlation can be explained by the similarities that exist between the intuitive experience and the process of awareness of the pre-thought of an experience.

On the one hand, the interior state which encourages an intuition — the intuitive state — and the interior state which encourages awareness of pre-thought — the state of evocation — are neighbouring states. Both are characterized by an 'embodied' attitude, a total presence in the singular situation, a situation which is present in the intuitive state, and past in the state of evocation.

On the other hand, the procedures used to access these two states are similar:
(1) In both cases access to the singular situation passes through a modification of the relation to the body:

- the pre-intuitive gestures essentially consist in finding the awareness of one's body, of one's breathing, of one's corporeal sensations;
- in the explicitation session, access to the past experience is set off by the evocation of the sensorial modalities of the experience. There too, the subject is brought back into his body. But this return to the body is guided by the interviewer, who accompanies the subject in the evocation of the sensorial details through the use of well-adapted questions.

(2) In both cases particular procedures are used to slow down the normal mental activity. This means:

- in the pre-intuitive phase, techniques of visualization, designed to calm down the interior dialog, the flow of memories and the projections into the future;
- in the explicitation session, procedures to slow down the reliving, the 'film' of the past experience, consisting, in particular, of helping the other to slow down his rhythm of speech.

Here again, the difference comes essentially from the presence or the absence of mediation. All of these procedures have these objectives:

- to provoke a return of the attention towards the immediate interior experience,
- to induce an attitude of non-voluntary, relaxed listening to the interior processes. For neither the awareness of the pre-thought nor the intuition can be provoked, forced.

This close relationship of the interior states and gestures explains the proportionality which we noticed, in the people interviewed, between degree of awareness and degree of intuitive expertise.

1.3 Familiarity of the Interviewer with the Pre-intuitive Gestures

We also noticed that a certain familiarity of the interviewer with the pre-intuitive gestures encouraged the process of awareness during the interview. The techniques of the explicitation session — techniques for guiding the other person into a state of evocation, techniques of questioning — are indispensable, but not sufficient. For the interviewee to access a position of embodied speech, the interviewer must show him the way: it is preferable that the interviewer set aside his own representations of the intuition, his own beliefs and expectations, that his interior attitude be open and welcoming, in order to guide the subject towards the same attitude. The interview is successful when concern about using techniques and reaching the objective — gathering the description of the experience — no longer creates an obstacle to this state of receptivity.

When this is the case, a particular kind of relation seems to be created between the interviewer and the interviewee for the duration of the interview. Everything happens as if the interior space liberated by the interviewer constitutes a sheath for the interviewee, not only psychic but almost visibly physical, which enables him to momentarily give up his representations, to relax, and to accept entering into relation with his own experience.

This relation resembles greatly the relation of connection which has often been described as one of the components of the intuitive experience. To really compare the two gestures, it should be necessary to carry out an explicitation of the internal processes of the interviewer and of the interviewee during the interview.

But if such is the case, if an intuitive connection exists during the interview, could it not bring about an influence of the interviewer on the interviewee, the former unconsciously communicating to the latter what he wants to hear ?

This possibility constitutes an additional argument in favour of the interviewer's familiarity with the pre-intuitive gestures: for the interviewee to be able to become aware of his own experience, it is necessary that the interior space liberated by the interviewer be completely cleared of his representations and beliefs, including the unconscious ones, through deep process work.

2. DIFFICULTIES IN MODELLING

2.1 Problem of the Models' Validity

An important difficulty in the modelling phase comes precisely from the influence of the beliefs of the interviewer and his own experience about the construction of models.

Indeed, each operation of analysis and each operation of abstraction carried out corresponds to an interpretation by the modeller. Whether it deals with dividing the description into phases, isolating descriptive traits in the text, bringing descriptive traits with close meaning into descriptive categories, or grouping these into yet more abstract categories, the modeller refers to his own understanding of the described experience.

To avoid this interpretation becoming pure, simple projection, the modeller must have undergone an update of his own implicit representations, beliefs and expectations. Is it then desirable that he set aside totally 'in parentheses' his own knowledge about intuition? On the contrary, it seems to us, as already said, desirable that the researcher should have a certain familiarity with the intuitive experience and that he uses it, in order to carry out his work of modelling.This familiarity enables him in particular to identify the aspects of the experience that he might not see or not be able to interpret if he had no understanding of it.

The fact that the modelling work includes an irreducible element of interpretation has a consequence for the objectivity of the models we have constructed; they are not 'true' in the sense of being the only representations possible; other choices, another dividing up of the descriptions of the subjective experience, could have been made. However, we have set up two kinds of validation:

(1) Each time that it was possible (that is in about 30% of the cases) we asked the interviewee to check the constructed model, which effectively led us to make some modifications, generally very slight.

(2) The fact that the generic structures which emerged enabled us on the one hand to guide the next people interviewed to the discovery of the pre-thought aspects of their experience and on the other hand to understand and to structure easily the ulterior descriptions, constitutes for us a very strong confirmation, not of the 'truth' of these models but of their fruitfulness. They are keys to exploring and understanding the intuitive experience.

2.2 Lack of Descriptive Categories

Another difficulty of this modelling phase comes from the lack of adequate descriptive categories. For example, our language provides few concepts to describe the interior movements of going down into the sensations of the body, of calming the mental activity and of renouncement, which make up the gesture of letting go.

In a general way, our language is very poor for describing the essential aspects of the intuitive experience: its corporeal anchoring, the return of attention to the interior, the absence of intentionality, the fine line of attention brought to the singular situation which is lived out here and now, the loss of a feeling of individual identity. There are even several aspects of the experience for which we have found no concept or adequate descriptive category. For example, in what category can we put the interior images which emerge during an intuition, which seem to be neither remembered nor constructed? How can we name as 'kinaesthetic' sensations which are strictly speaking neither interoceptive nor exteroceptive, because the subject no longer perceives the limits between his body and exterior space?

We find this same difficulty of vocabulary at higher levels of abstraction, when it is a question of choosing a unique term to name interior gestures which are close because of their objectives and the procedures set up: 'letting go', 'connection'..., we experienced difficulties in finding terms which were sufficiently generic without being too distant from the descriptive traits used by the different people.

Is this difficulty inherent to language? Is language, which aims at categorizing and abstracting, in essence unadapted to describe the singular, embodied, intuitive experience with that element of indifferentiation which it is made up of ? Or perhaps the poverty of our vocabulary to describe the intuitive experience is only due to the fact that this experience, like the subjective experience in general, has been little explored in our culture.

Are the vocabulary and structure of other languages better adapted?[25] Could we enrich ours with more specialized words and descriptive categories, transform its structure? Could we elaborate a language adapted to describing and comparing the results of the explicitation of the subjective experience at the same time that we develop the tools to clarify explicitly this experience?

CONCLUSION

This study confirms our hypothesis at the starting point: intuition does correspond to an experience, that is, a set of interior gestures which involve the entire being. Even if

---

[25] For example, Sanskrit includes about twenty terms for what we translate by 'consciousness' or 'awareness'.

intuition keeps an unpredictable, capricious character, it is possible to encourage its appearing, and to accompany its unfolding, by a very meticulous interior preparation. This preparation does not consist in learning, in progressively accumulating knowledge. It consists in emptying out, in giving up our habits of representation, of categorization, and of abstraction. This casting off enables us to find spontaneity, the real immediacy of our relation to the world. For, astonishingly, our most immediate, most intimate experience is also the most inaccessible for us. A long detour is necessary before we receive awareness of it.

It is in this immediate, pre-representational and pre-discursive experience of the world that all our cognitive activity seems to be rooted. In this perspective, far from being an exceptional mode of knowledge, intuition would be a burgeoning thought, the source of thought. The fact that the original genetic level of thought has been so little studied is one of the most inexplicable aspects of western thought, which probably pays heavily for this oversight. May the phenomenological description of the intuitive experience which we have sketched out contribute to reinstating this blind spot in our culture.[26]

References

Anzieu, D. (1981), *Le corps de l'œuvre, essai psychanalytique sur le travail créateur* (Paris: Gallimard)
Bandler, R. and Grinder, J. (1975), *Patterns of the Hypnotic Techniques of Milton H. Erickson* (Capitola, CA: Meta Publications).
Changeux, J.P. and Connes, A. (1992), *Matière à penser* (Paris: Editions Odile Jacob).
De M'Uzan, M. (1977), *De l'art à la mort* (Paris: Albin Michel).
Dilts, R. (1994), *Strategies of Genius* (Capitola, CA: Meta Publications).
Dilts, R., Grinder, J., Bandler, R. and Delozier J. (1980), *Neuro-Linguistic Programming: The Study of the Structure of Subjective Experience*, Volume 1 (Capitola, CA: Meta Publications).
Dreyfus, H. (1986), *Mind over Machine* (New York: Macmillan, Free Press).
Duplessis, Y. (1984), *Les couleurs visibles et non visibles* (Paris: Editions du Rocher).
Fox Keller E. (1983), *A Feeling for the Organism: The life and work of Barbara McClintock* (San Francisco: Freeman).
Grinder, J. and Bandler, R. (1976), *The Structure of Magic* (Science and Behavior books).
Gusdorf, G. (1951), *Mémoire et personne* (Paris: Presses Universitaires de France).
Heidegger, M. (1993), *Grund Probleme der Phänomenologie* (Frankfurt am Main: Vittorio Klostermann).
Miller, G., Galanter, E. and Pribram, K. (1960), *Plans and the Structure of Behavior* (Henry Holt).
Piaget, J. (1974), *La prise de conscience* (Paris: Presses Universitaires de France).
Piaget, J. (1974), *Réussir et comprendre* (Paris: Presses Universitaires de France).
Polanyi, M. (1962), *Personal Knowledge. Towards a Post-Critical Philosophy* (Chicago UP).
Reik, T. (1948), *Listening with the Third Ear: The inner experience of a psychoanalyst* (New York: Farrar, Straus and Giroux, 1983).
Schelling, F.W. (1856), *Philosophische Briefe über Dogmatismus und Kriticismus*, Sämtliche Werke, vol. I (Stuttgart-Ausbourg: Cotta).
Smith, J. and Smith, D. (1977), 'Database Abstractions: Aggregation and Generalisation', *ACM Transactions on Database Systems*, **2** (2), pp. 105–33.
Sowa, J.F. (1984), *Conceptual Structures: Information processing in mind and machine* (Addison-Wesley).
Stengers, I. and Schanger, J. (1988), *Les concepts scientifiques. Invention et pouvoir* (Paris: Editions La Découverte).
Sternberg, R.G. and Davidson, J.E. (1994), *The Nature of Insight* (Cambridge, MA: MIT Press).
Varela, F., Thompson, E. and Rosch, E. (1991), *The Embodied Mind: Cognitive Science and Human Experience* (Cambridge, MA: MIT Press).
Vermersch, P. (1994), *L'entretien d'explicitation* (Paris: Editions ESF).
Wittgenstein, L. (1968), *Philosophical Investigations*, trans. G.E.M. Anscombe (Oxford: Blackwell).

[26] **Acknowledgements:** This article summarizes a doctoral thesis carried out at CREA (Center for Research on Applied Epistemology, Ecole Polytechnique), and completed in November 1998. My thanks to Francisco Varela, my thesis adviser, for his support and the confidence he showed in me throughout my work, and to the Institut National des Télécommunications, for giving me the opportunity to carry out this research, and all who agreed to be interviewed and provided the material for this work.

Carl Ginsburg

Body-image, Movement and Consciousness:

Examples from a Somatic Practice in the Feldenkrais Method[1]

We think of consciousness as a thing. Observation of our experience indicates that we are actually consciousing, and that experiencing is closely related to movement and the muscular sense. The position of this paper is that mind and body are not two entities related to each other but an inseparable whole while functioning. From concrete examples from the Feldenkrais Method, it is shown that changes in the organization of movement and functioning are intimately related and that one cannot change without conscious experience. Implications for the resolution of controversies in the field of consciousness studies and the neurosciences are suggested.

Introduction: The Importance of Movement

It is odd that we have made the activity of sentience into a noun. We say consciousness and not consciousing, implying that consciousness is a thing. Yet for other related activities we say we are sleeping or that we are dreaming. The specific activities of a conscious mind are, however, verbs. We imagine, look at, think, listen, observe, feel, bring attention to, meditate, etc. We speak of consciousness as a state. Yet everything we know of consciousness is connected to movement. In order to see the book on the table across the room I must make an act of attention. I turn my head and eyes and focus at the distance. Whatever impinges on the retina is not what I see. This may be of a particular size shape and produce a certain colour, but I see a book. That means my perception is organized to see a particular thing.

Correspondence: Carl Ginsburg, Eschersheimer Landstrasse 70, D-60322 Frankfurt, Germany.
Email: 110633.450@compuserve.com

[1] The term The Feldenkrais Method® is a registered service mark of The Feldenkrais Guild , PO Box 489, Albany, OR 97321-0143, USA.

Journal of Consciousness Studies, **6**, No. 2–3, 1999, pp.79–91

If I fix myself so that nothing moves and the image stays on the retina for so many seconds I will no longer see. But this is hard to do. My eyes naturally move all the time. If I watch my own process, I find a continuous shifting. My attention moves; my thought moves; there is an arising and falling of each distinct thought or moment of where my attention is directed. And as this activity continues, I have the ability to also observe the activity, the mind watching itself. Do we confuse ourselves by making a noun, consciousness? As I continue I will use both the noun and verb form.

I take a walk with my dog. My vision puts me in spatial flow where the movement through the landscape is my walking itself, and at the same moment directing my path. A rock wall comes into view and I skillfully step over it. I know in my sensation of my moving when I have lifted my legs high enough so that my feet come over the wall. I do not have to stop and think about it. It is all part of my immediate conscious experience. And yet I am surely not consciousing all the workings of my biological system. I stop to look for a rock to sit on in a dry arroyo. I find what I seek. Sitting, I am facing the sandy bed of the arroyo, and about twenty yards away a twisted mountain oak sprouting out of the rocks of the arroyo wall spreads its branches over the arroyo. I feel my breathing become easier, a flowing in my chest. I am enjoying the beauty of this view. My dog approaches. He sits looking at me. I lift my hand to pat his head and he licks my hand. I am attending, intending, interacting in sequence, and continuing that activity until I sleep again.

I can describe all this (another activity of consciousing) through the movement of my breath, palate, voice box, lips and tongue, or through the movement of my fingers on the computer keyboard. I can describe it because I experienced it. We say it is now in my memory. My experience was not, cannot be, raw sense data. On the contrary I was perceiving space, flow, my self in moving, objects in the landscape, the dog, sounds of birds, the feel of myself that I describe as aesthetic enjoyment. My moving itself is irreducible because it is coordinated, flowing, integrated and not separate from what I am perceiving with my other senses. When I am remembering, I am not re-experiencing exactly, but bringing forth fragments of the experience. From this I rapidly make sentences. When I write, my fingers hit the keys in response to the rising words that at the same time I am sub-vocalizing, and the corresponding letters are struck without stopping to think which letters match the word. My finger awareness includes their orientation to the keyboard. My consciousing is shifting with each moment in time. The overall effect is a coordinated moving flow in time. My activity is organized and integrated. So are the perceptions that are essential for this integration of action and activity.

At the same time I am oriented in the space of my environment, and oriented in the body space so that when I lift my hand I *know* where my hand is relative to myself and relative to the environmental space. How precise this is can be tested by closing one's eyes and moving one's hand in front of one's face. You will see in your mind's eye some sort of image of your hand. It need not be very distinct but the image will correspond to a position in space. Open your eyes and check the correspondence. For almost everyone the image will correspond exactly to the position of your hand.

In the activity of my normal consciousing I am also oriented in time. I situate myself between past and future. I am aware that I have a history. I need not bring this up at any moment, but I can bring it up immediately when needed.

Imagine yourself waking up from sleep in a hotel in a foreign country. At first you may be disoriented. You wonder where you are located. You might imagine yourself in a familiar space only to realize that that is not where you are and you do not even know what time or day it is. You have an uncomfortable sensation within yourself. As you come more awake you then orient yourself. Now you are awake and consciousing. You know where the bathroom is. You can step on the floor, erect yourself in gravity and not trip over the chair.

I am gradually making an inventory of some of the mundane activities of consciousing and deliberately leaving out such issues as symbolic thinking, subjective qualia, etc., that take attention away from the biological roots of what we put under the heading of consciousness. Many of our activities are not in the realm of consciousing. When I erect myself in gravity, I normally direct myself to do so. I might on the other hand be in a somnambulistic state. I can still do so having previously organized this activity. In addition much of the muscular activity to accomplish this action is not under conscious control, but is directed through the vestibular system, the extra pyramidal muscular responses, the vestibular-optical reflexes. I can stand up without paying mind to my action and act habitually and probably inefficiently. On the other hand I can develop my awareness in such a way that my experience of my acting is rich with knowing my self-orientation, my relation to space and gravity, my sense of timing, and I will stand elegantly and efficiently using a minimum of muscular effort.

The Question of Consciousness

The fact that acts can be done with minimal awareness, or in some cases none at all is confusing to philosophers and scientists. It is thought then that consciousness has no biological function, that we could live without it. Paradoxically without consciousness no philosopher or scientist would ever be concerned about the issue. A more significant contention is that without consciousing no child could learn to erect himself or herself, and no child could self direct the activity needed for biological survival. The organization of erect standing and walking is undoubtedly the most complex thing a brain accomplishes in life, and at this moment in history well beyond the ability of the most sophisticated and rapid computers. My point here is that all human action requires an integration of conscious and non-conscious activity, and also requires immense and complex organization.

We do not usually study ourselves with this attention to what we experience. Nor do we consider the degree to which our activity results from the integration of so many different levels. On the contrary we tend to study the visual system as an isolated entity, or the behaviour of a subject in responding to a target stimulus. We do so because our analytical cognitive abilities are easy to use. We have organized cognitive systems available which, through complex organized entities such as language, symbolic pictorial representations, mathematics, we can represent ideas as images, sentences, or mathematical equations. Such complex organizations make simplicity possible. We tend not to consider how these capacities come into an organized state. We use these systems as if everything of significance can be expressed within them, without concern for the degree to which they also limit our thought processes. If we allow it to be so, we end up limited by the linearity of our communication systems, and specifically by the linearity of the logical structure of thought that is symbolically mediated, i.e. driven by the needs of language or other communication. Integration, coordination, interconnectedness is then hard to understand. It is easier to see functions as modularized and not worry how separate functions become integrated actions. Can we develop another way to think?

The question of consciousness is one, then, that has baffled attempts to deal with it in a structured analytical way. There is a gap between what we can know of our own lived experience, which depends on consciousness or consciousing itself, and what we can postulate as an explanation of how consciousness is possible. Thus the controversies so familiar to those involved in consciousness studies.

In this paper I wish to take an entirely different tack, and shift the thinking. My professional experience is in the area of movement learning in relation to developing awareness using The Feldenkrais Method. Although I work in the realm of a particular method, I believe that the success of this work reveals something quite general about the workings of the nervous system and indeed can show that the activities of consciousness or consciousing are essential to human biological life. What I propose is that the phenomenology of the Feldenkrais method allows one to connect changes in the domain of inner experience with changes in the organization of outer behaviour. It thus provides a way to observe the correlations between the domain of phenomenology and the domain of external observation.

The Somatic Insight

Moshe Feldenkrais wrote in 1964, 'My contention is that the unity of mind and body is an objective reality, that they are not entities related to each other in one fashion or another, but an inseparable whole while functioning. To put the point more clearly I contend that a brain without motor functions could not think or at least that the continuity of mental functions is assured by corresponding motor functions.' Feldenkrais goes on to note that, 'We have no sensation of the inner workings of the central nervous system; we can feel their manifestation only as far as the eye, the vocal apparatus, the facial mobilization and the rest of the soma provoke our *awareness*. This is the state of consciousness!' (Emphasis mine.) And lastly the conclusion resulting from these contentions: '. . . the state of the cortex is directly and legibly visible on the periphery through the attitude, posture, and muscular configuration, which are all connected. Any change in the nervous system translates itself clearly through a change of attitude, posture and muscular configuration. They are not two states but two aspects of the same state.' With one stroke we have eliminated the mind–body problem.

The stance taken here by Feldenkrais is hypothetical, and also operative. It is a working position, substantiated by the practical work he had been exploring for thirty years, and shared by a pioneering group of thinker-explorers of the twentieth century who were interested in finding practical ways of furthering human development. Among these people were F. Mathias Alexander, Heinrich Jacoby, Ida Rolf, Gerda Alexander, Elsa Gindler and her many students, Charlotte Selver, Emmi Pikler, Berta Bobath among them, and of course Feldenkrais, who was influenced by this movement through his contact with Jacoby, but also through his work in Judo and contact with oriental teachers. (For an overview see Johnson, 1995.)

Elsa Gindler, whose 'arbeit am menschen' (work on the human) was so influential, cured herself of tuberculosis by so refining her awareness of her breathing that she taught herself to rest her diseased lung and breathe more fully with the healthy lung. F. Mathias Alexander discovered through extensive self examination how he could inhibit habits of use of his head and neck that interfered with his voice, something essential for his original profession as an actor. Berta Bobath developed new approaches to physical therapy that involve a neuro-developmental approach, and Emmi Pikler, a radical way to rear children through her detailed observations of development. All of those mentioned developed practices of embodied awareness. Such practices show a correlation between a phenomenology of awareness and the refining and reorganization of human skills and capabilities.

In the short space of this essay, it is not possible to explore any of these practices in any depth. However, I will take some specific examples from my practice of the Feldenkrais method to illustrate what can be learned from these somatic practices. We can emphasize again that there is no mind–body problem from this perspective. What I hope to suggest is a direction to the solution of the other standing problems of consciousness.

Examples from the Feldenkrais Method

We call our processes in the Feldenkrais method 'lessons', and they are in two styles. Awareness Through Movement lessons are presented verbally, usually to groups. The presenter guides the lesson by directing the participants through a series of movement sequences that increase the level of self awareness of the participant, and at the same time increase the level of sensitivity to the nuances of kinesthetic sensation.

Here is a particular Feldenkrais Awareness Through Movement lesson. As with many of these lessons, it has a large element of exploration in which the learner is directed to explore different movements with the attention directed to the quality of execution rather than the size of movement. Everything is done softly with emphasis on expanding awareness. For the sake of brevity I will only describe the major elements of the lesson. At first one is directed to sit comfortably cross legged on the floor and to put the hands together as if praying with the elbows out. The instruction then is to keep the bases of the two palms together and separate the fingers from each other without moving the elbows. One tries both hands and then just the right and just the left. One then turns the hands so that the fingers point away from the body. The same movements are repeated. For many people it is quite difficult and only a small movement is possible to do comfortably. Now one is instructed to think that the right eye contains something like a small telescope where the lens is. One then looks to the right and then up and around so that one makes a slow careful circular movement with the right eye attending to any parts of the movement which are not smooth and easy. By moving very slowly, delicately and attentively through the difficult portions of the movement, one begins to improve the quality of moving the eye. One can then make circles in each direction. Finally one combines this movement with the movement of the hands. Returning to the movement of the hands, the following effects are generally noted. First the right hand is now more capable than the left in the movement of keeping the base of the palms together and lifting the fingers away. Secondly the distribution of tonus throughout the entire right side of the body has changed. This is observable to an outside person observing the face, the shoulders, etc.

What we have here is a clear demonstration of the effect of directed conscious awareness on the activity of the nervous system itself. Note that in moving the right eye the left eye automatically moves also. Thus the changes in the distribution of muscular activity are not the consequence of the movement *per se*. The change then can only have resulted from the directing of awareness to the movement of the right eye. And this change is not localized with the eye, but distributed through the musculature of the entire right side and the corresponding movement organization. Any theory of consciousness and nervous system functioning *must* take such phenomena into account. I believe this phenomenon, and many others not yet acknowledged, does indeed challenge a lot of our current thinking about mind, brain and consciousness.

Phenomenologically one feels one's right eye in a new way. Initially as I begin to move my right eye in a circular motion, imagining the eye as a telescope, I move the eye in accordance with this image, feeling the movement of the eye with an attention that I normally do not bring to moving my eye. At first I may find it difficult to make the circle round; at certain points I find that I cannot move the eye the way I want. Slowly as I move, directing my attention to where I can move with quality, i.e. a sense of ease and comfort, I find that I can approach the difficult places in the circle and begin to make a complete smooth and enjoyable movement. Now I experience a spreading ease throughout first the right side of my face, then with my breathing. Eventually I am directed to return to the movement of the hands, and find my right hand more supple and moveable. This is learning, however, not at the level of simple association, or conditioning.

Here is a story to show the same thing another way. I was teaching a Feldenkrais class to a group of people in a large corporation. Many were scientists, engineers and technical workers. The common characteristic of the group was that they all suffered with back pain at varying times. In one lesson we explored movements on one side of the body for almost forty minutes. In that space of time most class members improved their easy range of movement about seventy per cent or more. I then had them check the same movement on the other side. They found themselves about as restricted as when they first tried to move on the first side. I then had them imagine the same movements as they did in the forty minute sequence on this other side for about five minutes. Suddenly they found that they could move eighty per cent more on this side. One engineer looked up at me after experiencing this change and said, 'That doesn't compute.' What happened for him obviously challenged a belief he had that mind and material were separate and that immaterial mind could not influence matter, i.e. his body. Empirically he could not deny the experience; intellectually he could not account for it. Here a mental activity, imagining, affects the state of the organization of the nervous system as indicated by a new organization of movement. It is not an immaterial process in the sense that if one observes the person while that person imagines, one can detect subtle activity in the musculature which accompanies the imagining.

Our second lesson process is named Functional Integration. This is a hands on process in which the practitioner communicates with the participant through touch. Feldenkrais described this teaching process as 'dancing together'. The practitioner touches and feels where the person touched can move and the person touched feels what is wanted or intended and responds. The aim again is enhanced awareness in which the person touched realizes new possibilities of kinesthetic sensing and feeling, and experiences shifts in the body (movement) image. Often the experience of the lesson for the participant is beyond verbal description, but the reverberations of these shifts become clear after the lesson as the person experiences daily life with a changed self appreciation. How profound this can be will be illustrated with the specific examples cited below.

Over the years I have given thousands of Functional Integration lessons. On the surface it appears as if I use my hands to communicate with the person receiving the lesson. In fact I have trained myself to use the movement of my entire structure to make the contact and sense the other person. I produce within myself a very clear organization of my spine and pelvis so that what is communicated with my hands is produced with my entire self action. For myself, as practitioner, I find that I am effective when I shift to an open awareness, shut down my usual verbal self chatter, and give up any attachment to producing results. My thinking is embodied in the sense that I move directly from sensing and feeling into the action of communicating through my own movement to the person receiving the lesson. I find in this way that I can be very precise to the needs of the person I am working with. Many people I work with report that they feel I have contacted them and felt their presence in an unique way.

Here is an example from my individual practice that further indicates the relation of conscious experience to even the most reflexive activities of the nervous system. My client Jeff was recovering, very slowly, from Guillian-Barre Syndrome. This syndrome apparently involves an acute viral infection of the spinal nerve roots. Muscle weakness and paralysis results from disturbances of the lower motor neurons. Sensory symptoms involve loss of position sense, and some distorted sensations such as tingling. When he was acutely ill, Jeff was completely paralysed, but he had not lost body (touch) sensation. He had recovered, by the time I began to work with him, to the point that he could make any voluntary movement asked of him. However, he found himself very weak and needed two crutches to walk. Often he used a wheel chair. At this point he was two years past his acute illness.

As we did our weekly lessons, he improved his balance and his stamina. In a few weeks he was able to graduate to the use of one crutch. One day, as we started another lesson, my attention was drawn to Jeff's feet. I knew that he could feel my hand touching his feet, distinguish one toe from another, and wiggle the foot up and down, as well as the toes. Yet, when he wasn't trying to move his feet, they were lifeless. And when he walked, his feet slapped at the ground like floppy shoes.

I chose then to do an experiment with a flat board. I had Jeff lie on his back. I put a soft roller under his knees and a styrofoam roller under his ankles. This had two effects. First it took Jeff out of the gravity field so that he was not compelled to make an effort to stand up. Secondly I could feel how his feet moved without the heels pressing on the table and could move his entire self through pressure on his feet. I knew Jeff could make voluntary movements with the muscles of his lower legs, but from past experience I knew his weakness probably related to a lack of reflex tone in these same muscles. I also knew that by pressing his feet gently with a hard, flat surface, I could possibly elicit more so called reflex activity.

It was a good choice of a lesson for Jeff. I began by pressing my hard board gently against Jeff's left foot. His foot, initially floppy and toneless, did not respond at all to the pressure of the flat surface as I tilted the board one direction or another. The foot stayed where it was, unmoved by the stimulation. I would interpret what I felt as I moved the board against Jeff's foot as 'I am not connecting'. The foot had a quality I could most easily describe as lifeless. In a normal situation a person's foot would follow the movement of the board as the foot reacted to the stimulation of the surface. Slowly as I pressed the toes and the ball of the foot, small responses began and Jeff's foot began to follow my movements. I could detect each increase in response with my hands, which then resulted in my increasing the stimulation of Jeff's foot. After twenty minutes or so, Jeff's foot responded with a good approximation of normalcy. I was now able to move his entire skeleton through his foot in a simulation of the function of standing on that foot. I do this by moving the board with my pelvis well grounded so that the movement of my center is transmitted through my arms to the foot, knee, pelvis, spine and head of my client. In my own feeling sense, I could imagine his entire spine and detect how each vertebra connected in the movement. To my estimation his lower leg muscles had increased in tone. The skeletal structure carried the movement to his head.

But Jeff in fact was unaware at this point. I asked him to compare the left foot, the one we had worked with, with the right. He said that he felt no difference. I then asked him to get up slowly and take a few steps. I was pleased at this point. My work with Jeff had resulted in a discernible change in his foot and as he began to walk I could see that his left leg carried weight better than the right. His left foot no longer slapped the ground, but moved normally with the action of his walking. I let Jeff walk and didn't ask anything new of him. Jeff paused; a look of surprise passed across his face.

'I didn't realize,' he said. 'I didn't realize that I had lost my foot. It's unbelievable. I have a foot again. I can feel it clearly.' Jeff began walking more vigorously, feeling his left foot again and again.

Here the nuts and bolts of changing neurological organization appear first. He walks differently and then finds a profound shift in his body feeling. That he says, 'I have a foot again,' indicates that the spatial area of his conscious appreciation of himself has expanded. It is not just a question of sensation. Remember, he never lost touch sensation. The phenomenology of the body-image is a profound subject. Here the body-image is linked completely to the return of organized functioning. Oliver Sacks in his book *A Leg To Stand On* (1984) provides one of the best first-person descriptions of this relationship on record in writing about his recovery from a devastating injury to his leg. For Sacks the experience had an aspect of revelation as he realized the profound connection between his self image and his functioning, a phenomenological connection completely ignored in his medical training.

In this second example, again from my practice, the change in body-image provoked a crisis. On the surface it appeared that my client and I were dealing with a problem in physical structure. This client was born with congenital malformations of both her hip joints. In her growing up she learned to do the things she wanted, i.e. mobilize herself to walk, stand, run, erect herself in gravity, despite the fact that both hip joints did not have proper sockets, and the joints were supported only by the tissue of the joint capsule. What she did with herself she did in her own fashion, finding a way that worked so that she could be as much as possible like other children. As a normal child does, she constructed patterns of action/movement that allowed her to succeed to the best of her ability. These patterns were not the same as those of a child without her structural difficulties. One point about these movement patterns is that they had value. They were the ones that worked given the constraints of her physical difficulties.

At the age of twenty six, her physicians, having noted that her bone growth had ended, replaced through surgery both hip joints with stainless steel balls and implanted teflon sockets in her pelvis. Subsequent to this surgery and her convalescence she continued her life, but as time went on she began to experience increasing pain in her back. She continued with physical therapy. It was of no avail to her. Now in her thirties she was referred to me to see how my approach might aid her.

What I observed about her was that despite the new hardware that gave her perfectly usable hip joints, she still walked and erected herself with the same patterns that were useful to herself as a child. These patterns involved an extreme arching of her low back and a bringing of her knees together for support. What I knew was that she had no sensation or feeling of other patterns. This may seem like mind reading. Nevertheless it is important to the outcome of what I do to make educated assumptions about my client's experience. I needed to know what she needed to experience in order to find a new pattern. The new patterns could not be taught externally and certainly not through language. The fact that ordinary physical therapy was of no use indicated this. We had to create an *experiential* pathway to a new body-movement image. To do this she and I had to retrace the learning path of erecting herself in gravity.

I could feel in the quality of rigidity in her spine and ribs, which was unyielding even when she was lying down how little feeling she had of this middle part of herself. It was the consequence of the extreme efforting that she needed to hold herself erect. And indeed in standing one felt almost an impossibility of any change as she held her spine so strongly in fear of falling. In a more ideally organized person the spine is a flexible supporting column in which the muscles are of even tonus, ready for movement and action. The lessons that I did were created in part by watching how children learn the actions of coming up to stand, and imagining what needs to be felt internally in conjunction with this learning. Thus I began by getting her to move her pelvis and spine in relation to each other. It can only happen as an awareness. Even after a few lessons she had much less pain.

At one particular lesson a new pattern emerged for her more clearly. At the end of the session she appeared to me to be frightened. She told me that she felt very strange. The next day she reported that she was in a crisis and that she hadn't slept well. I asked her what she was experiencing. She said, 'I don't feel like myself. I don't feel like the same person. It's very disturbing.' Later in our discussion she said, 'But I know I also feel how much easier it is to walk.' It was this later observation that allowed her to go on with the lessons. The lessons were leading to patterns that were completely novel to her experience. She discovered with each change some sense of disturbance of her self feeling and thus her self identity. What was fortunate for her progress was that each time that she felt strange to herself, she allowed herself the feelings of fright and disturbance, knowing that what was new to her sensation of herself would be 'normal' in a few days. She thus found a way to transcend the identity of herself with a particular pattern of feeling of herself. The complexities we are approaching in this instance are beyond the scope of this paper. I will come back to the point, however, because one begins to appreciate that our issues do not exist in the vacuum of the isolated nervous system and person.

In any case my client had to make a conscious step at a higher level. She had to observe the quality of her changing and choose what best fit her life.

I would like to make a brief diversion to indicate that, phenomenologically, sensory perceptions are not in isolated sensory systems. From my own experience I discovered a relation of body-image to vision. On a visit to an optometrist, who specialized in a field called behavioural optometry, I explored wearing prism glasses that distorted the experienced visual spatial field. One set made the floor appear much closer than in my normal vision. My internal body space decreased so much that I felt about four feet tall. When I tried to walk, I could barely move my legs and had no idea where to place my feet. It took some minutes with the glasses to begin to recover normal movement. It is apparent that perceptions such as body-image are cross related within the many sensory systems. Any distortion in one place immediately produces disturbances in other perceptions as well as in functioning. And yet very quickly the nervous system begins to reorganize to restore the same coherence of perception and therefore the quality of action and movement. What interests me in all of this is the great plasticity of ourselves in self organizing to provide us with a biological stability. I think I have strongly made the case so far that although we do not control the learning process directly, the activities of consciousing are essential to this level of learning in which perceptions and actions are interlinked and constructed.

I would like to conclude with a description of a Functional Integration process that emphasizes how the nervous system responds much more directly to complete integrated action patterns rather than isolated parts of movement. I am working with Brenda who suffered a cerebral accident when she was in her twenties some twelve years before. She has pursued many avenues toward recovery of use of her paralysed left hand, this hand which contracts into a snarl of confused twisting along with her wrist and arm when she tries to use it. When she ignores the arm and hand, it hangs with the elbow partially bent. We have worked together for four sessions and have already discovered together a number of new things not made available before. First and foremost, Brenda finds it easier to progress when she doesn't push, use effort, or try hard to get the result. She can also progress when she shifts focus away from the hand and the details of the action. And there is her discovery that it is not just the hand and arm where there is loss of mobility and function.

I began my first lesson with Brenda by touching the ribs and spine on each side to reveal to myself that the affected left side was quite immovable compared to the right. When I passively moved the left arm, the ribs stayed glued to the table, an indication that her internal experience of this area is missing; this is in contrast to the right side where my lifting her arm led to the entire rib cage following and facilitating the movement. As I continued the lesson I spent a good bit of time with the 'good' right side exploring how pressing the foot moved the ribs and spine on this side as well as continuing with movements of the arm in conjunction with the trunk and pelvis. Only then did I approach the left side again, and in doing so I also brought Brenda's awareness to the differences. As I sensed improvement, such as feeling that ribs and spine began to respond when I pressed the left foot, I checked with Brenda to find out whether she felt the difference. She did and indicated that she really appreciated sensing herself in moving. Moving the arm, head and shoulder all together I was able to slowly, passively, move her hand to touch her shoulder and then her neck and finally her face. At no time did I attempt to move her past any resistance that I sensed in her.

Now in the fifth session I feel that when I move her arm, the ribs follow. I ask Brenda to take my hand and move it in space. This she does by catching my hand in her still spastically contracted fingers. But her arm and shoulder are no longer behaving in a spastic pattern of fixed contractions. I ask her to move me wherever she wishes. This she does lifting my arm, pushing it forward, pulling it back. Suddenly she realizes that she can move me, and, therefore herself to places that were unreachable when we started together. It is as if this functioning came out of nowhere. Later Brenda tells me that she has caught herself spontaneously using her left side in situations where previously she would never have considered it.

We work more with the hand. I have her touch and feel my hand, touch herself and stroke herself. In my moving her passively to bring her hand to herself in previous sessions, I arranged her fingers, as they diminished in their spasticity, to touch her neck or her face. We work also with her sensation and perception. How she feels and identifies each finger and feels where they are in space and in movement. It turns out that her sense of space and movement is not reliable whereas touch is. As she uses the hand in the small ways that are possible, in touching, feeling, her sensation becomes more accurate.

What is different about our work together? There are elements here of communication and contact, my ability to sense at all times what is going on with Brenda and stopping when it is too much, or when she begins to resist. There is the support I am able to give her, so that she trusts that my touch is safe, that I will respect her space and being. There are aspects of my skill that allow me to be intentional without being invasive, that allow me to guide without ever needing to be forceful. There is my constant reminder that there is no need to succeed, that success will follow process. I evoke a coupling that allows Brenda to find a new possibility. I do not give her any information, but out of the coupling, the dance we do together, she senses differences and in effect creates new information. Each one of us avoid the arrogance of thinking that we are responsible for what happens in the lesson.

How is such a dance possible without consciousing, aware-ing at an expanded level? I must take into account Brenda as a thinking, feeling, breathing being. There is no way to achieve any result without accounting for the phenomenological, how she is experiencing the exchange between us, and what I am experiencing. We are coupled together so that although I cannot get inside her feelings, I can still respond to that through my feeling of her movement, and response to me. Consciousness can be eradicated in abstract thought, not in the lived world.

Some Conclusions

The perspective we have outlined here has, as I have shown through a number of concrete instances, empirical justification. I believe such a perspective has the power to resolve a number of continuing difficulties in the ongoing debates about consciousness, AI, cognition, etc. It is not my purpose here to do this. I would like, however, to point out that we can make some conclusions and actually eliminate some approaches to the problem at hand. I am forced to conclude through the medium of my approach, that I come close to a very direct contact, nervous system to nervous system in the practice of my lessons. The kinds of ways that the people that I work with change their patterns is indicative of this, as is the ways that I can work with myself. I make my conclusions, then, based on the practical consequences.

One conclusion is that the nervous system responds to the impress of entire connected functions and structurally shifts to a better state of organization. Bits and pieces which have no particular meaning or relation to anything else have no effect. That's why trying to move the fingers of a person whose hand is paralysed by stroke has very limited effect, but as in Brenda's case getting her to move me results in a profound reduction in her muscular spasticity, and the beginnings of her own movement capability. Similarly with Jeff, the contact with his entire skeleton simulating the function of standing on his leg brings back the image of his foot. It is clear then, for human beings, and for other living creatures, the whole is indeed greater than the parts. A corollary of this is that the level of change in the nervous system is the level of meaning. Change must be connected to life.

The phenomenological perspective cannot be eliminated. One could say that one operates one's nervous system through the highest level of organization, which implies experience and consciousness.

Reductionism, one can conclude, is neither a pragmatic, nor effective approach to working with people at this level, nor to understanding the integrative aspects of the nervous system. To cite the example of movement science, years of attempts to understand coordinated human movement experimentally by trying to work at the level of individual motor units or some such bottom up approach has been spectacularly unproductive. Latash (1996) writes of this kind of approach as 'trying to understand its [a complex system's] function on the basis of the summed activity of its elements'. 'Apparently,' he concludes, 'this is a dead end route.'

If this is so for a supposedly tractable problem such as the integration of the muscular system for movement, what then for studying consciousness? Fortunately this kind of impasse is leading to new directions. There is certainly research that is beginning to show that some kind of dynamic systems approach will be necessary. To cite one example: Walter Freeman in his investigations of the olfactory bulb in rabbits showed a number of startling things (Freeman, 1995). First that the initial signals from the smell receptors vanished in the cerebral cortex, and were replaced by a new pattern of cortical activity. Second that when the rabbit was reconditioned to a different response to the same stimulus (smell), a new pattern emerged, and that all the conditioned patterns to other smells shifted also. There may be good reason to believe that a nervous system does not deal with nor store raw sense data. If the responses of a higher animal relate to the meaning of a stimulus in regard to how the animal will act in the environment, we are dealing with a high level of biological complexity. This includes for higher animals the social environment. One could conclude that any project to explain even such a direct observable as behaviour on the basis of knowing the precise state of the nervous system is doomed to failure.

How then can we enlarge our understanding of our nervous system and its relation to the phenomenological realm, and consciousness? The organization of such a system requires the organization of effective action and movement as a ground for all further cognitive development. This is the major task of a nervous system. The corollary is that movement is essential to the task of self organizing the system. Very little has been explored scientifically in this realm. Some authors, for example Maturana and Varela (1987) and Gerald Edelman (1987), have seen the essential importance of movement to understanding the nervous system and biological systems in general.

Recently there has been a revival of dynamic systems theory in understanding movement and the brain. I suggest Kelso (1995) and Thelen & Smith (1994) for overviews.

Whatever we want to say about the act of consciousing, we are always in it, and cannot escape to independently corroborate anything. Nor can we escape the fact that we live, develop, learn and organize our nervous systems in connection with a community of fellow beings. We have to assume that this is so for all higher living creatures. We cannot have a separate understanding of the brain or consciousness without understanding experiencing, without accounting for the details of the phenomenology of lived experience. This experience can indeed be shared. What is needed is more exploration at the top level, which includes accurate study of the influence of consciousing on consciousness itself. Such a project has been endorsed by at least a few investigators recently. I mention particularly Núñez (1997), Varela (1996) and Wilber (1997). I hope what I have contributed here helps further this understanding. Hopefully it will lead also to new explorations at the lower level of the operations of the nervous system itself.

References

Edelman, G. (1987), *Neural Darwinism* (New York: Basic Books).

Feldenkrais, M. (1964), 'Mind and body', *Systematics: The Journal for the Correlative Study of History, Philosophy, and the Sciences*, **2** (1). Reprinted in *Your Body Works*, ed. G. Kogan, 1980 (Berkeley, CA: Transformations).

Freeman, W. (1995), *Societies of Brains* (Hillsdale, NJ: Lawrence Erlbaum Associates).

Johnson, D. (1995), *Bone, Breath, and Gesture: Practices of Embodiment* (Berkeley, CA: North Atlantic Books).

Kelso, J.A. Scott (1995), *Dynamic Patterns: The Self-Organization of Brain and Behavior* (Cambridge, MA: MIT Press).

Latash, M.L. (1996), 'The Bernstein Problem: How does the central nervous system make its choices?', in *Dexterity and its Development*, ed. M.L. Latash and M.T.Turvey (Mahwah, NJ: Lawrence Erlbaum Associates).

Maturana H. and Varela, F. (1987), *The Tree of Knowledge* (Boston, MA: New Science Library).

Núñez, R.E. (1997), 'Eating soup with chopsticks: Dogmas, difficulties and alternatives in the study of conscious experience', *Journal of Consciousness Studies*, **4** (2), pp. 141–65.

Thelen, E. and Smith, L. (1994), *A Dynamic Systems Approach to the Development of Cognition and Action* (Cambridge, MA: MIT Press).

Sacks, O. (1984), *A Leg To Stand On* (London: Duckworth).

Varela, F.J. (1996), 'Neurophenomenology', *Journal of Consciousness Studies*, **3** (4), pp. 330–49.

Wilber, K. (1997), 'An integral theory of consciousness', *Journal of Consciousness Studies*, **4** (1), pp. 71–92.

Part 2
Phenomenology

Natalie Depraz

The Phenomenological Reduction As Praxis[1]

> ... through the *epochè*, the gaze of the philosopher in truth first becomes fully free. ...
> [F]ree of the strongest and most universal, and at the same time most hidden, internal
> bond, namely, of the pre-givenness of the world.
>
> (Husserl, *Krisis,* § 41)

I: Introduction — Theory vs. Practice at the Foundation of Phenomenology

This paper is concerned with the method of phenomenological reduction understood
as a disciplined embodied practice. However before we embark in the discussion that
gives this paper its title, it is essential to provide the context from which these questions sprang at the turn of the century, when phenomenology was founded.

At least since Kant, we have become accustomed to sharply distinguishing
between the theoretical interest of reason (which takes knowledge as its goal) and its
practical interest (which deals with ethical and moral considerations). On this basis,
scientific research, whose rigour is grounded on objectification, is frequently contrasted with a quest for wisdom, whose truth is guaranteed by an internal feeling of
intuitive order of well-being and of the authenticity of the individual who makes it his
aim as an aspiration to freedom (i.e. personal salvation or collective emancipation).

In both these cases it is a question of 'knowing': the first is knowledge of an object,
while the second is knowledge of *self*. In a certain way, one could say that the Socratic
'know thyself' gave rise to a kind of practical philosophy, which cultivated a return to
self and whose bearing is ethical and individual. This trend is also preserved in an
exemplary fashion in classical eudaimonism, scepticism, and beyond them in diverse
spiritual traditions (notably Orthodox Christianity, Sufism and Buddhism). By
contrast, Descartes' *ego cogito ergo sum* (with its important variant: *ego sum, existo*)
provides the clear foundation for modern scientificity by yielding the only certainty
which can be posited.

Correspondence: Natalie Depraz, 45 bis, rue Pouchet, 75017 Paris, France.

---

[1] This enquiry seeks to actualize the requirement of a return to the experience, which I formulated in
Depraz (1995a) but which remains a dead letter if it does not result in a concrete enactment. With
regard to such an appeal to experience, cf. also Waldenfels (1993), pp. 263–77.

The founder of phenomenology at the beginning of the twentieth century, Edmund Husserl, subscribes to this Cartesian heritage. He even goes one step further in positing a 'transcendental' ego, an apodictic repository of a radicalized scientificity whose unique 'object', he argues in the *Cartesian Meditations*,[2] is precisely the subject. Subjectivity, however, appears only when we pull away from prejudices rooted in the taken-for-granted character of the world. The challenge represented by phenomenology's claim to scientificity resides, in effect, in the following internal tension: (i) a maximum objectifying ambition on the part of the subject, the only guarantee of universality, and (ii) the recognition of the need to do justice to this subjective experience in its own intuitive quality.

So the intrinsic ambivalence built into phenomenology is simply this duality of the subject, at once both *theoretical* and *existential*. In this respect, the beginning of the Lectures from 1923–24, entitled *First Philosophy*,[3] is eloquent in alternating — even while trying desperately to hold them together — a subject situated in the world, therefore embodied, and a purely theoretical subject preoccupied solely with apodictic evidence. Carried along by a theoretical interest in establishing a new foundation for science, Husserl never ceased to rely upon that operative subjectivity which remains the initial motor for the theoretical interest in phenomenology. This is a way of saying that the interests of the theoretician are inhabited and stimulated by a disciplined existential practice which is rarely thematized in its own right.[4]

This co-existence of a practical embodied and existential dimension and of a theoretical one is at the heart of the very gesture of the *reduction*, set up from 1904–5 onward as the cardinal and definitive *method* of phenomenology. Of course there remains the difficulty that one is then situated upon a watershed where the practical tends to be persistently obliterated by the theoretical, even while allowing the practical to re-appear into the theoretical. It appears at least sufficiently so to make it possible to raise questions with regard to it, to examine it, to track it down. A watershed which is all the more crucial for phenomenologists since it stands at the very heart of the phenomenological method in question and precisely there, where it takes on an embodied dimension.[5]

---

[2] Husserl (1950a), §2 'Need for a Radical New Beginning in Philosophy', and §8 'The Ego Cogito as Transcendental Subjectivity'.

[3] Husserl (1959), lessons 28 to 32 and notably lesson 32.

[4] Such a practice only emerges in a particularly exemplary way when Husserl insists upon the philosophical discipline as a vocation (*Berufung*), as an ethics of any absolute justification functioning as both the first and the last requirement of theoretical research:

> [From the defects] of science . . . there proceeds the philosophical demand for a presuppositionless beginning, for a new life of knowledge, a truly radical life; the demand for a life inaugurating a science founded on an absolute justification. . . . But this absolute radicalism, for him who wishes to become a philosopher in this most authentic sense of the word, implies his submitting to a corresponding decision which will engage his life in an absolutely radical manner, a decision which will make of his life an *absolutely devoted life*. This is a decision through which the subject becomes self-determining, and even rigourously so — to the very depths of his personality — committed to what is best in itself in the universal realm of intellectual values and committed, for his entire life-time, to the idea of the supreme Good . . . the subject chooses [supreme knowledge] as his veritable 'vocation', for which he decides and is decided once for all, to which he is absolutely devoted *as a practical ego*. (Husserl, 1959; see also *Cartesian Meditations* [1950], §1.)

[5] See also Depraz (1998a), representing our first attempt to deal with this subject.

The question we have to ask with regard to the status of the reductive attitude is therefore a double question:

First: it is important to ask ourselves again today to what extent the gesture of the reduction is not simply a formal method making possible a theoretical analysis, a justification in principle *(Begründung)* of subjective experience, but is wholly rooted in an effective *praxis* which yields intuitive access to internal experience. This entails revising the method of the reduction on the basis of early indications — however fragile and incomplete they might be — which bear witness to this experiential underpinning.

Second: it will be necessary to show how this *praxis* is an exercise which is itself open to scientificity since potentially animated by necessary and universal rules. It therefore amounts to more than describing either the anecdotal and fortuitous biographical facts concerning the individual subjectivity of the private subject Husserl. It is also more than a purely preparatory, provisional and contingent instrument permitting pedagogical access to a theoretical dimension which is alone significant. What is really at stake in this experiential revision of the reductive method, thanks to its concrete *praxis,* is nothing less than an approach to a new *phenomenological scientificity* inhabited by a regulated and concerted (that is intersubjective) practice which functions as its central engine. In other words, it is not just a matter of disclosing the unknown practical roots of the reductive method but of drawing attention to the way in which this practice is itself scientific, that is, capable of giving rise to a new type of objectification.

II: The Phenomenological Reductions

Reduction harbours, then, a tension between the practical and the theoretical. At one and the same time, it is an effective act, an immanent operation, an activity *(Leistung)* which makes of me both an agent working at a transformation of the world *via* the transformation of my-self, and a state, a mode of self-observation, an attitude *(Einstellung)* which places me in the overreaching position of an impartial and disinterested spectator.[6] And yet, I am proposing to bring to light a renewed reductive method, whereby the spectator is given a specific embodiment, and where the operation inherent in the reductive gesture is taken up again through the logic of its own reflexivity. By thus aggravating the oxymoron of the practical and the theoretical, internal to the reduction in its Husserlian heritage, my point is that, in fact, reflection and incarnation, contemplation and action are not opposed until each begins to fertilize the other, thereby intensifying each other to the point of becoming virtually indistinguishable from each other.[7]

1. The psychological reduction as a reflective conversion

When I operate the reduction I do not limit my domain of experience, according to a current conception of the verb *reducere* in the natural sciences. Instead, in a philo-

---

[6] This is the impartial (alias *cosmotheoros*) spectator which Merleau-Ponty talked so well about, for example, in the Preface to his *Phenomenology of Perception* (1945, p. xv) where he adopts a critical stance inspired by Fink.

[7] For first steps in this direction cf. Depraz (1995c; 1997). It is the way that I, as a philosopher, am able to capture what is at stake in my work with Varela and Vermersch (forthcoming).

sophical sense, the point is to disengage and free up another quality, another modality of a subjective experience which remains identically my own.[8] Literally, I lead back (re-ducere, zurückführen, Ritter & Gründer, no date, Bd. 8, p. 370) my own experience, which gives itself immediately to me. This means explicating layers of the experience and freeing myself from the object in order to take note of the act of consciousness directed towards this object. In this way, I enlarge my field of experience by intensifying it, by allowing another dimension to emerge from it, a dimension which precisely frees me from the ordinary pre-givenness of the world. We have to do here with a specific mode of conscious apprehension, by means of which, quite simply, I learn to see the world and objects differently. I learn to look at the world in another way, not that the first is negated or even radically altered in its being, nor that certain objects are henceforward substituted for others but, from the simple fact that my manner of perceiving, my visual disposition, has changed, objects are going to be given to me in another light.

As such, this alteration of my way of seeing things (Umkehrung des Blickes), which leads me to envisage each object not in itself but in accordance with the act of consciousness which bears it and is directed towards it, remains fragile, because momentary. At every moment I am once again caught up and absorbed in the perceived object, that is, in the perception of some flower whose lively and warm colour, whose gracefully shaped petals I admire, or of a house which, in the growing shade of the evening, is outlined against a flamboyant sky. And on each occasion I have to make a special effort to return to the perceptual act, to the visual act in its very occurrence.

However, this return to the act is rarely simultaneous with the perception of the object. When I turn my attention from the colourful and elegant vision of the flower to take note of the manner in which I see it, of the experienced quality of this seeing, notably of its focusing character, I am already in the aftermath of the first viewing. When I take a step back from the arris of the roof of the house, there where the distinction between light and shade gets obscured, with a view to taking account of the modality of the act in which I am engaged, of the way in which it remains open to the countryside's twilight, I am no longer so attentive to the flamboyance of the sky or to the darkness of the walls of the house; I am already further off in time. The return to the perceptual act is situated in an aftermath of the perception of the object, whether it is a question of the *immediate* past, retentionally held in mind, or more easily of a present *remembering* of the past situation (Husserl, 1959, lessons 41, 43 & 45). In this regard it should be noted that to designate this temporal lag, seemingly constitutive of the passage from the object to the act, Husserl uses the substantive *Nachträglichkeit,* which signifies a typical structure characterizing the deferment of the impression in relation to the retention or to the perception in relation to reflection.[9]

But here again, one should distinguish between these two types of temporal lag. The *retentional* lag more properly corresponds to this thematic disengagement of an act attentive to itself, even to the perception of the object. In a fraction of a second (maybe even less),[10] one passes from an attention directed toward the object to an

---

[8] Cf. the distinction between *Beschränkung* (liberation)/ *Einschränkung* (delimitation) developed after Husserl (1950b), 2nd Lesson, then in Husserl (1959), 42nd Lesson, p. 98.

[9] Cf. Brand (1955), which also makes use of the choice expression *Reflexion im Ansatz.*

[10] On the the neuro-biological roots of retention, see Varela (this issue).

attention directed to the act,[11] and there is a retention of the object in the act by which it is immediately apprehended, even a possible to and fro between the object perceived and the perceptual act, but never, it seems, complete coincidence of the two. In the case of the *remembering* of the perception of the flower or of the house, I re-member the complex 'object perceived/perceptual act'. But at the precise instant of this re-membering, long after the event, I no longer take note of the act of re-memorizing as it unfolds (for example of its discontinuous, laborious or luminous quality) to the extent that I now concentrate on a new object, which is the 'past act of perception' in all its complexity. In short, at no matter what level one is situated,[12] it really seems as though the structure of the reflexive transformation most usually assumes the form of a constitutive recapitulation, which renders the two perceptual registers (object/act) non contemporaneous.[13]

2. The epochè as a transcendental reduction

In order to relieve, in however small a measure, the fragile instability of this re-turning of attention from the object towards the act of consciousness, and so to confer upon its fleeting evanescence a form of stability, Husserl recognized the need for an *epochè* very early on (Husserl, 1950c, 2nd section, §§30–3).

Literally, the *epochè* corresponds to a gesture of suspension with regard to the habitual course of one's thoughts, brought about by an interruption of their continuous flowing. *Epekhô*, 'I stop', as Montaigne used to say in his *Essais*,[14] taking up again a key-word from the Pyrrhonians.[15] As soon as a mental activity, a thought anchored to the perceived object alone, turns me away from the observation of the perceptual act to re-engage me in the perception of the object, I bracket it. It continues to exist in front of me. I have neither eradicated nor negated it — it would come back in force — but it is there in front of me, lacking any real efficacy, without validity

[11] Husserl (1966), third section entitled *Association*, is devoted to the complex correlation of affection and attention, to which we will come back when describing the Psychological Way.

[12] What emerges here corresponds to the level of a phenomenological psychology (cf. Husserl, 1959, 3rd and 4th Sections, and 1962). The rereading of the Husserlian texts proposed here has largely benefited from the work undertaken over the past year (1996–97) in the context of the 'Séminaire de Pratique phénoménologique' organised by P. Vermersch in collaboration with N. Depraz and F. Varela. For more details of an empirical and procedural kind concerning the different descriptive planes of these acts and experiences, see Vermersch (this issue).

[13] No doubt this last suggestion should be refined by indicating to what extent this non-coincidence or non-simultaneity is dependent upon an on-going and familiar experiential context which brings to light a temporality constitutive of the lag, of evasiveness, of loss, of opaqueness. Cf. in this respect Bernet (1994), especially 'La présence du passé', pp. 215–43. An educated experience cultivated out of the dually co-occuring attention (cf. Varela *et al.*, 1991; Wallace, 1998) makes it possible for us to approach an unprecedented temporality where the perceptual act ends up anticipating the perceived object itself. (Regarding this original temporality sketched within phenomenology cf. Depraz, 1998b).

[14] Montaigne (no date), II, pp. 229–30: 'Leur mot sacramental (il s'agit des 'Sceptiques' ou 'Epéchistes'), c'est *epekhô*, je ne bouge. Voilà leur refreins, et autres de pareille substance. Leur effect, c'est une pure, entière et très parfaite surséance et suspension du jugement.' Cf. Sextus Empiricus, *Adversus Physicos,* I, 132; also Coussin (1929), pp. 373–97. Husserl's references to the sceptical *epochè* need to be unearthed, for example, using P. Natorp's Lectures between 1902–1906 which Husserl followed. (I thank B. Besnier who drew my attention to this link.)

[15] If, for the Pyronnians, the *epochè* is already a state of abstention, of suspension of judgment, designed to promote *ataraxia*, the 'Epéchistes', as Montaigne called them, are nevertheless not the only ones. The Stoics also made frequent use of this expresion, less however to mark a suspension than a consent (*assensus*). Cf. Cicéron, *Académiques,* 2, 32, 104, etc. See in this respect Migniosi (1981).

(*Geltung*). I have already, as it were, left it to itself; I am no longer interested in it and so am able to contemplate it at a distance. This is the meaning of what Husserl quite rightly calls 'neutralization' of validity, thereby sharply distinguishing the *epochè* from any destructive negation.[16]

In this way, one can say that the *epochè*, the putting out of validity upon the world, develops further the precarious structure of the reflective conversion. It is a guiding thread for its ability to maintain itself, of its own accord, over time.[17] Basically, in order that the reduction should always be a living act whose freshness is a function of its incessant renewal in me, and never a simple and sedimented habitual state, the reflective conversion has to be operative at every instant and at the same time permanently sustained by the radical and vigilant gesture of the *epochè*.

But since (unlike the provisional character of Cartesian doubt) the *epochè* is only definitive if it is reactivated at each instant as a general gesture of suspension with regard to any positively given *datum*, it is unable of itself to ensure the complete maintenance of the reflective conversion. In fact, it turns out to be itself subject to a fragile temporalization arising from the need for ceaseless renewal. Because of this, the transcendental reduction, which is supposed to break us away from taking the world as simply there, is, at every moment redirected away from its task of suspension and slipping into a habitual attitude. It then becomes a mere formal husk which is no longer on guard against itself. The risk of 'methodologism' appears to be a very real one.

3. The status of the eidetic reduction

In fact, Husserl brings under the general rubric of a 'phenomenological reduction' different forms of reduction, each of which possesses a different meaning not only by virtue of the peculiarity of its object but, even more, by virtue of the function it fulfills in the context of the search for a new scientificity.

With this first clarification of the distinction between reflective conversion and transcendental *epochè* I have already outlined the basic differentiating characteristics of two of the major forms of phenomenological reduction:

(1) The reflective conversion covers *grosso modo* what Husserl names the 'psychological reduction' in the form of a return of the perceiving subject to itself, that is, more precisely, to its acts of lived awareness stemming from the perceptual apprehension of a given object. Its fragility lies in its instantaneous temporality.

(2) Through the radicality with which it suspends the thesis of the existence of the world, the *epochè* supplies the internal transcendental pre-requisite necessary for any reductive procedure and which is therefore constitutive of the latter. It furnishes the psychological reduction with a more stable temporal support by virtue of its temporalization (primarily, as ceaseless reiteration) but is itself limited to this level on account of the need to repeat the operation on each occasion.

Confronted with this first delimitation of the reductive functions, the question then arises as to what role should be reserved for what Husserl calls, finally, the 'eidetic

---

[16] On this tendency to confuse *epochè* and negation, cf. Husserl, 1950c, § 30, and Lowit (1957).

[17] It should however be noted that Husserl does not always distinguish clearly between reduction and *epochè*, and differs in this from, for example, J. Patocka. Cf. on this point Patocka (1988), pp. 249–63, and (1992), pp. 117–43.

reduction'. By contrast with the psychological reflective conversion which is rooted in the particular perceptual intensity of the subject, or of the transcendental *epochè*, which brings on the scene the vertiginous spectacle of a subject which no longer has any confidence in even the most obvious worldly structure, the eidetic reduction takes as its theme the essence of any object whatsoever, understood as a concrete essence. We are perceiving beings, beings embodied in the world. The first two forms of reduction shatter the evidence of these links and so confront us with the reflexive abyss and the *vertigo* which arises from the falling away of the world.

The task of the eidetic reduction is to get us to question our inviolable attachment to the particular sensible *datum* and, in so doing, to free up for us the interior space of the purely *possible*. In fact, the obsession with the empirical arises from the attachment to the simple efficacity of fact, which gives rise to potential alienation. On the other hand, taking account of the infinite variations of the real, of the possible internal differentiation of the latter, presupposes an imaginative capacity whose initial strength is sufficient to move beyond effective reality and so allow us to envisage the infinite plurality of possibilities.

For Husserl, fact (*Tatsache*) is in consequence abstract and the essence, concrete.[18] The abstract character of fact proceeds from its being limited to the actualization of one possibility alone, which unilaterally controls events to the exclusion of any other possibility. The essence is concrete because it is rich, full of all kinds of potentialities internal to the field of subjective experience and proceeds from the variation of all facts in their indefinite multiplicity. The essence acquires its concreteness from a variation of that very factual realm from which it itself stems; it draws its universality from its having been torn away from the arbitrariness of the contingent.

The practical gesture which presides over any eidetic reduction is a mental gesture arising out of each sensible datum (*Empfindungsdatum*). For example, it varies all existing reds (the sombre red of the hearth, the flamboyant red of the setting sun, the vermilion hue of lips, the brown red of coagulated blood, etc.), places them on imaginative parade — not necessarily in the mode of visual perception — with a view first to disengaging the specific quality of this red of the setting sun, then, with a view to deriving the invariable essence, the concrete essence of red. Such a mental gesture of identification results from the richness of the given, itself enlarged because exceeded by the imaginary, a gesture which ensures its own universality by unfolding the latter from within itself, that is, by ending up being indifferent to it. The particular example of such and such a red, illustrating the procedure of variation by furnishing a guideline for it, is confirmed, just as soon as the purely arbitrary invariant emerges from it.

The function of the eidetic reduction is basically that of making possible a procedure of categorization by way of the *identification of invariants*. Husserl very clearly draws his inspiration (though in a non-technical way) from the calculus of variations which he himself studied closely in the 1880s under Weierstrass and then developed further in the context of his first research projects in mathematics.[19] The specificity of this categorization stems from its double source, perceptual and imaginative. The

---

[18] See Husserl (1950c), first section, devoted to fact and essence.

[19] 'The general description of the method of ideation is obviously itself a description of the generality of the essence; in a free variation we can let every exemplary object with respect to which it is practised become a something in general, even, in a certain sense, become a variable in the mathematical sense of that word.' (Husserl, 1973a, n° 13, §10, p. 92.)

perceptual and so sensiblé anchorage confers a dose of individual singularity upon the categorial experience; the imaginative support un-ties the real from its exclusively empirical efficacy to open it up upon the infinity of the possible, which latter confers its universality upon the category.

Thus, in the precise context of a descriptive categorization of subjective experience, the realm of the eidetic offers a second way of shoring up the transcendental *epochè*, a second way of enabling the first gesture of reflective conversion to be sustained, no longer in a perceptual, but in a mental-imaginative way. In this regard, it could be said that the eidetic practice of descriptive categorization tips the scales in the direction of a form of omni-temporality (*Allzeitlichket*) which no longer has anything individual about it but already plays a trans-individual role.[20]

In short, for Husserl, the categorial *scientificity* of phenomenology derives from the specific form of this eidetics; its *radicality* from the transcendental *epochè*, its experiential *individuation* from the reflective conversion.

III: Pathways — From Methodological Solitude to the Community of Reduced Subjects

In the 1920s, the reductive act, ensured and maintained by the *epochè*, categorized and idealized by eidetic variation, gets systematized in the context of a regulated plurality of modes of access to the reduction. Should this process of successive buttressing of the fragility of the reflective conversion be regarded as a search for an explicit practical means, which is on each occasion singular and always fragmentary and precarious? We are now once again situated on the famous watershed between theory and practice.

However, the description of different steps pertaining to each of the reductive pathways leads one to believe that it is less a matter of a fixed 'doctrine of paths' (*Lehre der Wege*)[21] than an attempt, even a clumsy, but certainly a valiant attempt at a coherent pluralisation of the possible ways of access to the reduction. In their very plurality, these pathways lay things out in relief, in sharp contrast and in such a way as to accentuate the singularity of the subjective experience. Let us now go back to the varieties of reduction from the point of view of the many paths along which the reduction can be practised.

1. The Cartesian way

Moved by a radical concern with the indubitablity of the known and the perceived, the subject which sets out along this way seeks:

(1) To put out of operation, and by means of the most complete *epochè* possible, any admixture in knowledge of the sedimented values left over from a pre-given world. Keeping to a pre-given world makes it difficult to appeal to a purely theoretical truth.

---

[20] Husserl (1948), 2nd Section, §64 'The unreality of intellectual objects and their temporality'.

[21] Husserl (1950a), §53 and so on. Cf. (1922), n. 13: 'Acting in a personal way, living in a familiar and harmonious way with others', p. 269: 'The other for whom I experience empathy can remains external to me and not form any unity with me'.

(2) Only such a transcendental suspension of the mundane thesis, that is, of the pre-judice of the world, makes it possible to affirm the existence of an ego divorced from the world. Such an ego can feature as the source of the sought-after certainty (apodicticity in Husserlian language).

(3) However, this ego has to be related in some way to the world, in the first instance *via* the objects given for perception. Containing in myself, and in an intrinsic fashion, this intentional directedness toward an objective correlate, I reapprehend myself as a subjectivity originally linked to the world.

(4) Through the *epochè*, my view of the world is modified: the latter is no longer naively posited alongside of me, it is integrated from the first in me, carried along by my consciousness as meaning-giving.

This first way of the reduction is, in certain respects, a copy of the way taken by Descartes in his *Metaphysical Meditations*: (1) practice of doubt, (2) bringing to light of the *ego cogito* as absolute certainty, (3–4), long reconquest of the sensible world starting from its relentless destruction through doubt.

But aside from the phenomenological absence of God as the initial and continual motor propelling the ontological perpetuation of the ego and of the world, Husserl's 'Cartesian' way presents the *epochè* as a definitive neutralization of the world and not as its provisional negation. What is at stake in this modification is the status of the subject at work in the reduction: Husserl sees it as a subject continually renewing in itself the act of neutralization, Descartes as a possible foundational axiom for objective scientificity. In other words: is the operative subjectivity strictly constituted by the very act of the reduction, or is it only invoked as a means of obtaining scientific validation? With Husserl himself, this alternative is not so easily decided.

The properly 'Cartesian' risk of this pathway obviously lies in the emphasis it places upon the second fork of the alternative, in which subjective experience is obliterated, or at least covered over, to the point of nipping in the bud the experiential potentiality which initially resided in it. One might think that what is at issue here is the difficulty of setting up a 'science of the subjective' as a science of the singular. What already appeared to Aristotle in his *Second Analytics* as an internal contradiction — remember the famous disclaimer: 'there can only be a science of the general!' — is now recycled by Husserl in the first thirty years of the 20th century with all the ambiguity which surrounds the quest for foundations and for an objectifying apprehension in the context of an experiential access to the lived experience of a singular subject.

2. The psychological way

With a view to facing up to just such a difficulty the phenomenologist, from the beginning of the 1920s, will seek to set up other possible modes of access to the experience of the reduction and, in the first place, the way proper to the 'phenomenological psychologist'.

When I adopt this way, what strikes me in the first place is the withdrawal, even the obliteration, of the transcendental motif *stricto sensu,* that is, of the radical concern with an *epochè*.

(1) First, I become progressively more dis-interested in the world by inhibiting it: not that I cut myself off brutally by means of a transcendental *epochè*, rather, I adjust myself to the prospect of no longer being able to make use of it, I leave it to itself,

even to the extent of being able to contemplate it at a distance — as an impartial spectator (*unbeteiligter Zuschauer*).

(2) Even more than in the context of the Cartesian way, the world continues to exist; more still, it exists *for me* and not simply in itself as a legitimate reality from which I have, at all costs, to detach myself. I can be all the more involved in it, the more I have conclusively left it to itself. I am all the more capable of acting and of entertaining specific goals the less I remain attached to it.

(3–4) We encounter here an un-interested and detached way of acting which is nourished, activated and intensified by holding oneself at a distance from any immersion or absorption in the world. The latter can in consequence flood in upon me all the more powerfully for never having ceased to be there. And for my part, I am also able to welcome it quietly and impassively.

Thus the psychological way represents an essential modification of the action of the phenomenologist in view of a quality of *attentive observation*, disengaged from any voluntarism. An extract from a manuscript from the 1930s, among many others, recaptures beautifully the tenor of this singular quality of dis-interested attention:

> We should here bear in mind the fact that this way of 'doing nothing' [*des Nichtstuns*] when one is at rest and remains upright in a kinesthetic constellation is completely different from that which consists in a veritable non-activity [*eines...Nicht-aktivseins*]. For I am still active, I am still, as being myself, in some mode of being preoccupied with something, I am still oriented in some direction, even though in the 'stop mode'. But if I renounce my object, if I turn towards another object, if I have ceased altogether to be concerned with the first object, then touching this object, being touched by it, is to be occupied with it in a completely different sense. It is no longer a matter of being directed toward it, of being actively oriented toward it (being in the form of willfulness). But one can be easily led astray. For the active contact, with its horizon of potentiality as an active horizon of possibilities of action, has passed over into the mode of passive apperception, to that of simple association, just as the *datum* of sensation (the sensation of contact) is something of which I am 'conscious' in an originally associative temporalisation, removed from any effective activity. If I pay attention, if this thing touching-touched 'affects' me in the background, this affection is really an egoistic mode which breaks up the pure association (which is operative in the sphere of 'non-egoity' [*Ichlosigkeit*], of the 'non-awakenedness' [*Unwachheit*] of the I — for whoever exists and acts 'in the passive background', or the subterranean strata of active or, better still, active and affective, egoistic life) (Husserl, 1973b, Beil. XVIII, pp. 304–5).

In the larger context of an analysis of corporality and, more exactly, of the sensation of tactile movement (*Betasten/Berührung*), *affection* is presented as a specifically active way of being attentive. Beyond the opposition between (focused voluntary) activity and (receptive, purely associative) passivity, affection defines a singular open quality of perceptual attention, indeed the very way of potentializing attention itself, which Husserl sometimes talks about in terms of a delicate 'keeping hold of (*Im Griff-Halten*)' (Husserl, 1948, §23b). This is what it means to think of affection as a power of attention rather than as a sheer potential in the sense of possible attention. Far from being opposed to attention, as is the opaque to what is lucidly transparent, affection means being vigilant, evokes the very power of attention (Husserl, 1973b, Beil. XVIII, pp. 303–4.)

This is where the question of the status of the lived-body, of the affect, as much as of their reference to a communitarian context, imposes itself, a question to which the psychological way does not have any direct response. To make of the reductive act an incarnate and shared act, a new effort is required, another way has to be adopted, that of the 'life-world'.

3. *The way of the life-world revisited:*
   the co-reductive community as inter-affection

The first two ways remained solipsist or, at the very least, individual. Intersubjectivity is presented there either as a second constitutive extension of individually reductive solitude (Cartesian way), or as an inter-individual sharing of reductive acts deployed by each subject for itself (psychological way). Only the way which passes by way of the life-world takes account of the communitarian dimension of the reductive experience. I am not the only one to apprehend myself at every instant as an operative subject and, in addition, others, co-actors in this experience, may equally work to develop this experience more correctly and more intensely in me. However, the intersubjective sharing of the reductive experience — what I called elsewhere co-reduction (Depraz, 1995b, chapters IV–VI) — is the culmination of two previous steps which are originally implied in it, that is, the taking account of corporeal sensibility and the management of the affect.

The displacement of the attention directed toward the object in the direction of the act aimed at this object, just like the detachment with regard to interests and ends in daily activity, could at first create the impression that the experience of the reduction is of a purely mental or cognitive order. But the power of the mind alone is not enough to render this experience effective if corporality and affect do not contribute their share and are not thereby transformed and intensified. Rather than seeking, like Descartes, a way of violently rejecting the corporeal sense and, more extensively, the sensible world (and this with a view to obtaining a purely mental presence of the self to itself, a presence freed from all resistance, from any contingency and from any material opacity), the reductive path of the life-world proceeds towards an immersion in an embodied sensibility in which we all share as incarnate subjects. We are each of us the repository of such an interior sensibility without always having properly taken account of it for itself. So it is a matter of taking command of a higher freedom at the very heart of our sensorial — and so also affective — rootedness.

The result is decisive. Sense and affect, far from being — as Descartes naively thought — enemies which lead us astray and deceive us, are rather to be regarded as our 'allies' that can help us. They are the privileged support of the transformation, of the alteration (*Veränderung*) of ourselves in which, in the end, the reductive experience consists. In working on them and with them, the sensibility of the body become finer, more ductile. In being sharpened, it is intensified (see Depraz, forthcoming).

Also, this third way leads in the first instance to a new kind of *epochè* which is retrogressive, which leads back to our primordial sensible incarnation in the world (Husserl, 1954, §§44, 45 & 47), then to a clearing of sedimentation of our habitus, not just our individual (onto-genetic) habitus, but especially that engaged in a common (philo-genetic) history (Husserl, 1992, notably n°4 and n°28). On the basis of the recovery of this sensible foundation taken up again in a new way, a foundation in which we can recover affections and actions long since stowed away, that splitting of the level of vigilant consciousness required by the reduction can be put into effect.

The life-world is the daily world of all our actions and activities, of all our simplest and most immediate ways of knowing-how, of all our interactions, of our intercourse (*Verkehre*) with others. In coming to understand our lived-corporality as a *Urpraxis*, we are assured that the vital world which surrounds us and where we live with others is really there, totally present in each of our perceptual and kinaesthetic acts. So the practice of the reduction reaches right down to our flesh (*Leib*):

> . . . the reign of perception in the lived-body (*Leib*), a reign which confers upon all the movements of the lived-body the meaning of egoistically accomplished movements, presents itself to us as a praxis of the I in the world, and, in truth, as an originary praxis *(Urpraxis)* which co-operates with, and has already in advance already operated for every other *praxis*. At the same time, it pertains to such a *praxis* to be available only for a fleshly body (*Leibkörper*) and as an 'originally practical object'. Qua perceptual lived-body, this object possesses a practical significance, a functional significance which characterizes it as the point of departure for any *praxis* and, above all, as the original locus for a constantly foundational *praxis* through which any ulterior *praxis* intervening immediately in the bodily world finds its origin, inhabited, as it is, by new, originally practical layers (Husserl, 1973b, n° 18, 1931, p. 328).

If in fact I seek to experience the potentialities, the affections and the activities of my lived-body at every on-going moment I can no longer treat it as my instrument, my external machine; rather I feel it to be the concrete and indispensable support of all spiritual labour. Following up on Husserl, Merleau-Ponty already put it quite succinctly when he said: I do not have a body, I am my lived-body. If our flesh is our original *praxis*, this means that we are always working on it and that it is on this basis in us we practise the activity of reflective conversion, of a transcendental *epochè* and even of eidetic variation. It is also on the basis of this primordial practical incarnation that a possible intersubjective sharing of the reductive act becomes meaningful.

Such a reductive[22] community is radically co-empathic without being in any way fusional or mystic. It is to be distinguished from any simple empathic relation by virtue of an analogizing experience (*Analogisierung*) by means of which I put myself imaginatively in the place of the other, never ceasing to remain in my 'absolute here' while the other remains in his 'over there'. [23]But it also has to be distinguished from a simple 'pathos-with', where [24]I am literally con-fused and so fuse with the other, two affections reduced to the initial unity. Neither an analogization which is experienced but still constructed because mediated, nor a pathic fusion operating in pure immediacy, are able to serve to explain how the reductive community emerges from an 'interaffection' where the always unique and individual encounter of two egos is played out (and replayed across the generations). As a remarkable illustration of this third way of understanding empathy as an inter-affection, let me quote Husserl *in extenso*:

---

[22] In the 30s, Husserl does speak of such a community as a 'gnostic community' (*gnostische Gemeinschaft*), as a community of savants (cf. Kelkel, 1959, n. 4); in a more pragmatic way, Spiegelberg (1975) has tried to describe the concrete procedures of a phenomenological community, of a 'co-subjectivity' engaged in the exercise of the reduction.

[23] Husserl (1950a), §53 and so on. Cf. (1922), n. 13: 'Acting in a personal way, living in a familiar and harmonious way with others', p. 269: 'The other for whom I experience empathy can remains external to me and not form any unity with me'.

[24] Henry (1990), third part. It is important to notice that Henry uses as his exemplary model for pathic co-empathy the mother–child relationship, as originally non-intentional and so fusional empathy.

In the world human beings exert 'spiritual influences' upon each other, they enter into contact on the spiritual plane, they act upon each other, I to I; the fact that I do this is known to the other and that determines him to 'orient himself' accordingly from his side. But they also act upon each other more internally. I take upon myself what the other wants, I do what he wants. What I do is not simply done out of myself, but the will of the other is accomplished in my service, in my doing. In being compassionate, in rejoicing with the other, I do not simply suffer as myself, it's the other's suffering which lives on in my suffering, or again, inversely, I am absorbed in the other and I live in his life; in particular, I suffer his suffering. In the same way that I reach a conclusion with him about the conclusion he has reached (not that, so to speak, I am 'in agreement' with him to the extent that the conclusion which I reached myself coincided, harmonized with the conclusion he reached, but I evaluate with him the conclusion he reached by understanding it and without necessarily sharing it), so I re-live his suffering with him. It is not possible for me to will his willing in the same way that he does, but I can be associated with his action, or again, I can be united with him by doing what he wants or by exercising authority over him.

And my 'I' can be united with another 'I' (a Thou). Each 'I' is in touch with itself, coincides in a certain way with the I which confronts it, the action of the one and the action of the other are not just separate actions running in parallel but form one similar action, mutually adjusted in a harmonious way and uniting in a unitary agreement. This unitary character can however take diverse forms. The other with whom I empathize can remain external to me and not form any unity with me. I take care of him, I understand him after the event, I can think and feel with him by establishing contact with him and taking up a position with him. But I can also live a part of my willful life in him, put my will into him, to the extent that he is subjected to me and 'it' then lives in him in a conscious way in the extent of his duties or the sphere of his 'service', in as much as it carries my will over into him, into his will, carrying out my action in his action. I can also take the other into myself by taking him as my model, a model which I have entirely built into my own I. In so doing, I act as if he were in my place (Husserl, 1973a, n° 13, 1922, §10 & §11).

We are dealing here with a radically intersubjective reduction which relies upon a de-centering of the individual in relation to himself, such that he is able to apprehend the inter-subjective quality of the affection at work, a sort of ability to grasp the 'feeling' that is given here as shared. An analogical lived experience based on changing places still presupposes the duality of the two individuals, an external relation. A more profound empathy, which is not however a fusion (a pure *pathos*), brings into being a co-singularity *via* a process of co-singularization.

As Spiegelberg clearly recognizes in his own way, co-reduction, as co-subjectivity, does not in any way preclude a solitary practice of the reduction. Both before and after the intersubjective exchange, I, and I alone, engage in the internal work which allows me, on the one hand, to intervene intelligently in the exchange and, on the other, to make this exchange fruitful for myself. To put intersubjectivity in a leading position in the practice of the reduction does not in any way mean that the enigmatic reduction can be practised together, and at the same moment, in a sort of mystical or pathic fusion. To talk of an 'intersubjective reduction' as does Husserl[25], implies that one determines with precision the moment, or the exact moments, when intersubjectivity is operative, as also the periods of recuperation and of solitary re-engagement when the only criterion that makes sense is that of internal intuitive evidence. There again, it is appropriate to trace this distinction back to its rootedness

[25] Cf. on this point Depraz (1995b), chapter IV.

in the concrete practice of the reduction, a practice which enjoys its own temporality, its own moments and rhythms.

In a certain way, the others are always there in the exercise of the reduction but, in each instance, their presence is linked to a differentiated functionality:

(1) The most intense intersubjectivity is that of active exchange where the verbal unfolding of experience leads to confrontation with one another, to opposition to one another, even to conflicts with one another, in which, through discussion, the maximum breadth of experience is uncovered, together with all its inter-individual variations but also its principal invariant or invariants.

(2) But intersubjectivity plays a second role at the very heart of the work each one conducts in isolation and becomes, so to speak, 'intra-subjectivity'. Others are no longer present in flesh and blood as in the context of an exchange in which propositions and contradictions are mingled, but the other become an intimate presence in itself, one from which is born a specific quality of alterity to self.[26] Either, I already have in mind some criterion formulated by someone else which I did not consider at the moment of expressing this experience, and I try to determine its significance for me. Or, more fundamentally, the other is present in me in a form which guides the exploration of the experience in question. I interiorize his demands, his difficulties. I take advantage of his competence, his accumulated experience. The other lives at the very heart of this solitary labour, so bound up with me that — at a certain stage — he could fast be ignored, even disregarded . . .

Only a plurality of such inter-subjective (syn-chronic and dia-chronic) empathies avoids a fusional crystallization by giving 'play' to the intensity of the interaffection in question. So the co-reductive *Urpraxis* consists not only in radically de-centering oneself on the basis of one's individual ego-self and in inhabiting the intimacy of the other, this being the concrete guideline for action which is recuperated as my own, but also in de-centering the uniqueness of every inter-individual co-affective relationships. That the other may appear as a lead to be followed up lets it be understood that he is capable of leading the individual beyond himself, that is, of enabling him to free himself from individuality but also to inter-individuality. I am then able to gain access to a strictly transindividual dimension of the reductive experience, and this, by opening the horizon of the generative tradition itself, of the transmission (*Tradierung*) of a heritage (*Erbschaft*) which can always be re-activated with each new interaffective encounter (cf. Steinbock, 1995). Such an inter-affection therefore reaches back beyond the individuals personally concerned and into the generative history of previous interpersonal encounters, the long tracks of history.[27]

IV: Conclusion

As we have already been able to confirm in the course of this presentation of the different act forms and of the different reductive paths, there exists a methodological

[26] Cf. Depraz (1995b), especially chapter V.

[27] One finds an interesting re-reading of this quasi-pathic intersubjectivity in Schütz (1964), in connection with his typification of social relations among contemporaries (*Mitwelt*), ancestors (*Vorwelt*) and future generations (*Folgewelt*). In addition, in his phenomenology of music, elements of which are to be found in this second volume then, at greater length, in the fourth (1996), Schütz describes the community of musical auditors as the primordial locus for the unfolding of affective inter-individual, but also trans-individual syntheses.

richness capable of breathing life back into the theory of the reduction by putting it concretely into operation. Not only does one come to understand better what is at stake with the phenomenological method, a primordial *experience* and not just a report bearing upon experience, or even a simple theory which enjoys no subjective embodiment. In addition it becomes possible to gain a *genuine and disciplined* access to this multi-stratified act.

This has nothing to do with anything mysterious or esoteric, even if it is true that what is at issue is difficult, 'contrary to nature' as Husserl used to say, something which is far from being self-evident and which presupposes a certain amount of work, even of labour. The operation of the reduction implies a concrete *praxis*, whose peculiar character we have tried to bring out by appealing to Husserlian texts but also by offering an extension of the theory. It makes use of a certain number of procedures whose different aspects we have sought to enumerate across the reflective conversion, the transcendental *epochè* and the eidetic reduction but also across certain formative stages, certain pathways which pass by way of a confrontation with oneself, with the other subject, with the world and with others, as different forms of the so-called intersubjective reduction.[28]

It is interesting to point out in conclusion the extent to which this practical reconsideration of the reduction allows one to untie the sterile philosophical dilemmas which have been constantly set up as so many logical antinomies and which have continually blocked the work of phenomenological philosophers: voluntary/existential motivation, active/passive praxis, solipsism/intersubjectivity contents. These dilemmas, which are so many dualist pairs formulated in terms of alternatives, establish in advance the framework for the inquiry. They obviously point to a genuine difficulty and at the same time rest upon a failure to understand the concrete dynamic of the reductive activity. If one comes up against such conceptual knots, it can only be because the question has been wrongly posed and this because the experiential elucidation of the act has remained inadequate!

Acknowlededgements
I thank Valérie Kokoschka et Marc Maesschalck (Centre de philosophie du droit, Université de Louvain-la-Neuve), for allowing me to present this work as part of their Seminar. Special thanks to Francisco Varela for inviting me to contribute this article, and for working with me to find a less 'continental' voice for it.

References
Bernet, R. (1994), *La vie du sujet, Recherches sur l'interprétation de Husserl dans la phénoménologie* (Paris: P.U.F.).
Brand, G. (1955), *Welt, Ich und Zeit* (den Haag: M. Nijhoff).
Coussin, P. (1929), 'L'origine et l'évolution de l'*epochè*', *Revue des études grecques*, **42**.

[28] With regard to the '*phänomenologische Praxis durch die Epochè*', which proposes immanental descriptive procedures with no other mode of acces or of reappropriation than imitation, cf. the testimony of Plessner (1959):

> Den minutiösen Beschreibung war nicht leicht zu folgen und oft verlor ich den Faden, gleichwohl gebannt von der abwägend-betulichen Stimme österreichisch-mährischer Färbung. . . . Das dauerte bis gegen halb eins und dann war man in Gnaden entlassen: 'Machen Sie nur so weiter'. Husserl war viel zu sehr Monologist, um nach landläufigen Vorstellungen ein guter Dozent zu sein (pp. 32–3).

110 N. DEPRAZ

Depraz, N. (1995a), 'Phénoménologie et non-phénoménologie', Recherches husserliennes, 4.
Depraz, N. (1995b), Transcendance et incarnation, le statut de l'intersubjectivité comme altérité à soi chez Edmund Husserl (Paris: Vrin).
Depraz, N. (1995c), 'Phenomenological Reduction and the Political', Husserl Studies, 12 (1).
Depraz, N. (1997), 'Le spectateur phénoménologisant : au seuil du non-agir et du non-être', in Eugen Fink, Actes du Colloque de Cerisy-la-Salle, Juillet 1994, ed. N. Depraz et M. Richir (Amsterdam : Rodopi).
Depraz, N. (1998a), 'Das Ethos der Reduktion als leibliche Einstellung', in Der Anspruch des Anderen, Perspektiven phänomenologischer Ethik, ed. B. Waldenfels and I. Därmann (München: W. Fink Verlag).
Depraz, N. (1998b), 'Can I anticipate myself? Selfaffection and temporality', in Temporality, Selfawareness and Alterity, ed. D. Zahavi (Dordrecht: Kluwer, Contributions to Phenomenology).
Depraz, N. (forthcoming), Lucidité du corps. Pour un empirisme transcendantal en phénoménologie, First Part : 'Hyperesthésie du corps'.
Depraz, N., Varela F. and Vermersch P. (forthcoming), On becoming aware. Steps to a phenomenological pragmatics.
Henry, M. (1990), Phénoménologie matérielle (Paris: P.U.F.).
Husserl, E. (1948), Erfahrung und Urteil, Untersuchungen zur Genealogie der Logik (Hamburg : Glaassen und Goverts).
Husserl, E. (1950a), Cartesianische Meditationen, Hua I (den Haag: M. Nijhoff).
Husserl, E. (1950b), Die Idee der Phänomenologie, Hua II (den Haag: M. Nijhoff).
Husserl, E. (1950c), Ideen I, Hua III (den Haag: M. Nijhoff).
Husserl, E. (1954), Die Krisis der europäischen Wissenschaften und die transzendentale Phänomenologie, Hua VI (den Haag: M. Nijhoff).
Husserl, E. (1959), Erste Philosophie, Hua VIII, 'Theorie der phänomenologischen Reduktion' (den Haag: M. Nijhoff).
Husserl, E. (1962), Phänomenologische Psychologie, Hua IX (den Haag: M. Nijhoff).
Husserl, E. (1966), Analysen zur passiven Synthesis, aus Vorlesungs- und Forschungsmanuskripten (1918-1926), Hua XI (den Haag: M. Nijhoff).
Husserl, E. (1973a), Zur Intersubjektivität (1921-28), Hua XIV (den Haag: M. Nijhoff).
Husserl, E. (1973b), Zur Intersubjektivität (1929-35), Hua XV (den Haag: M. Nijhoff).
Husserl, E. (1992), Die Krisis der europäischen Wissenschaften und die transzendentale Phänomenologie. Ergänzungsband. Texte aus dem Nachlass (1934-37), Hua XXIX (Dordrecht: Kluwer).
Kelkel, A. (1959), 'Réflexions husserliennes', Etudes philosophiques.
Kern, I. (1962), 'Die drei Wege zur transzendental-phänomenologischen Reduktion in der Philosophie E. Husserl', Tidjschrift voor Filosofie. Engl. Trans. in Husserl. Expositions and Appraisals (London : Notre Dame Press, 1973).
Lowit, A. (1957), 'L'épochè de Husserl et le doute de Descarte', RMM, 4.
Merleau-Ponty, M. (1945), Phénoménologie de la perception (Paris: Gallimard).
Mignosi, R. (1981), 'Reawakening and Resistance : the stoic source of Husserlian épochè', Analecta Husserliana, 11, p. 311–19.
Montaigne, Essais, II, chap. XII, 'Apologie de Raimond Sebond', Ed. Strowski, II.
Patocka, J. (1988), Qu'est-ce que la phénoménologie ? Fr. Trans. by E. Abrams (Grenoble: J. Millon).
Patocka, J. (1992), 'Premier exposé de la réduction phénoménologique', pp. 117–43 et 'Epochè et réduction', pp. 249–63, in Introduction à la phénoménologie de Husserl, Fr. Trans by E. Abrams (Grenoble: J. Millon).
Plessner, H. (1959), 'Bei Husserl in Göttingen', in Edmund Husserl 1859-1959 (La Haye: M. Nijhoff).
Ritter, J. and Gründer, K., Historisches Wörterbuch der Philosophie.
Schütz, A. (1994), Collected Papers II (den Haag: M. Nijhoff).
Schütz, A. (1996), Collected Papers IV (Dordrecht: Kluwer).
Spiegelberg, H. (1975), Doing Phenomenology. Essays on and in Phenomenology (den Haag: M. Nijhoff).Spiegleberg, H. (1975), Doing Phenomenology, Essays on and in Phenomenology (den Haag : M. Nijhoff).
Steinbock, A. (1995), Home and Beyond, Generative Phenomenology after Husserl (Evanston, IL :Northwestern University Press).
Varela, F. (1998), 'The Specious Present : a neurophenomenology of time consciousness', in Naturalizing Phenomenology, ed. J. Petitot, F. Varela, B. Pachoud & J.-M. Roy (Stanford: Stanford University Press).
Varela, F., Thompson, A. & Rosch. E. (1991), The Embodied Mind : Cognitive Science and Human Experience (Cambridge, MA : MIT Press).
Waldenfels, B. (1993), 'Husserls Verstrickung in die Erfahrung' in Edmund Husserl, Arbeit an den Phänomen (Frankfurt: Fischer).

Francisco J. Varela

Present-Time Consciousness

I: Introduction

My purpose in this article[1] is to propose an explicitly naturalized account of the experience of present nowness on the basis of two complementary sources: phenomenological analysis and cognitive neuroscience. What I mean by naturalization, and the role cognitive neuroscience plays will become clear as the paper unfolds, but the main intention is to use the consciousness of present time as a *study case* for the phenomenological framework presented by Depraz in this Special Issue.

It would be foolish to claim that one can tackle this topic and expect to be satisfied. The experience of temporality addresses head-on the fundamental fact that we exist only within a transparent web of time. Its elucidation occupies a central place in the history of thought altogether, and most certainly in the phenomenological tradition. Edmund Husserl considered temporality a foundational axis of his phenomenological research: all other forms of mental activity depend upon temporality, but it does not depend upon them. He worked on these questions until his death. Unlike his many illustrious predecessors (including James) Husserl *did* manage to bring about essential progress in the formulation of the basic structures of intimate time (Gallagher, 1998). Drawing from the phenomenological account developed by Husserl does not represent some kind of Husserlian scholastic obsession. I cannot overemphasize that my use of Husserl's use of the phenomenology of time is not concerned with a close textual reading in order to prove or disprove a point in the author's thought. I prefer to take my cues from Husserl's *style* as an eternal beginner, always willing to start anew; this is the hallmark of phenomenology itself (but it has not always been the case in practice). What interests me most is the unfinished motion of his writings: only in

Correspondence: Francisco J. Varela, LENA (Neurosciences Cognitives et Imagerie Cérébrale), CNRS UPR 640, Hôpital de la Salpètrîere, 47 Blvd. de l'Hôpital, 75651 Paris, Cedex 13, France.

---

[1] This paper is adapted from 'The specious present: The neurophenomenology of inner time consciousness', in *Naturalizing Phenomenology*, edited by Petitot, Varela, Pachoud and Roy, forthcoming from Stanford University Press. Copyright 1999 by the Board of Trustees of the Leland Stanford Junior University. I am grateful to Stanford University Press for authorizing this version here.

their turns and jumps do we get a glimpse of how his description contains, among many other ideas in germ, a dynamical bent which is key for a naturalization project.

These phenomenal data will provide the bridges to cognitive neuroscience discussed here in relation to recent results from neural dynamics and the emergence of large-scale assemblies that provide a counterpoint to the constitution of temporality. My approach to temporality is a case study of a general research direction I have called *neurophenomenology*, in which lived experience and its natural biological basis are linked by *mutual constraints* provided by their respective descriptions (Varela, 1996). Given the importance of the topic of the experience of temporality, let it be clear that I consider this as an acid test of the entire neuro-phenomenological enterprise.

II: Lived Time Is Not Physical-Computational

As is common to any true phenomenological study, the exploration of time involves the gesture of reduction,[2] followed by the identification of descriptive invariants. As soon as we enter a study of present time with this kind of philosophical attitude it becomes apparent that the familiar account of time inherited from our modern western cultural background is inadequate. In fact, we have inherited from classical physics a notion of time as an arrow of infinitesimal moments, which flows in a constant stream. It is based on sequences of finite or infinitesimal elements, which are even reversible for a large part of physics. This view of time is entirely homologous to that developed by the modern theory of computation. As a refined expression of general computation, a Turing machine and its writing head inscribes symbols one by one in an infinite string, giving rise to time as a sequence-stream, exactly as in classical mechanics.

As computational views entered into cognitive science in the form of the computationalist (or cognitivist) viewpoint, computational time was unquestioningly used in the cognitive study of time. Some research continues to base experimental studies on an 'internal timer' giving rise to duration at various scales. A (hypothetical) clock emits pulses which translate into behaviour; judgments on duration depend on pulse counting, and are reflected on memory and decision (Church and Broadbent, 1990). This strict adherence to a computational scheme will be, in fact, one of the research frameworks that needs to be *abandoned* as a result of the neuro-phenomenological examination proposed here. But I will return to this conclusion later, after presenting my main argument.

Even under a cursory reduction, already provided by reflections such as those of Augustine and James, time in *experience* is quite a different story from a clock in linear time. To start with, it does not present itself as a linear sequence but as having a complex *texture* (whence James' 'specious present',[3] it is not a 'knife-edge' present), and its fullness is so outstanding that it dominates our existence to an important degree. In a first approximation this texture can be described as follows: There is always a centre, the now moment with a focused intentional content (say, this room with my

---

[2] In this paper the term 'reduction' and its cognates are used in their technical Husserlian sense, not with their more usual meaning in the philosophy of science.

[3] The expression is James'. In fact Husserl carefully underscored in his copy of *Principles* the term 'specious present' and suggested, in Gabel shorthand, a German translation which remains undeciphered! I am grateful to Shaun Gallagher for bringing this to my attention.

computer in front of me on which the letters I am typing are highlighted). This centre is bounded by a horizon or fringe that is already past (I still hold the beginning of the sentence I just wrote), and it projects towards an intended next moment (this writing session is still unfinished). These horizons are mobile: this very moment which was present (and hence was not merely described, but lived as such) slips towards an immediately past present. Then it plunges further out of view: I do not hold it just as immediately, and I need an added depth to keep it at hand. This basic texture is the raw basis of what I will be discussing *in extenso* below. In its basic outline, we shall refer to it as the *three-part structure of temporality*. It represents one of the most remarkable results of Husserl's research with phenomenological reduction.

Another important complementary aspect of temporality as it appears under reduction, is that consciousness does not contain time as a constituted psychological category. Instead, temporal consciousness *itself* constitutes an ultimate substrate of consciousness where no further reduction can be accomplished, a

> universal medium of access to whatever exists. . . . Constitutive phenomenology can well be characterized as the consistent and radical development of this privilege of consciousness into its last ramifications and consequences (Gurwitsch, 1966, p. xix).

We find a converging conclusion in James concerning the apparent paradox of human temporal experience: on the one hand there is the unity of the present, an aggregate we can describe where we reside in basic consciousness, and on the other hand this moment of consciousness is inseparable from a *flow*, a stream (Chapter IX of *Principles*, 1898). These two complementary aspects of temporal consciousness are the main axes of my presentation.

This rough preliminary analysis of time consciousness leads, then, to three distinguishable levels of temporality which will guide my argument:

(1) A first level proper to *temporal objects and events* in the world. Thus it is close to the ordinary notions of temporality in human experience which grounds the one currently used in physics or computation, but also in the experimental psychology of time.

(2) The phenomenologist starts from this level, but reduction makes apparent the second level, that of *acts of consciousness* that constitute objects-events.[4] This is the 'immanent' or 'internal time' of acts of consciousness. Their structure forms the main body of the phenomenological analysis in Husserl's *Lectures*.

(3) Finally (and this is the most subtle level of analysis), these first two levels are constituted from another level where no internal–external distinction is possible, and which Husserl calls the 'absolute time constituting *flow of consciousness*' (PZB 73).[5]

III: The Duration of Object-events

1. Duration: The experience of visual multistability

Time never appears detached but as temporal object-events which are the correlates or the intentional focus of the temporal consciousness: temporal object-events are what these acts are *about*. In contrast to what might be of interest for the psychologist

---

[4] In this paper I prefer to use the conjoint expression object-event to render *Zeitobjekte*. Although the terminology used by G. Granel (1968), tempo-object would be better, it is ungrammatical.

[5] The section or page numbers correspond to *Zur Phänomenologie des Inneren Zeitbewusstseins, Husserliana X* (1966), abbreviated here PZB. The English translation used here is from the texts by J. Brough, J. Churchill or R. Bruzina when available, or else I have modified them or provided my own.

or the neuroscientist, for the phenomenologist the content of the object is not as important as the manner of its appearance.

At various points in his research Husserl returns to the basic observation that what is proper to temporal objects is their double aspect of *duration and unity* (PZB 23, 113–14). Duration is correlative to the intentional direction: *this* house I am walking by, *that* bird that flew from here to there. . . . These are actual durations, and refer to the object having a location in time. Unity is correlative to the individuality of the object-events in question, standing out as a distinct whole against the background of other events. Thus a temporal object-event covers a certain span T, a complete act. However the entire act is a continuous process in the course of which *moments of nowness are articulated,* not as a finished unity but in a succession. It is this mode of constitution of object-events, whatever their duration T and their content, that interests me here. It must be the case that consciousness of succession derives from structural features of the acts of consciousness. Our problem is the characterization of these structures.

In his writings Husserl is characteristically sparse with examples. In PZB he uses one recurrent illustration: listening to a melody (a choice most later commentators have followed as well). I think it is important to examine this issue more carefully for various reasons. First, because when Husserl brings his example to hand, it is, strangely enough, as an un-situated subject in an abstract mode: we don't know in what circumstances the music is being listened to (is he alone, in a concert hall?), nor whether this is background listening or an intense emotional concentration (is it a moving piece, is he familiar with it?). All this is not merely peripheral, since without these particularities the mode of access to the experience itself is lost.

A TASK IN VISUAL PERCEPTION

- Consider the following image:

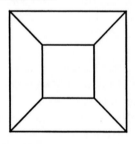

  α

  Out of context, most western subjects naturally see either a 'pyramid' or a 'hallway':

- Suspend habitual interpretations and consider the multiple variations together. We may infer that since α depicts neither pyramid nor hallway, it is an ambiguous or multi-stable perception.

- These variations can be *practised* by the following strategy:

    1. Fixate on the centre of the figure.
    2. Blink your eyes.
    3. 'Aim' at its alternative.

We are still missing a phenomenology of internal time-consciousness where the reductive gestures and the textural base of the experience figures explicitly and fully. The entire phenomenology of internal time-consciousness should be rewritten with the precision of a mode of access to experience that serves as support for reduction; what transpires in Husserl's writing is often far from such texture. Here I depart from usage by inviting the reader to actually engage in a specific experience of multi-stable visual perception that will provide reader and author with an explicit *common phenomenal ground*. Multi-stable perceptions are a good case study: they are precise and complex enough for the analysis, while still providing corresponding neurocognitive correlates. Indeed, multi-stable visual perception phenomena are deceptively clear.

These instructions turn the subject into an active agent, as the condition of possibility of the perception, the constitution of meaning itself illustrated here in a minimal case. There is a lot more to explore in this experiment concerning the perceptual horizon used for changing perception, as well as in regard to the strategy of language (the naming of the alternative, the 'aiming' at the other possibilities).[6] But let me stay with the temporal aspects of this perception. We notice, as it has been known since the Gestaltists, that as we acquire proficiency, the reversal can be accomplished with little effort and upon request. It is also clear that the reversal has in itself a very complex dynamics that takes on a 'life' of its own (more on this later). We also notice that the gesture of reversal is accompanied by a 'depth' in time, an *incompressible* duration that makes the transition perceptible as a sudden shift from one aspect to the other, and not as a progressive sequence of linear changes.

Granted, this well-known phenomenon is not common in ordinary life. A more 'ecological' case would be when I open a door, and as I move across the threshold I run into somebody who is directly in front of me. Both through body motion and visual orientation the person's face comes spontaneously into focus: I recognize a colleague, and thrust out my hand for a greeting. In both the multi-stable visual perception and the vignette just presented, I want to highlight what happens as one moves away from object-events dominated by passive attitude as in listening to music.

In the example of multi-stable perceptions we do not need to actively move our entire body. However an important layer of motion is actively present, whether in head adjustment, frowning and blinking, and, surely, in eye movements of various kinds. This is important, for little can be concluded from cases where motricity is absent. As phenomenological research itself has repeatedly emphasized, it is on the active sensori-motor interdependence that perception is based.[7] Independently, several traditions in cognitive research have, in their own way, underlined perception-action as a key.[8] It is this *active* side of perception which gives temporality its roots in living itself. Within this general framework, I will concentrate more precisely on the structural basis and consequences of this sensori-motor integration for our understanding of temporality.

---

[6] See for example Ihde, 1977, chap. 6.

[7] This is usually attributed to M. Merleau-Ponty's work, but it is very explicitly articulated by Husserl in materials available only recently. See Zahavi (1994).

[8] Some classics are E. von Holst, J.Piaget, and J.J. Gibson. For recent discussion see Varela *et al.* (1991); Kelso (1994).

2. The neurodynamics of temporal appearance

My overall approach to cognition is based on situated, embodied agents. I have introduced the name *enactive* to designate this approach more precisely. It is comprised of
two complementary aspects.

(1) On the one hand, the ongoing coupling of the cognitive agent, a permanent coupling that is fundamentally mediated by sensori-motor activities.

(2) On the other hand, the autonomous activities of the agent whose identity
is based on emerging, endogenous configurations (or self-organizing patterns) of
neuronal activity.

Enaction implies that sensori-motor coupling modulates, but does not determine,
an ongoing endogenous activity that it configures into meaningful world items in an
unceasing flow.

I cannot expand this overall framework more extensively,[9] but it is the background
of my discussion of temporality as a neurocognitive process. Enaction is naturally
framed in the tools derived from dynamical systems, in stark contrast to the cognitivist tradition that finds its natural expression in syntactic information-processing models. The debate pitting embodied-dynamics vs. abstract-computational as the basis
for cognitive science is still much alive.[10] For some time I have argued for the first
and against the second, and this choice justifies the extensive use of dynamical tools
in this paper.

From an enactive viewpoint, any mental act is characterized by the concurrent participation of several functionally distinct and topographically distributed regions of
the brain and their sensori-motor embodiment. It is the complex task of relating and
integrating these different components that is at the root of temporality from the point
of view of the neuroscientist. A central idea pursued here is that these various components require a *frame or window of simultaneity which corresponds to the duration of
lived present*. In this view, the constant stream of sensory activation and motor consequence is incorporated within the framework of an endogenous dynamics (not
informational-computational one), which gives it its depth or incompressibility. This
idea is not merely a theoretical abstraction: it is essential for the understanding of a
vast array of evidence and experimental predictions.[11] These endogenously constituted integrative frameworks account for perceived time as discretized and not linear,
since the nature of this discreteness is a horizon of integration rather a string of temporal 'quanta'.

At this point it is important to introduce *three scales of duration* to understand the
temporal horizon as just introduced:

(1) basic or elementary events (the '1/10' scale);
(2) relaxation time for large-scale integration (the '1' scale);
(3) descriptive-narrative assessments (the '10' scale).

This recursive structuring of temporal scales composes a unified whole, and it only
makes sense in relation to object-events. It addresses the question of how something

---

[9] See Varela (1979); Varela *et al.* (1991); Thompson and Varela (1999).

[10] Port and van Gelder (1995), provide an excellent survey of contemporary issues, including an
     accesible discussion of dynamical tools for the cognitive scientist.

[11] Cf. Varela *et al.* (1981); Dennett and Kinsbourne (1991); Pöppel (1988); Pöppel and Schill (1995).

temporally extended can show up as present but also reach far into my temporal horizon. The importance of this tri-level recursive hierarchy will be apparent all through this paper.

The first level is already evident in the so-called fusion interval of various sensory systems: the minimum distance needed for two stimuli to be perceived as non-simultaneous, a threshold which varies with each sensory modality.[12] These elementary events can be grounded in the intrinsic cellular rhythms of neuronal discharges, and in the temporal summation capacities of synaptic integration. These events fall within a range of 10 milliseconds (e.g. the rhythms of bursting interneurons) to 100 msec (e.g. the duration of an EPSP/IPSP sequence in a cortical pyramidal neuron). These values are the basis for the 1/10 scale. Behaviourally these elementary events give rise to micro-cognitive phenomena variously studied as perceptual moments, central oscillations, iconic memory, excitability cycles and subjective time quanta. For instance, under minimum stationary conditions, reaction time or oculo-motor behaviour displays a multimodal distribution with a 30–40 msec distance between peaks; in average daylight, apparent motion (or 'psi-phenomenon') requires 100 msecs.

This leads us naturally to the second scale, that of long-range integration. Component processes already have a short duration, on the order of 30–100 msec; how can such experimental psychological and neurobiological results be understood at the level of a fully constituted, normal cognitive operation? A long-standing tradition in neuroscience looks at the brain basis of cognitive acts (perception-action, memory, motivation and the like) in terms of *cell assemblies* or, synonymously, *neuronal ensembles*. A cell assembly (CA) is a distributed subset of neurons with strong reciprocal connections.[13]

In the language of the dynamicist, the CA must have a *relaxation time* followed by a bifurcation or phase transition, that is, a time of emergence within which it arises, flourishes, and subsides, only to begin another cycle. This holding time is bound by two simultaneous constraints: (1) it must be longer than the time of elementary events (the 1/10 scale); (2) it must be comparable to the time it takes for a cognitive act to be completed, i.e. on the order of a few seconds, the 1 scale) (e.g. Varela *et al.*, 1981; Pöppel, 1988). In brief, as we said before, the relevant brain processes for ongoing cognitive activity are not only distributed in space, but they are also distributed in an expanse of time that cannot be compressed beyond a certain fraction of a second, the duration of integration of elementary events.

What kind of evidence is there to postulate that every cognitive act, from perceptuo-motor behaviour to human reasoning, arises from coherent activity of a sub-population of neurons at multiple locations? And further, how are such assemblies transiently self-selected for each specific task? Since this will be a recurrent topic for the remainder of this article, I'd like to formulate it as a working hypothesis. The basic intuition that comes from this problem is that a specific CA emerges through a kind of temporal *resonance* or 'glue'. More specifically, the neural coherency-generating process can be understood as follows: *A specific CA is selected*

---

[12] In Chapter XV of *Principles*, James (1898) provides an elegant description of these data which were extensively explored in the last century.

[13] This section draws substantially from a previous publication (Varela, 1995) which discusses more extensively the literature and history of these ideas.

through the fast, transient phase locking of activated neurons belonging to sub-threshold, competing CAs.

The key idea here is that ensembles arise because neural activity forms transient aggregates of *phase-locked* signals coming from multiple regions. Synchrony (via phase-locking) must *per force* occur at a rate sufficiently high so that there is enough time for the ensemble to 'hold' together within the constraints of transmission times and cognitive frames of a fraction of a second. However, if, at a given moment, several competing CAs are ignited, different spatio-temporal patterns will become manifest and hence the dynamics of synchrony may be reflected in several frequency bands. This view has been supported by widespread findings of oscillations and synchronies in the gamma-range (30–70 Hz) in neuronal groups during perceptual tasks. The experimental evidence now includes recordings during behavioural tasks at various levels, from various brain locations — both cortical and sub-cortical — from animals ranging from birds to humans, and from signals spanning broad-band coherence from single units, local field potentials and surface evoked potentials (electric and magnetic). (See Singer, 1993; Varela, 1995, for history and summary of this literature; Lachaux *et al.*, 1998, for recent results).

This notion of synchronous coupling of neuronal assemblies is of great importance for our interpretation of temporality, and we will return to it repeatedly below. Here is the point where things get really interesting in our development of a view of cognition which is truly dynamic, making use of both recent advances in nonlinear mathematics and of neuroscientific observations. In brief, we have neuronal-level constitutive events, which have a duration on the 1/10 scale, forming aggregates that manifest as incompressible but complete cognitive acts on the 1 scale . This completion time is dynamically dependent on a number of dispersed assemblies and not a fixed integration period; in other words it is the basis of the origin of duration without an external or internally ticking clock.[14]

Nowness, in this perspective, is therefore pre-semantic in that it does not require a re-memoration, (or as Husserl says a 'presentification') in order to emerge. The evidence for this important conclusion comes, again, from many sources. For instance, subjects can estimate durations of up to 2–3 secs quite precisely, but their performance decreases considerably for longer times; spontaneous speech in many languages is organized such that utterances last 2–3 secs; short intentional movements (such as self-initiated arm motion) are embedded within windows of this same duration. This brings to the fore the third duration, the 10-scale, proper to descriptive-narrative assessments. In fact, it is quite evident that these endogenous, dynamic of nowness horizons can be, in turn, linked together to form a broader temporal horizon. This temporal scale is inseparable from our descriptive-narrative assessments, and linked to our linguistic capacities. It constitutes the 'narrative centre of gravity' in Dennett's metaphor (Dennett, 1991), the flow of time related to personal identity (Kirby, 1991). It is the continuity of a self that breaks down under intoxication or in pathologies such as schizophrenia or Korsakoff's syndrome.

---

[14] The precise timing is necessarily flexible (30–100 msec; 0.5–1.3 secs) since such events can naturally vary in their detailed timing depending on a number of factors: context, fatigue, type of sensorial mode utilized, age and so on. This is why I speak of an order of magnitude, not of absolute value.

I am now ready to advance the last key idea I need to complete this part of my analysis: *The integration-relaxation processes at the 1 scale are strict correlates of present-time consciousness.*

We are thus referred back to the phenomenal domain, and the nature of this link is what we need to explore carefully. Distinctions between ongoing integration in moments of nowness, and how their integration gives rise to broader temporal horizons in re-membrance and imagination are at the core of the Husserlian analysis of intimate time, to which we now return.

IV: The Just-past Is Not Memory

Temporal objects appear to us as such only because of the correlative *acts* of consciousness which have specific modes of appearance that are at the very heart of the issue of immediate temporality. Normally we designate these modes by the terms present now, past and future. Beyond this cursory designation however, reduction clearly points to the mode of 'now' as having a unique or *privileged status* (PZB 35). Two lines of analysis lead to this. First, the texture of now which James calls 'specious'. In effect, 'now' is not a temporal location for it has a lived quality as well: it is a space we dwell in, rather than a point where an object passes transitorily. Second, it is in relation to the rich structure of present nowness that all other modes of temporality take form.

Nowness, thus, is not an object, but a field with a structure analogous to the *centre and periphery* structuring of the visual field. Husserl himself speaks of nowness as a 'temporal fringe' (PZB 35). In other words, the very mode of appearance of nowness is in the form of extension, and to speak of a now-point obscures this fact: '... present here signifies no mere now-point but an extended objectivity which modified phenomenally has its now, its before and after' (PZB 201).

Husserl is grappling here with what Gallagher (1998) calls the cognitive paradox of temporal consciousness: the present has an extension which is perceived by an act that is in the present. A temporal object-event such as my identifying the figure as a pyramid has a unity which first appears as present nowness. It then slips away when it appears anew as a hallway. The previous recognition (and its given-ness) has now sunk into the past, as when an object moves from centre to periphery in space. This marks the beginning of the resolution of the apparent contradiction between sameness and difference, constancy and flow, which we will elaborate more below. To do so, I must now move to another level of detail in the study of the structure of consciousness, one which is constitutional (in Husserlian jargon), insofar as it provides the temporal features of mental acts that unify them into a single *flow* of consciousness.

The key issue in this stage of my examination of temporality is the contrast between the mode of appearance of now and of the just-passed, the act which reaches beyond the now. As Husserl points out, commenting on similar reasoning in Brentano:

> We could not speak of a temporal succession of tones if . . . what is earlier would have vanished without a trace and only what is momentarily sensed would be given to our apprehension (PZB 397).

But how can this structure of time perception be constituted? What is preserved is also modified. If when I see a pyramid I could still hold unchanged the nowness of when I saw the hallway, all temporal structure would disappear. The relation of now to just-past is one of slippage organized by very strict principles:

> ... new presentations each of which reproduces the contents of those preceding attach themselves to the perceptual presentation and in so doing *append* the continuous moment of the past (PZB 171, my emphasis).

This phrase expresses the intuitions behind the analysis of *dynamics intrinsic to these slippages of appearance*, as developed in the following section. It is key to my search for bridges between naturalization and the texture of temporal experience.

What form does this slippage from nowness to immediate past take? Brentano's postulate was that the constitution of the past is re-presentation or memory presentification of what preceded. In several remarks dispersed over the years, Husserl actually gets close to a demonstration that the now-to-just-past slippage is not the same as immediate memory retrieval or *presentification*.[15] To the appearance of the just-now one correlates two modes of understanding and examination (i.e. valid forms of donation in the phenomenological sense):

(1) remembrance or evocative memory and
(2) mental imagery and fantasy.

There are at least two main arguments for Husserl's observation. First, the nature of memory retrieval is one that is created now, and there is surely a nowness to the act of remembering . Thus we cannot account for the past with an act that is supposedly happening in the now. Second, when I remember having seen the hallway (as opposed to being in the embodied situation seeing it now) the past and the successive past that receded into oblivion have an immediacy, an evidence to them. In the present I 'see' what just passed; in memory I can only hold it in a representation as if through a veil. Thus memory and evocation have a mode of appearance that is qualitatively different from nowness.[16]

Let us turn back to the visual task, and resume our examination. As I look at the pyramid, I experience the near side at that moment of now, and as well there is the unity of the object as a durable unity (the pyramid is namable). This reveals the play between the primal impression of the near side of visual perception-action and the constituting unity that makes an identifiable object-event appear. It is the manifold of retentions, as illustrated by the exercise, that makes sense of the entire event: the now is experienced in an 'original' way.

> For only in primary remembrance do we see what is past; only in it is the past constituted, i.e. not in a representative but in a presentative way. . . . It is the essence of primary remembrance to bring this new and unique moment to primary, direct intuition, just as it is the essence of the perception of the now to bring the now directly to intuition (PZB 41).

Accordingly Husserl makes a disciplined distinction between impressional as opposed to *re-presentational* consciousness. In impression an object is originally

---

[15] This unusual term translates well *Vergegenwärtigung*, a rich mixture of waiting (*Warten*), present (*Gegen-wart*), and moving-from-present (*Ver-gegen-wärtigung*). This translation marks also the contrast with presentation (*Gegenwärtigung*). A non-literal translation in a psychological context could be that of evocative memory (including remembrance and imagination), in contrast to short-term or iconic memory.

[16] Thus the usual association between St. Augustine's and Husserl's views on time are misleading, since Augustine's examination does not distinguish between the presence of past as evocative memory of man's entire life and the past as living present.

constituted, and is thus given as present (I am now looking into the page and see the pyramid). In representation an object-event already given to impression is re-evoked (I evoke seeing the pyramid a little while ago for the first time). Similar conclusions can be drawn from neurocognitive evidence. For a long time cognitive psychology has distinguished between evocative memory, as implied above, and other forms of immediate retention. For instance, comparing rote vs. elaborate mnemonic recollection of items, yields a substantial (200-400 msec) shift in the corresponding ERPs (see e.g. Rugg, 1995). More recently, brain imaging methods have begun to establish

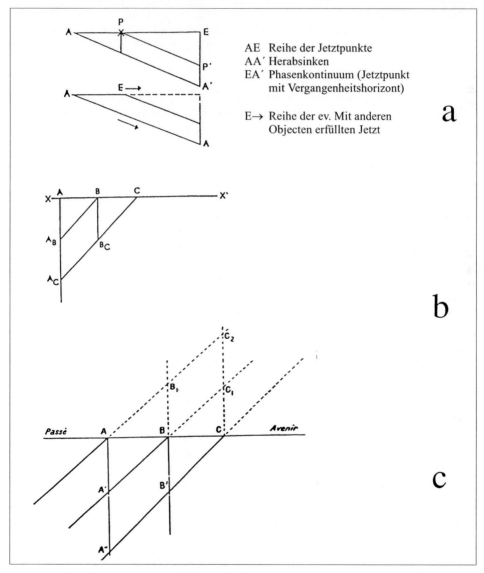

AE Reihe der Jetztpunkte
AA′ Herabsinken
EA′ Phasenkontinuum (Jetztpunkt
    mit Vergangenheitshorizont)

E→ Reihe der ev. Mit anderen
    Objecten erfüllten Jetzt

Figure 1. The 'figures of time' as introduced by Husserl.

(a) The diagram chosen by Stein published in the Lessons (PZB 28).
(b) One of several variants kept by Husserl prior to 1905.
(c) The version by Merleau-Ponty (1945, p. 477), which prolongs the lines into retentional time, as suggested by Husserl himself (cf. PZB 331).

that quite different structures are mobilized during active presentational tasks —
whether they are a form of memory (episodic, operational), or imagination. All these
presentational tasks mobilize a whole new set of capacities which add to the flow of
time but are obviously not required for it.

V: The Dynamics of Retention

1. The figures of time: retention as present

Husserl introduces the terms *retention* and *protention* to designate the dynamics that
follows impression in the present which *intends the just-past* and *the immediate
future*. This is the key innovation in the Husserlian analysis: to introduce a level of intentional direction in temporal consciousness. Retention is the attribute of a mental
act which keeps a hold of phases of the same perceptual act in a way that is distinguishable from the experience of the present (but that is not a re-presentation, as we
just saw). The key feature for retention is its direct contact with earlier perceptions,
making perception at any given instant contain entities that show up as temporally extended. Under reduction, object-events have a duration (they are specious), but the
conscious act of temporal perception also displays a temporality in the three-part layering. Similarly (but not symmetrically) another distinction seeks future threads or
*pro*tentions.

   This is the three-part structure that transforms an intentional content into a temporal extension. Figure 1 reproduces three sketches for these 'figures of time' taken
from different sources, but all expressing a geometrical depiction of the three-part
structure of temporality. The now and the degrees of pastness are what Husserl refers
to as *Ablaufsmodi*, slippages or elapsing modes, and which are depicted in reference
to a source-point, whence the discreteness in this diagram. The use of lines and points
is unfortunate, since it distracts from Husserl's remarkable insight; one might guess
this is an echo of his training as a mathematician. The fate of these figures of time has
been curious. Since they are easily grasped they have been used extensively as sum-
maries of Husserl's position. Yet these 'figures of time' hardly represent the scope of
his explorations; at best they illustrate an earlier and static view (Fig.1).[17] The appeal
of the diagrams came through in Merleau-Ponty's *Phenomenology of Perception*
(1945, p. 477) where the author comments approvingly on these depictions. However
Merleau-Ponty was well aware of the shortcoming as he added next to the diagram:
'Time is not a line but a network of intentionalities' (p. 477). Further on:

> The emergence of a present now does not *provoke* a piling behind of a past, and a pulling
> of the future. Present now *is* the slippage of a future to the present, and the just-past to the
> past: it is in one single movement that time sets in motion in its entirety (p. 479).

However, many have retaken uncritically this and several other diagrams in
Husserl's writings.
   In brief then:

> primal impression intends the new and actual phase of the temporal objects-events, and
> presents it as the privileged now. Retention presents just elapsed phases and presents
> them as just past in various degrees (Brough, 1989, p. 274).

---

[17] For a more detailed discussion see Larrabee (1994) and Miskiewicz (1985).

Retention is then a specific intentional act intending the slipping object constituting it as just past. Retention is not a kind of holding on to the now by its edge; it is an active presentation of an absence that arises from the modifications and dynamic apprehension of the now. Metaphorically it is more like moving from centre to periphery than the after-effect of an image, which is like the present modified only in intensity. But in the temporal realm, it is a curious structure indeed: it is present-living past, retention belongs to a 'living present (*lenbendig Gegenwart*)'.[18] Or, as Husserl quipped in a hand-written marginal scribbling on his working notes: 'But "perceived past" doesn't that sound like a "wooden iron"? (*hölzernes Eisen*)' (PZB 415).[19]

2. Retention as dynamical trajectories

It is indeed a wooden iron, unless we take a dynamical view of how the origin of the now can be formulated on the basis of our earlier hypothesis. The use of 'append' and 'slippage' in the phenomenological description already evokes this viewpoint, but it needs to be developed fully. Besides the fact that there is substantial experimental support for these hypotheses, it is essential to recognize that we are dealing with a *bona fide* candidate for the synthesis of a temporal space where cognitive events unfold.

Why is this of importance here? Because it leads us directly to an explicit view of the particular *kinds* of self-organization underlying the emergence of neural assemblies. These arise from collections of a particular class of coupled nonlinear oscillator, a very active field of research (e.g. Mirollo and Strogartz, 1990; Winfree, 1980; Mackey and Glass, 1988; Kelso, 1994). These dynamical processes, in turn, illuminate the mechanism whereby neuronal assemblies 'now' possess a three-part structure.

The key points to keep in mind for our discussion are the following. Self-organization arises from a *component* level, which in our case has already been identified as the 1/10 scale of duration, and re-appears here as single or groups of non-linear oscillators. Second we need to consider how these oscillators enter into synchrony as detected by a *collective* indicator or variable, in our case relative phase. Third, we need to explain how such a collective variable level manifests itself at a global level as a cognitive *action* and behaviour, which in our case corresponds to the emergence of a percept in multistability. This global level is not an abstract computation, but an embodied behavior subject to initial conditions (e.g. what I 'aimed' at, what was the preceding percept), and non-specific parameters (e.g. changes in viewing conditions, attentional modulation). The local–global interdependence is therefore quite explicit: the emerging behaviour cannot be understood independently of

---

[18] B. Besnier remarks: 'This is what is usually expressed by saying that retention belongs to a "living present" (lebenhaftig or *lebendig*). But there is something that retention de-presents (*démomentanéise*) which one could translate by *ent-gegenwärtigung*, but this choice might create confusions . . .' (Besnier, 1993, p. 339). For the relations with the term *Ent-gegenwärtigung* as 'de-presentation', see the previous footnote on presentation and presentification.

[19] T. van Gelder called my attention to this telling remark; it gives the title to his contribution to this topic (van Gelder, 1998). Our respective ideas were presented simultaneously (yet developed independently) at the Conference 'Contemporary Issues in Phenomenology and Cognitive Science', Bordeaux, October, 1995.

the elementary components; the components attain relevance through their relation
with their global correlate.

What have we gained? Very simply that these kinds of emergent processes give us a
naturalized account for the apparent discrepancy between what emerges in the living
present and the presence of the past. In effect, the fact that an assembly of coupled oscillators attains a transient synchrony and that it takes a certain time for doing so is the
explicit correlate of the origin of nowness. As the models and the data show, the synchronization is dynamically *unstable* and thus will constantly and successively give
rise to new assemblies. We may refer to these continuous jumps as the *trajec- tories* of
the system. Each emergence bifurcates from the previous ones from its initial and
boundary conditions. Thus the preceding emergence is still present in the succeeding
one.

This brings to the fore the important role of *order* parameters in dynamical accounts. Order parameters can be described under two main aspects:

(1) the current state of the oscillators and their coupling, or initial conditions;
(2) the boundary conditions that shape the action at the global level: the contex-
     tual setting of the task performed, and the independent modulations arising
     from the contextual setting where the action occurs (i.e. new stimuli or en-
     dogenous changes in motivation).

Order parameters are defined by their embodiment, and are unique to each case.
The trajectories of this dynamics, then, enfold both the current arising and its sources
of origin in one synthetic whole as they appear phenomenally. A wooden iron indeed.

3. *The dynamics of multistability*

The kinds of specific dynamics we have brought to bear to the understanding of retention and the just-past are not simple. In particular, arrays of coupled oscillators are interesting because they do not in general behave according to the classical notion of
stability that derives from a mechanical picture of the world. Stability here means that
initial and boundary conditions lead to trajectories concentrated into a small region of
phase space wherein the system remains, a point attractor or a limit cycle. In contrast,
biological systems demonstrate *in*stability is the basis of *normal* functioning rather
than a disturbance that needs to be compensated, as in a mechanical picture of causality.

Let us return once again to our experiential ground of visual multistability. The
origin of multistability is due to properties that are *generic* to coupled oscillators and
their phase relations. In other words their mode of appearance is an invariant under
certain conditions and reporting subjects. This is further clarified by recent experiments performed in order to study the dynamics of multistability in visual perception.
Kelso *et al.* (1994) presented observers with *variant perspectives* of the classical
Necker cube, a close relative of our first visual task. By asking the observer to push a
button when the perceptual reversal occurs, one obtains a time series of reversal
which obeys a stochastic distribution (a gamma function with a mean at around 1 sec).
Kelso *et al.*, however, requested observers to perform the same task of time measurement while noting separately the time series as a function of perspective, which is
thus used as an order parameter.

The interesting observation is that, again, at the extremes of the cube the distribution of reversal intervals is considerably flattened. The subject is more likely to have

sporadic figure reversal, or to be 'fixed' on one mode for a longer duration. At these extremes subjects report getting 'blocked' by an interpretation. As before, one can think of these results as the way the coordination of a wide array of oscillators appears via a common variable of phase. By introducing perspectival variants, the location in phase space is accordingly modified, and new dynamical modes appear, in this case revealing a saddle instability.

That this dynamical interpretation is actually linked to neuronal ensembles as we have been assuming here is shown by recent experiments (Leopold and Logothetis, 1996). A monkey was rigorously trained to voluntarily 'aim' at reversing a set of ambiguous figures, (binocular rivalry, a visual task known to be similar to Necker cube figure reversal), and then to indicate the moment at which this reversal appeared for his perception. At the same time, individual neurons were recorded from a number of its visual cortical areas. The authors report that in motion sensitive area MT, a percentage of neurons correlate with reversal and can be modulated by the perceptual requirements of the tasks; this percentage is diminished in primary regions V1/V2. This kind of evidence strongly supports the notion that multistability arises through the large-scale collaborations between neurons at many different places in the visual cortex and elsewhere in the brain, a concrete example of an emerging CA for a specific task which has perceptual and phenomenal correlates.

VI: The Dynamics of Flow

1. The genetic analysis of temporality

I need to turn now to the last step in my analysis, a step that is taken on far less trodden ground than the intentionality of object-events and retentional dynamics, two 'classical' topics in the phenomenology of time after Husserl. Since the discussion so far has been concentrated on a particular kind of intentional act, retentional dynamics still belongs to the type of constitutional analysis referred to as '*static*', the classic level at which most commentators on Husserl's time analysis have remained. It is called static since it is intentionally directed to object-events and to what appears (either as external processes or immanent duration, for instance the completion of a movement). In other words, so far we have considered the more accessible levels of temporarily, the appearance of temporal object-events and the acts of consciousness which constitute them.

Husserl brings to the fore a third and last level of analysis which has been less explored by later work. This is 'the absolute time-constituting flow of consciousness' (PZB 73). In the context of the present use of dynamical ideas it is interesting that Husserl's choice to refer to this level of study as the 'flow' is suggestive:

> It is absolute subjectivity and has the absolute properties of something to be denoted metaphorically as 'flow' (*Fluss*) as a point of actuality, primal source-point, that from which springs the 'now', and so on (PZB §36; also t. No. 54, p. 368).

The idea of flow opens up to two less 'classical' issues that I will dwell on here: (1) the *genetic* or *constitutional* analysis of time, just introduced above as the flow of absolute time, and (2) its close relation to the *affective* dimension (cf. Section VII). Husserl established the distinction between static and constitutional analyses of time during the years 1917–23. These topics are notoriously more difficult to explore, not only because they are grounded on Husserl's late production, but also because they touch on subtle areas, which is what makes them more attractive. Accordingly the reader is asked to consider what I propose in the remainder of this text as a *sketch* of future work more than anything else.[20]

Return to the first visual task (Do it!). Aim for a change in percept, and return to the initial one. It is clear that we have been given two distinct experiences with a similar content. The link joining both as two-of-the-same demonstrates the basic fact that there is an underlying temporalization which has a relative independence of the particular content of the views. As Husserl concisely remarks,

> Every experience is 'consciousness' (*Bewusstsein*) and consciousness is always consciousness-of... Every experience is itself experienced (*selbst erlebt*) and to that extent also intended (*bewusst*). *This* being intended (*Bewussst-sein*) is consciousness of the experience (*Erlebnis*) (PZB 291).

The link is a *reflection,* which is not always present but that may always be put into action, it accompanies all my acts. This reflection is temporal since experiences *are* (immanent) object-events with duration: they appear slipping into the past and gradually disappear into the fringes of time. It is against this background of the flow of experiencing that the duration of object-events and the experience of temporality is constituted. This underlying flow raises then a new apparent paradox: it can be detached from the temporal object-events but at the same time it appears inseparable from them, since a flow without object-events does not manifest itself.

The nature of this immanence is given by Husserl in the following (remarkable) passage which summarizes his previous analysis:

> I may express the situation thus: What is perceived, what manifests (*selbstgegeben ist*) as an individual object, is always given in unity (*Einheit*) with an absolutely non-manifest domain (*nicht gegeben Mannigfaltigkeit*) (PZB 284).

Proper immanent temporality is that of lived experiences themselves. Here we reach what might rightly be perceived as the second aporia of temporality: the coexistence of permanence and change. Consciousness is an unceasing background where distinct temporal acts and events with their own duration appear. In around 1911 Husserl introduces the name of 'double intentionality' (PZB 80, 379) for this articulation, since not only is there a retention (of the object event) but also a *retention of retention* (a reflective awareness of that experience). These two aspects of intentionality work together and are inseparably interwoven into the unitary flow of consciousness. Consciousness could not exist apart from the acts which it intends or experiences, but it remains distinct from it, a pregnant unity of appearance and non-appearance.

We may now ask what avenues of access or exploration are available to study the immanent flow? As discussed before, one main source is the *reflexive* act, the becoming-aware of experience as temporal. This is quite immediate and the most convincing argument to establish that flow is an essential phenomenon. However, al-

---

[20] These difficulties have been discussed eloquently by Besnier (1993). In fact this Section owes a lot to him: I have liberally let myself be guided by some of his arguments and textual indications. I have been unable to take into consideration the material from Fink's unpublished time manuscripts (Bruzina, 1993; 1994). The analysis of flow seemed to have arisen in close parallel to Husserl's efforts to study intersubjectivity, the question of common time and the phenomenological basis of historicity. This is surely one of the most fascinating and still largely unexplored areas in phenomenological research. The paucity of published sources does not make things easier (see Depraz, 1992; 1995).

though accessible, immediate reflection is a task made difficult by the simple fact that to provide description we need to keep up with the shiftiness of changing experience. As we have said, shifts concern mere fractions of a second, and even diligent observation makes it hard to provide useful distinctions.[21]

The second royal avenue of access to the flow is remembrance, if we understand that such presentification must be done in a 'pure' manner, i.e. with a view to its nature and not its specific content. I can very clearly re-live the last visual percept in the task. But this evocation is complete only when it pulls with it also the embodied context in which that image arose (my posture, the car passing in the background, the concurrent fragments of ideation as I was doing the task). In other words, although an evocation intends an object which it brings to presence in a specific mode (cf. Section IV) it does so as a field: the intended object is a centre, but it is also a periphery full of the context of the embodied experience. This fringe, although not intended, is nevertheless brought to life by remembrance:

> In order to examine properly (in its 'genetic' constitution) the temporality of immanent experience, it is necessary to direct one's reflexive focus during an experience of *Erinnerung* on the experiences that are re-produced by themselves. This is difficult (Besnier, 1993, p. 347).

Indeed it is, but at least it is feasible enough that we can concur that there is such a thing as the bringing into life of the fringes of a memory. Where one could have found an isolated item sought by remembrance, we find, without specifically looking for it, the appended re-lived threads of the experience itself. Or if I may speak figuratively: in re-membering an intended object, it comes out bristling with retention threads of the original experience. Stated positively: what makes remembrance have such a retentional fringe must be *the manner in which these very retentions have been constituted.*

In our attempt to naturalize retentional acts, we attempted to solve the wooden iron nature of the past-always-present. Further examination of the mode of appearance of immanent temporality confronts us again with a new apparent paradox, not unlike that of the 'wooden iron', which we may call the *constitutional* paradox of temporal consciousness. The process of slippage itself (i.e. de-presentation, *Entgegenwärtigung*, *dé-momentanéisation*) has the marks of being an active or even *self-generated* process. Can there be a process that is a cause of itself? In this case the paradox takes the more classical form of a *regressum ad infinitum*. Is there an angle to illuminate this second apparent contradiction?

2. The geometry of nonlinear flows

An answer has already been sketched in passing and it now needs to be unfolded more fully. The neurodynamics of time we have been pursuing is essentially based on nonlinear coupled oscillators. As we saw, this class of dynamical systems finds its wealth of behaviour in the fact that constitutional instabilities are the norm and not a nuisance to be avoided. The case of multistability makes this quite evident experien-

---

[21] This is also a statement about the relative poverty of examples of the continued cultivation of reductive capacities, a main motivation for this Special Issue. In the *Abhidharma* corpus of Buddhism, long term cultivation of a variant of phenomenological reduction is reported to give access to very detailed description of the rapid successions of immediate reflection (see Varela *et al.*, 1991 for more on the *Abhidharma* corpus).

tially: the percepts flip from one to another by the *very nature* of the geometry of the phase space and the trajectories.

This is a widespread characterization not only applicable to this case study. Complex, non-linear, or chaotic systems in general provide a self-movement that does not depend (within a range of parameters) on where the systems are. In other words whether the content of my visual percept is a man/girl or a pyramid/ hallway, the intrinsic or immanent motion is *generically* the same. If the specific place in phase space is a correlate of the intentional content of an object-event, the system never dwells on it, but approaches, touches and slips away in perpetual, self-propelled motion. Cognitively this corresponds to the observation that in brain and behaviour there is never a stopping or dwelling cognitive state, but permanent change punctuated by transient aggregates underlying a momentary act (1 scale of duration). Formally this is expressed by the pervasive presence of stable/unstable regions, so that any slight change in initial and boundary conditions makes the system move to a nearby stable/unstable region.

This notion has been and is still explored by dynamicists under various guises. In the specific case of multistability of the Necker cube, we assume the coordination of a wide array of oscillators via a common variable of phase. By introducing perspectival variants, the dynamical landscape is accordingly shifted to new dynamical modes appearing in the phase portrait. This saddle instability implies that at that point there is mixture of tendencies to be attracted into that position (i.e. perceptual content) or to move away from it, and the slightest perturbation will push and pull the trajectories.

More generally, many apparently 'noisy' natural events (such as the transition times between Necker cube reversals) have recently yielded unexpected deterministic patterns under nonlinear dynamical analysis beyond the reach of traditional linear analysis. The main feature of these methods is to give us a view of dynamics not only based on trajectories, but in the more encompassing frame of *the geometry of the phase space landscape*.

This is not merely a formal description. These geometrical patterns can be studied even in a highly localized grouping of neuronal activity such as that measured by an electrode on the surface of the brain (a few cubic millimeters of cortex). For instance, in a local temporal epileptic focus which seems like a noisy oscillation, we have found evidence for such multiple determinism and instabilities (Le van Quyen *et al.*, 1997 a,b). While recording from a subject's brain he was asked to perform simple visual and auditory discrimination. We then studied the interval between these discharges much like the time series from Necker percept reversal. This provided consistent indications that these temporal dynamics cannot be characterized as simple 'noisy' periodicity. Even a simple first-return map (the value of one time interval plotted against the value of the following one), reveals detailed changing geometrical patterns depending on experimental conditions, but shows consistent evidence of a saddle instability with stable and unstable manifolds. This observation suggests that the phase space landscape can be characterized by *departures from strict periodicity in a non-random manner* (Auerbach *et al.*, 1987). In particular the different perceptual discriminations 'pull' this local dynamics towards a distinct unstable periodicity. Although the positions of the periodic points are shifted between the behavioral conditions studied, the related slopes of approach to the instabilities appear as invariant features of the dynamics for all our experimental conditions.

   In this study case we stress the relevance of local nonlinear properties in brain events which are often lost when global, averaging methods (like spectra, or even dimension estimators) are applied. There is a surprising degree of detail displayed by the trajectories or orbits of the epileptic dynamics as modulated by perceptual tasks. A paradigmatic manifestation of this is the fact that a chaotic trajectory typically includes an *infinite* number of unstable periodic orbits. These orbits are unstable in the sense that the smallest deviation moves the state away from the periodic orbit. Thus, a nonlinear deterministic (or chaotic) system never remains long in any of these unstable motions but continually switches from one periodic motion to another, thereby giving an appearance of randomness (Artuso *et al.*, 1990).

3. The double intentionality

We have gained, then, a renewed intuition to resolve the riddle of this second wooden iron of the mixture of passivity and activity, of invariance and change of double intentionality. 'The self-appearance (*Selbsterscheinung*) of the flow does not require a second flow, rather it constitutes itself as phenomenon itself (*in 'sich' selbst*)' (PZB 381). Merleau-Ponty refers to this paradoxical aspect of reductive description by saying that to exist time 'must be already in me (*fuse en moi*)', and, as it arises as a flow of retentions, it also self-manifests (*Selbsterscheinung*).[22] In fact: 'I have not chosen to be born, but once born, time must already permeate me (*le temps fuse a travers moi*), whatever I do' (Merleau-Ponty, 1945, p. 488).

   Husserl develops his descriptive account of this paradoxical appearance of 'double intentionality' in the notions of transversal and longitudinal intentionality (*Quer-* and *Längsintentionalität*).[23] The first is retentional dynamics, the static constitution. Longitudinal intentionality, in contrast, is the genetic constitution of the temporalization of experiences themselves, their self-manifestation. These are necessarily interdependent, but their mode of dependence and the root of their difference is what is difficult to express : 'For all of that we have no names' (PZB 371).

   Now, longitudinal intentionality acts by an integration from within the now itself, it provides an unchanging substrate from which the flow emerges. As Besnier remarks (p.350), there is a great temptation to transpose the analysis of perceptual intentionality by envisaging this as a 'pure' substrate or *Ur-hyle*. I do not have to enter into the thorny technical debate this mode of analysis has produced since Husserl (Depraz, 1996). My contribution is to bring to the fore the intuition derived from the generic nonlinear flows. Self-manifestation appears in our analysis as self-motion or generic instability, which is not a mere artifact of description, but an invariant formal description for self-organization. Thus its relevance to temporality is appropriate. The flow, in the neurodynamical sense, is precisely a wooden iron that exists as flow only to the extent that it is constituted in individual trajectories (not an inert geometrical magma) as ongoing self-propelled transient trajectories visit various regions in phase space (corresponding to an intended object-event, an appearance).

   The inseparability of these two intentionalities here is not only descriptively accurate, but part of the intrinsic logic of complex non-linear dynamics. It would be inconsistent to qualify the self-motion as a 'deeper layer' of the dynamical process, and to

---

[22] Merleau-Ponty (1964), pp. 244–5, 296–8, as discussed by Besnier, 1993, footnote 9, p. 356.

[23] Cf. PZB §39, t. No. 54.

describe trajectories as mere appearance (Gallagher, 1979). *Mutatis mutandis*, it seems illusory to isolate a 'deeper' layer of genetic constitution where experience would be constituted from an absolute time, and only then made manifest in conscious intentionality. What is deep is the *link* between self-motion (immanence) and trajectories (appearance).

Enough has been said about the immanent or absolute flow to suggest its importance and perspicacity. It is surely a topic that needs exploration, and it is the natural ground for bridges into other varieties of experience and towards other traditions concerned with human consciousness. Indeed, this level of analysis touches more than any other on the ground of self, pure ego, or basic consciousness. Brough (1989) summarizes:

> And thanks to the infinite horizon opened up by the absolute flow, we can be sure that we can go right on changing and accumulating a past, while still remaining the same. There is a fissure, then, in consciousness. Thanks to this fissure, any one of my acts, asserting itself and holding sway for a more or less brief time . . . is able to 'slide off' without taking my whole self with it. If my internal awareness were glued without gap to my fleeting experiences, the passage of time would rip my ego to shreds (p. 288).

But we must now leave these considerations and turn to our last topic which is the closely related issue of the appearance of this self-motion from the perspective of affect.

VII: Protention — Transparency and Emotional-tone

1. *Immanent temporality and affect*

Return again to the first task and re-examine more closely the nature of the switching, as it happens. One essential component of the experience is that the shift is sudden and accompanied by a (more or less distinct) emotional change when the visual perception shifts abruptly. Thus, the mode of slippage of nowness into just-past, the retentional trajectory, appears as presence of the past not only in a way that is distinct from representational memory. It also gives us the cue that the *emotional tone* is an integral part of the phenomenon. What is the role of emotion or affect in the self-movement of the flow? And what is its role, if any, in the anticipation of what is to come, protention?

In Husserl's published texts, protention is not extensively analysed and I have the impression that he implicitly assumes a certain symmetry with retention, as if the same structure of invariance for the past could be flipped towards the future. But protention intends the new prior to an impression and thus can only be a pre-figuration. Husserl speaks of ' empty constitution' (PZB 52), but it is not expectation or anticipation in the sense of containing a representation of what the next now will bear. To see why this is so, one need only to apply the same arguments as used for distinguishing retention and evocative memory. Indeed protention has a mode of openness: '. . . the only thing definite is that without exception something will come'; in listening to a melody (his example) there is a predictable side to protention since it intends further phrases of the music (PZB 106, 84). These and similar remarks from the *Lessons* seem to have provided the basis for the symmetrical view of the three-part structure of time, and as indicated in the oft-used figure of time discussed above (Fig. 1).

This analysis can be substantially enriched. There are at least two main sources of evidence to conclude that protention is generically *not* symmetrical to retention. The first is, precisely, that the new is always suffused with affect and emotional tone that accompanies the flow. In fact, protention is not a kind of expectation that we can understand as 'predictable', but an openness which is capable of self-movement, an indeterminate that is about to manifest. In this quality it provides the natural link into affection, or, more aptly with some form of self-affectedness (see below). The second is that retention has the structure of a continuum, but protention can only be a bounded domain, since we cannot anticipate an anticipation that is yet to come. While the threads of retention set the stage for protention, it cannot modify the retentional threads retroactively.[24]

Time and affect were never systematically treated by Husserl. A substantial part of his notes are still unpublished or are accessible only from secondary sources. However, a deepening of late analysis of time makes it possible to trace some important fragments of a view of affection as initiating the drive of the lived flow itself (Depraz, 1993). Thus my propositions in the remainder of this Section are not entirely at variant with Husserl's later research, but go beyond it. As he says:

> How is the self (*Ich*) the centre of this life it experiences? How is it experienced? It is affected by that which consciousness is conscious of (*Buwusstsein bewusst ist*), it follows affect, or still it is attracted, held, taken in by that which affects it (Ms. C III/1).

Husserl's notes contain recurrent references to this primordial aspect with regards to the child's early life where one finds an 'instinctive' intentionality (*Triebsintentionalität*). As Depraz remarks:

> Affect is thus this non-form which makes constitution of the self by itself, that affects it in the strict sense of structure, that of constitutive temporality. . . . Affect is there before being there for me in full consciousness: I am affected before knowing that I am affected. It is in that sense that affect can be said to be primordial (Depraz, 1993, pp. 73, 75).

How is this pertinent for the three-part structure of time? Husserl remarks that during a melody the sounds affect me differently as it creates its retentional threads, an attentional tendency (*eine Tendenz der Zwendung*). Or we may say it provides a *disposition* which is marked by a gradual intensities. This temporalizing effect puts protention at the centre stage: '. . . it is not only the impressions from hyle that affect, but already "hyletical anticipations of data"' (*ibid.*, p. 79).

Time as a royal road to the study of affect continued after Husserl, especially by Heidegger and Merleau-Ponty, where the discussion about self-affectedness is considerably enriched. The main innovation is in their treatment of time as self-affectedness. As Merleau-Ponty says: 'Le temps est 'affection de soi par soi', and notes that the expression derives from Kant as modified by Heidegger in his *Kantbuch*.[25] Self-affectedness becomes a key insight into the nature of consciousness:

> . . . even the most precise consciousness of which we are capable is affected by itself or given to itself. The very word consciousness has no meaning apart from this duality (Merleau-Ponty, 1945, p. 488).

---

[24] Gallagher (1979) discusses this asymmetry as well, and points out that Husserl speaks of the differences in 'style' between protention and retention (*Hua. XI*, pp. 323–4).

[25] Merleau-Ponty, 1945, p. 487; 'Die Zeit ist ihrem Wesem nach reine Affektion ihrer selbst', *Kant und das Problem der Metaphysik*, p. 180–1.

With Levinas (1988), a further sphere of affection, hetero-affection, is brought to the fore: The Other, alterity, is the primary clue for time's constitution. We are not only affected by representations and immanent affection ('affection de soi par soi'), but alterity as inseparable from the sphere of an ego-self. In this move the very distinction between auto- and hetero- ceases to be relevant, since in all cases it is all brought down to the same manifestation: it is a question of 'something other', the experience of an alterity, a difference in the identity of the present, whether by the inevitable slippages to retention, or by the anticipations in protention.

But these philosophical refinements are not central for us here in all their detail. We are seeking to move beyond the apparent paradox between an original impression in time that would be coloured by affection, or, conversely, the primacy of affection that would underlie temporality. We seek a non-dual synthesis whereby affect is both constitutive of the self, and at the same time contains a radical openness or unexpectedness with regards to its occurring.

2. *Disposition for action*

In order to move further in our analysis we need to have a concrete base on which to base our examination, much as the visual tasks provided the basis for the static analysis. Many alternatives exist, but I have chosen to explore the role of affection in the constitution of time in the context of active involvement in the world and through the dispositional quality of affect and its gradations, since — from the point of view of enactive cognitive neuroscience — coping plays a central role. Coping is a readiness or dispositional tendency for action in a larger field, an *ontological readiness*, that is, an expectation as to the way the world will show up. For this very same reason coping has everything to do with habitus, the recurrence of our lives. Learning a skill is a prototypical example of acquisition of transparency for action.

The loss of fluidity in coping is never distant from a dispositional affective-tone, as we have seen. But we can now see that different degrees of breakdown in transparency and the multiple manners in which it happen opens a panoply of affective tonalities: fear, jealousy, anger, anxiety, self-assurance and so on. Accordingly, the word emotions is used here in its specific sense: the *tonality of the affect that accompanies a shift in transparency*. Affect, on the other hand is a broadening of the dispositional orientation which will pre-condition the emotional tone that may appear.

As I write now, I have a dispositional attitude that engages me in an anticipation of writing and shaping my thought into sentences. As I write this word now, the disposition is coloured by an emotional charge, a moderate resentment for not finding the proper expression. But that emotional tone appears against a background of the exalted mood of a productive day devoted to finishing this text.

More explicitly, I want to distinguish three scales for affect, homologous (but not isomorphic) to the three scales of temporality used above.

(1) The first scale is *emotions*: the awareness of a tonal shift that is constitutive of the living present.
(2) The second is *affect*, a dispositional trend proper to a coherent sequence of embodied actions.
(3) Finally *mood*, the scale of narrative description over more or less long duration.

3. Emotional-tone as dynamical landscaping

For the ethologist, affect and emotions are a relatively small repertoire of immediate dispositions that are physiologically inscribed in a species inheritance, although in most mammals habit and sustained learning may shape it significantly.[26] Neuro-biologically, they can be associated to a relatively stable set of neural correlates (e.g. Damasio, 1994). Studies of human emotional responses, even in relatively artificial situations, reveal the extent to which the biological endowment of 'basic' emotional patterns is enfolded in the historical recurrence of an individual, its historicity and language. Individual habits, historicity and language, constitute the palette of human emotional life incorporating the biological make-up to an end which is but which is historically and individually unique.[27]

Homologously, we can say that the experience of time has a biological base in elementary events (1/10 scale), but this basis is enfolded with other structures of temporalization into the specious present that is our theme. To deny that such a deeply rooted biological basis plays a role in the appearance of temporality is fruitless. Similarly, I am not reducing emotions to their empirical correlate in a reductionistic move. As considered here, emotions are an integral part of an ontological readiness. This should not obscure the fact that such an ontological constitution has roots in basic emotional dispositions inseparable from our history as living beings and minute events in brain physiology.

When I induce a break in habitus by exercising reduction when looking at the visual image of our task, I bring to it an emotional disposition which pre-figures the change in my perception. In saying 'I expect to see' I also provide exogenous, additional order parameters that alter the geometry of the phase space. This process of 'sculpting' a dynamical landscape is intrinsically distinct from the trajectories that move within it, but form an inseparable unity.

In fact, it has been known for some time that the intention to carry out a movement is coupled with a change in emotional tone that varies in degree. As a global variable, induced changes in dynamical landscape can be detected. One well known case is the readiness potential. For a finger movement, a large slow electrical potential can be measured over the entire scalp which *precedes* by a fraction of a second the beginning of the motion, and the subject can report that he has decided to initiate the movement.[28] This is not a correlate of intention (as it is sometimes said), but it does give a concrete idea of how vast a reconfiguration of a dynamical landscape is involved at the origin of a fully constituted now (moving the fingers). In the results of Leopold and Logothetis (1996) already mentioned, a similar reconfiguration of the disposition for firing of individual neuronal responses is visible some 100–200 msecs *before* the monkey indicates that it has switched to a new percept.

Why is all this relevant here? Because it is direct evidence of the manner in which emotional tonality plays into the dynamics of flow. Emotional tonality is, by its very action, a major boundary and initial condition for neurodynamics. This diffuse, con-

[26] For the basic studies of instinct and emotion in animals see the foundational studies of K. Lorenz (1972), which are still useful. For a more recent and provocative survey see der Waals (1995).

[27] See Ekman and Davidson (1994) for a recent survey of psychological studies, and Rorty (1980) for cognitive views.

[28] The original description is due to Deecke et al. (1969). A vast literature on these pre-conscious electrical correlates has been produced since.

stitutive effect is in accord with the mechanism of action via neurotransmitters that
have been know for some time to condition the modes of response at the neuronal
level, as the body of knowledge of psycho-pharmacological agents attests.

This sketch of the nature of protentions via affective-tonality has taken us to a third
and final step of what seems to be formally a genetic constitution of temporality. I
have introduced a last dynamical principle that applies to neurocognitive dynamics as
well. I refer to the mutual bootstrap between the phase space landscape and the
specific trajectories that move in it, and the fact that the very same trajectories
provide the very conditions for an embodied coupling, since through their coupling
they shape their dynamical landscape. Metaphorically, the walker and the path are
intrinsically linked.

This bootstrap principle seems to be present in a variety of natural systems, and has
recently been referred to as 'operating at the edge of chaos', or 'self-organized criti-
cality'. For example, this idea provides a renewed view of evolution since it provides
an answer to the old nature (genetic expression) vs. nurture (environmental coupling
conditions) dilemma. In this synthetic view (cf. Kauffman, 1993) the relation between natural forms, (the *Baupläne* of organisms), and the selection process in their
ecological embeddedness, is not one of contradiction but precisely a mutual imbrica-
tion when seen through dynamical glasses.[29] This built-in mobility, enfolding trajectories and geometry, gives a natural system a possibility of always staying close to
regions in phase space that have multiple resources (e.g. at least two in bistable visual
perception).

To conclude: The generic structure of double intentionality proposed by Husserl is,
I submit, of this class of dynamical bootstrap, and the phenomenal analysis of affect
and emotional tonality provides evidence for it.

VIII: Nowness — New Figures of Time

To gather all the threads that have been developed here, and to echo the tradition
started by Husserl himself, I would like to propose a new figure of time, the *fourfold
structure of nowness* (see below, Fig. 2).

This is not so bold or farfetched. By now it seems clear that the point-by-point,
linear time depiction at the base of the figures of time is insufficient. One major
improvement is to introduce, not points and lines, but flows, *dynamical* trends. A
second major improvement is to take into explicit account what surfaced in the later
work of Husserl himself, the central role of double intentionality, static and genetic
constitution. This final ingredient gives to the homologies between the constitution of
space and times the preeminence they deserve. I do this by taking the *centre/fringe*
structure as the very core of a new figure of time. Once these three basic aspects have
been incorporated a new representation falls into place quite naturally.

1. To start let us consider the role of dynamics that has been central in our development, and hence move away from the use of discrete points in a line as in the traditional diagram. Not only do we leave behind a line geometrical figure, but also we
must introduce an *asymmetry* into it. With regards to static constitution, we have discussed two different kinds of dynamical ideas: retentional trajectories (the past) and
order parameters for anticipation (the future). In the new diagram arrows on lines, as

---

[29] This is referred to as evolution by natural drift in Varela *et al.*, 1991.

is traditional in mathematics display the dynamical quality, but I distinguish trajectories from anticipatory landscaping by dropping the arrowheads. With regards to genetic constitution, we also have two distinct ideas: the immanent temporization of self-motion, and the directed intentionality relative to a position in phase space.

Dynamical Ingredients

	order parameters	**Static**
trajectories of retention	of anticipation	past/future
transient attractors	self-motion of	**Genetic**
intentional content	generic instabilities	change/permanence

2. Next we consider the spatial ingredients, that is, the role of a centre–periphery configuration at the core of temporalization. With regard to static constitution, we of course recover the retention–protention axis. Again, these are asymmetrical, since retentions recede into past, but the protentional fringe is an open horizon of anticipation. Thus we again find that the centre–periphery structure does not provide all the necessary distinctions, since the fringes as they move away from centre, become qualitatively different. As to genetic constitution, the fringe re-appears in the preconscious, affective substrate (permanence) on one direction, and the conscious, embodied ego, aware of emotional change on the other (change).

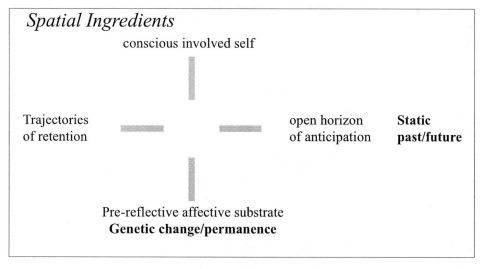

Spatial Ingredients

conscious involved self

| Trajectories of retention | | open horizon of anticipation | **Static past/future** |

Pre-reflective affective substrate
Genetic change/permanence

We thus arrive at ingredients that come in *two sets of four*, a suggestive fourfold. The centre/periphery configurations are analogous in the spatial and dynamical schemes, since they underscore the paradoxical nature of past in the present, and of change within permanence that puzzled Husserl (and many others) throughout his work. These pairs are the wooden irons of the figure of time, which appear here under a new, non-paradoxical light.

Fundamentally, the added insight comes from the fact that the component ingredients have a *generic* link between them, an internal interdependence that has been explored throughout this paper. In other words, the new figures of time are not only graphical combinations of items, but they display effective links, which are not only descriptive. Phenomenologically, I have stressed the full *interdependence* of both intentionalities, the inseparability of the static and genetic analysis, and the mutual determination of instinctive and cognitive constitution of self. In parallel, trajectories and the landscape of their phase space are a unity in a complex nonlinear system.

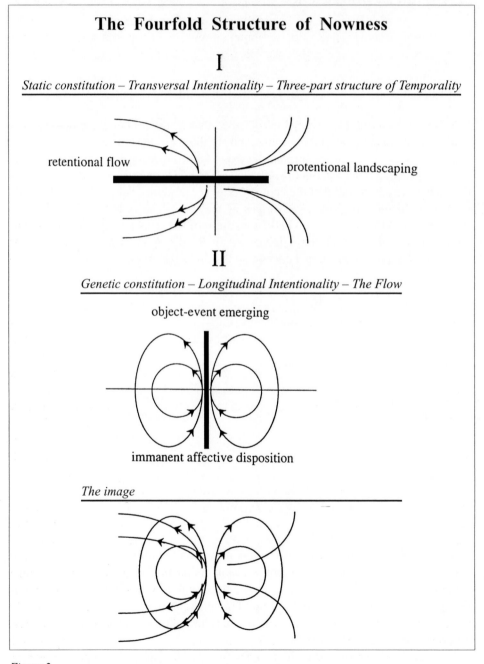

Figure 2.
The new figures of time resulting from the neurophenomenological analysis presented here. For explanations see Section VIII.

Correspondingly, we have examined the many aspects under which determinism, trajectories, regions in phase space, adaptive geometrical landscapes are complementary. I consider these mutual interdependencies and their role in the constitution of temporality the most immediate insight that naturalization can provide.

With these elements in position, the figure of time, as I said, falls naturally into place. Figure 2 places these ingredients in relation to each other, in regards to both the role of dynamics and space, and the circular causality for the longitudinal but not for the transversal intentionality. Since the order parameters for protention do not influence retroactively the system's history, we arrive at an asymmetrical four-fold figure of time.

IX: Coda — The Triple-braid of Neurophenomenology

We are now in a position to stand back and reconsider our analysis of temporality. Has neurophenomenology passed the acid test? Let us return to the neurophenomenological research programme: the circulation between the external and the experiential. In Varela (1996) the neurophenomenological working hypothesis was stated as follows:

Phenomenological accounts of the structure of experience and their counter parts in cognitive science relate to each through reciprocal constraints.

On the one hand, we are concerned with a process of external emergence with well-defined neurobiological attributes; on the other, with a phenomenological description, which stays close to our lived experience. The nature of the circulation one seeks is no less that of *mutual constraints* between both accounts, including both the potential bridges and contradictions between them. What is the specific nature of the passages between these two accounts in the case at hand? What have we learned in the specific case of immediate temporality?

One thing is clear: the specific nature of the mutual constraints is far from a simple empirical correspondence or a categorical isomorphism. Three ingredients have turned out to play an equally important role: (1) the neuro-biological basis, (2) the formal descriptive tools mostly derived from nonlinear dynamics, and (3) the nature of lived temporal experience studied under reduction. What needs to be examined carefully is the way in which this triple-braid, these three ingredients are *braided together in a constitutive manner* (see Varela, 1997 for more on this non-isomorphic neurophenomenology). What we find is much more than a juxtaposition of items side by side. It is an *active* link, where effects of constraint and modification can circulate effectively, modifying both partners in a fruitful complementarity. I believe that this triple-braided analysis of temporal consciousness has introduced a substantial novelty, which both renews the phenomenological analysis beyond its traditional descriptive tools, and at the same time links the neurobiological to the phenomenal realm in an explicit manner.

First, it allowed us to solve the cognitive paradox since in its current point in time a dynamical system has no 'representation' of its past. But the past acts into the present in a causality that is best described as 'invisible' or 'subtle' since it can only be revealed by geometric reconstructions from raw data. In that sense the name retention introduced by Husserl, as well as 'slippage', are adequate descriptive terms that acquire here a fuller sense. The present state wouldn't be what it is except for its past, but the past is not actually present (it is a nonlinear causality) and it is not represented, so no cognitive paradox.

Second, we have also seen that the present account solves the constitutional paradox of temporality, a dimension of temporality which has received much less attention. This is the disposition for action that appears in temporality in the affective
dimension. This dimension is novel because it is not only the retentional-presence,
but also the sedimented dispositions of a living being. Thus these disposition go into a
larger temporality of their history and situatedness, they are pre-noetic to use again
the apt description provided recently by Gallagher (1998). So the dynamical model is
not only relevant to static, retentional time but also that of constitutional layering of
the past. Here again the dynamical link between phenomenal and empirical data is
crucial for it offers the complementary dimensions of order parameter determining
trajectories, as well as the bootstrapping effect of action modifying the dynamical
landscape itself, hence no constitutional paradox. If the dynamical model arguably
provides a naturalization bridge to the internal relations among the temporal phases
of mental acts, the constitutional relations are in fact richer than what can be captured
by Husserl's notion of retention.

Clearly there is much to be done to transform dynamical tools into precise concepts
for cognitive neuroscience, and to make more precise the triple-braids for temporality
and other important phenomenological dimensions (such as space and intersubjectivity). But at least it can be said that the neurophenomenological research programme
emerges from this study beyond a hopeful declaration, as an open road for exploration.

Acknowledgments
Amy Cohen-Varela, Shaun Gallagher, Natalie Depraz, Jean Petitot, Evan Thompson
and Pierre Vermersch gave me many hours of essential exchange and encouragement.
The work carried on with my Neurodynamics research group at LENA has provided
me much of the empirical substrate for this discussion; I am specially grateful to Jacques Martinerie, Jean-Philippe Lachaux and Michel Le Van Quyen. To all of these
friends my heartfelt thanks; I am fully responsible for the remaining errors and short-
comings.

References

Arbib, M.A. (1995), *Handbook of Brain Theory and Neural Networks* (Cambridge, MA: MIT Press).
Amitt, D. (1991), *Attractor Neural Networks* (Cambridge: Cambridge University Press).
Artuso, R., Aurell, E. and Cvitanovic, P. (1990), 'Recycling of strange sets. I. Cycle expansions',
    Nonlinearity, **3**, pp. 325–59.
Auerbach, D., Cvitanovic, P., Eckmann, J.P., Gunaratne, G. and Procaccia, I. (1987), 'Exploring
    chaotic motion through periodic orbits', *Phys. Rev. Lett.*, **58**.
Bernet, R. (1985), *Texte zur Phänomenologie des Inneren Zeitbewusstseins: Texte nach
    Husserliana X,* (Hamburg: Felix Meiner).
Bernet, R. (1994), *La Vie du Sujet* (Paris: Presses Universitaire de France).
Besnier, B. (1994), 'Remarques sur les *Leçons sur la Conscience Intime du Temps* de Husserl', *Alter*
    No. 1, pp. 319–56.
Brand, G. (1955), *Welt, Ich und Zeit* (The Hague: M. Nijhoff).
Brough, J. (1989), 'Husserl's phenomenology of time consciousness', in *Husserl's
    Phenomenology: A textbook*, ed. J.N. Mohanty and W.R.McKenna (Washington, DC: Univ. Press
    of America).
Bruzina, R. (1993), 'The revision of the Bernau time-consciousness manuscripts: Status questionis
    — Freiburg 1928–1930', *Alter* No.1, pp. 357–83.
Bruzina, R. (1994), 'The revision of the Bernau time-consciosuness manuscripts: New questions —
    1930–1933, *Alter* No.2, pp. 367–95.

Church, R.M. and Broadbent, H. (1990), 'Alternative representation of time, number and rate', *Cognition*, **37**, pp. 55–81.

Damasio, A. (1994), *Descartes' Error* (New York: Grossman-Putnam).

Deecke, L., Scheid, P. and Kornhuber, H. (1969), 'Distribution of readiness potentials preceding voluntary finger movements', *Exp.Brain. Res.*, **7**, pp. 158–68.

Dennett, D. and Kinsbourne, M. (1991), 'Time and the observer: The where and when of time in the brain', *Beh.Brain Sciences*, **15**, pp. 183–247.

Depraz, N. (1992), 'Les figures de l'intersubjectivité. Etudes de Husserliana XIII-XV', *Arch.Philosophie*, **55**, pp. 479–98.

Depraz, N. (1994), 'Temporalité et affection dans les manuscrits tardifs sur la temporalité (1929-1935) de Husserl', *Alter* No.2, pp. 63–86.

Depraz, N. (1995), *Incarnation et Transcendence* (Paris: J.Vrin).

Depraz, N. (1996), 'Qu'est-ce que la *hylè* transcendentale?', *Analecta Husserliana*, **50**, pp. 115–23.

Depraz, N. (1998), 'Can I anticipate myself?', in *Consciousness and Temporality*, ed. D. Zahavi (Dordrecht: Kluwer; in press).

der Waals, F. (1995), *Good Natured* (Cambridge, MA: Harvard University Press).

Ekman, P. and Davidson, R. (ed. 1994), *The Structure of Emotions* (New York: OUP).

Gallagher, S. (1979), 'Suggestions towards a revision of Husserl's Phenomenology of time-consciousness', *Man and World*, **12**, pp. 445–64.

Gallagher, S. (1997), 'Mutual enlightenment: Recent phenomenology and cognitive science', *Journal of Consciousness Studies* **4** (3), pp. 195–214.

Gallagher, S. (1998), *The Inordinance of Time* (Evanston, IL: Northwestern University Press).

Glass, L. and Mackey, M.C. (1988), *From Clocks to Chaos* (Princeton: Princeton University Press).

Granel, G. (1968), *Le Sens du Temps et de la Perception chez E.Husserl* (Paris: Gallimard).

Gurwitsch, A. (1966), *Studies in Phenomenology and Psychology* (Evanston, IL: Northwestern University Press).

Held, K. (1966), *Lebendige Gegenwart* (The Hague: M.Nijhoff).

Heidegger, M. (1928/67), *Sein und Zeit* (Hamburg: Max Niemeyer).

Husserl, E. (1964), *The Phenomenology of Internal Time Consciousness*, trans. James S. Churchill (Bloomington, IN: Indiana University Press).

Husserl, E. (1966), *Zur Phänomenologie des Inneren Zeitbewusstseins (1893-1917), Husserliana X*, ed. R. Bohm (The Hague: M. Nijhoff).

Ihde, D. (1977), *Experimental Phenomenology: An Introduction* (New York: Putnam & Sons).

James, W. (1898/1988), *Principles of Psychology*, 2 vols. (New York: Dover).

Kelso, J.A.S. (1995), *Dynamic Patterns: The self-organization of brain and behavior* (Cambridge, MA: MIT Press).

Kelso, J.A.S., Case, P., Holroyd, T., Horvath, E., Raczaszek, E., Tuller, E. and Ding, M. (1994), 'Multistability and metastability in perceptual and brain dynamics', in *Multistability in Cognition*, ed. M. Staedler and P. Kruse (Berlin: Springer Series on Synergetics).

Kerby, A.P. (1991), *Narrative and the Self* (Bloomington, IN: Indiana University Press).

Ladraux, J.P., Rodriguez, E., Martinerie, J., Adam, C., Harbour, D. and Varela, F. (1998), 'Gamma baud activity in human intracortical recordings triggered by cognitive tests', *Journal of Neuroscience* (forthcoming).

Larrabee, M. (1994), 'Inside time-consciousness: Diagramming the flux', *Husserl Studies*, **10**, pp. 181–210.

Leopold, D. and Logothetis, N. (1996), 'Activity changes in early visual cortex reflect monkey's percepts during binocular rivalry', *Nature*, **379**, pp. 549–53.

Le Van Quyen, M., Schuster, H. and Varela, F. (1996), 'Fast rhythms can emerge from slow neuronal oscillators', *Int.J.Bifurcation Chaos*, **6**, pp. 1807–16.

Le Van Quyen, M., Martinerie, J., Adam, C., Lachaux, J-Ph., Baulac, M. Renault, B. and Varela, F. (1997a), 'Temporal patterns in human epileptic activity are modulated by perceptual discriminations', *Neuroreport*, **8**, pp. 1703–10.

Le Van Quyen, M., Martinerie, J., Adam, C., Schuster, H. and Varela, F. (1997b), 'Unstable periodic orbits in human epileptic acivity', *Physica E*, **56**, pp. 3401–11.

Levinas, E. (1988), *En découvrant l'existence avec Husserl et Heidegger* (Paris: J. Vrin).

Llinás, R. (1988), 'The intrinsic electrophysiological properties of mammalian neurons', *Science*, **242**, pp. 1654–64.

Lorenz, K. (1972), *Gesammelte Abhandlungen*, 2 vols (Münich: Piper Verlag).

Mackey, D. and Glass, L. (1988), *From Clocks to Chaos* (Princeton: Princenton University Press).

McInerney, P. (1991), *Time and Experience* (Philadelpia: Temple University Press).

Merleau-Ponty, M. (1945), *Phénomenologie de la Perception* (Paris: Gallimard).

Merleau-Ponty, M. (1964), *Le Visible et l'Invisible* (Paris: Gallimard).

Miskiewicz, W. (1985), *La Phénoménologie du Temps chez Husserl*, Ph.D. Thesis, University of Paris Sorbonne.

Miller, I. (1984), *Husserl, Perception and Temporal Awareness* (Cambridge, MA: MIT Press).

Mirollo, R. and Strogartz, S. (1990), 'Synchronisation of pulse-coupled biological oscillators SIAM', *J.Appl.Math.*, **50**, pp. 1645–62.

Nuñez, A., Amzica, F., Steriade, M. (1993), 'Electrophysiology of cat association cortical cells in vivo: intrinsic properties and synaptic responses', *J. Neurophysiol.*, **70**, pp. 418–30.

Ott, E., Sauer, T. and Yorke, J. (Ed. 1993), *Coping with Chaos*(New York: Wiley).

Petitot, J. (1992), *Physique du Sens* (Paris: Editions du CNRS).

Petitot, J., Varela, F., Pachoud, B. and Roy, J.M. (ed. 1999), *Naturalizing Phenomenology: Contemporary Issues in Phenomenology and Cognitive Science* (Stanford University Press; in press).

Pöppel, E. (1988), *Mindworks: Time and conscious experience* (Boston, MA: Harcourt Brace Jovanovich).

Pöppel, E. and Schill, K. (1995), 'Time perception: Problems of representation and processing', in *Handbook of Brain Theory and Neural Networks*, ed. M.A.Arbib (Cambridge, MA: MIT Press).

Port, R. and van Gelder, T. (1995), *Mind as Motion: Explorations in the Dynamics of Cognition* (Cambridge, MA: MIT Press).

Rorty, E. (ed. 1980), *Explaining Emotions* (Berkeley, CA: University of California Press).

Rugg, M. (1995), 'Event-related potential studies of human memory', in *The Cognitive Neurosciences*, ed. M. Gazzaniga (Cambridge, MA: MIT Press).

Singer, W. (1993), 'Synchronization of cortical activity and its putative role in information processing and learning', *Ann. Rev. Physiol.*, **55**, pp. 349–74.

Thompson, E. and Varela, F. (1999), *Why the Mind is not in the Head* (Cambridge, MA: Harvard University Press; forthcoming).

Traub, R.D., Whittington, M., I.Stanford, I. and Jeffreys, J. (1996), 'A mechanism for generation of long-range synchronous fast oscillations in the cortex', *Nature*, **383**, pp. 621–4.

van Gelder, T. (1999), 'Wooden iron: contemporary cognitive science meets Husserlian phenomenology', in Petitot *et al.* (1999).

Varela,F., Toro, A., John, E.R. and Schwartz, E. (1981), 'Perceptual framing and cortical alpha rhythms', *Neuropsychologia*, **19**, pp. 675–86.

Varela, F. (1979/1995), *Invitation aux Sciences Cognitives* (Paris: Seuil).

Varela, F. (1995), 'Resonant cell assemblies: A new approach to cognitive functioning and neuronal synchrony', *Biol.Research*, **28**, pp. 81–95.

Varela, F. (1996), 'Neurophenomenology: A methodological remedy for the hard problem', *Journal of Consciousness Studies*, **3** (4), pp. 330–50.

Varela, F. (1997), 'The naturalization of phenomenology as the transcendence of nature: Searching for generative mutual constraints', *Alter: Revue de Phénoménologie*, **5**, pp. 355–85.

Varela, F., Thompson, E. and Rosch, E. (1991), *The Embodied Mind: Cognitive Science and Human Experience* (Cambridge, MA: MIT Press).

Winfree, A. (1980), *The Geometry of Biological Time* (New York: Springer Verlag).

Zahavi, D. (1994), 'Husserl's phenomenology of the body', *Etudes Phénoménologiques* No.19, pp. 63–84.

Andrew R. Bailey

Beyond the Fringe:

William James on the Transitional Parts of the Stream of Consciousness

One of the aspects of consciousness deserving of study is what might be called its subjective unity — the way in which, though conscious experience moves from object to object, and can be said to have distinct 'states', it nevertheless in some sense apparently forms a singular flux divided only by periods of unconsciousness. The work of William James provides a valuable, and rather unique, source of analysis of this feature of consciousness; however, in my opinion, this component of James' theory of the mind has so far gone under-emphasized in the scholarly literature. This paper undertakes some philosophical geography, trying to draw out and elucidate some of the relevant ideas from James' corpus, and also subjects those ideas to some analysis to try and assist in judgements of their current importance.

> Like a bird's life, [the stream of consciousness] seems to be made [up]
> of an alternation of flights and perchings.
>
> (William James, *Principles of Psychology*, p. 243)

This rather well known metaphor lucidly captures a rather neglected, but very significant, aspect of William James' account of phenomenal consciousness: his distinction between substantive states of consciousness and the transitive ones which intervene temporally between them. James insists that though consciousness is a flux, it is also differentiated: the bird's life is a seamless unity, but it also contains two different kinds of activity, flying and perching.

However, as James himself presciently noted (1890, pp. 243 ff.), we tend to concentrate our attention — both phenomenological and theoretical — upon our substantive mental states.[1] And so it has come to pass that, in the scholarly literature

Correspondence: Andrew R. Bailey, Department of Philosophy, The University of Calgary, Calgary, Alberta T2N 1N4, Canada.

---

[1] Ralph Barton Perry, James' student and first and perhaps best commentator, phrased it thus: 'The practically habituated mind flies from perch to perch, and is aware of the perch rather than of the passage.' (1938, p. 81.)

Journal of Consciousness Studies, **6**, No. 2–3, 1999, pp. 141–153

on James, interest in the transitional parts of the stream of consciousness, or in their distinction from substantive synchronic mental states, has been sparse. Such as it is, it has tended to come from those working within the framework of traditional Continental phenomenology,[2] such as Alfred Schuetz (1941), Aron Gurwitsch (1943), and Bruce Wilshire (1968). Partly for this reason, perhaps, interest in the transitive parts has not yet found its way into contemporary philosophical debates on the problem of consciousness, and in particular not into the emerging new interdisciplinary field of 'consciousness studies', even for those most influenced by the work of William James. Thus, for example, thinkers like W.E. Cooper (1990) and Owen Flanagan (1991) generally place almost no emphasis on the transitive parts. Tim Shallice (1988, heavily influenced by James here) enumerates what he calls the two 'structural' properties of consciousness — being sensibly continuous, and being divided into foreground and background — but takes the first property as being more or less just obvious, by contrast with the second to which he devotes several pages. David Galin (1996), likewise, takes James to be an important thinker on the flow of consciousness, and inveighs against a lack of interest in James' notions of the fringe and the nucleus, but he tacitly treats the fringe as a synchronic phenomenon, and never mentions its connection with the transitive parts of the stream of consciousness.

Another part of the reason for this lack of attention to the transitive parts is perhaps the status that has been accorded James' other description of consciousness as a stream or river, which has been called the 'master metaphor' in his account (Flanagan, 1992, p. 155).

> Consciousness, then, does not appear to itself chopped up in bits. Such words as 'chain' and 'train' do not describe it fitly as it presents itself in the first instance. It is nothing jointed; it flows. A 'river' or a 'stream' are the metaphors by which it is most naturally described (James, 1890, p. 239).

But over-attention to this passage has tended to elide the other Jamesian notion of the passage of phenomenal consciousness *as* being nevertheless, in a sense, jointed or variegated. The *contents* of the flow of consciousness

> ... are discrete and discontinuous; they do pass before us in a train or chain.... But their comings and goings and contrasts no more break the flow of the thought that thinks them than they break the time and space in which they lie.... The transition between the thought of one object and the thought of another is no more a break in the *thought* than a joint in the bamboo is a break in the wood (1890, p. 240).

In other words, the contents of thought — the substantive parts — are not in fact a stream, in James' sense; they *were* correctly described by James' psychologist predecessors as a 'chain', a differentiated 'sequence of differents'.[3] What makes consciousness akin to a stream is the embedding of these thoughts into *transitional* parts—conscious activity that intervenes without break between one thought and the next. Conscious awareness, then, is really more accurately described as a bird's life or

---

[2] Perhaps this circumstance would not have pleased James, who apparently took some pleasure in deflating the 'unspeakable Meinong'; that 'humbug' Wundt; Kant, whom he called a 'mere curio'; and the 'sour grapes' of his nemesis Hegel; and who completely ignored the publication of Husserl's *Logische Untersuchungen* in 1901, despite Husserl's idolisation of his own *Principles of Psychology* and probably despite the urgings of James' close friend Carl Stumpf — indeed James was even influential in preventing its publication in translation in America until the second half of this century.

[3] Shadworth Hodgson, *The Philosophy of Reflection*, cited by James in *Principles*, p. 230.

bamboo pole than a flowing river; the dominance of the stream metaphor is apt to allow us to lose sight of this.

In this paper I will critically examine James' notion of the transitive parts of the stream of consciousness, and make some suggestions about the contemporary philosophical importance of this concept. My aim is to do two things: to show it is a more problematic notion than has usually been realized, but to suggest that it is also a more important and fruitful idea than it is usually given credit for in contemporary philosophy of mind.

The Unity of Consciousness

I need first to briefly outline some of the main points of James' view of the stream of consciousness: partly in order to place James' theory of the transitive parts into some sort of context, but also because some of these points become very important in deciding exactly what James must mean by transitive parts. James begins by noting the following:

> Naming our thought by its own objects, we almost all of us assume that as the objects are, so the thought must be.... As each object may come and go, be forgotten and then thought of again, it is held that the thought of it has precisely similar independence, self-identity, and mobility (1890, p. 196).

However, he suggests, we are misled by such considerations. In fact, James holds, there are five, and only five, facts we can introspectively discover about consciousness:

(1) 'Every thought tends to be part of a personal consciousness';
(2) 'Within each personal consciousness thought is always changing';
(3) 'Within each personal consciousness thought is sensibly continuous';
(4) 'It always appears to deal with objects independent of itself';
(5) 'It is interested in some parts of these objects to the exclusion of others, and welcomes or rejects — *chooses* from among them, in a word — all the while.' (1890, p. 225)

The aspect that interests us here is that thought is *sensibly continuous*. 'Consciousness . . . does not appear to itself chopped up in bits' (1890, p. 239; 1892, p. 145). In what does this continuity consist? What more can we say about it? We can distinguish between five different ways in which consciousness is a unity, rather than chopped up.

i. The non-complexity of mental states

Mental feelings are not compound: we should not confuse 'the combining of objects for that of feelings' (1890, p. 158n). The taste of lemonade, for example, does not combine the tastes of sugar and lemon; rather the *physical object* combines lemon and sugar, and the resulting taste *resembles* both. 'A higher state is not a lot of lower states; it is itself' (1890, p. 162n). Rather, James, suggests, any 'units' of sense data (as discrete tones combining to form a chord) are integrated below the level of consciousness: 'the [resulting idea] is itself an immediate psychic fact and bears an immediate relation to the neural state which is its unconditional accompaniment' (1890, p. 157).

What is combined, James says, is the nerve processes in the brain, and not anything 'mental' (1890, pp. 150–158). Furthermore, all combinations (in this sense), logically speaking, are the effects of their various causes, and not the set of those causes themselves. For example, water consists in the combination H_2O, but all this means is that those constituent atoms, arranged in a certain way (H–O–H) have certain effects upon external media such as our sense organs and various reagents (1890, p. 159). The atoms do not combine in any more substantive way than this: they do not cease to be themselves and blend and become 'one.' In summary: combinations involve distinct units operating upon some external body or medium to produce an 'atomic' effect within that medium. So, even if it were the case that separate ideas could 'combine' to form new ones, '. . . the compounded idea is an altogether new psychic fact to which the separate ideas stand in the relation, not of constituents, but of occasions of production' (1890, p. 161).

(In 'The knowing of things together' James modifies this doctrine somewhat. In this later article, he admits that there is a sense in which mental states may be called complex, just as their objects are — but still *not* because their parts are separable, and certainly not because their parts have an existence more fundamental or long-lived than the complex ideas of which they are a part [1895, p. 81].)

ii. Temporal connectedness

> . . . [E]ven where there is a time-gap [as in sleep or unconsciousness] the consciousness after it feels as if it belonged together with the consciousness before it, as another part of the same self (1890, p. 237; 1892, p. 145).

Thus consciousness is continuous in the sense of 'the parts being inwardly connected and belonging together because they are parts of a common whole' (1890, p. 238). As James memorably puts it: if two people wake up in the same bed, there is no risk of them getting confused about which past stream of thought is connected with which person. 'Peter's present instantly finds out Peter's past, and never by mistake knits to that of Paul' (1890, p. 238). Even if Peter were to have detailed knowledge of Paul's 'last drowsy states of mind . . . as he sank into sleep,' there would be no danger of confusion. His knowledge of Paul's states is of a very different character from that of his own: he remembers his own, but only conceives of Paul's, and the object of remembrance is 'suffused with a warmth and intimacy' that makes it *ours* (1890, p. 239; 1892, p. 145).

iii. Associational connectedness

'The changes from one moment to another in the quality [or, roughly, content] of the consciousness are never absolutely abrupt' (1890, p. 237; 1892, p. 145). There are no breaks in thought produced by sudden contrasts of the 'quality' of the successive segments, 'so abrupt that the segment that followed had no connection whatever with the one that went before' (1890, p. 237). Transitions are *part* of consciousness just as the joint in bamboo is part of the wood.

There is always, James says, some affinity between any two apparently contrasting, juxtaposed thoughts. 'What we hear when the thunder crashes is not thunder *pure*, but thunder-breaking-upon-silence-and-contrasting-with-it' (1890, p. 240). It follows from this, then, that thoughts cannot be identified simply with the object of their attention: at any one time, our thought includes consciousness of:

1. some of what has just passed, 'things known a moment ago more clearly'.
2. some of what is to come, 'things to be known more clearly a moment hence'.

3. some awareness of present conditions, such as 'our bodily position, attitude, condition' and/or 'that peculiar warmth and intimacy that make [thoughts] come as ours' (1890, pp. 241–2).[4]

Among other things, this gives consciousness its sense 'of the *whence* and the *whither* that always accompanies its flows' (1890, p. 242).

iv. The transitive parts

Now we come to the transitive parts themselves. When we introspect we are aware, James asserts, of passages or transitions between our more stable thoughts. In lieu of interpretation for the moment, let me quote James wholesale:

> As we take, in fact, a general view of the wonderful stream of our consciousness, what strikes us first is this different pace of its parts. Like a bird's life, it seems to be made of an alternation of flights and perchings…. The resting-places are usually occupied by sensorial imaginations of some sort, whose peculiarity is that they can be held before the mind for an indefinite time, and contemplated without changing; the places of flight are filled with thoughts of relations, static or dynamic, that for the most part obtain between the matters contemplated in the periods of comparative rest.
>   Let us call the resting-places the 'substantive parts,' and the places of flight the 'transitive parts,' of the stream of consciousness. It then appears that the main end of our thinking is at all times the attainment of some other substantive part than the one from which we have just been dislodged. And we may say that the main use of the transitive parts is to lead us from one substantive conclusion to another (1890, pp. 243; 1892, pp. 146).

It is hard to introspect the transitive parts for what they are, James says: to focus on them is to annihilate them. They necessarily cease, thereby, to be flights to a conclusion, and become substantive things themselves. Nor can they be studied by moving to a conclusion and then looking back, James claims: 'if we wait till the conclusion *be* reached, it so exceeds them in vigor and stability that it quite eclipses and swallows them up in its glare' (1890, pp. 244–5; 1892, p. 147). So to ask the proponent of transitive parts to *produce* them is unfair, just as it was unfair of Zeno and his camp to demand of the advocates of motion to produce the place an arrow *is* when it moves (1890, p. 244; 1892, p. 147). We must therefore beware of emphasizing the substantive elements unduly—for example, ignoring the transitive feeling between silence and thunder, 'and of treating their boundary as a sort of break in the mind' (1890, p. 244). James suggests that to ignore transitive elements is to treat breaks between substantive parts as breaks in the mind (1890, p. 244).

James notes that both the 'Sensationalists' and the 'Intellectualists' deny transitive parts because they are 'equally unable to point to any distinct substantive feelings in which they were known' (1890, pp. 244–5; 1892, p. 148). But, James insists, we *do* have feelings which correspond to the relations between things: '*so surely as relations between objects exist* in rerum naturâ, *so surely, and more surely, do feelings exist to which these relations are known*' (1890, p. 245; 1892, p. 148). We should admit to feelings of *and* and *if* and *by* just as readily as *blue* and *cold*, James asserts (1890, pp. 245–6; 1892, p. 148).[5]

---

[4] This phenomenon, James says, is paralleled in brain activity: any nervous state of the brain co-exists with, and is affected by, the dying vibrations of the previous states and the waxing excitement of incipient processes.

[5] Consider, again, the brain: it is in a continual process of rearrangement. 'And if a lingering rearrangement brings with it one kind of consciousness, why should not a swift rearrangement bring

v. The fringes

There are also *other* 'unnamed states or qualities of states' that, James claims, are also important and unrecognized: the 'fringes' of consciousness (1892, p. 149). These feelings denote relations, tendencies, connections, expectancies. For example:

(a) 'Hark!' brings about an attitude of expectancy — 'a sense of the direction from which an impression is about to come' (1890, pp. 250–1; 1892, p. 149). And this sense differs from that conjured by other words, such as 'Look!' or 'Wait!'

(b) The effort of trying to recall a forgotten name involves a gap in our consciousness, but one where 'a sort of wraith of the name is in it, beckoning us in a given direction,' and immediately rejecting wrong names (1890, p. 251; 1892, p. 149). And this 'gap' is different for different words: they have different 'shapes,' mould themselves to different possible sounds or rhythms — e.g. they reject different candidates. This difference, James asserts, is one of feeling. They are the feelings of different absences, not the absence of feeling (1890, pp. 252–3; 1892, p. 149).

(c) Experiences sometimes can be 'recognized as familiar, as having been enjoyed before, though we cannot name it or say where or when' (1890, p. 252). The only name we have for this is 'sense of familiarity'.

(d) Words and phrases denoting relations — such as 'but', 'either one or the other', 'although it is, nevertheless' — have a 'felt meaning' which is more than simply their sound: it is not true that, as we read them, 'there is nothing more in our minds than the words themselves as they pass' (1890, p. 252). The same is true of all the other parts of speech that are nothing but 'signs of direction' in thought, such as 'who?', 'when?', 'no' or 'not yet'.

(e) The intention to say (or perhaps think) *x*. 'One may admit that a good third of our psychic life consists in these rapid premonitory perspective views of schemes of thought not yet articulate' (1890, p. 253).

Consciousness, then, has a field of view — a horizon: 'this permanent consciousness of whither our thought is going' (1890, p. 255) These feelings are not sensorial images, however,[6] and they are a very important part of our stream of thought.[7]

> Let us use the words *psychic overtone, suffusion*, or *fringe*, to designate the influence of a faint brain-process upon our thought, as it makes us aware of relations or objects but dimly perceived (1890, p. 258).

---

another kind of consciousness as peculiar as the rearrangement itself?' (1890, p. 246; 1892, p. 149). However, 'as the brain-changes are continuous, so do all these consciousnesses melt into each other like dissolving views. Properly they are but one protracted consciousness, one unbroken stream' (1890, pp. 247–8).

[6] 'Sensorial images are stable psychic facts; we can hold them still and look at them as long as we like. These bare images of logical movement, on the contrary, are psychic transitions, always on the wing, so to speak, and not to be glimpsed except in flight' (1890, p. 253).

[7] 'Every definite image in the mind is steeped and dyed in . . . the sense of its relations, near and remote, the dying echo of whence it came to us, the dawning sense of whither it is to lead. The significance, the value, of the image is all in this halo or penumbra that surrounds and escorts it — or rather that is fused into one with it and has become bone of its bone and flesh of its flesh; leaving it, it is true, an image of the same *thing* it was before, but making it an image of that thing newly taken and freshly understood' (1890, p. 255; 1892, p. 151).

The Transitive Parts

Our concern here is the transitive parts. But what exactly are they supposed to be? And are they consistent with the rest of what James says about the stream of thought? Despite the somewhat cavalier way the temporal unity of consciousness can sometimes be treated in the modern literature, these things are not, on the face of it, fully clear. There are two major issues here: the way in which a unitary flux can also be partitioned; and the problem of making consistent James' claims about the transitions in consciousness.

The partitioning of consciousness

James says, often and at length, that the stream of consciousness is a flux — that it does not come divided into parts. How then can it come divided into transitive and substantive parts?

> Consciousness, as a process in time, offers the paradoxes which have been found in all continuous change. There are no 'states' in such a thing, any more than there are facets in a circle, or places where an arrow 'is' when it flies. ... [T]he *actual* present is only the joint between the past and future and has no breadth of its own. Where everything is change and process, how can we talk of 'state'? (1892, pp. 399–400)

The solution must be to read on to James the following position: that the flux of consciousness comes undivided,[8] but that *we* individuate 'states' within it, after the fact. James mentions that the way we tend to do this is by identifying ideas by their objects (1890, p. 196). This *seems* fairly straightforward for mental imagery—these mental states are to be individuated along the same lines as the things they are images of.[9] But what of the transitive parts? Do they have objects with which to be identified? James thinks so—in the shape of *relations*. James believes in the empirical reality of relations, conjunctive as well as disjunctive.

> Every examiner of the sensible life *in concreto* must see that relations of every sort, of time, space, difference, likeness, change, rate, cause, or what not, are just as integral members of the sensational flux as terms are, and that conjunctive relations are just as true members of the flux as disjunctive relations are. (1909, p. 293)

However, the members of the *fringes* also seem to be identified in exactly the same way: as being felt but non-imagistic relations. What, then, differentiates the fringes from the transitive parts?

The issue of transition

The problem here is the following: are there, consistently with James' writings, temporal intervals *between* substantive thoughts, which are filled up with transitive parts? Or, to put it another way, what is to prevent transitive parts from simply collapsing into the 'temporal' aspects of substantive parts—that is, what holds the fringes and the transitive parts apart?[10]

---

[8] 'The concrete pulses of experience appear pent in by no such definite limits as our conceptual substitutes for them are confined by. They run into each other continuously and seem to interpenetrate. What in them is relation and what is matter is hard to discern.' (1909, p. 294)

[9] Although, since both mental and physical are for James but two aspects of the reality of 'pure experience,' there seems no reason to assume that 'the physical world' comes divided itself (in order to act as a kind of template for the cutting up of the mental).

[10] 'Between all [the substantive elements of thought] there is 'transitive' consciousness, and the words and images are 'fringed,' and not as discrete as to a careless view they seem' (1890, p. 271).

James provides an analysis of what passes through our mind when we utter the phrase *the pack of cards is on the table* (1890, pp. 278–83). He rejects the notion that this time-slice can be divided up such that, at one point, we have only the thought *the pack* and at a somewhat later time only the thought *the table*. His claim is as follows:

> I say of these time-parts that we cannot take any one of them so short that it will not after some fashion or other be a thought of the whole object 'the pack of cards is on the table.' They melt into each other like dissolving views, and no two of them feel the object just alike, but each feels the total object in a unitary undivided way (1890, p. 279).

Rather, what happens is that parts of the thought are to the fore at certain times — certain objects will be 'more emphatically present to the mind' (1890, p. 280).

All this seems in conflict with the notion of transitive parts: there is no part of such a thought which is separable from the substantive part of the thought, and which can be identified with a relation. The relation expressed by 'on' in this sentence, for example, is, at every time slice, all wrapped up with the rest of the thought.

> The tiniest feeling that we can possibly have comes with an earlier and a later part and with a sense of their continuous progression (1909, p. 294).

Further, James explicitly asserts that transitive parts are *not* to be seen as some kind of connective tissue between separated substantial parts. They are not 'some sort of psychic material by which sensations, in themselves separate, are made to cohere together' (1890, p. 258n).

Possible readings

What are we to do here? How, specifically, are we to understand the transitive parts? I think there are at least three interpretative possibilities:

(a) *Content/object*: we could rely on the difference between the objects of these different kinds of thought. Thus, the distinction to be made between imagistic and non-imagistic types of thought is reasonably clear; perhaps we can find a similar distinction *within* the domain of non-imagistic thought to divide up transitive parts and fringes.

(b) *Stability*: we could place great weight on James' comment that some kinds of thought 'can be held before the mind for an indefinite time, and contemplated without changing' whereas the transitive parts cannot (1890, p. 243; 1892, p. 146).[11]

(c) *Speed*: we could seize upon James' comments to the effect that transitive parts 'obtain between the matters contemplated in the periods of comparative rest' and that the distinction is based upon 'this different pace of [the] parts' of the stream of consciousness (1890, p. 243; 1892, p. 146).

My view is that the last is the most plausible — the least bad of a set of rather unsatisfactory alternatives. The first seems to hold out little prospect of uniquely identifying transitive parts within James' account of the stream of thought: it seems to irremediably blur the distinction with the fringes *qua* elements of the unities which are the substantive parts. For example, both the fringes and the transitive parts,

---

[11] Schuetz, for example, appears to uncritically hold that substantive parts differ from transitive parts just in that the former 'can be held before the mind for an indefinite time,' while the transitive parts are 'thoughts of relations, static or dynamic, between the substantive parts' (1941 p. 448).

according to James, include feelings of relations of continuity and connection of a temporal and logical sort — 'the dying echo of whence it came to us, the dawning sense of whither it is to lead' (1890, p. 258).

The second also appears unable to bear the weight of interpretation. Is it, for example, true that we *cannot* 'hold the concept of a relation before the mind indefinitely' — have not philosophers been able to do so at least long enough to write a weighty tome on, for example, the 'or' relation? Surely what James means to say here is that *when we do so* the relation ceases to be a transitive part and becomes a substantive part. And, again, the prospects of using this criterion to differentiate fringes and transitive parts seem bleak.

So we are left with the third possibility: transitive parts are precisely those phases of consciousness that we move through rapidly and more or less imagelessly in order to arrive at a substantive 'conclusion'. Thus, in contradistinction from the fringes, they are fast-moving *segments of subjective time* rather than *aspects* of a substantive time-segment. This does seem to mesh fairly well with most of what James has said about the transitive parts, and fits nicely with the 'bird's life' metaphor with which we began. The most basic distinction between transitive parts and the rest of the stream of thought, on this reading, is *pace*; so the analogy of 'an alternation of flights and perchings' seems an apt one. There are also happy overtones to the simile: for instance, a bird's flight is, in some way, directed and guided—and so, according to James, are the swift transitions of the transitive parts. 'Relation . . . to our topic or interest is constantly felt . . . particularly the relation of harmony and discord, of furtherance or hindrance of the topic' (1890, p. 259). And, like a bird's life, the stream of thought, including its transitive parts, is a unity.

However, it arguably requires the assumption that we have frequent moments of imageless thought, so to speak *between images*. I do not recall coming across this assertion in James. And there are certain problematic quotes: consider, for example, his description of the *fringes* as 'psychic transitions, always on the wing, so to speak, and not to be glimpsed except in flight' (1890, p. 253).

Philosophical Importance

What is the philosophical import of all of this? On the face of it, the notion of transitive parts is simply a more or less empirical psychological claim about the contents of our mental life—though this should itself have a great deal of interest to workers in the field of consciousness studies. However, contained within the notion of the transitive parts are a nest of important and substantive philosophical claims and implications. A substantial book could be written on these issues and their connection with the temporal flow of consciousness: here I intend only to give a brief rundown, in order to flag some of the main areas of interest.

The reality of relations

The transitive parts consist in the direct mental apprehension of relations. For James, relations are not hypotheses about the connections between experience; they are not patterns imposed upon a neutral universe; they are an empirical and ontological reality.[12]

---

[12] 'Consciousness does not leap from one "substantive" state to another, but rather is always in "felt" continuity by virtue of the experiencing of "transitive" relationships' (McDermott 1977, p. xxxvi). See also the discussion of time below.

Pure experiences exist and succeed one another; they enter into infinitely varied relations; and these relations are themselves essential parts of the web of experiences. There
is a 'Consciousness' of these relations for the same reason that there is a 'Consciousness'
of their terms. As a result, fields of experiences are observable and distinguishable (1905,
p. 9).

James' defence of this notion is basically in terms of his introspective intuitions
about the reality of conscious experience, and his views of the eventual usefulness of
this idea for further thought. We might see three clauses here:

(a) Relations appear to us as immediately 'perceived' reality. Thus the evidence
     we have suggests the reality of relations.
(b) To accept this appearance as truth is pragmatically useful in further theoriz-
     ing, such as James' *Principles*.
(c) We in fact have independent theoretical evidence for the truth of conscious
     'seemings' of this kind: the doctrine of pure experience. What we 'have in our
     minds' is not a *representation* of the object of thought; it is an aspect of *the
     thing itself.*

Should we accept all this? Even if we accept his introspective conclusions, it is certainly still open to us to hold to the possibility of James' hypothesis about relations in
the world being false. We might also profess ourselves dissatisfied with the weight of
the evidence he produces, and suggest that the burden of proof remains with him.

One reason for doing this, it seems, is that James' theory makes all relations
equally 'real,' and we might find that conclusion uncomfortable. He need not elide
the distinction between, say, stable, lawlike relations and 'arbitrary' ones, or between
'physical' relations and 'mental' ones. But he cannot say that, properly speaking,
such and such a relation is a real one (in the sense of being a property of the universe)
and this and so is not — *any* relation we perceive, apparently, we perceive *as a genuine property of pure experience.*

The possibility of imageless thought

Another important idea to be found in James on this point is the following: transitive
parts are a kind of *imageless thought*. Thinking (by which we mean here the phenomenal flow of thought), therefore, need not consist in visual or aural imagery, as
was often previously assumed. As Aron Gurwitsch puts it:

In these cases we . . . experience specific mental states from which all imagery either of
words or things is absent, and for which it is impossible to account as long as consciousness is assumed to be composed, on the one hand, of sensations, and on the other hands,
of ideas, representations, and images of a perfectly definite nature (1943, p. 458).[13]

James on this point is plausible, but we may still entertain *caveats*. In particular, he
spends at least the bulk of his argumentative efforts in the chapter on 'The Stream of
Thought' demonstrating that all thought *contains* or involves non-imagistic feeling.[14]
However, one may hold this and still hold that it is impossible for the mind's eye,

---

[13] Further, he goes on, 'we may see that, in James' opinion, the "transitive parts" not only make up a
considerable part of conscious life, but also possess more importance, significance, and value than the
"substantive parts" to which they are attached' (p. 462).
[14] Though he does spend time, for example in Ch. XVIII of *Principles* (on imagination), trying to show
that particular *ideas* we may think to be visual need not be so.

while conscious, to be completely black and silent — that, though there are other elements as well, mental experience always contains *some* imagery.

The inadequacy of intellectualizing

A third philosophical consequence which may be distilled from the doctrine of the transitive parts is a critique of the adequacy of the very tools of linguistic philosophy. Here are some reasons:

(a) A large, varied and important part of our mental reality is immune to linguistic analysis because its 'contents' cannot be named.

(b) Concepts do not, at bottom, properly describe the flux of thought and reality, since they necessarily divide it up arbitrarily — it has no joints at which to be cut.

(c) It is perhaps the case that much of our logical reasoning is performed through transitive parts. As such, the 'logical' relations we actually rely on are, it seems, by definition vague, indescribable, and *different* every time.

> In principle, then, ... intellectualism's edge is broken; it can only approximate to reality, and its logic is inapplicable to our inner life. ... I must deafen you to talk, or to the importance of talk, by showing you, as Bergson does, that the concepts we talk with are made for purposes of *practice* and not for the purposes of insight. Or I must *point*, point to the mere *that* of life, and you by inner sympathy must fill out the *what* for yourselves. ... Philosophy [has] been on a false scent since the days of Socrates and Plato (1909, pp. 296–7).

Relations are sensations, and sensations are fleeting, momentary, particular and unnameable (because constantly changing). They are not the stable, abstract entities of analytic fantasy. 'The real units of our immediately-felt life are unlike the units that intellectualist logic holds to and makes its calculations with' (1909, p. 296).

The impression of time

Fourthly, it is significant that the experience of continuity, encapsulated in the transitive parts, is felt and not just posited, James asserts.[15] Gurwitsch suggests that for James continuity 'is identical with phenomenal time' (1943, p. 449). That is, every single mental state is *also* an awareness of time passing, since it must contain some elements pointing to the past and future.

Hume, by contrast, felt that a *succession* of ideas was necessary: a single idea cannot give rise to the impression of time. In fact, there *is* no separate impression of time: the idea of time (like space) stands for the very succession of contents, not for some specific, distinguishable content. It is not an idea of an object, 'but merely [one] of the manner or order in which objects exist' (1740, pp. 39–40).

> The idea of time is not deriv'd from a particular impression mix'd up with others, and plainly distinguishable from them; but arises altogether from the manner, in which impressions appear to the mind, without making one of the number (1740, p. 36).

Thus, for Hume, time is atomistic, in the same manner as the succession of discrete contents: there are 'indivisible moments' in time (e.g. 1740, p. 39). Therefore there can be no real connection between the thoughts of the flow of consciousness, or, then,

---

[15] The main importance of the transitive parts then, for Gurwitsch, is that they make 'temporality ... the fundamental structure of conscious life' (1943, p. 467).

between moments of time. Perceptions are each self-sufficient entities, entirely independent of any other perception.[16]

But, James objects:

(a) A succession of feelings is not the same thing as a feeling of succession. Indeed, a succession is not sufficient, because there must also be simultaneous knowledge of previous phases at later stages in order to know that a succession has taken place (1890, pp. 627–31).

(b) To be a 'memory' of past phases, Hume claims, an idea must 'resemble' its original, while being of a lesser 'vivacity' — but how can we identify this 'resemblance' across time? In order to be correlated, both parts must be known (Gurwitsch, 1943, pp. 455–6).

(c) For Hume, there is no experience of intrinsic connection between time-slices. We know only that another impression *has succeeded* a first — we do not experience the *succession* itself. Succession is merely inferred after the event (Gurwitsch, 1943, pp. 456–7). This conflicts with our 'life experience' of consciousness, James asserts.

The self

James' account of the unity of consciousness has a well-known impact upon accounts of the self. For James, personal identity consists neither in an immutable, introspectible self (criticised by Hume as having no empirical warrant), nor merely a bundle of perceptions and ideas (attacked in turn by the Rationalists). Selves, rather, are constructed out of the phenomenological data of our continuity.[17] There is no distinction between the thinker and the thought: we are, more or less, just the unbroken flow of our experiences.

Concluding Remarks

The precise philosophical content of the notion of the transitive parts turns out to be this: that certain moments in our stream of thought consist in rapid, imageless motion towards a substantive 'conclusion,' during which we do not hold up the feelings we experience before our attention to deliberately inspect them. These feelings are ones of *relation*, in particular of various kinds of continuity and connection; and they reveal that relations are just as much a part of our 'life-world' as the objects they relate.

The philosophical importance of aspects of this doctrine is considerable: in particular, if true, it has significance for views on the ontology of relations, the ontology of thought, the practice of logic, and our sense of time. I have here merely indicated that some central planks of the transitive part doctrine do seem introspectively accurate: these are the direct apprehension of relations, a sense of movement through thought, and the existence of imageless elements in thought. Certain other elements seem less well demonstrated, I have hinted, in particular the existence of segments of *purely* imageless thought, and the identity relation between the structure of our experience and that of 'external reality' or of time.

---

[16] If a substance is '*something which may exist by itself*,' then they 'are … substances, as far as this definition explains a substance' (1740, p. 233).

[17] On this see for example Flanagan (1991), pp. 32–3; Cooper (1992); and Parfit (1979).

References

Cooper, W.E. (1990), 'William James' theory of mind', *Journal of the History of Philosophy*, **28**.

Cooper W.E. (1992), 'William James' theory of the self', *Monist*, **75**.

Flanagan, Owen (1991), 'Naturalizing the mind: The philosophical psychology of William James', in *The Science of the Mind* (Cambridge, MA: MIT Press).

Flanagan, Owen (1992), *Consciousness Reconsidered* (Cambridge, MA: MIT Press).

Galin, David (1996), 'The structure of subjective experience: sharpen the concepts and terminology', in *Toward A Science of Consciousness: The First Tucson Discussions and Debates*, ed. S. Hameroff, A. Kaszniak and A. Scott (Cambridge, MA: MIT Press).

Gurwitsch, Aron (1943), 'William James' theory of the "Transitive Parts" of the stream of consciousness', *Philosophy and Phenomenological Research*, **3**.

Hume, David (1740), *A Treatise of Human Nature*, 1978 edn., ed. L.A. Selby-Bigge (Oxford: Oxford University Press).

James, William (1890), *The Principles of Psychology*, Vol. 1, 1918 edn. (New York: Dover).

James, William (1892), *Psychology: Briefer Course* (Cambridge, MA: Harvard University Press, 1984).

James, William (1895), 'The knowing of things together', *Essays in Philosophy* (Cambridge, MA: Harvard University Press, 1978).

James, William (1905), 'The notion of consciousness', *Essays in Radical Empiricism* (Cambridge, MA: Harvard University Press, 1976).

James, William (1909), 'The continuity of experience', in McDermott [1977].

McDermott, John J. (ed. 1977), *The Writings of William James* (Chicago: University of Chicago Press).

Parfit, Derek (1979), 'Personal identity', in *Philosophy As It Is*, ed. T. Honderich and M. Burnyeat (New York: Penguin).

Perry, Ralph Barton (1938), *In the Spirit of William James* (New Haven: Yale University Press).

Schuetz, Alfred (1941), 'William James' concept of the stream of thought, phenomenologically interpreted', *Philosophy and Phenomenological Research*, **1**.

Shallice, Tim (1988), 'Information-processing models of consciousness', in *Consciousness in Contemporary Science*, ed. A.J. Marcel and E. Bisiach (Oxford: Clarendon Press).

Wilshire, Bruce (1968), *William James and Phenomenology: A Study of 'The Principles of Psychology'* (Bloomington: Indiana University Press).

Jean Naudin, Caroline Gros-Azorin
Aaron Mishara, Osborne P. Wiggins
Michael A. Schwartz and Jean-Michel Azorin

The Use of the Husserlian Reduction as a Method of Investigation in Psychiatry

Husserlian reduction is a rigorous method for describing the foundations of psychiatric experience. With Jaspers we consider three main principles inspired by phenomenological reduction: direct givenness, absence of presuppositions, re-presentation. But with Binswanger alone we refer to eidetic and transcendental reduction: (1) to establish a critical epistemology; (2) to directly investigate the constitutive processes of mental phenomena and their disturbances, freed from their nosological[1] background; (3) to question the constitution of our own experience when facing a person with mental illness. Regarding the last item, we suggest a specific kind of reduction, typically intersubjective from the start, which we call the 'looking-glass reduction'. The schizophrenic experience — understood as a 'loss of taken-for-grantedness' implying the constitutions of the body, of the other, and of internal time — is a real 'epochal provocation' for the psychiatrist. As the horizon it opens seems to be both corporeal and narrative, this 'provoking' of an epochè in the attitude of the psychiatrist himself and the resistances it implies raise important issues regarding the general constitution of human experience.

In this article we propose to examine the possibilities opened up by the use of the Husserlian method of reduction in psychiatric experience. In discussion of Husserl's 'reduction' or *epochè* the reader frequently encounters two distinct senses of the term. The first sense we might call 'the early sense of reduction' or the epochè of Husserl's early book, *Logical Investigations* (Husserl, 1970a). In this sense epochè simply

Corresponding author: Jean Naudin, 55 bis Bd Rodocanachi, 13008 Marseille, France. E-mail: artsnaud@aix.pacwan.net

[1] Nosology is the branch of medicine that deals with the systematic classification of diseases.

Journal of Consciousness Studies, **6**, No. 2–3, 1999, pp. 155–171

means setting aside all preconceived theories and presuppositions in an attempt to get 'back to the things themselves'. This is the sense in which Karl Jaspers in his seminal book *General Psychopathology* (Jaspers, 1963) may be said to be employing a phenomenological reduction: Jaspers asserts the need to set aside all 'prejudices' (*Vorurteile*) in order to obtain an unvarnished look at the phenomena precisely and exclusively as they present themselves to the observer.

The second sense of epochè or reduction is the later sense as it appears in Husserl's 1913 book, *Ideas Pertaining to a Pure Phenomenology and to a Phenomenological Philosophy, First Book* (Husserl, 1982). In this book the epochè must be performed in order to set out of operation what Husserl calls 'the natural attitude'. Within the natural attitude we simply assume that the world is real and that we ourselves are real beings who exist among other objects in the world. Within the natural attitude, in other words, we do not see that the world and ourselves as worldly beings have been 'constituted' by mental processes of consciousness (*Bewusstsein*). This more fundamental consciousness which constitutes the world and even itself as one object among others within the world Husserl terms 'transcendental consciousness' or 'transcendental subjectivity'. In order to get back behind the already constituted world and subject (the empirical subject) and to regard them as they are being constituted by transcendental consciousness, we need to perform what Husserl calls a 'transcendental epochè'. The transcendental epochè, by suspending the natural attitude, allows us to view the world, not as a pre-given reality, but rather as constituted by consciousness; it allows us to examine carefully the processes of consciousness which are unified or synthesized in certain ways and thereby presents us with objects and indeed with an entire world of objects, including our empirical (worldly) selves.

As we shall see in what follows, both the earlier and the later senses of epochè or reduction are relevant to psychiatry. But one can easily imagine lively discussions regarding the legitimacy of such an application of the phenomenological approach to psychiatry. One can even read into such words as 'use' or 'application' the idea that the phenomenological method should be just another *technique* in the field of psychiatry. However, far from being a technical application, the true originality of phenomenology consists in proposing a way of returning to a pure experience situated beneath or below any such immediately theoretical or technical preoccupation.

Nevertheless, we do hold to the idea that a method must have as its goal the obtaining of some result and cannot in consequence be examined independently of this goal. In this sense, the reduction has to be thought of as a conceptual tool, the need for which is enforced by a practice. The idea of a possible use for the phenomenological method in psychiatry relates to the practices which actually take place in psychiatric life, and to the need for a progressive clarification of their foundations, with a view to sorting out the results from the artifacts created by the very conditions of clinical work. This use presupposes, accordingly, a constant oscillation between a purely intuitive practice, engaged in the immediately present experience with a patient, and a theorizing activity which tests present clinical experience against psychopathological concepts inherited from the past (Lanteri-Laura, 1991).

The phenomenological method in psychiatry offers a way of clarifying the modes of access to the basic givens of experience (the clinical observation of patients, the diagnostic intuition of the psychiatrist, self-observations, the evaluation of the subjective experience of the illness, the interpretation of a biographical narrative, personal feelings about the situation), modes of access which may very well turn out not to be phenomenological in themselves, and to refer to the realm of technique (varied techniques of diagnosis, questionnaires and semi-structured interviews, evaluation scales, therapeutic devices). The goal is the rigorous description of these ultimate givens just as they make their appearance in the context of the specific knowledge represented by modern psychiatry, and despite whatever previous theories might have been foisted *a priori* upon the realm of experience. The use of the phenomenological method in psychiatry therefore clearly belongs in the context of a philosophy which finds its application in a scientific domain. In this respect it is in conformity with the use advocated by Husserl (1955) of philosophy as rigorous science.

In psychiatry, as elsewhere, the phenomenological method can only be practised and described independently of the technico-empirical features which define a discipline as a realm of scientific investigation. However, this method still provides a means of observing phenomena as they arise, or, to put it otherwise, in the pre-scientific situation which provides the basis for such phenomena (Schutz, 1964). This is also why the specifics of the phenomenological reduction, in so far as it is implied in psychiatric experience, have to be described. For these specifics depend upon the circumstances surrounding the use of the method, in this case, psychiatric experience as a working reality. It is in fact possible to identify as many reductions as there are specialized fields of application.

Among the peculiarities proper to the psychiatric use of the reduction (Azorin, 1996), the following will prove to be particularly important:

(1) the field of psychiatry is that of mental pathology;
(2) a key result of the practice of phenomenology is to grasp the disturbance itself not so much as the mark of a deviation *vis-à-vis* the norm, as rather that of the autonomous development of a possibility already potentially present in normal experience;
(3) the problem of consciousness and of its disturbances in the field of psychiatry is doubly difficult because what we see here is a collapse of the usual foundations of consciousness. These are the foundations which usually anchor consciousness both in its body, as the seat of its habitualities, and in everyday reality, as the customary movement which constitutes its field of development;
(4) in the most radical types of experience we are dealing with a reduction which is intersubjective from the start and which has to be distinguished in consequence from the phenomenological reduction in solipsistic variant (cf. Depraz's contribution to this Special Issue).

In these last two peculiarities we can see the most specific use of the method of reduction in psychiatry (Naudin, 1997). This applies especially to the use of the reduction in the encounter with someone afflicted with schizophrenia. In this essay, we will limit ourselves to problems which can be related to this diagnosis.

I: Return to the Origins of the Phenomenological Approach in Psychiatry — Binswanger against Jaspers

We have recently insisted upon the need to return to the origins of phenomenological psychiatry, that is, to a consideration of the way in which Husserlian phenomenology is implied in Jaspers' *General Psychopathology* (1963), and this with a view to understanding both the persistent interest in the method as well as its misconceptions which, even today, considerably limit its impact on psychiatric literature (Naudin *et al.*, 1997). In 1911, Jaspers (1963) was the first psychiatrist who referred to Husserlian philosophy as a means for enriching the knowledge the psychiatrist might be able to derive from the mental states of his patients. In his *Psychopathology*, Jaspers is particularly optimistic about the fruitfulness of the notion of intentionality and bases his critique of the prejudices which both obscure and obstruct direct access to clinical phenomena upon the use — perfectly evident even though not further explained — made of the phenomenological reduction.

In fact his method rests on three principles which share in common the suggestion that any pre-established theoretical knowledge should be provisionally set aside, which is precisely what the phenomenological reduction is all about. Most notably this knowledge concerns 'cerebral mythology', so-called 'philosophical' prejudices, and the postulate of the unconscious. The three major principles announced by Jaspers are the following (Wiggins & Schwartz, 1997):

(1) direct givenness: only with resort to intuition can clinical matters of fact be experienced directly;
(2) the absence of presuppositions: methodological suspension of prejudices which stand in the way of direct access to phenomena (the proper result of epochè as described by Depraz);
(3) making intuitively present: re-presentation (*Vergegenwärtigung*) in Jaspers' sense has nothing to do with Kantian representation; re-presentation signifies the act by means of which I can 'make present what is not itself directly present'; in other words, the act of re-presenting consists in the attempt to produce in oneself the experience of the other.

To be sure, already in Jaspers one encounters the Husserlian watchword 'return to the thing itself', together with the phenomenological reduction in its first meaning of an initial setting aside of any constituted theoretical knowledge. But it is necessary to criticise Jaspers, and even to abandon a good number of prejudices which still link his work to German romantic psychiatry, if one wants to understand, with Binswanger (Binswanger, 1963; 1965; 1978; Gros-Azorin, 1997; Mishara, 1997), the relevance of pure phenomenology to the understanding of psychiatric experience.

Jaspers' is a descriptive phenomenology of empathy which is limited to describing and ordering the subjective experiences of the mentally ill. As a result, it never questions the atavistic prejudice of clinical psychiatry, which is that of basing itself upon a constant reference to the norm. As Tatossian & Giudicelli (1973) sum the matter up:

> [Jaspers'] phenomenology relates to the experiences of the normal man with a view to distinguishing with regard to the sick: those experiences which remain the same; those experiences which differ from them quantitatively or by virtue of some still imaginable, if not altogether evident, combination; finally, those experiences which are unknown to the sane, and therefore incomprehensible to them and so only intelligible by analogy (p. 129).

When it concerns itself with genesis, Jaspers' phenomenology limits itself to noting how the lived experiences in question can succeed one another with the evidence that goes along with comprehension (*Verstehen*); in this way it is able to show how 'the emergence of the psychic coincides with the development of psychic evidence', how, for example, the deceived lover can become jealous. But it sets aside the fundamental question concerning the genesis of the process itself as the emergence of a possibility peculiar to human experience. In the same way, it also sets aside the question of the structure of human experience, a question which lies at the root of that part of Husserl's thought which falls under the head of 'constitutive genesis'. Constitutive genesis, in Husserl's sense, would not distinguish *a priori* the lived experience of the sane individual from that of the mentally sick. Refusing any deepening of the reduction towards constitutive genesis, Jaspers then stays on the plane of psychological comprehension.

Jaspers' descriptive pyschopathology has to be set off against that of Binswanger (Gros-Azorin, 1997). From the very beginning, Binswanger understands the importance of undertaking a radical critique of the dualism of subject and object, together with its consequences in psychiatry. In the implications of the phenomenological reduction and its further extensions in the transcendental philosophy of Husserl and the philosophy of Heidegger, he sees a method capable of bequeathing to psychiatric experience a greater self-understanding and a way of pressing back the frontiers of our psychological understanding in the direction of a structural comprehension of experience (Tatossian, 1996). In this article, we have deliberately decided not to develop the implications of Heidegger's philosophy in Binswanger's *Daseins* analysis in order to be able to accord greater emphasis to the methodological problems posed by the Husserlian project in the field of psychiatry.

II: Methodology for a Phenomenological Approach in Psychiatry

With a view to gaining a better understanding of both the rigour and the diversity of the uses to which the reduction can be put in psychiatry, one first has to understand in what way, and upon what stages of experience, it can be applied. Simplifying matters, one can begin by saying that these stages are, strictly speaking, the technico-medical stages which characterize the psychiatric encounter in its own medical context of reference. Diagnosis, treatment and prognosis make up the medical context of psychiatric practice. These stages are characterized by professional objectives seeking to distinguish practical conceptual instruments from the different ways in which the subjectivity of the patient makes its appearance. These stages are much more tightly entangled in psychiatric practice than in current medical practice. All the same, it will sometimes prove practical to distinguish them in order to bring out more clearly the particular mode of application of that reduction which is appropriate to them.

On the methodological plane, direct application of the Husserlian reduction furnishes psychiatry with both: (1) the basis for a critical epistemology (Lanteri-Laura, 1991; Tatossian, 1996) and, (2) a rigorous means of access to direct experience (Azorin, 1996; Naudin, 1997; Varela, 1996).

(1) By critical epistemology, we mean a philosophy applied to critically examining the foundations of scientific knowledge (here psychiatric knowledge). This epistemology is 'critical' because it places in question ideas that are widely accepted in the field of psychiatry. It criticizes and modifies these ideas in the light of what the psychiatrist encounters in the patient's behaviour. This critical attitude is particularly fruitful when it is a matter of understanding the structures of those experiential stages which appear to be the most technical — and notably that of the diagnosis. It is also primarily linked to the eidetic reduction (Husserl, 1962) since it bases its methodology upon: (a) a prior suspension of the theories in circulation, a suspension which

makes it possible to avoid prejudging their validity; (b) imaginative variations bearing upon clinical phenomena with a view to allowing invariants to appear — in other words, those essential features without which the phenomena would not be what they are — and (c) a return to the clinical experience itself with a view to allowing the encompassing regularity of an essential structure to make its appearance.

Take for example the case of a person living alone and isolated from the world, engaging in no activity and indulging in delusional ideas, based upon the presence of voices which insult her and hold her under their control. The voices convince her that an alien has taken possession of her body, lives in her inner ear, steals each one of her organs while she sleeps, and this causes her considerable fatigue. This alien being sells her organs to rich mutants for grafting and the patient considers herself to be an injured party since the money generated by this business should have been paid to her. Technically, a diagnosis of schizophrenia could easily be justified on the basis of the following symptoms: social withdrawal, a-pragmaticism, bizarre and delusional ideas, and acoustico-verbal hallucinations. But a psychiatrist inspired by phenomenology would not be satisfied with any devaluing of these delusional and hallucinatory ideas by typifying them as erroneous judgments and perceptions in the manner recommended, if not required, by the present classification of mental disturbances. He would be more inclined to bracket any such diagnosis as technical/criteriological. He would be equally inclined to neutralize such judgments bearing upon reality as would lead him to invalidate the experience of the other on the grounds of its being delirious, because mistaken. He would seek to open up a reflective space within which the meaning of the symptoms alone would count. Varying the delusional themes bit by bit he would try to extract the invariable elements. The fact that the ideas of the patient are directed essentially towards her body might lead one to invoke melancholic hypochondria but these ideas would hardly be modified in their essence if, in place of the theme of grafting and of an exchange of organs with mutants, one were to envisage, for instance, the theme of making a soup out of the organs which could be given to pigs, or again the theme of the Nazi doctor undertaking hidden experiments in the patient's inner ear. The bodily obsessions would however be profoundly modified if they were to be integrated into a delusion of ruin, where the loss of organs and bodily collapse appeared as the inevitable outcome of a past mistake.

One does not have to perform these variations upon a theme for very long before one grasps that the characteristically invariant theme of the delusion of this patient is not that of a loss or of a mistake, as it would be in the case of a melancholic, but rather the intrusion into, and the lack of any determination with regard to, the constitutive limits of the lived body, themes which figure among those most characteristic of persons with schizophrenia. In the same vein, it is not the erroneous nature of the judgment which makes one think of delusion but rather its incorrigibility, the fact that no other judgment is permitted to contradict the evidence on the basis of which the conviction of the experiencing subject is founded. This is what indicates an invariant type characteristic of the existential style of the person with schizophrenia rather than a collection of criteria indicative of the presence of an organic disturbance. The psychiatrist cannot ignore the fact that before him others have already described these disturbances. Schneider called them 'mineness disturbances'. But in this case, he is able to go much further in his analysis by referring these disturbances to a modification of the living body, of the body in so far as it can be mine, that is, endowed with its own intentionality. This connection is not just established in theory, by relating an already given dogmatic presupposition to the experience in an external way. He is able to establish this relation in a much more intimate way in the face of the emergence of a clinical phenomenon which is given in accordance with its own coherence, its own style — a style which is just as readily recognizable in the thematic of delusional discourse, in what the voices say, in the type of intrusion which they effect in a non-delusional bodily experience. This is thus akin to the stylization in the rather mannered style of a patient who takes herself to be in her body — as if her body didn't really belong to her, as if her gestures are those of a marionette or an automaton. It is this mannered style which enables the psychiatrist to think of schizophrenia right away, even before any assembling of criteria or any in depth discussion. Schizophrenia appears to him as it has already appeared so often to so many other psychopathologists as a disturbance in the belonging of the self to its bodily being. The subjective experience of persons touched by this disturbance are intentionally organized around an attempt at reappropriating the self. On the basis of the eidetic method we have just described, it becomes possible to claim that any intentional horizon is constituted around this preoccupation with the reconstruction of the self. This eidetic method therefore explores the horizon of the possibilities proper to a given style of existence. It discloses the characteristic features of a typology (Kraus, 1982; Lanteri-Laura, 1991; Tatossian, 1980; 1996; Wiggins and Schwartz, 1994).

The typological/eidetic approach is particularly valuable in teaching and research. Moreover, it leads us to a progressive modification of practice itself. Purely practical questions concerning daily life, the degree of freedom, the correspondence between the personal projects of the patient and reality, can be discussed in the light of this eidetic orientation. The psychiatrist who adopts such a point of view comes to question what is given in the phenomena of every day life (Husserl, 1970b; Schutz, 1964; Tatossian, 1980), which of course forms the common foundation of his own experience and that of the patient he encounters. At this stage in any case, the typological/eidetic approach, which still reflects the nosological categories it seeks to critically refine (Naudin *et al.*, 1997; Rossi-Monti and Stanghellini, 1997) comes up against a fundamental objection: it fails to call in question one of the most radical *a prioris* surrounding the psychiatric encounter, namely, the primacy of the experience of the observer over that of the observed. Hence the need for more elaborate methods of access to direct experience.

(2) By the method of direct access to experience we mean an attitude close to that of the transcendental reduction (Husserl, 1955; 1957; 1960) and of its further developments in a philosophy of the lifeworld (Husserl, 1970b; Schutz, 1964). By suspending the very thesis of reality, the transcendental reduction leads Husserl to a disclosure of the originary underpinnings of experience and especially its foundation in corporality, temporality and intersubjectivity. At the same time, it brings to light the fundamental split in the subject (Husserl's *Ich-Spaltung*), a split which is marked by the natural engagement in the world of everyday life: on the one hand, (a) a constituted (or *empirical*) subject which is the subject in the psychological sense and, on the other, (b) a constituting (or *transcendental*) subject which is the experiential source of the constituted subject and the constituted world.

Moreover, the transcendental reduction discloses two types of intentional process: (a) active processes — processes in which the ego lives, and which appear as processes through which objects are *thematized*, processes in which the subject is active, thinks, decides or speaks; (b) passive processes — processes which are self-regulating, take place by themselves and without being actively produced by an ego, processes which are, so to speak, 'automatic' and which, for Husserl, can be characterized as *pre-thematizing*. The unity of experience, more exactly, the unity of the objects intended by consciousness, including the unity of the self, takes place consequently on the basis of processes of passive synthesis, processes which unite the multiple features of an identical object. The totality of these processes unfolds on the constantly renewed basis of a certainty, of a primordial *faith* (Merleau-Ponty, 1962), an unshakeable faith in the world, a primordial belief which constitutes the horizon of confidence in, and receptivity towards, experience. This constant renewal of the intentional horizon of present experience presupposes the stability of an experiential temporal structure which Husserl describes as an interweaving of retentions (an intending of what has just taken place and which still remains attached to present experience), of presentations (an intending of what is immediately present to consciousness) and of protentions (an intending of what is expected to be presented) [Husserl, 1964].

The totality of the processes which we have just described is obviously put into operation in the encounter with the other, an other who is, at one and the same time, an empirical and a constituting subject. The question of the encounter with the other is a serious problem for the transcendental reduction, which Husserl describes as only applied in direct self-reflection, i.e., only in direct examination of one's own consciousness. By its very essence, the subjectivity of the other is not accessible in the immediacy of direct givenness. Access to the constituting subjectivity of the other is not possible save through the mediation of his body. The article by Depraz in this volume makes particularly clear the need to rethink the reduction on the basis of inter-subjectivity and the method which leads in that direction. It is no longer enough to accept the transcendental solipsism of Husserl's Cartesian way to the reduction. Nor will it suffice to share inter-individually the results of reductions operated by each individual for his own account. Only a way which passes by way of the lifeworld is capable of taking account of the communitarian dimension of the experience of the reduction. This intersubjective sharing of the experience of the reduction merits the title of a co-reduction (Depraz, 1995). This co-reduction at the heart of the lifeworld takes account of more primary dimensions already constitutive of affectivity and bodily sensibility. It arises out of a total immersion in the incarnate sensibility which we all share from the first with others as incarnate subjects.

This reminder of Husserl's transcendental philosophy and its overcoming in a co-reduction — unfortunately much too brief to be explicit and much too long to be simply introductory — enables us to grasp some of the most problematic aspects of the encounter with the mentally ill. One characteristic aspect is bizarreness. The bizarre appears right away as an intersubjective phenomenon. It appears to be constitutively linked up with a certain incomprehension on the part of the observer; it attests to a primordial astonishment *vis-à-vis* the encounter, an astonishment whose meaning has to be reconstituted. I judge the behaviour of the other to be bizarre when I am unable to understand it with reference to our common world, when relying upon psychological inferences which allow me to anticipate the motives of the other no longer suffices for understanding, when the initial empathic movement which links me to him turns out to be restricted. As a symptom, the bizarre therefore appears as a fact of communication since it arises out of the impossibility of mutual understanding between myself and the other based upon common references (Tatossian, 1996). In fact, the bizarre refers back to originary and inter-affective evidence which lies at the root of the intersubjective experience as such.

With regard to our patient, from a thematic point of view (that is, conceptually, above and beyond the bare fact of her obvious hallucinations) the bizarre arises for example from the fact that the referential connections between her bodily experience of intrusion and the financial compensation to which she aspires presuppose a type of commercial relation. Although commercial relations of this kind are potentially justifiable in every day life and do indeed contribute to the legitimacy of the self at the heart of the social organization, the motive for such commercial relations seems totally inadequate on the intersubjective plane given the actual nature of the intrusion and its far-reaching context. In order to evaluate reflectively the adequacy of this motive, the observer has to understand the intersubjective basis upon which he establishes his own certainty and so has to call into question the solidity and the spontaneity of his own experience. Only on the basis of a primordial inter-affectivity is the observer able to understand in what sense the commercial context is incongruent with the painful experience of intrusion. More fundamentally still, the experience of the bizarre arises from a modification of the pre-thematic level of the experience, in particular, from the mannered way in which the patient carries through the gestures of daily life (walking, dressing, engaging in conversation). The impression of the bizarre arises from the impossibility of being together with others in the solidarity of gestural communication and, for the observer in particular, from the difficulty he experiences in being natural in a situation marked by a primordial lack of harmony. The essence of the schizophrenic bizarreness shows itself as a modification of the intercorporeal dimension, one which precedes any thematization of psychological motives.

With the help of this example, we see that what is bizarre about the encounter with a person with schizophrenia bears upon the affective and corporeal dimension which links us up originally, myself with the other, as embodied subjects. The body which we each of us are as subjects is affected by a basic modification with regard to the inter-human encounter. This basic modification bears upon the constitution of the experience, in Husserlian terms: its transcendental genesis.

If, for example, I find that I am very tired after a long engagement with the patient, this is due to the constitutive effort imposed upon me by the encounter. What seems to me to be lacking in meaning is more properly to be regarded as lacking in solidity. By my own constitutive efforts I seek to restore the bodily solidity which the encounter lacks. This can only be done at the cost of a dual transcendental effort, upholding my own self as an embodied subject on the one hand, and, on the other, upholding the intersubjective stratum of the world as the locus of the emergence of the self, the perceived thing and the other.

The encounter with a person with schizophrenia does not simply call into question the bodily being of the other but also my own bodily being. This cannot be understood save by following the path opened by a co-reduction — to talk the language of Depraz (1995). The encounter with a person with schizophrenia can only be thought out of inter-affection. From a didactic point of view, it might therefore be interesting for us to now take up our analysis again in terms consistent with the transcendental reduc-

tion in order to understand the processes which might lead to the necessary fundamental modification of the inter-affective dimension.

Schizophrenia has been described by psychoanalysts as a deficiency in the processes by which identity is constituted, more specifically, the identity of the empirical
ego (the supposed weakness of the ego). But a closer investigation shows that mental
illness does not call in question the empirical subject save in so far as its transcendental foundations are shaken (Blankenburg, 1971; Tatossian, 1980). The weakness of
the ego in schizophrenia is never anything other than a 'transcendental weakness'.

The psychiatrist who undertakes the transcendental reduction for himself gains
access to a deeper understanding of those transcendental processes which prove to
have been undermined in psychotic experience. Access to such phenomena of *transcendental weakness* as those which characterize mental sickness is conditioned by
the practice of the transcendental reduction in psychiatry, in the absence of which
they would be taken to be no more than organic/empirical problems (in other words,
brain diseases) or else as problems for the empirical ego (in other words, problems of
identity). Whenever he functions under the auspices of the reduction, the psychiatrist
gains access to the pre-thematic dimension of experience, that very dimension which
is itself *specifically* deranged in the experience of the mentally ill. We claim to have
shown with our concrete example of the bizarreness of a patient that it is the wholeness
of the experience which is called into question by this pre-thematic deficiency, not just
the experience of the patient but also that of the psychiatrist who encounters her.

By grasping what is specific about the experience of persons with schizophrenia,
the psychiatrist grasps at the same time the whole meaning of the split in the subject at
the centre of the reduction and especially the conditions of the possibility of the unity
of the experience (Binswanger, 1978). By interpreting the tiredness which follows
upon the encounter with his patient as a tiredness linked to the effort of constitution,
namely, that of a *transcendental asthenia* (Blankenburg, 1971), the psychiatrist at the
same time grasps the meaning of his own constitutional efforts. Only the practice and
the knowledge of the transcendental reduction is able to give the psychiatrist the
means of interpreting the language, and more generally the behaviour, of his patients,
in so far as they are the expression of a fundamental disturbance in their experience.

At this stage one question still lacks adequate clarification. Would it even be possible to undertake an authentic overcoming of the primacy of the experience of the
observer *vis à vis* the observed given that the reduction could only be carried through
by the psychiatrist alone? At any rate, one may be forgiven for entertaining doubts on
the matter, and the methodological limits of transcendental reduction, in its strictly
Husserlian sense, are felt here. In addition, the transcendental analysis of schizophrenic asthenia shows that a co-reduction founded upon empathy demands, on the
part of the psychiatrist, a dual transcendental effort, a dual effort which challenges the
primordial spontaneity of empathy. We now hope to be able to show conceptually
what is most specific to the psychotic experience. And this, we hope, will also
enrich our understanding of the constitution of normal experience (Naudin, 1997;
Naudin *et al.*, 1997).

III: The Schizophrenic Epochè

Binswanger (Gros-Azorin, 1997) analyses what is specific to the psychotic experience as being a matter of the how the transcendental deficiency proper to psychotic

experience displays a failure on the part of the temporal structure fundamental to experience, a slackening, even a telescoping, of retentions, presentations and protentions. He clearly situates the problem of delusion in the perspective of pure phenomenology, to the extent that horizonal intentionality and the presumptive evidence of worldly experience are implied in the patient's own psychopathology (Binswanger, 1965; 1978). He quotes Husserl (1957): 'the real world only exists to the extent that it is constantly taken for granted that experience will continue to unfold in accordance with the same constitutive style'. If the person with delusions no longer simply follows the 'logic of facts', the logic of what presents itself, it is because 'the whole constitutive structure of transcendental subjectivity and objectivity, the natural experience of the world, of reason, of truth and of reality has broken down'. The essence of delusion is to be grasped in terms of a disturbance of the basic time structure. This profoundly impacts what the patient takes as evident for the basis of delusional judgments (Mishara, 1997).

Blankenburg (1971) has shown that Binswanger's claims regarding a modification of the natural production of evidence could equally well be confirmed in nondelusional schizophrenic experience. The case of a person with a simple schizophrenia, Anne, capable of lucid reflections concerning her experience, makes it possible for him to show how persons with schizophrenia suffer from a veritable 'loss of natural evidence', in the very words of the patient. Anne is aware 'that she lacks something which is both minimal and basic for life and which other people possess effortlessly and without even looking for it.' She says that she does not know how to do the simplest and most routine things, like for example getting dressed or venturing her opinion in a discussion. It is not a matter of a lack of knowledge or of information but of a radical and imprecise lack, bringing about, so to speak, a genuine 'crisis of common sense'. Far from proposing yet another description of this *schizophrenic deficit*, Blankenburg describes this crisis as a *dynamically dialectical disequilibrium* in the production of evidence. Natural experience achieves an equilibrium between evidence and non-evidence. Moments of doubt lead to a thematization which replaces non-concordant evidence with a new concordant evidence. Confronted with doubt, schizophrenic experience does not succeed in re-establishing this equilibrium and lets non-evidence proceed forth without any possibility of overcoming it.

Wiggins, Schwartz and Northoff (1990) have developed the idea that, in the initial stages of the psychosis, one finds a profound modification of the Self and the World which bears on a deficiency in the synthetic unification of mental life, a unification which is normally accomplished spontaneously on the basis of the structures of corporality and of constituting temporality. This modification corresponds to a severe and invasive weakening of the process of intentional synthesis, leading to a disintegration of the self, which is experienced as if it were associated with aspects of the not-self. This estrangement from the world and from the self, experienced as an incapacity for everyday life, leads the ego to thematize what would normally be taken for granted. This thematization can bring with it valuable and varied information about the constitution of psychotic experience as well as about the constitution of normal experience. In itself, it is not necessarily pathological and can constitute a valid form of knowledge. Blankenburg (1971) shows how this thematization refers to a specific form of the epochè which is expressed just as well by the adoption of a pragmatic stance as in strange conduct or again in the hallucination of persons with schizophrenia.

This 'proneness to epochè' (Stanghellini, 1997), peculiar to persons with schizophrenia, is rooted in a weakness inherent in transcendental experience. Just like the Husserlian epochè, it presupposes a giving up of the natural attitude, but it is radically distinct from the epochè of the philosopher with regard to two principal features: (1) the person with schizophrenia undergoes it and cannot avoid the deficiency of his own experience, whereas the philosopher seeks it out and strives deliberately to maintain it; (2) it bears upon evidence of a pragmatic rather than of a theoretical kind.

In the person with schizophrenia, the radical erosion of the constituting subject lays bare the very process of constitution. The fact that the schizophrenic epochè bears specifically upon pragmatic evidence is related to the fact that this pragmatic evidence corresponds, for the most part, to corporeally and intersubjectively constituted evidence. More fundamentally still, this pragmatic evidence sets in motion the dialectical equilibrium between the processes by which the other is constituted by my I, and I myself by the other. The constitution of the world of everyday life presupposes our incarnation in a living body and, as a result, a multiplicity of perspectives. There is a common *now* as well as a *here* and a *there*, all of which are oriented on the basis of our corporeal engagement in the world. This perspectival character is constitutive of the world of everyday life. In the experience of the person with schizophrenia, and as a result of the break-down in the process of appresentation and the slackening of the temporal structure, this perspectival character is radically undermined, calling into question the possible foundation of the constitution of time in corporality and intersubjectivity (Blankenburg, 1997; Naudin, 1997; Naudin & Azorin, 1997b). A method therefore has to be employed to rethink the questions linked with corporality as intercorporality and to follow up the implications of the intersubjective perspective, even while bearing in mind its originary modification at the centre of experience of the person with schizophrenia. And this modification must be conceived as a co-reduction on the basis of the encounter with a person with schizophrenia as a modified encounter.

In order to be more explicit let us consider another example of our own observation of a patient. J.P., 41 years of age, hardly exhibits more than a certain apragmaticism as the residual sign of a schizophrenic condition which began 20 years earlier. This apragmaticism finds its subjective meaning in a profound tiredness which is highly evocative of transcendental asthenia. He signals his own difficulties by saying:

> I cannot enjoy a now as others do. For example, when I see men bustling around me I don't understand it. I don't understand what they are doing, more particularly, I don't understand why they do it. Others all live in accordance with the same rhythm; they have a daily life, their daily banalities. They engage in these banal occupations because they have a now, because they know how to get oriented, I don't have any such orientation, I do not know how to set out from here. That I should be here or over there is all the same to me. Telephoning is banal, for example; but I am sure that I do not do it like others, not in accordance with the same rhythm, that's easy to see. My funny rhythm on the piano. Wait. Record that. It would be a way of confirming my illness! What I lack is a visual field, a field open before me. It's on the basis of such a visual field that others are able to have a now. You see that picture on the wall, well, I ask myself why it is there. Someone must have put it there, have chosen it, have hung it up, there and not somewhere else, even though tomorrow he might very well be dead. I don't understand why men do that kind of thing, I don't understand their stories, how they stick to them.

This clinical observation reflects the questions we pose concerning our embodied anchoring in a commonsensical world which has its localities (its heres and theres), its time organization, its nows and thens, and its perceptual horizons which the subject can share with others. It serves as a practical confirmation of what we want to describe in the name of a 'looking-glass reduction'.

IV: The Encounter with Persons with Schizophrenia as a Looking-glass Reduction

Encountering the person with schizophrenia enforces a kind of (phenomenological) reduction, whether the clinician be seasoned or the novice resident. Such an epochè cannot be understood as issuing from a philosophical motive but rather involuntarily and pervasively touches upon the intersubjective roots of how we meaningfully experience. The phenomenological psychiatrist is able to enhance this experience and express it in technical language by the mindfulness which reduction as a disciplined practice brings (see Depraz in this issue; Mishara, 1994). That is, such a psychiatrist is well prepared to recognize and describe what is spontaneously provoked in encountering the seeming 'bizarreness' of the patient. The rules of exchange (and the meaningful 'co-constitution' of situations) which habitually preside in the encounter with others in everyday life have been put in abeyance. A doubt is introduced in the psychiatrist's own experience which for the moment undermines the basis of daily life in the community and the so-called *a priori* conditions of competent dialogue or exchange (Goffman, 1981; Naudin & Azorin, 1997b). The psychiatrist must employ her own subjective response as part of the diagnostic process and attempt to restore clinical rapport. As has been so often demonstrated in the experiments of social psychologists, a falling short of these rules or conditions provokes a value judgment in social cognition, and 'implicit processes' of stereotyping may be brought into play to protect her experience of social identity. The other (in this case, the patient) seems 'different' with such pervasive insistence that the psychiatrist's own relationship to others in the world (i.e. her intersubjective rootedness) is itself called into question.

The phenomenological social theorist Schutz (1964) states that the man in the street lives in a specific form of the epochè. This is the inverse of that described by Husserl, and is marked by the exclusion of any doubt with regard to the reality he experiences in the natural attitude (i.e. the 'thesis' of the existence of the natural world as a non-assailable belief). This 'epochè of everyday life', however, is abruptly and fundamentally called into question by the schizophrenic epochè. This calling in question has to be thought in terms of constituting intersubjectivity. The psychiatrist practising the clinical epochè is compelled, when encountering a person with schizophrenia, to grasp this primordial possibility of an epochal provocation at the heart of the natural attitude. More precisely, the psychiatrist should recognize that at bottom this is what she has been doing all along without knowing it when she sincerely tried to understand, listen and make vividly present (*vergegenwärtigen*) to herself the experience of the patient who has schizophrenia. This is why, with a view to describing this specific epochè, we shall from now on speak of a 'looking-glass epochè' (or 'face-to-face' epochè) [Naudin, 1997; Naudin et al., 1997].

This looking-glass epochè stems from the denaturalization of common experience, an intersubjective outcome of the failure of passive synthesis and of the slackening of the fundamental temporal structure which characterizes the experience of a person with schizophrenia. More profoundly, it marks the initial setback in any spontaneous attempt to constitute the common present of the encounter, a present bodily constituted in inter-affection, in a reciprocal fashion. It is important to note that it is not initially a matter of the person afflicted with schizophrenia deliberately refusing to communicate or of an absence of any intention to communicate but rather of a deficiency in the very basis out of which such intentions are possible and so can be sustained or disavowed.

Clinically, this makes it possible to take account of the fact that some individuals with schizophrenia seem purely passive *vis à vis* such a denaturalization while others seem able to reappropriate this deficiency subjectively by thematizing it as a theoretical tenet, as conscious refusal or disavowal. Faced with this initial rupture, the psychiatrist trained in the epochè can only make progress by analysing the resistances which, in leading him *either* to detach himself from the other with schizophrenia *or* to identify with him by imposing upon him the psychiatrist's own vision of reality, and thereby constantly bring him back to natural life. The analysis, by the psychiatrist, of his own resistances to the epochè make it clear to him that, in the time of the encounter, they go along with the difficulty his schizophrenic counterpart experiences in maintaining an involuntary epochè with regard to day-to-day life and, at the same time, in holding his own experience open to the constant renewal of the thesis of reality.   By following this path thus far, we ourselves have linked these questions with a fundamental sharing of embodiment on the basis of which the ego and the other are co-constituted in intercorporality. We are going to conclude this work by pointing to a flagrant contradiction which arises out of the privilege accorded to perception by Husserl, a contradiction which seems to us to be partially resolved by the looking-glass epochè imposed upon us by the encounter with someone who is hallucinating. The contradiction is the following: the hallucinatory epochè leads us to question the privilege accorded to perception by any phenomenology of Husserlian inspiration and to criticize it from a narrative perspective (Mishara & Schwartz, 1995; Naudin & Azorin, 1997b; Schapp, 1983). In the looking-glass epochè, and especially in the epochè presupposed by the experience of hallucinatory voices, the horizon within which all experience arises is shown to be narrative in essence.

One of our patients hears a voice which tells him to kill himself. Another hears the voice of a famous television commentator who 'comments' upon his every movement from continuously observing perspective. Our first patient heard insults and submitted passively to the orders of an alien inhabiting her ear. Such patients claim to hear voices which (in a manner which no doubt frustrates them) cannot be heard by others. The clinician may be genuinely inclined to want to empathize with the patient and believe the patient's report but is unable to summon up any experience in the natural attitude to grasp this experience. The clinician may be quite ready to lend her the phonological characteristics of her own voice, even sometimes of the voice of her associates. In all such cases this voice in the clinician is oriented in accordance with her own body as a reference point. This type of spatial orientation protects her from hallucination. On the contrary, hallucinatory voices speak from some other locus. They don't have their own body as would an embodied, speaking agent who addresses us in the natural attitude. These bodiless voices dominate the one who hallucinates.

In listening to the patient's complaint, the psychiatrist, nevertheless, inevitably compares the symptom with the nearest available analogies available in her everyday experience, the experience of voices issuing from other embodied agents with locations in the world. By means of a series of variations in steps of abstraction, by removing non-essential features or aspects of the symptom of hallucination (such as issuing from an embodied and localizable agent), the clinician arrives at transitional phenomena (e.g. the 'voice of conscience', or hypnagogic hallucinations before falling asleep) that ever approach the symptom he/she wishes to define. Still, he/she does not arrive at the essential structure till he/she has abdicated all ties to the phenomenon in natural reality as he/she knows it. Gradually the patient's experience is approached by means of abstracting/removing aspects (such as the attaching of voices to an embodied localized agent) in a reconstructive effort to make the patient's subjective experience vividly present. Using this method, close to Husserl's eidetic reduction, the psychiatrist is then able, by means of variation which begins with his/her everyday experience of hearing voices issuing from others, to abstractly conceptualize the experience of hearing disembodied voices which appear to issue from some other(s) who are not localizable in the patient's hallucinations. The patient, for her part, is unable to distance from these voices precisely because they do not appear to emerge from any locus from which the subject could remove himself. Even when the voices are reported to arise from within the patient's own body, as in the inner ear of our one patient, they are no less disturbing and afford no distance which the subject could impose between herself and the irritating stimulus in order not to no longer listen because now the other is located in her body. Hearing voices is a variant of those situations in which there is an inability of the subject to remove herself (physically or mentally) from the irritating stimulus — for example in the case of the increasing physical pain of a toothache).

In the place of perceptual experience which allows for perspectival distance and motility, hearing voices assume the form of multiple narrative fragments (e.g. commands or commenting voices). The experience itself seems to be denaturalized by the irruption of a narrative fragment which is itself devoid of bodily form. The patient's strategy is to bring these voices into some kind of narrative which makes sense to the patient and share this narrative with others. The patient then states narratively that it is the television personality, the alien, God, the devil or the CIA who is speaking to his/her in this disembodied way. Narrative allows the distance to what is narrated by sharing a meaning with others in which the narrator is able to impart (from a new perspective assumed with the narrative attitude) disturbing experiences with a certain sense of closure (Mishara, 1995). By spontaneously mirroring the patient's experience, the clinician who listens validates the reduction from (natural) reality which the schizophrenic involuntarily experiences and helps her gain a certain sense of perspective with regard to it. At the same time, one is perhaps forced to concede that one's own perceptions are themselves originally engaged at the heart of narrative, or of multiple narrative's fragments (Carr, 1991). Hallucinatory voices reveal some general meaning of human experience; it might be possible that a narrative configuration structures the basis of any perceptual, and more generally bodily experience (Schapp, 1983).

As we have seen, eidetic reduction often begins with exemplars in perceptual experience (as in the above example of beginning with the hearing or locatable voices of other embodied agents — in the natural attitude) in an abstractive movement to the invariant generalizable meaning structure (the hallucination of disembodied voices during psychosis). Owing to this emphasis on perception, Husserl's phenomenology is sometimes accused of being trapped within a methodology that needlessly privileges perception. We argue, from what we called the hallucinatory epochè, that it is possible to supplement the Husserlian approach with considerations from a narrative perspective which does not overlook the significance of language (Mishara & Schwartz, 1995; Mishara, 1995; Naudin & Azorin, 1997b). In both the mirroring epochè, as it is imposed on the clinician in her encounter with the patient with schizophrenia, and in the context of the epochè presupposed by the patient's experience of hallucinatory voices, the opposition verbal/non verbal can no longer be maintained so clearly. It gives way to an even more fundamental and inextricable 'interweaving' between these seemingly separate modes of experience.

Conclusion

We have shown how the Husserlian method of an epochè can be applied both to experience of the patient with schizophrenia and the clinician who encounters the patient. The latter becomes disarmed of her own commonsensical prejudices but thereby invites the patient to a narrative exchange in the shared context of a 'looking-glass epochè'. Reduction is not merely a clinical technique which can be employed consciously but throws us back on our most fundamental roots of being human: intersubjectivity, time-consciousness and embodiment. Because the encounter is at once foreign and yet disarming, it opens a realm of questioning which can further the interface between phenomenology, cognitive neuroscience, and psychopathology. In the present paper, only methodological paths were explored, but this kind of clinical research suggests some possible developments in the field of neurosciences, regarding namely the processes implicated in the internal structure of time, embodiment, and narrative structures of horizon. The encounter with persons with schizophrenia affords a number of indications regarding the directions to be taken by this research.

References

Azorin, J-M. (1996), 'Position du psychiatre phénoménologue par rapport aux névroses et aux psychoses', *Confrontations Psychiatriques*, **37**, pp. 197–218.

Binswanger, L. (1963), *Being-in-the-world: Selected Papers of Ludwig Binswanger* (New York: Basic Books).

Binswanger, L. (1965), *Wahn. Beiträge zu seiner phaenomenologischen und daseinsanalytischen Erforschung* (Pfullingen: Neske).

Binswanger, L. (1978), 'Le problème du délire dans la perspective de la phénoménologie pure', in *Présent à Henri Madiney* (Lausanne: L'âge d'homme).

Blankenburg, W. (1971), *Der Verlust der natürlichen Selbstverständlichkeit. Ein Beitrag zur Psychopathologie symptomarmer Schizophrenien* (Stuttgart: Enke).

Blankenburg, W. (1997), 'Rapport non délirant à la réalité et délire', *L'Évolution Psychiatrique*, **2**, pp. 285–97.

Carr, D. (1991), *Time, Narrative, and History* (Indianapolis: Indiana University Press).

Depraz, N. (1995), *Transcendance et incarnation, le statut de l'intersubjectivité comme altérité à soi.* (Paris: Vrin).

Goffman, E. (1981), *Forms of Talk* (Garden City, NY: Anchor Books).

Gros-Azorin, C. (1997), *Phénoménologie et expérience psychiatrique chez Ludwig Binswanger* (Paris: Université de Paris XII).

Husserl, E. (1955), 'Philosophy as a rigorous science', in *Phenomenology and the Crisis of Philosophy*, tr. Q. Lauer (New York: Harper and Row).

Husserl, E. (1957), *Formal and Transcendental Logic* (The Hague: Martinus Nijhoff).

Husserl, E. (1960), *Cartesian Meditations*, tr. D. Cairns (The Hague: Martinus Nijhoff).

Husserl, E. (1962), *Ideas: General Introduction to Pure Phenomenology,* tr. B. Gibson (New York: Collier).

Husserl, E. (1964), *The Phenomenology of Internal Time-consciousness*, trans. J.S. Churchill (Bloomington: Indiana University Press).

Husserl, E. (1970a), *Logical Investigations*, tr. J.N. Findlay (New York: Humanities Press).

Husserl, E. (1970b), *The Crisis of European Sciences and Transcendental Phenomenology*, tr. D. Carr (Evanston, IL: Northwestern University Press).

Husserl, E. (1982), *Ideas Pertaining to a Pure Phenomenology and to a Phenomenological Philosophy, First Book*, tr. F. Kerstern (The Hague: Martinus Nijhoff).

Jaspers, K. (1963), *General Psychopathology*, tr. J. Hoenig & M.W. Hamilton (Chicago, IL: University of Chicago Press).

Kraus, A. (1982), 'Identity and psychosis of the manic-depressive', in *Phenomenology and Psychiatry*, ed. A.J. De Koning (London: Academic Press).

Lanteri-Laura, G. (1991), *Psychiatrie et connaissances* (Paris: Sciences en situation).

Merleau-Ponty, M. (1962), *Phenomenology of Perception*, tr. C. Smith (New York: The Humanities Press).

Merleau-Ponty, M. (1974), *The Visible and the Invisible*, tr. A. Lingis (Evanston, IL: Northwestern University Press).

Mishara, A.L. (1994), 'A phenomenological critique of commonsensical assumptions of DSM-III-R: The avoidance of the patient's subjectivity', in *Philosophical Perspectives on Psychiatric Diagnostic Classification*, ed. J. Sadler, M. Schwartz & O. Wiggins (Baltimore: Johns Hopkins University Press).

Mishara, A.L. (1995), 'Narrative and psychotherapy — the phenomenology of healing', *The American Journal of Psychotherapy*, **49** (2), pp. 67–78.

Mishara, A.L. (1997), 'Binswanger and phenomenology', in *Encyclopedia of Phenomenology*, ed. L. Embree, E.A. Behnke, D. Carr, J.C. Evans, J. Huertas-Jourda, J.J. Kockelmans, W. McKenna, A. Mickunas, J.N. Mohanty, T.M. Seebohm and R.M. Zaner (Dordrecht: Kluwer Academic Publishers).

Mishara, A.L. and Schwartz M.A. (1995), 'Conceptual analysis of psychiatric approaches: phenomenology, psychopathology, and classification', *Current Opinion in Psychiatry*, **8**, pp. 312–16.

Naudin, J. (1997), *Phénoménologie et psychiatrie. Les voix et la chose* (Toulouse: PUM).

Naudin, J., Dassa, D., Giudicelli, L. and Azorin, J.M. (1995), 'Binswanger avec Schapp: analyse existentielle ou analyse narrative', *L'Évolution Psychiatrique*, **3**, pp. 575–91.

Naudin, J. and Azorin, J-M. (1997a), 'Commentary to Wiggins & Schwartz's "Edmund Husserl's influence on Karl Jaspers's phenomenology"', *Philosophy, Psychiatry and Psychology*, **1**, pp. 41–3.

Naudin, J. and Azorin, J-M. (1997b), 'The hallucinatory epochè', *Journal of Phenomenological Psychology*, **28** (2), pp. 171–95.

Naudin, J., Azorin, J-M., Stanghellini, G., Bezzubova, E., Kraus, A., Dörr-Segers, O. and Schwartz, M.A. (1997), 'An international perspective on the history and philosophy of psychiatry: the present day influence of Jaspers and Husserl', *Current Opinion in Psychiatry*, **9**, pp. 390–4.

Rossi Monti, M. and Stanghellini, G. (1996), 'Psychopathology: an edgeless razor', *Compr. Psychiat*, **3**, pp. 196–204.

Schapp, W. (1983), *In Geschichten verstrickt. Zum Sein von Mensch und Ding* (Frankfurt: Klostermann).

Schutz, A. (1964), *Collected Papers I, II, II*. (La Haie: Martinus-Nijhof).

Stanghellini, G. (1997), 'For an anthropology of vulnerability', *Psychopathology*, **30**, pp. 1–11.

Tatossian, A. (1980), *Phénoménologie des Psychoses* (Paris: Masson).

Tatossian, A. (1996), 'La phénoménologie: une épistémologie pour la psychiatrie?', *Confrontations Psychiatriques*, **37**, pp. 177–91.

Tatossian, A. (1997), *Phénoménologie et Psychiatrie: A. Tatossian* (Paris: Acanthe-Lundbeck).

Tatossian, A. and Giudicelli, S. (1973), 'De la phénoménologie de Jaspers au retour à Husserl: l'anthropologie compréhensive de Zutt et Kulenkampff', *Confrontations Psychiatriques*, **11**, pp. 127–61.

Tellenbach, H. (1980), *Melancholy: History of the problem, endogeneity, typology, pathogenesis, clinical considerations*, tr. E. Eng (Pittsburgh: Duquesne University Press).

Varela, F. (1996), 'Neurophenomenology. A methodological remedy for the hard problem', *Journal of Consciousness Studies*, **3** (4), pp. 330–49.

Wiggins, O.P., Schwartz, M.A. and Northof, G. (1990), 'Toward a Husserlian description of the initial stages of psychosis', in *Philosophy and Psychopathology*, ed. M. Spitzer & B.A. Maher (Berlin: Springer-Verlag).

Wiggins, O.P. and Schwartz, M.A. (1994), 'The limits of psychiatric knowledge and the problem of classification', in *Philosophic Perspectives on Psychiatric Diagnostic and Classification*, ed. J.Z Sadler., O.P. Wiggins and M.A. Schwartz (Baltimore: John Hopkins University Press).

Wiggins, O.P. and Schwartz M.A. (1997), 'Edmund Husserl's influence on Karl Jaspers's phenomenology', *Philosophy, Psychiatry and Psychology*, **1**, pp. 15–39.

Part 3

Contemplative
Traditions

B. Alan Wallace

The Buddhist Tradition of Samatha:

Methods for Refining and Examining Consciousness

The Nature and Purpose of *Samatha*

Buddhist inquiry into the natural world proceeds from a radically different point of departure than western science, and its methods differ correspondingly. Early pioneers of the scientific revolution, including Copernicus, Kepler, and Galileo, expressed an initial interest in the nature of physical objects most far removed from human subjectivity: such issues as the relative motions of the sun and earth, the surface of the moon, and the revolutions of the planets. And a central principle of scientific naturalism is the pure objectification of the natural world, free of any contamination of subjectivity. This principle of objectivism demands that science deals with empirical facts testable by empirical methods entailing testability by third-person means; and such facts must, therefore, be public rather than private, which is to say, they must be accessible to more than one observer.

Another aspect of this principle is that scientific knowledge — paradigmatically knowledge of astronomy and physics — must be epistemically objective, which is to say, observer-independent. A profound limitation of this ideal is that it cannot accommodate the study of subjective phenomena, which presumably accounts for the fact that the scientific study of the mind did not even begin until three hundred years after the launching of the scientific revolution. And it was roughly another hundred years before the nature of consciousness came to be accepted as a legitimate object of scientific inquiry. In short, the principle of objectivity excludes the subjective human mind and consciousness itself from the proper domain of natural science.

In stark contrast to this objective orientation of western science, Buddhism begins with the premise that the mind is the primary source of human joy and misery and is

Correspondence: B. Alan Wallace, Department of Religious Studies, University of California, Santa Barbara, CA 93106, USA.

Journal of Consciousness Studies, **6**, No. 2–3, 1999, pp. 175–187

central to understanding the natural world as a whole. In a well known discourse attributed to the Buddha he declares, 'All phenomena are preceded by the mind. When the mind is comprehended, all phenomena are comprehended.'[1] The mind and consciousness itself are therefore the primary subjects of introspective investigation within the Buddhist tradition. Moreover, just as unaided human vision was found to be an inadequate instrument for examining the moon, planets and stars, Buddhists regard the undisciplined mind as an unreliable instrument for examining mental objects, processes, and the nature of consciousness. Drawing from the experience of earlier Indian contemplatives, the Buddha refined techniques for stabilizing and refining the attention and used them in new ways, much as Galileo improved and utilized the telescope for observing the heavens. Over the next 2,500 years, Buddhist contemplatives have further developed and made use of those methods for training the mind, which they regard as the one instrument by which mental phenomena can be directly observed. As a result of their investigations, they have formulated elaborate, sophisticated theories of the origins and nature of consciousness and its active role in nature; but their inquiries never produced anything akin to an empirical study or theory of the brain.

They did, however, develop rigorous techniques for examining and probing the mind first-hand, and the initial problem in this endeavour was to train the attention so that it could be a more reliable, precise instrument of observation. With no such training, it is certainly possible to direct one's awareness inwards, but the undisciplined mind was found to succumb very swiftly to attentional excitation, or scattering; and when the mind eventually calms down, it tends to drift into attentional laxity in which vividness is sacrificed. A mind that is alternately prone to excitation and laxity is a poor instrument for examining anything, and indeed the Buddhist tradition deems such a mind 'dysfunctional'.

Thus, the first task in the Buddhist investigation of the mind is to so refine the attention and balance the nervous system that the mind is made properly functional, free of the detrimental influences of excitation and laxity. To do so, those two hindrances must be clearly identified in terms of one's own experience. Excitation, the first obvious interference to observing the mind, is defined as an agitated, intentional mental process that follows after attractive objects,[2] and it is a derivative of compulsive desire.[3] Laxity, on the other hand, is an intentional mental process that occurs when the attention becomes slack and the meditative object is not apprehended with vividness and forcefulness. It is said to be a derivative of delusion.

The types of attentional training Buddhists have devised to counteract excitation and laxity are known as *Samatha* (pronounced 'shamata'), the literal meaning of which is *quiescence*. It is so called, for *Samatha* is a serene attentional state in which

[1] *Ratnameghasutra*, cited in Santideva (1961), p. 68. This passage is found in the English translation of Santideva's work (1981), p. 121. A similar point is made by the Buddha in the opening verse of *The Dhammapada*: 'All phenomena are preceded by the mind, issue forth from the mind, and consist of the mind.' (1989, Ch. 1, v. 1.) All translations from the Pali, Sanskrit and Tibetan in this paper are my own.

[2] Wallace (1998) p. 168. A mental process is said to be *intentional*, not because one intends for it to occur, but because it has its own cognized object or objects.

[3] Compulsive desire is a mental affliction that by its very nature superimposes a quality of attractiveness upon its object and yearns for it. It distorts the cognition of that object, for attachment exaggerates its admirable qualities and screens out its disagreeable qualities. Cf. Guenther & Kawamura (1975), p. 96; Rabten (1979), pp. 74–5.

the hindrances of excitation and laxity have been thoroughly calmed. The discipline of *Samatha* is not bound to any one religious or philosophical creed. Such attentional training is found to varying extents in many of the contemplative traditions throughout history, including Hinduism, Buddhism, Taoism, Christianity and Sufism. It may be understood as a 'contemplative technology' that has been used in diverse ways by people holding widely different philosophical and religious views.

The central goals of the cultivation of *Samatha* are the development of attentional stability and vividness. To understand these two qualities in terms of Buddhist psychology, one must note that Buddhists commonly assert that the continuum of awareness is composed of successive moments, or 'pulses', of cognition each lasting for about ten milliseconds.[4] Moreover, commonly in a continuum of perception, many moments of awareness consist of non-ascertaining cognition, that is, objects *appear* to this inattentive awareness, but they are not *ascertained*.[5]

In terms of this theory, I surmise that the degree of attentional stability increases in relation to the proportion of ascertaining moments of cognition of the intended object; that is, as stability increases, fewer and fewer moments of ascertaining consciousness are focused on any other object. This makes for a homogeneity of moments of ascertaining perception. The degree of attentional vividness corresponds to the ratio of moments of ascertaining to non-ascertaining cognition: the higher the frequency of ascertaining perception, the greater the vividness. Thus, the achievement of *Samatha* entails an exceptionally high density of homogenous moments of ascertaining consciousness.

To return to the analogy of the telescope, the development of attentional stability may be likened to mounting one's telescope on a firm platform; while the development of attentional vividness is like highly polishing the lenses and bringing the telescope into clear focus. Tsongkhapa (1357–1419), an eminent Tibetan Buddhist contemplative and philosopher, cites a more traditional analogy to illustrate the importance of attentional stability and vividness for the cultivation of contemplative insight: in order to examine a hanging tapestry at night, if you light an oil-lamp that is both radiant and unflickering, you can vividly observe the depicted images. But if the lamp is either dim, or — even if it is bright — flickers due to wind, you would not clearly see those forms.[6]

The Use of a Mental Image as the Object in *Samatha* Practice

Among the wide variety of techniques devised for the cultivation of *Samatha*, one of the most commonly practised methods among Tibetan Buddhist contemplatives entails focusing the attention upon a mental image. This image may be of a visual object, such as a stick or pebble, although Tibetan Buddhists generally tend to prefer mental images having great religious significance to them, such as an image of the Buddha.[7]

[4] Vasubandhu, 1991, II, p. 474; cf. Jamgön Kongtrul Lodrö Tayé (1995) pp. 168–9.

[5] For a detailed account of non-ascertaining cognition see Lati Rinbochay (1981), pp. 92–110.

[6] I have translated a definitive presentation by Tsongkhapa of the cultivation of *Samatha* in Wallace (1998). The above analogy is found in the section entitled 'The reasons why it is necessary to cultivate both'.

[7] The technique of focusing on a pebble or stick is found in the section entitled 'Instructions on quiescence with signs' in Padmasambhava (1998). Tsongkhapa opts for focusing on an image of the Buddha in the section entitled 'A presentation of actual meditative objects' in Wallace (1998). For a

Regardless of the kind of technique one follows in the pursuit of *Samatha*, two mental faculties are said to be indispensable for the cultivation of attentional stability and vividness, namely, mindfulness and introspection. The Sanskrit term translated here as *mindfulness* also has the connotation of *recollection*, and it is the faculty of sustaining the attention upon a familiar object without being distracted away from it. Thus, when using a mental image as one's meditative object, mindfulness is fixed steadily upon that image. Moreover, that image must be clearly ascertained, otherwise the full potency of attentional vividness cannot arise, subtle laxity is not dispelled, and one's concentration will remain flawed.

Mindfulness of a mental image is said to be a kind of mental perception. In the actual practice of *Samatha* it is common first of all to attend visually to an actual physical object, such as a pebble; and once one has grown thoroughly familiar with its appearance, one proceeds to reconstruct a mental image of it and focus on that. In that phase of practice, mental perception apprehends the form of the pebble by the power of the visual perception of it. Thus, mental perception does not apprehend the pebble directly, but rather *recollects* it on the basis of the immediately preceding visual perception of that object.

According to Buddhist psychology, the mental image of the pebble is not a mental faculty or process, for it does not cognize its own object, but nor is it material in the Buddhist sense of being composed of particles of matter. Rather, it is regarded as a form for mental consciousness (cf. Hopkins, 1983, pp. 232–4), of the same type of qualia as the forms that appear in the dream-state. In this practice, one's mindfulness is focused on that mental image itself, not on the physical pebble of which the image is a likeness. In other words, it is the function of mindfulness to sustain the recollection of the image of the pebble, steadily observing it 'internally' in a manner analogous to the visual observation of the pebble itself.

Mindfulness is the principal means of accomplishing *Samatha*, but it must be accompanied by the mental faculty of introspection. While it is the task of mindfulness to attend, without forgetfulness, to the meditative object, introspection has the function of monitoring the meditative process. Thus, introspection is a type of meta-cognition that operates as the 'quality control' in the development of *Samatha*, swiftly detecting the occurrence of either excitation or laxity. In the Buddhist tradition, introspection is defined as the repeated examination of the state of one's body and mind (Śāntideva, 1997, V:108), and it is regarded as a derivative of intelligence.[8]

The Buddhist assertion of the possibility of introspection as a form of metacognition raises the interesting problem of whether or not it is possible for the mind to observe itself. Buddhists generally assert that at any given moment consciousness and its concomitant mental processes have the same intentional object; and at any given moment only one consciousness can be produced in a single individual (Vasubandhu, 1991, Vol. I, pp. 206 & 272). Moreover, a famous discourse attributed to the Buddha declares that the mind cannot observe itself, just as a sword cannot cut itself and a fingertip cannot touch itself; nor can the mind be seen in external sense objects or in the sense organs (*Ratnacutasutra*, cited in Śāntideva (1971) pp. 220–1.)

---

clear discussion of the technique of focusing on a Buddha-image by a contemporary Tibetan contemplative, see Lamrimpa (1995).

[8] Intelligence is defined as a mental process having the unique function of differentiating specific attributes or faults and merits of objects that are maintained with mindfulness. Cf. Rabten (1979), p. 63.

I suspect the rationale behind that assertion is that even when one is aware of one's own subjective experience of an object, there is still a sense of separateness between the observer of that experience and the experience itself. The sense of duality remains. Within the context of ordinary, dualistic cognition, there can be no subjective awareness that has no object, just as there can be no object without reference to a subject that cognizes or designates that object. According to Tibetan Buddhist philosophy, subject and object are mutually interdependent. All phenomena experienced as subjects and objects arise within, and in dependence upon, the conceptual framework in which they are designated.

When one observes one's own subjective experience of an object, the observer seems to be distinct from that experience; and if one takes note of that observer, there remains a sense of duality between the noted observer and the one who notes that observer. This hypothesis of an observer perceiving a simultaneously existing observer perceiving a simultaneously existing observer leads to an infinite regress. The eighth-century Indian Buddhist contemplative Śāntideva avoids this problem by suggesting that instead of such metacognition occurring with respect to a simultaneously existing cognition, one is rather *recollecting* past moments of consciousness. In short, he hypothesizes that it is possible to recollect a subjective experience that was not previously cognized as a distinct, isolated entity. In his view, when one remembers seeing a certain event, one recalls both the perceived event and oneself perceiving that event. The subject and object are recalled as an integrated, experienced event, from which the subject is retrospectively identified as such; but he denies that it is possible for a single cognition to take itself as its own object (Śāntideva, 1997, IX: 23; cf. Dalai Lama, 1994, pp. 26–31).

To take an example, when one's attention is focused on the colour blue, one is not observing one's perception of that colour. However, when one's interest shifts to the experience of blue, one is in fact *recalling* seeing that colour just a moment ago. In this process, one conceptually and retrospectively isolates the subjective element from the remembered experienced event, in which the blue and one's experience of it were integrated. Thus, when the attention is shifted back and forth between attending to the colour and to remembering seeing the colour, it seems as if such a shift is comparable to shifting the attention from the objects at the center of consciousness to those at the periphery; but according to Śāntideva, the attention is instead shifted from the perceived object to a short-term recollection of a previous event. And in remembering that event, the subject is isolated and recalled, even though it was not its own object at the time of its own occurrence. When one is recalling a perception of an earlier event, there is still a sense of duality between oneself and the perception that one is recalling. A single cognition does not perceive itself, so the subject/object duality is sustained.

In this case, introspection, functioning as a kind of mental perception, *recalls* intentional mental processes, such as excitation and laxity, from a prior moment of experience. Experientially, when one concentrates fully on a visual object, mental perception is focused on that object, and it does not apprehend the *experience* of that object. Then when the attention is shifted to the visual experience itself, the visual object becomes indistinct, though it does not fade out altogether. This apparent shift of the attention from the object to the subject seems to entail a shift within a subject/object field, or matrix, of visual experience: as one focuses more closely on the object, one becomes less conscious of the subject; and as one focuses more closely on the subjective experience, one becomes less conscious of the object. Śāntideva's point in this regard seems to be that although one is not conscious of the subjective experience of a visual perception while it is occurring, one may later recall the entire subject/object matrix, thereby bringing the initial subjective experience into consciousness.

The Stages of Development of *Samatha*

Progress in the gradual cultivation of *Samatha* is mapped out in terms of nine successive attentional states. The initial challenge in this training is to develop a continuity of sustained, voluntary attention, but in the first state, called *attentional placement*, the mind is strongly dominated by excitation. Indeed, because one is now consciously trying to sustain the attention unwaveringly on a single object instead of allowing it to roam about freely, it seems as if the mind were more overwhelmed by compulsive ideation than usual. One brings the mental image to mind, but almost immediately it is lost and the attention is scattered.

This initial, limited capacity for sustained attention is born out by modern experiments that have measured transient, focused attention on the basis of the performance of simple sensory tasks. Such research indicates that this transient, high level of focused attention lasts between one and three seconds (cf. Posner, 1978). Scientific investigation of attention during the late nineteenth century also indicated that voluntary attention cannot be sustained for more than a few seconds at a time. Such research led William James to conclude, '*No one can possibly attend continuously to an object that does not change.*' (James, 1950, I, p. 420.)

According to the Buddhist tradition, it is very difficult to attend continuously to an object that does not change, but that ability can be enhanced. During the successive stages of *Samatha* training, even the presence of mindfulness and introspection is no guarantee that progress will be made in sustaining the attention, for one may recognize the presence of laxity or excitation and still fail to take steps to counteract them. The remedy, Tsongkhapa declares, is the cultivation of the will, which is here closely associated with intervention and effort. According to Buddhist psychology, the will is the mental process that intentionally engages the mind with various types of objects and activities. In this case, when either laxity or excitation occurs, the mind is stimulated by the will to intervene in order to eliminate them. Tsongkhapa likens the relationship between the mind and the will to iron that moves under the influence of a magnet. The will to eliminate laxity and excitation is aroused by recognizing the disadvantages in succumbing to those hindrances and the advantages in overcoming them.[9] Thus, the initial two phases of this training are accomplished by learning about the nature of the practice and by contemplating the benefits of pursuing it.

At the outset of this training, one is encouraged to practise for many short sessions each day — as many as eighteen, fifteen-minute sessions — with as few distractions between sessions as possible. As a result of persevering in this practice, it is said that one ascends to the second attentional state called *continual placement*. During this phase, the mind is still subject to so much excitation that the attention is more often

---

[9] This topic is discussed in the section entitled 'Identifying the will and the means of stopping laxity and excitation' in Wallace (1998).

not on the object than on it, but at times one experiences brief periods of attentional continuity, for up to a minute or so. In other words, on occasion, for up to a minute, the attention does not completely disengage from the chosen mental image. But even during those periods of sustained attention, the mind is still prone to subtle excitation, which manifests as peripheral 'noise', or mental chitchat. Experientially, it seems as if one's attention is still fixed on the mental image even while other thoughts and sensory impressions come to mind. According to Buddhist psychology, however, it seems more likely that the attention is disengaged from the mental image during those interludes, but the breaks are so brief that there seems to be an unbroken continuity of attention to the main object. In any case, at this point only a gross level of attentional stability has been achieved, and that, too, is interspersed with periods of gross excitation, in which the meditative object is forgotten altogether.

As one continues in the training, one gradually reduces the number of sessions per day, while increasing the duration of each one. The emphasis in this regard is always on maintaining the highest quality of attention, rather than opting for mere quantity of time spent in the training. The next attentional state in this development is called *patched placement*, at which point the attention is mostly on the meditative object, and its continuity needs only to be patched up now and then when gross excitation occurs. Thus, there are more frequent periods of sustained attention, and they are of longer duration.

When one accomplishes the fourth attentional state, called *close placement*, the attention is stabilized to the point that one does not entirely disengage from the meditative object for the full duration of each session. The third and fourth states are achieved chiefly by the cultivation of mindfulness, and the principle emphasis up to that point is on the development of attentional stability, rather than vividness. In fact, Buddhist contemplatives have found that if one strives initially for ever greater vividness, that effort will actually undermine the development of stability. With the attainment of close placement, the power of mindfulness is well exhibited, gross attentional stability is achieved, and one is free of gross excitation.

Particularly at this point in the training, it is very easy to fall into complacency, feeling that one has already achieved the aim of sustained, voluntary attention. In reality, one is still very much subject to subtle excitation and to both gross and subtle laxity, and Tsongkhapa warns that if one fails to recognize these flaws, continued practice of this sort may actually impair one's intelligence. William James was also aware of pathological cases in which the mind is possessed by a fixed and ever monotonously recurring idea, and he concluded that those were the only cases in which the attention does become fixed on an unchanging object (James, 1950, I, p. 423). Buddhist contemplatives maintain that mental health can be retained and even enhanced as long as one cultivates a high degree of vividness in such sustained attention.

Thus, the fifth attentional state, called *taming*, and the sixth, called *pacification*, are achieved with the force of introspection, with which one closely monitors the meditative process, watching for the occurrence of laxity and subtle excitation. In the stage of taming, gross laxity, in which the vividness of the attention is missing, is dispelled; and in the phase of pacification, subtle excitation is eliminated, so that even peripheral distractions have disappeared.

By that time, an increasing sense of joy and satisfaction arises while meditating, so the seventh and eighth attentional states of *complete pacification* and *single-pointed attention* are achieved by the force of enthusiasm. In the seventh state even subtle laxity, in which the full potency of attentional vividness is not brought forth, is eliminated; and at the point of single-pointed attention the mind can dwell with utter stability and vividness on its chosen object for hours on end, without the occurrence of even subtle laxity or excitation. William James predicted that if the attention were concentrated on a mental image long enough, it would acquire before the mind's eye almost the brilliancy of a visually perceived object (*ibid.* p. 425), and this is exactly what Buddhist contemplatives report from their experience at this point in the development of *Samatha*.

With the attainment of the ninth state called *balanced placement*, accomplished with the force of familiarization, only an initial impulse of will and effort is needed at the beginning of each meditation session; for after that, uninterrupted, sustained attention occurs effortlessly. Moreover, the engagement of the will, of effort, and intervention at this point is actually a hindrance. It is time to let the natural balance of the mind maintain itself without interference.

The Attainment of *Samatha*

Even when one has reached the state of balanced placement, *Samatha* has still not been fully achieved. Its attainment is marked first by a dramatic shift in one's nervous system, characterized briefly by a not unpleasant sense of heaviness and numbness on the top of the head. This is followed by an obvious increase in mental and then physical pliancy, entailing a cheerfulness and lightness of the mind and a buoyancy and lightness of the body. Consequently, experiences of physical bliss and then mental bliss arise, which are temporarily quite overwhelming. But that rapture soon fades, and with their disappearance, the attention is sustained firmly and calmly upon the meditative object, and *Samatha* is fully achieved. The above claims concerning a shift in one's nervous system and its consequences have to do with first-hand, empirical, physiological experiences. It remains to be seen how, or whether, such a theory and the corresponding physiological changes can be detected objectively and understood in modern scientific terms.

With the achievement of *Samatha*, one disengages the attention from the previous meditative object, and the entire continuum of one's attention is focused single-pointedly, non-conceptually, and internally in the very nature of consciousness; and the attention is withdrawn fully from the physical senses. Thus, for the first time in this training, one does not attempt to recall a familiar object or mentally engage with it. One's consciousness is now left in an absence of appearances, an experience that is said to be subtle and difficult to realize. Only the aspects of the sheer awareness, clarity, and joy of the mind appear, without the intrusion of any sensory objects. Any thoughts that arise are not sustained, nor do they proliferate; rather they vanish of their own accord, like bubbles emerging from water. One has no sense of one's own body, and it seems as if one's mind has become indivisible with space.

While remaining in this absence of appearances, even though it is still not possible for a single moment of consciousness to observe itself, one moment of consciousness may recall the experience of the immediately preceding moment of consciousness, which, in turn, may recall its immediately preceding moment — each moment having no other appearances or objects arising to it. Thus, due to the homogeneity of this mental continuum, with each moment of consciousness recalling the previous moment of consciousness, the experiential effect is that of consciousness apprehending itself.

The defining characteristics of consciousness recollectively perceived in that state are first a sense of *clarity*, or implicit luminosity capable of manifesting as all manner of appearances, and secondly the quality of *cognizance*, or the event of knowing. Upon attaining *Samatha*, by focusing the attention on the *sheer* clarity and the *sheer* cognizance of experience, one attends to the defining characteristics of consciousness alone, as opposed to the qualities of other *objects* of consciousness.

The Use of Non-ideation as the Object in *Samatha* Practice

If one's chief aim in developing *Samatha* is to ascertain the nature of consciousness, one might ask whether a more direct strategy — without mentally engaging with a mental image or any other object — might be used. Many Buddhist contemplatives have in fact trained in an alternative technique of cultivating non-conceptual attention from the outset, without focusing on any other object such as a mental image. In this method the eyes are left open, gazing vacantly into the space in front of one. According to Buddhist psychology, this space is a type of form that is apprehended by mental, and not sensory, perception (Hopkins, 1983, p. 233). Mentally, one completely cuts off all thoughts of the past, future, and present. Bringing no thoughts to mind, one lets the mind remain like a cloudless sky, clear, empty, and evenly devoid of grasping onto any kind of object.

In this, as in all other techniques for the development of *Samatha*, attentional stability and vividness are cultivated by means of mindfulness and introspection. Here, the object of mindfulness is the mere absence of ideation, and with introspection one monitors whether the mind has come under the influence of excitation or laxity. Tsongkhapa especially emphasizes that while following this method, one must *ascertain* the absence of ideation as one's meditative object, rather than simply letting one's mind go blank. His concern here, I presume, is to ensure that the meditator does not mentally drift into a nebulous trance, but maintains an actively engaged intelligence throughout this training. In this way, one progresses through the nine attentional states explained previously. Eventually *Samatha* is achieved, and — as in the previous method — it is characterized by joy, clarity and non-conceptuality.[10]

Buddhist contemplatives raise the question as to whether this non-conceptual state of *Samatha* actually transcends all conceptual structuring and modification and whether the mere suppression of ideation is sufficient for entering a totally non-conceptual state of awareness. The eminent Tibetan Buddhist contemplative Karma Chagmé (1612–1678) voices the general consensus within the Tibetan tradition when he asserts that although this state may easily be mistaken for conceptually unstructured awareness, it is not unmodified by ideation; for one still maintains the conceptual sense that one's attention is being sustained in the absence of conceptualization (Karma Chagmé, 1998, p. 82) .

---

[10] A clear discussion of this technique is found in the section entitled 'The cultivation of attention' in Karma Chagmé (1998).

Settling the Mind in Its Natural State

There is something contrived about the above state of non-conceptuality, for during the training that leads to it, the mind has been artificially withdrawn from appearances and ideation has been suppressed. The consciousness of which one perceives the characteristics of joy, clarity, and non-conceptuality is one that has been conceptually isolated from its normal conceptual processes and from the variety of appearances with which it is normally engaged. The question may then be raised, 'Is it not possible to identify the natural characteristics of consciousness *in the midst of the mind's activity, without suppressing ideation*? After all, consciousness is obviously present and active while thoughts arise, so in principle there seems no reason why it could not be identified.

It was for this purpose that the technique of 'settling the mind in its natural state' has been devised and taught within the Indo-Tibetan Buddhist tradition (Dalai Lama & Berzin, 1997, pp. 37–142; Karma Chagmé, 1998, p. 80). This method, like all other techniques for developing *Samatha*, entails freeing the mind from distraction, so that one's attention is not compulsively carried away by either mental or sensory stimuli. However, this method is exceptional in that the attention is not fixed upon any object. Here one gazes steadily into the space in front of one, but without visually focusing on anything. Mentally, one brings the attention into the domain of the mind, and whenever any type of mental event is observed — be it a thought, an image, a feeling, a desire, and so on — one simply takes note of it, without conceptually classifying it, and without trying to suppress or sustain it. Letting one's mind remain at ease, one watches all manner of mental events arise and pass of their own accord, without intervention of any kind. Settling one's awareness in the present, the attention is not allowed to stray off in thoughts concerning the past or the future, nor does one latch onto any object in the present.

Normally when thoughts arise, one conceptually engages with the *referents*, or intentional objects, of those thoughts, but in this practice one perceptually attends to the thoughts themselves, without judging or evaluating them. The heart of the practice is allowing one's consciousness to remain in its 'natural state', limpid and vivid, without becoming embroiled in fluctuating emotions and habitual thought patterns.

While following this practice, one alternately seeks out the consciousness that is engaging in this meditation and then releases one's awareness once again. This is said to be an effective means of dispelling laxity. The eighth-century Indian Buddhist contemplative Padmasambhava (1998) describes this technique as follows:

> Having nothing on which to meditate, and without any modification or adulteration, place your attention simply without wavering, in its own natural state, its natural limpidity, its own character, just as it is. Remain in clarity, and rest the mind so that it is loose and free. Alternate between observing who is concentrating inwardly and who is releasing. If it is the mind, ask, 'What is that very agent that releases the mind and concentrates the mind?' Steadily observe yourself; and then release again. By so doing, fine stability will arise, and you may even identify awareness (p. 106).

The result of this practice, he says, is that flawless *Samatha* arises, such that wherever the awareness is placed, it is unwaveringly present, unmoved by adventitious thoughts, and vividly clear, without being sullied by laxity, lethargy, or dimness. In this way, too, the sheer clarity and cognizance of consciousness can be recognized.

The Alleged Trait Effects of Accomplishing *Samatha*

In addition to various, valuable state effects of attaining *Samatha*, which were mentioned earlier, a number of trait effects are also claimed by Buddhist contemplatives. Following such meditation, afflictive emotional states such as aggression and craving are said to occur less frequently and are of briefer duration than previously. Even when negative mental processes arise, one does not readily succumb to them, and one's mind remains calm and dispassionate. Moreover, particularly as a result of settling the mind in its natural state, one experiences a non-conceptual sense that nothing can harm one's mind, regardless of whether or not ideation has ceased. In between meditation sessions, as one goes about normal, daily activities, one experiences a heightened sense of attentional vividness; and it seems as if even one's sleep were suffused with exceptional concentration, and one's dream-life takes on special significance. These claims are psychologically and physiologically significant, and they lend themselves to being tested scientifically so that we can understand more precisely what is meant by 'attentional vividness' and the other purported shifts in consciousness while sleeping and dreaming.

The Buddhist tradition also claims that once one has accomplished *Samatha*, various forms of extrasensory perception and paranormal abilities can be developed with relative ease. These include such abilities as perceiving the minds of others, recalling one's previous lifetimes, moving through solid objects, walking on water, multiplying one's own form, and so on. For an intelligent person educated in the modern west, one's first reaction to such claims may be to dismiss them without a second thought. I personally do not know whether any or all of these claims are valid. It does seem to me, however, that many of the Buddhist contemplatives making such assertions have engaged in rigorous, sustained, attentional training that are either undeveloped or long forgotten in the West. In short, they have run experiments in consciousness that are unknown to modern science. Therefore, dismissing such claims without any attempt to put them to the empirical test is an unscientific, purely dogmatic response. On the other hand, to accept such claims without any attempt to put them to the empirical test is just one more unscientific, dogmatic response.

Claims of extrasensory perception and paranormal abilities are quite common within the Buddhist tradition, in which no theoretical principles refute the possibility of such attainments, and numerous methods are taught and practised to acquire them. Recall the earlier cited statement of the Buddha, 'All phenomena are preceded by the mind. When the mind is comprehended, all phenomena are comprehended.' This is followed by an equally provocative assertion, 'By bringing the mind under control, all things are brought under control.'[11] Modern science, on the other hand has apparently assumed the opposite perspective: When the environment and the body, and specifically the brain, are brought under control, the mind is brought under control. Hence, in order to bring about a sense of comfort and well-being and freedom from suffering and fear, the modern west has sought techniques to control the environment, and maintain fine physical health; and it has produced a stunning array of drugs to control the mind, enabling people to relax, to become mentally aroused and alert, to sleep, to relieve anxiety, to overcome depression, to counteract attentional disorders,

[11] *Ratnameghasutra*, cited in Śāntideva (1961), p. 68.

to improve the memory, to experience euphoria, bliss, and even alleged mystical states of consciousness.

While the modern western approach is remarkably empowering to those who create, market, and distribute the above types of technology and drugs, it is profoundly disempowering for the individual. The Buddhist approach, on the other hand, provides little incentive to the rigorous, sustained, extraspective investigation of physical processes and to the development of technology. Given the current, unprecedented encounter of the ancient Buddhist tradition and modern science, there is no reason that we should be forced to choose one to the exclusion of the other; though the question of which one to emphasize more strongly is a matter of personal inclination.

The ultimate aim of the practice of *Samatha* is not simply to ascertain the primary characteristics of consciousness or to attain exceptional mental powers. Rather, it is to realize the ultimate nature of awareness, free of all conceptual mediation and structuring, transcending even the concepts of existence and non-existence. Such primordial awareness, known in this tradition as 'the Buddha-nature', is said to be our essential nature, and it is the fathomless well-spring of intuitive wisdom, compassion, and power. For exceptional individuals, the previously described method of settling the mind in its natural state may be sufficient for gaining such realization; but for most people, further training beyond *Samatha* is required, but that would take us beyond the scope of this paper.[12]

Prolegomena to a Future Contemplative Science

By the end of the nineteenth century, many physicists were utterly convinced that there were no more great discoveries to be made in their field — their understanding of the physical universe was in all important respects complete. One of the few lingering problems to be solved was known as the 'ultraviolet catastrophe', which had to do with the incompatibility of entropy-energy formulae derived from classical thermodynamics. The solution to this problem came from Max Planck, who thereby laid the foundation for modern quantum theory, which shook the very foundations of physicists' views of the universe.[13]

While there is certainly no comparable sense that the cognitive sciences have formulated a comprehensive theory of the brain and mind — far to the contrary! — many experts in this field have concluded beyond a shadow of a doubt that consciousness is produced solely by the brain and that it has no causal efficacy apart from the brain. The fact that modern science has failed to identify the nature or origins of consciousness and that it is far from even discovering the brain correlates of consciousness in no way diminishes the certainty of those holding materialist views of the mind. When empirical knowledge of the nature and potentials of consciousness replace these current metaphysical assumptions, I strongly suspect that the 'problem of consciousness' will turn out to have a role in the history of science comparable to that of the ultraviolet catastrophe.

The most effective way to acquire such knowledge, I believe, is by a concerted, collaborative effort on the part of professional cognitive scientists and professional

---

[12] For a discussion of such techniques for realizing the primordial nature of awareness, see Karma Chagmé (1998), chs. 4–6, and Padmasambhava (1998), pp. 114–40.

[13] For a fascinating account of this problem and its radical solution, see Whittaker (1954), Ch. 3.

contemplatives, using their combined extraspective and introspective skills to tackle the hard problem of consciousness. This might entail, among other things, longitudinal studies of the gradual development of *Samatha* by people devoting themselves to this training with the same dedication as displayed by the scientists and engineers employed for the Manhattan Project. The successful completion of those efforts to tap atomic and nuclear power changed the face of the modern world. The successful completion of a Samatha Project might do so as well, and if such an endeavour were pursued with the altruistic aims promoted by Buddhism and the other great contemplative traditions of the world, the consequences for humanity may be more uniformly beneficial.

References

Dalai Lama (1994), *Transcendent Wisdom: A Teaching on the Wisdom Section of Shantideva's Guide to the Bodhisattva Way of Life*, trans., ed., and annot. B. Alan Wallace (Ithaca: Snow Lion).

Dalai Lama & Alexander Berzin (1997), *The Gelug/Kagyü Tradition of Mahamudra* (Ithaca: Snow Lion).

Dhammapada, The (1989), ed. Nikunja Vihari Banerjee (New Delhi: Munshiram Manoharlal Publishers).

Guenther, Herbert V. & Kawamura, Leslie S. (1975), *Mind in Buddhist Psychology* (Emeryville: Dharma).

Hopkins, Jeffrey (1983), *Meditation on Emptiness* (London: Wisdom).

James, William (1890/1950), *The Principles of Psychology* (New York: Dover).

Jamgön Kongtrul Lodrö Tayé (1995), *Myriad Worlds: Buddhist Cosmology in Abhidharma, Kalacakra, and Dzog-chen*, trans. & ed. by International Translation Committee (Ithaca: Snow Lion).

Karma Chagmé (1998), *A Spacious Path to Freedom: Practical Instructions on the Union of Mahamudra and Atiyoga*, comm. Gyatrul Rinpoche, trans. B. Alan Wallace (Ithaca: Snow Lion).

Lamrimpa, Gen. (1995), *Calming the Mind: Tibetan Buddhist Teachings on the Cultivation of Meditative Quiescence*, trans. B. Alan Wallace (Ithaca: Snow Lion).

Lati Rinbochay (1981), *Mind in Tibetan Buddhism*, trans. and ed. Elizabeth Napper (Valois: Gabriel/Snow Lion).

Padmasambhava (1998), *Natural Liberation: Padmasambhava's Teachings on the Six Bardos*, comm. Gyaltrul Rinpoche, trans. B. Alan Wallace (Boston, MA: Wisdom).

Posner, M.I. (1978), *Chronometric Exploration of Mind* (Lawrence Erlbaum Associates).

Rabten, Geshe (1979), *The Mind and Its Functions*, trans. Stephen Batchelor (Mt. Pèlerin: Tharpa Choeling).

Śāntideva (1961), *Siksa-samuccaya*, ed. P.D. Vaidya (Darbhanga: Mithila Institute).

Śāntideva (1971), *Siksa-samuccaya: A Compendium of Buddhist Doctrine*, trans. from the Sanskrit by Cecil Bendall and W.H.D. Rouse (Delhi: Motilal Banarsidass).

Śāntideva (1997), *A Guide to the Bodhisattva Way of Life*, trans. Vesna A. Wallace and B. Alan Wallace (Ithaca: Snow Lion).

Vasubandhu (1991) *Abhidharma Kosabhasyam*, French trans. Louis de La Vallée Poussin, English trans. Leo M. Pruden (Berkeley, CA: Asian Humanities Press).

Wallace, B. Alan (1993), *Tibetan Buddhism From the Ground Up*, with Steven Wilhelm (Boston, MA: Wisdom).

Wallace, B. Alan (1996), *Choosing Reality: A Buddhist View of Physics and the Mind* (Ithaca: Snow Lion).

Wallace, B. Alan (1998), *The Bridge of Quiescence: Experiencing Tibetan Buddhist Meditation* (Chicago, IL: Open Court).

Whittaker, E.T. (1954), *A History of the Theories of Aether and Electricity, Modern Theories 1900–1926* (New York: Philosophical Library).

Jonathan Shear and Ron Jevning

Pure Consciousness:

Scientific Exploration of Meditation Techniques

I

How can consciousness be studied scientifically? Science, of course, is fundamentally a matter of methodology, and the bedrock of scientific methodology is objective corroboration. Thus studying consciousness scientifically requires that we study it objectively, and take the results of methodologically sound examination of its publicly observable underpinnings, correlates and effects as the proper means of determining the truth and falsity of proposed theories. By itself, however, this objective approach, while necessary, is also necessarily inadequate. For consciousness is essentially an *interior* phenomenon, something we experience *as* subjectivity. Thus if we weren't able to identify the subjective phenomena of consciousness directly, that is, subjectively, we would have no way to know which externally observable phenomena were relevant to what phenomena of consciousness, or in what ways. Indeed, as the extensive discussions of the 'hard problem' make clear, no accounts of phenomena in purely 'third-person' objective terms would ever by themselves even suggest the existence of, much less explain, the subjective qualities of feelings, smells, thoughts, and other 'qualia' that constitute the bulk of our conscious life.[1] On the other hand, any purely subjective approach to the study of consciousness would also obviously be inadequate. For the only consciousness that one can examine directly is one's own, and the distinction between objectivity and subjectivity, crucial to anything we can call 'science', requires reference to, and corroboration in terms of, perspectives outside of one's own subjectivity. What is required then is some combination of objective and subjective approaches.

Such combinations are of course standard fare in psychophysiological studies that examine, for example, correlations between mental tasks and phenomena on the one

Corresponding author: Jonathan Shear, Department of Philosophy, Virginia Commonwealth University, Richmond, VA 23284-2025, USA.

---

[1] For twenty-seven articles reprinted from *JCS* 'Hard Problem' Special Issues, see Shear (1997).

hand and various sorts of brain imaging and other physiological measures on the other. Yet, useful and exciting as such studies can be, they suffer from a significant asymmetry. For while their objective side employs sophisticated scientific method-ologies, capable of isolating and evaluating variables completely outside the ken of ordinary sense perception, their subjective side typically uses mere everyday sorts of introspection, capable of isolating only ordinary internal phenomena such as sense perception, imagining and verbal thought. That is, while the objective side of con-sciousness studies is supported by sophisticated scientific methodologies, the subjec-tive side typically appears to be little more than Aristotelian. The need for systematic first-person methodologies here is thus starkly apparent.

There have, of course, been attempts to rectify this asymmetry. Introspectionism was the first, and phenomenologists have been working on another methodology. Both of these approaches are discussed at length by other contributors to this volume. This paper will explore a third approach, one that integrates elements of traditional Eastern meditative procedures with modern objective scientific methodologies. In contrast to the introspective methods usually relied on in modern Western treatments of consciousness, the Eastern procedures in question have the possible advantage of being the products of centuries of effort to develop systematic first-person explora-tory methodologies. But since these methodologies developed outside of the context of our traditions of science, their reported results of course cannot simply be taken at face value. Nevertheless, aspects of their internal logic and putative results appear to be cross-culturally congruent, despite great differences of metaphysical frameworks and social milieux. Thus examining them and their effects in the context of modern scientific methodologies and criteria may well prove useful to us in our own task of developing a significant science of consciousness.

In the paper that follows we will accordingly describe some common methodologi-cal features and claimed results found in several major Eastern meditative traditions, discuss conceptual and methodological problems they raise, review some relevant scientific research on contemporary meditating subjects, and suggest some implica-tions for the scientific study of consciousness. In particular, it will be suggested that the existing meditation-related research already indicates that Eastern varieties of meditative procedures should prove to be a useful component of any future science of consciousness.

II

The literature of Asian meditation traditions (Vedanta, Yoga, Buddhism, Taoism, etc.) contains repeated claims to the effect that it is possible to learn to go beyond the surface of human awareness to its depths and gain systematic experience of the ground, structures and dynamics of consciousness underlying all human experience. What is needed, according to these accounts, is to 'reverse' the direction of one's attention and turn it from its ordinary 'outward' orientation to feelings, thoughts, sen-sations, and objects 'inward' towards consciousness itself. We normally, of course, tend to think of awareness of such things as feelings and thoughts as 'inward' in contrast to 'outer' awareness of the physical world in general. Indeed, this distinction between inward and outward is fundamental to the child's learning to distinguish between the public physical realm and the private realm of his or her own mind, as cognitive developmental studies have repeatedly pointed out. But the notion of 'inward' used here is much more radical. For here even awareness of one's own most private, internal thoughts and feelings is still external to one's awareness itself, for they still appear *to* one's awareness, in front of one's 'mind's eye', so to speak, and the 'inward' referred to here is intended to indicate a complete reversal of attention, away from thoughts and feelings as much as from external objects, back into *awareness itself*.[2] This radical redirection of awareness, away from all of its ordinary objects, whether sensations, images, or thoughts, is then said in time to produce experience of both the ground and deep structure of all of our consciousness awareness.

There are of course serious conceptual problems with such traditional accounts. In the first place, it is not easy to understand how one could redirect one's attention away from all thoughts, sensations and graspable mental contents while at the same time actually practising a procedure that one has had to grasp and learn. Secondly, the standard descriptions of some of the experiences that will concern us indicate that they are completely unimaginable; indeed their absolute ungraspability is a recurrent theme in the relevant literature. Thirdly, objections have been raised against the possibility of the existence of culture-independent experiences in general, and the type of experiences we will discuss in particular. And questions have been raised about the propriety of inferring cross-cultural congruence of experiences from congruence of description, given the necessarily culture-embeddness of all descriptions. Any serious attempt to integrate traditional meditation procedures and experiences into contemporary scientific studies of consciousness will have to come to grips with these questions, and each will be addressed below, if only briefly.

III

The difficulty of even imagining practising a procedure that could allow the mind to divert its attention from all mental content whatsoever is that it would seem that the very practice of any procedure would have to keep one's attention on the mental content and guidelines of the procedure being practised. Thus the practice itself would seem to preclude success. Yet there is nothing in principle paradoxical in the notion of

---

[2] As the Zen Master Hsu Yun (1840–1959), for example, put it:

> [Y]ou should unremittingly and one-pointedly turn the light [of awareness] inwards. . . . 'To turn inwards' is 'to turn back'. When hearing and looking follow sound and form in the worldly stream hearing does not go beyond sound and looking does not go beyond form. . . . However, when going against the mundane stream, the meditation is turned inwards to contemplate the self-nature (Lu K'uan, 1961, Series One, p. 14).

Hsu Yun, studied Ch'an throughout China, Tibet, and Southeast Asia in his youth, was 'the Dharma successor' to all five major sects of Ch'an (or Zen) Buddhism, reuniting them after many centuries of separation.

Compare also Plato in the West:

> [T]he true analogy . . . is that of an eye that would not be converted to the light from the darkness except by turning the whole body. Even so this organ of knowledge must be turned around [180 degrees] from the world of becoming together with the entire soul, like the scene-shifting periactus in the theater. . . . [Otherwise] it possesses vision but does not rightly direct it and does not look where it should

to gain knowledge of the source and deep structures of intelligence [i.e. the Good and the other Forms] (Plato, 1973, p. 750 [518b-d]).

For a discussion of this notion of 'reversal' in Plato, Zen and Vedanta, see Shear (1990b), Chs 1–3.

a procedure which could first bring all of one's awareness to a single point, and then transcend its own activity — whether through fatigue or relaxation — thus bringing both itself and all other mental activity to a halt.

Consider, for example, procedures used in two Asian meditation systems most widely known in the West, Zen Buddhism and the Transcendental Meditation (TM) technique from Advaita Vedanta. Zen employs a variety of techniques, but by far the best known are those involving meditation with paradoxical *koans*.[3] There are many different types of *koans,* ranging from shouts to conceptual paradoxes, and different ways of practising with them. But, generally speaking, the *koan* practices are designed so that one focuses one-pointedly on the *koan* problem while every solution one can *conceive of* is portrayed as a dead end, rejected emphatically by one's teacher — until, finally, all discriminative activity becomes utterly blocked. Then, as Lu K'uan Yu[4] puts it,

> after all thoughts, whether good or evil, have been stopped so as to realize singleness of mind . . . the mind is reduced to impotency, it ceases to function and its condition is compared in the Ch'an [Zen] texts to that of a withered log, an unconscious skull, a wooden horse, a stone girl and an incense-burner in a deserted temple. . . . [T]he mind . . . is now on the wane and is on the point of vanishing completely to return to its bright essence (Lu K'uan, 1961, Series Two, p. 20).

Bringing the mind to absolute stillness in this way is, of course, not easy, and takes a 'strong will' and 'dogged determination to control . . . [one's] thoughts'. But the logic of the process is straightforward: using one's will to put an end to all thinking, including the act of willing itself, 'so that the mind can be calmed and the self-nature can be perceived' (Lu K'uan, Series Two, p. 14). One should bore into the *hua t'ou* (understood alternatively as the point of the *koan* and its 'head' or source in one's self-nature itself) continuously.

> [t]he important thing is to stick to your Hua Tou at all times — when walking, lying, or standing — from morning to night (Hsu Yun, in Chang, 1959b, p. 81).

Then

> [a]s time goes on, this concentration will . . . freeze the mind and isolate it from all externals resulting in the achievement of singleness of mind. The practiser is engulfed in the hua t'ou, thus forming an homogeneous block which no externals can penetrate. . . . Some practisers can even give up the habit of sleeping at night (Lu K'uan Yu, 1961, Series Two, pp. 21–2).

A major mechanism for this freezing of the mind is, according to Chang Chen Chi, the raising of the 'doubt-sensation' (*hua t'ou*),

> a special type of doubt — a doubt without content — or more succinctly, the pure sensation of 'doubt' *per se* . . . like a great mass or load weighing upon one's mind (Chang, 1959b, p. 225)

---

[3] Other Zen techniques include, for example, *i ch'ing* (raising the doubt-sensation), often practised in conjunction with *koans*, and keeping one's attention on the *tan t'ien* (a specific point or 'centre' about three finger-widths below the navel). All of these techniques, however, follow the logic discussed here, namely, bringing all thought to a halt in order to display the fundamental nature of mind or consciousness itself. See Lu K'uan, 1961, Series Two, pp. 13–22.

[4] Lu K'uan Yu (Charles Luk) was a long-time disciple of Hsu Yun, and a major early translator of Chinese Buddhist and Taoist texts.

that can naturally be expected to develop when every item of discursive knowledge rejected as inappropriate to 'solving' the *koan*. Finally, with successful practice, whether with a *koan, hua t'ou* or other procedure,

> The time comes when no reflection appears at all. One comes to notice nothing, feel nothing, hear nothing, see nothing. . . . But it is not vacant emptiness. Rather it is the purest condition of our existence (Katsuki Sekida, in Austin, 1998, p. 473).

Turning from Zen to TM, we find that the mechanics of this latter technique are quite different from those used in Zen in general, and *koan* (and *hua t'ou*) practices in particular. In the standardized TM practice one is taught to use a *mantra*, a sound without any associated meaning, and repeat it effortlessly until the mind becomes absorbed and settles down relaxedly. The *mantras* are said to be so well suited to the nature of the mind that, acting purely as 'resonances', they prompt the mind to relax and, following its natural tendency, settle down, and enjoy the experience of 'deeper levels' of consciousness within. As to the procedure itself, the instructors insist that there is not much to be said in general (that is, independently of reference to the individual's own experiences). All that one does is to think the *mantra* effortlessly. Indeed, the simplicity of the technique and the importance of effortlessness are major foci of the standardized instruction procedure. The crucial points of this instruction are said to be the proper choice of the particular *mantra* or sound for each individual, and the personal instruction tailored to the particular experiences of the new meditator, so that he or she learns to use the *mantra* 'properly', that is, effortlessly and without concern for whatever thoughts and experiences that may come and go. In this way, according to Maharishi Mahesh Yogi, [5] the new meditator

> actually experiences the subtle states of thought without having to imagine, anticipate, or aim at any particular experience (Maharishi, 1966, p. 58).

Maharishi attributes this settling to the fact that the 'subtler' levels of mind are more enjoyable to experience. Thus as the mind settles down 'it finds the way increasingly attractive' (*ibid.*, p. 55), spontaneously experiencing progressively 'finer' aspects of the *mantra*, until finally it settles entirely, transcending all experience of the object (the *mantra*) that had been engaging it. Here, as Maharishi puts it,

> When the subject is left without an object of experience, having transcended the subtlest state of the object, he steps out of the process of experiencing and arrives as the state of Being . . . beyond all seeing, hearing, touching smelling and tasting — beyond all thinking and beyond all feeling. This state of . . . unmanifested, absolute, pure consciousness . . . is easily experienced (*ibid.*, p. 52).

In this way the TM technique reportedly

> allows the active mind to settle down to transcendental consciousness, the field of pure intelligence, where the mind is silent, unbounded, and fully awake within itself (Roth, 1987, p. 29).

There are thus, to be sure, important differences between Zen and TM, both in their procedures and in the metaphysically tinged terms ('bright essence', 'Being', etc.) used to refer to the states reportedly produced. But there are also important similari-

---

[5] Maharishi, the major disciple of the late Swami Brahmananda Saraswati, the Shankaracharya of Jyotir Math in Northern India (i.e. head of one of the four traditional centres of Advaita Vedanta), introduced the TM technique to the rest of the world.

ties. For the Zen practices described above[6] and the TM technique both use mental processes designed to annihilate themselves, whether through effort, doubt, or relaxation, until a purely contentless wakeful mental state is reportedly achieved. Also, it appears that both types of procedures are, as their respective teachers insist, non-ratiocinative, and rely on specific (if different) types of feeling (doubt, positive affect) rather than any sort of intellectual analysis.[7] Finally, and most importantly for our discussion, both traditions contain descriptions of what appears to be the same, empirically contentless experience as produced by their very different procedures.

<h1 style="text-align:center">IV</h1>

Let us suppose for the moment that it is in fact possible to gain experiences corresponding to the above accounts, and through means such as those described, and also, again for the moment, that the various above accounts do in fact refer to (qualitatively) one and the same experience. This experience would appear to be one of consciousness alone by itself — pure, silent, and empty of all 'phenomenal' objects.[8] Here, as Zen texts often put it, the active mind has been left behind, and one's 'Void' self-nature, pure-consciousness alone by itself, is experienced.[9] Or, as Vedantan texts and the exponents of TM put it,[10] when the mind has become completely settled

---

[6] It should be reemphasized that Zen itself is a diverse, ancient tradition, with many subtraditions with significant differences of procedures and metaphysical claims. Nevertheless it is clear that the above account reflects at least a major component of the Zen traditions, which is all that is required for the present discussion. Indeed, this component is so great that Zen teachers such as Lu K'uan Yu will claim that 'All the devices used in [Zen] Buddhism . . . have only one aim: the stoppage of all thinking for the realization of mind.'

[7] We can also note that in both (traditional) Zen and TM, a sharp distinction is made between knowing how to meditate and knowing how to teach others to meditate. Becoming a Zen *Roshi*, or teacher, for example, may (depending on the particular tradition) require knowledge of many hundreds of *koans*, and how to assign them and how to evaluate students' progress, above and beyond practising Zen successfully oneself, 'breaking through' with a *koan*, and even becoming 'enlightened'. And while it takes only a few hours over four successive days to learn to practise the TM technique, learning to *teach* it — assign *mantras*, ensure effortlessness, 'check' students' practice, etc. — typically requires thousands of hours of meditation and lectures during ten-months of full-time in-residence training. A conspicuous difference between the two traditions, however, is that while *Roshis* are supposed to be enlightened 'Masters', TM teachers are supposed only to be expert technicians, capable of passing on knowledge of how to meditate successfully, without any presumption (or need) of their having become 'enlightened'.

[8] It should perhaps be noted that while this experience may be understood as the immediate goal of the meditation practices described above, both the Zen and the Vedantan sources referred to above are explicit that this experience is only a step in their traditions' real goal, namely, 'enlightenment' as they respectively understand it.

[9] As Chang puts it,

this self-witnessing or self-awareness portion is considered by Yogacara as pure consciousness itself. . . . It is also found in Zen. . . . This *chih*, or self-awareness, is intrinsically non--dualistic. It can be aware of itself, and can be aware as such, without any outer object . . . whereby thoughts within the dualistic pattern are brought into play. . . . The cultivation of self-awareness or pure consciousness will . . . eventually annihilate all dualistic thoughts and bring one to Buddhahood (Chang, 1959b, pp. 168–9).

Of course, non-Zen Buddhists may disagree that this is all there is to gaining 'Buddhahood'. But such questions are not germane to our own topic, which is not one of a correct understanding of Buddhism or Buddhahood, but only of particular experiences and procedures described.

[10] The TM technique derives from the tradition of Advaita Vedanta. See note 5 (above).

(while nevertheless remaining alert) one steps outside all activity of perception, and, silent and fully awake inside, experiences pure, unmanifest, absolutely objectless, consciousness. What is this experience like? By all accounts it is not *like* anything. For it has no content in it at all to make it more like any one thing than any other. And inasmuch as it contains no phenomenal content at all, no colours, sounds, thoughts, anticipations, etc. — or even any subjective manifold where such content could be located — whatever one can *imagine* is necessarily irrelevant to it. In short, the experience is simply awareness itself, unimaginable and, as the Zen are fond of saying, ungraspable.

Nevertheless, while the experience cannot be imagined, its defining characteristic — the complete absence of empirical phenomenal content — can readily be specified conceptually. This allows us to think about the experience coherently, even if we can't *imagine* it. The seemingly merely negative definition of the experience might seem odd or contrived, if one has never had the experience. Nevertheless it is still useful. For if one has never had the experience, one can recognize that one has never had any experience corresponding to this odd definition, and by the same token, after having the experience, one can, by all reports, equally readily recognize that one *has* had it.[11] Thinking about the experience in this (or any other) way is, of course, useless for *gaining* it, as traditional texts often emphasize. But the definition will serve as a useful beginning point for scientific investigation into the status of the experience itself.

V

The first question that needs to be addressed is why we should even entertain the idea that such an unusual experience can actually be had. One reason, of course is the reports in the texts of so many cultures. But these are merely anecdotal, and much more is needed before anything like scientific knowledge about consciousness could be thought to be had. Plausibility is one thing, objective fact quite another. Here, real research, following normal scientific protocols, is clearly necessary. And this is especially important when the topic involves the subjective experience of people who have invested their time, and often their hearts, in meditation procedures hoping to gain significant, even life-changing, experiences. For this kind of investment can naturally be expected to lead people to want to think they have the hoped-for experiences, whether or not they actually do.

Fortunately, however, a growing body of meditation-related research relevant to questions of the existence and significance of the experience in question has been accumulating over the past twenty-five years. This research began, naturally enough, by evaluating some of the traditional claims of physiological correlates of the pure consciousness experience.[12] One striking cross-cultural claim (found in texts of Yoga, Vedanta, Taoism, Zen, etc.) about physiological correlates of the experience is that it is accompanied not only by significant reduction of metabolic activity but complete

---

[11] When people learn to meditate effectively and settle down completely, one often hears comments like 'Oh, *that's* what was being talking about. Very simple. And nothing like anything I'd imagined!'

[12] Pre-scientific cultures were, of course, not oblivious to the distinction between actually having experiences and merely claiming to have them, and they naturally developed various means, some of them behavioural (witness the famous, and often seemingly bizarre Zen testing-stories), others physiological, to evaluate meditators' experiential claims.

cessation of the normal respiratory activity of inhalation and exhalation. As the *Yoga Sutras*, the central text of Yoga, puts it, the processes of 'taking in the breath and exhaling . . . do not appear in [conjunction with] a reposeful mind', that is, in a mind in the pure consciousness state of *samadhi*, where, as Vyasa's ancient commentary explains, 'breathing generally stops' (Patanjali, 1977, p. 81). Or, as Maharishi puts it,

> to create transcendental consciousness [the state of pure consciousness by itself] the brain must . . . be held . . . in a state of suspension. . . . For this to be possible the breath must be held in a state of neither breathing out nor breathing in. The breath must be between flowing and not flowing, and must be suspended there (Maharishi, 1967, p. 296).

And, as Chang puts it within the Zen tradition,

> Another major characteristic of *Samadhi* is the stoppage of breath. Without a complete cessation of breathing, the progressive thought-flow will never cease its perpetual motion. A number of different names have been used to designate *Samadhi*, one of them being 'stopping the breath' (Chinese: *chih shi*), which unmistakably points to the fact that *Samadhi* is a state related to this condition . . . this common and very natural phenomenon. (Chang, 1995b, p. 204)

This rather surprising physiological claim has now received support from contemporary scientific studies showing high correlation between periods of complete respiratory suspension and reported episodes of experiences of pure consciousness in subjects practising the TM technique. And other studies show biochemical indicators of significantly reduced metabolic activity on the levels of cells, tissues, and body during entire meditation periods among experienced meditators. These studies also report, as might be expected, correlations between episodes of pure consciousness experiences and physiological parameters quite outside those mentioned, or even suggested by, the traditional literature, such as, for example, unusually high inter-hemispheric EEG coherence.

Given the historical accounts, the correlations of respiratory suspension and reports of pure consciousness are particularly interesting. The most relevant contemporary studies have been carried out in conjunction with meditators using the TM technique. An article in *Psychosomatic Medicine* (Farrow and Hebert, 1982), for example, reports the results of several studies.[13] 'Many practitioners of TM report frequent experience of complete mental quiescence, the pure consciousness state described above [in the article],' and the experiments reported were 'designed to test for a possible relationship between breath suspension episodes and experiences of pure consciousness.' 'Breath suspension' here refers to episodes where largely vertical pneumotachograph tracings (indicating rather ordinary, if slightly slower than normal) respiration are sharply punctuated by essentially straight horizontal lines for half-minute or so periods of breath suspension.[14]

In the first study reported, meditators had roughly 10 times the number of periods of respiratory suspension (5.9 vs. 0.6) per 30 minute session than the non-meditating controls (sitting, instructed to relax) did. In another of the studies, examining correlations between button pushes indicative of subjective assessment of just having had a

---

[13] Compare also Travis and Wallace (1997) and Badawi *et al.* (1984).

[14] 'Breath suspension' here thus indicates the absence of normally detectable inhalation and exhalation; air flow does not stop entirely, however, and continues by virtue of ordinarily undetectable low amplitude 2–7 Hz fluttering of the lungs revealed by Fourier analysis.

'pure consciousness' episode, 36 of 84 button pushes by the 11 meditating subjects occurred within 10 seconds of the offset of one of the 57 breath suspension episodes (of sufficient length to meet the experimenters' criteria). The authors state that

> The probability that 36 or more of 84 randomly distributed event marks would occur within 10 seconds of the offset of 57 breath suspension episodes over 249 minutes is $p<10^{10}$.

A third study by the same authors, examining a single 'advanced' meditator, reported a 100% correlation between button pushes and breath suspension episodes. The authors also contrast the physiology of the reported pure consciousness state with those of sleep apnea, drowsy-state sleep onset, and epilepsy (*re* slow rolling eye movements, compensatory hyperventilation, etc.)

To date such studies, specifically exploring correlations between reported episodes of pure consciousness and respiration patterns, appear to have been carried out only on meditators practising the TM technique. One of the reasons for this is that reports of this experience are widespread among meditators practising this technique, often within the first few weeks of practice, while other meditation systems generally consider this particular experience more 'advanced'. The neurophysiologist (and long-time Zen practitioner) James Austin, reviewing the literature on meditation and respiration in his book, *Zen and the Brain*, concludes that

> These studies of TM subjects link clear, thought-free consciousness with two quite different sets of physiological evidence. The most impressive of these events suspends respiratory drive and causes a relative hypoventilation [in which 'respiration *stops*' with 'no compensatory overbreathing' afterward]. The second cluster of associated findings are more subtle and variable. They include peripheral autonomic changes and tendencies toward increased EEG coherence (Austin,1998, p. 97).

Moreover, Austin observes,

> [S]uch brief, clear, and quietly aware moments are not merely the typical normal drowsy prelude to sleep. Instead, when we are drowsy, the signs are shallow abdominal breathing, slow mentation and reaction times, and flatter alpha waves in our EEG [none of which characterize the moments in question]. Nor can anyone produce such moments of mental clarity *voluntarily* by choosing to hold the breath (*ibid.*).

VI

Let us now apply these results[15] to the methodological question raised above of how seriously to take meditation-related accounts of pure consciousness experiences. The above research indicates that a particular, highly unusual respiratory pattern, namely the complete *suspension* of the normal activity of inhalation and exhalation, is significantly correlated with episodes of the experience as reported in conjunction with the practice of the TM technique. Furthermore, it is apparent that this unusual respiratory pattern is an unconscious physiological correlate of the experience, for the identifying criterion of episodes of pure consciousness experiences is the complete absence of all empirical content. Thus, when we find an unusual, unconscious physiological parameter highly correlated with reports of episodes of an unusual experience, we surely have reason to think that the reports reflect something above and beyond mere cognitive factors such as metaphysical beliefs, expectations, desire to be

---

[15] See the Appendix (p. 205 below) for a review of research on a variety of physiological parameters related to the respiration studies discussed above.

thought successful or to please experimenters, etc. — especially since such cognitive factors have never even been suggested to be correlated with the physiology in question. The natural conclusion is that both the unusual experiential reports and the correlated unusual, unconscious physiological parameters both appear to be reflections of a specific underlying psycho-physiological state.

This conclusion would appear to be strengthened when the experimental results are evaluated in the context of the traditional accounts from Yoga, Vedanta and Zen that suggested the above research in the first place. The laboratory results on TM subjects do not of course establish the truth of these claims of the relevant correlation of experience and respiratory pattern in Yoga and Zen meditators. But they certainly agree with these claims, and it is difficult to see how such claims would ever have arisen in the absence of actual observations of the correlation in question.[16] The fact that the correlation between the unusual experience and unusual physiology in question is reported and emphasized in widely diverse cultural settings and even contradictory conceptual contexts (Indian Yoga and Vedanta; Chinese and Japanese Zen; modern Catholics, atheists, Protestants, etc. practising TM), and often as a result of explicitly non-cognitive procedures, thus provides further support for the conclusion that the commonality of experiential reports reflects a commonality of experience that is independent of the variables of culture and beliefs.

Indeed, it would strain credulity to suppose that phenomenologically different (and explicitly unimaginable) experiences should just happen by chance not only (i) to be described equivalently in different cultures with their diverse, often incompatible belief systems, but also (ii) to be correlated with the same unusual set of unconscious physiological parameters. Thus it seems reasonable, even given the absence to date of specific studies of meditating subjects from many of the traditions, both (1) to conclude that the cross-cultural equivalence of reports reflects actual phenomenal equivalence, and (2) to take the reports themselves as significant descriptions of the natural, culture-invariant subjective response to the physiological state in question.

VII

We have so far been talking about 'the' pure consciousness experience, as though it is obvious that there is precisely one experience that can be identified and referred to. But from the perspective of both phenomenological and hermeneutical analyses, this is not as obvious as it might seem. To begin with, our use of cross-cultural comparisons of experiences above makes it important to address hermeneutical objections to such comparisons in general. When one reads the relevant descriptions from different meditation traditions around the world, or even from subtraditions within a given tradition (as, for example, the different schools of Buddhism), it is clear that they are often embedded in different conceptual systems, and that different metaphysical terms (e.g. 'Being', 'Void', 'suchness', etc.) are used to refer to it. Thus it might well seem that the experiences referred to are likely to be significantly different, despite the fact that they all are also referred to in common as being devoid of all empirical

[16] This is a far cry from actually corroborating the claims with regard to various, very different meditation procedures. This would require direct laboratory testing, and the authors know of no studies conducted to date that specifically examine the traditionally claimed correlation in Zen and Yoga meditators.

phenomenal content whatsoever. And respectable hermeneutical thinkers have often taken this position.

Their argument goes as follows. All of our experience, as well as our language, occurs in particular social contexts, unique to each culture and subculture. As a result they are all also built up out of culturally-dependent components (language, symbols, expectations, etc.). Consequently all experiences in general, and the (supposedly single) experience we have been discussing in particular, are in fact culture-specific. Thus there are *no* experiences that are culture-independent and the same across different cultures. Consequently it is simply a mistake to think that there is any single experience being referred to here. Indeed, it is argued, this is made clear by the different metaphysical terminology different traditions and cultures use to refer to the set of experiences under discussion.[17]

It is not hard to see, however, that this sort of hermeneutical reasoning, however useful it might be to highlight the culture-dependent aspects of our experiences in general, does not apply to the pure consciousness experience in particular. For while hermeneutical thinkers argue that 'images, beliefs, symbols, and rituals define *in advance*, what the experience . . . will be like' by 'shaping' it and 'building' it up from such 'elements' as 'memory, apprehension, expectation, language . . . prior experience' (Katz, 1978), it is clear that no such 'elements' can be found in any experience fulfilling the defining characteristic of the experience we have been discussing. For any experience properly identifiable as a pure consciousness experience has to be devoid of *all* empirical phenomenal content in general, and thus all of *these* sorts of contents in particular. Thus, whatever experiences (and to whatever degree) the hermeneutical arguments may properly apply to, they clearly cannot apply to any experience fulfilling the defining characteristic of pure consciousness experiences.

Moreover, it is easy to see, purely logically, that all experiences fulfilling the defining characteristic of pure consciousness experiences have to be phenomenally equivalent. For suppose, to the contrary, that two pure consciousness experiences are phenomenally different. Then at least one of them must have phenomenal content that the other does not. But this contradicts the defining characteristic of pure consciousness experiences, and implies, contrary to our supposition, that this experience is *not* a pure consciousness experience. Thus the supposition must be false, and no two experiences fulfilling the defining characteristic of pure consciousness experiences can be phenomenally different.

We can also note that meditation traditions throughout the world regularly and explicitly insist that the kinds of content that hermeneutical thinkers are concerned with are precisely the ones that have to be left behind before the experience in question can be gained, and also that there is a great difference between the experience and the metaphysical terms and implications that they think may or may not be appropriately associated with it.[18] Thus whether or not there have ever been any experiences that fulfill the defining characteristic of the experience we have been discussing, as meditation traditions throughout the world have repeatedly insisted, it would

---

[17] Compare, for example, Katz (1978).

[18] Compare, for example, the methods of 'forgetting' emphasized by Taoism's Chuangtze, the anonymous medieval Christian 'Cloud of Unknowing', a wealth of Zen techniques, Vedanta's *neti neti*, the Western *via negativa*, etc.

appear on purely logical grounds that all experiences that actually do fulfill this characteristic must in fact be phenomenally the same, hermeneutical protestations notwithstanding.[19]

VIII

These purely logical arguments, however, leave something to be desired. For they proceeded as though we can be sure about what the various experiences really *are*, while all that we actually had to go on was *reports* of experiences. Here phenomenological and hermeneutical questions really do deserve more close attention. Let us begin with a basic phenomenological point. In ordinary conversation we generally take it for granted that experiences are *given* to us, and that their content is generally *transparent*. We know what our experiences are precisely because they are our experiences; all we need to do is introspect and report. In reality, however, as phenomenological thinkers effectively point out, it is not so simple. For our experiences often have unnoticed nuances. And the training in phenomenological methods is designed, among other things, to enable us to become aware of just such otherwise unnoticed features of our experience.

Applying this to the case at hand, let us suppose that descriptions of the experiences in question are often conceptually transparent, and also that we know unambiguously what it would mean to have an experience (definitive of 'pure consciousness') in which all determinate content (colours, sounds, feelings, thoughts, spatio-temporal extension, etc.) are absent. Let us further suppose that people reporting having experiences fulfilling the definition of 'pure consciousness' experiences are reporting their experiences quite honestly. These suppositions, however, are not enough to imply that the people reporting were *having* such contentless experiences, but only that they were having experiences that *seemed to them* to be contentless. For they might have been having experiences which only seemed contentless to them, because of the absence of any *noticed* colours, sounds, feelings, thoughts, spatio-temporal extension, etc., despite the fact that there actually *was* some content that they simply hadn't noticed. Philosophers of various sorts can of course raise a host of questions about the intelligibility of this possibility. But commonsensically, it does not seem at all out of the question that one could have an experience with some unobtrusive kind of content that one had not noticed, but which, once one's attention is drawn to it, one could look back at one's memory and conclude, 'Oh, yes. Now I see — *that* was there, after all.' Indeed, it is possible that phenomenological training could be just the kind of thing that could enable someone to notice such previously unnoticed, extremely unobtrusive content.

Practically speaking, however, this objection poses no problem for our present analysis. For the experiences in question would still be identifiably 'the same' by virtue of their complete absence of any ordinarily observable content: colours, thoughts, extension, etc. — even if there *were* some differences potentially articulatable in terms of as yet unnoticed, abstract content. That is, we would still have a readily identifiable class of highly unusual experiences that were 'the same' insofar as our ordinary criteria (colours, extension, etc.) for distinguishing the contents of experiences are concerned.

---

[19] For fuller development of these points, see Shear (1990a). For arguments on both sides of the issue, see Forman (1990).

One more hermeneutical objection still needs to be addressed, however. This concerns the difference between (i) experiences and (ii) experiences *as described*. Hermeneutical thinkers are quite correct in pointing out that to make cross-cultural experiential comparisons we generally rely on people's descriptions of experiences, rather than on the experiences themselves. And descriptions are necessarily couched in the language and concepts of the describers' own particular cultures. Thus, when the language and concepts and cultures are as different as those of Indian Hinduism, Chinese Zen, and American meditators (of whatever persuasion), even congruent descriptions cannot be presumed to refer to the same experiential content. Generally considered, this argument clearly has merit.

But in the particular case in question it would seem to have no force. This is because the terms used to identify and characterize the experience in question, namely 'colours', 'sounds', 'thoughts', 'extension', etc. (the complete absence of which identifies the experience), are all the sorts of terms that we take to be basic to the languages of all developed (and even most aboriginal) cultures. Indeed, the presumption of the cross-cultural sameness of meaning of precisely such terms (with the possible exception of 'extension') is basic to all translation whatsoever. Thus, whatever difficulties we may properly need to emphasize in regard to evaluating purported sameness of more complicated experiences, they would not seem to apply much, if at all, to such simple experiences as, for example, 'gold spot' and 'waves on a blue sea' — and even less to the particular experience in question, which, as empirically contentless, is even *simpler* than any of these quality-filled, perceptually-extended experiences. Indeed, the very fact that comparable descriptions, formulated in terms of (the absence of the referents of) such simple, cross-culturally identifiable terms, are found in the context of widely diverse cultural and conceptual contexts, in itself argues for the independence of both the descriptions and the experiences from their embedding cultural contexts. In sum, whether we look to the logic of the experiences themselves or to the very simple language and concepts by means of which they are identified, we see that the hermeneutical objections to referring to these experiences as qualitatively the same do not apply.

Thus, given the above considerations, it should be clear that the burden of the argument has to be on those who claim the necessary (or even likely) cross-cultural difference of these experiences, to specify the kinds of differences they have in mind. To be consistent with the cross-cultural descriptions in question, these differences cannot of course be differences of colour, sound, thoughts, etc., and it then becomes unclear what kinds of differences they could have in mind, even in principle. And in the absence of specification of such putative differences, the abstract hermeneutical arguments appear to remain empty of empirical significance as well as logical force.

IX

Let us now turn briefly from questions of identifying the experience in question to the more difficult ones of understanding its significance. We have been referring to the experience of awareness without any phenomenal content as the 'pure consciousness' experience, in accord with texts from a wide variety of meditation traditions. But why should this experience be thought of as 'pure' *consciousness* itself, rather than merely some odd experience among others? Two responses can readily be given. The first is

that it is natural to think that if one removed all the phenomenal content of consciousness while still remaining alert, what was left ought to be bare consciousness itself.
The second reason is a bit more abstract. Common sense holds that we are each conscious of our own consciousness, if only subliminally, throughout all of our conscious
experiences. Indeed, it seems apparent that, as Locke put it, each of us either is or has
'a consciousness' which 'owns and imputes its various experiences to itself'. Just
what such a consciousness itself, as distinct from its phenomenal objects, might be,
however, has proven to be an extraordinarily difficult question. One of the biggest
difficulties is that since Hume it has become apparent that ordinary introspection is
unable to locate any component of experience that is ubiquitous in the way experience of consciousness itself ought (according to commonsensical reflection) to be.

This topic is a complex one, and no attempt to unpack the many problems will be
made here. Nevertheless, it can readily be shown that the experience we have been
talking about is the only one that could possibly display such a supposed ubiquitous
component of experience. For to be truly ubiquitous, any component of conscious
experience would have to be compatible with all possible experiences; and only a
component of experience that has no empirical quality (i.e., one that can be recognized as present in some experiences and absent from others) of its own could have
such omni-compatibility.

The logic is as follows: Suppose (i) that consciousness itself is an ubiquitous component of experience and (ii) that it is also characterized by some empirical quality Q.
Then (iii) it must be logically possible (by the definition of 'empirical') to have an experience where that quality Q was absent. This absence, however, would imply (iv)
that consciousness (with its presumed characteristic property) was *not* ubiquitous,
contrary to the supposition (i).[20] Thus if consciousness is in fact ubiquitous, as common sense would have it, it must be devoid of all empirical qualities.[21] In short, the
experience we have been calling 'pure consciousness' is not only a uniquely good
candidate, but the only logically possible candidate, for clarifying the supposed subliminal experience of consciousness throughout our everyday experience, as well as
for consciousness by itself, independent of all the ordinary contents of experience.

Much more needs to be said for this line of reasoning to be really convincing, of
course.[22] Nevertheless, this brief account should be enough to suggest at least the
intelligibility of the widespread claims, often found in Vedanta, Zen and other

---

[20] Put more concretely: Suppose Q were a particular (phenomenal) colour, say yellow. Then *every
conceivable* experience would have to have yellow as an ubiquitous component. This would imply,
among other things, that yellow was not an empirical quality, not a colour among colours which could
be identified ostensively by its presence in some experiences and absence in others. Thus, by analogy,
if one were to wear yellow glasses, one would neither be able to specify anything within one's field as
yellow, nor, indeed, one be able to experience any other colours at all — for *everything* would look
yellow, and 'yellow' itself would not be identifiable as an empirical quality.

[21] Compare also Kant's arguments for the necessary empirical qualitylessness of consciousness itself (as
'pure original unchanging consciousness' having 'no special designation of its own', etc.) in Kant
(1964), pp. 129 ff.

[22] For further discussion of these issues see Shear (1996). The idea that the experience of 'pure
consciousness' by itself is naturally followed by experiential recognition of consciousness itself as the
pervading component of all our ordinary experience (raising what had, it seems, been merely
subliminal to the level of clear recognition) is, of course, found in many meditation traditions.

meditation-related traditions, that the experience we have been discussing ought to be taken to be experience of consciousness itself.

X

Quite aside from such abstract logical considerations, we can at least note, if not properly evaluate here, one purportedly experiential reason found in texts of various traditions for taking the 'pure consciousness' experience to display the ground of consciousness within. Texts found in both Zen and Vedanta, for example, refer to eight distinguishable 'layers' of our inner awareness: the five senses, the discursive mind, the experiencing ego, and finally pure consciousness itself.[23] We are, of course, all readily familiar with the first six, namely, the five senses and the thinking mind. The seventh, the ego, is a topic discussed at length in Western thought (with conflicting conclusions here, to be sure, as in the East). The eighth, that of pure consciousness, is, on the other hand, hardly ever even alluded to in Western thought. The relevant point for our discussion, however, is that each of these 'layers' is said to be experienceable directly, as attention moves from the surface to the depths of consciousness. Thus, for example, Austin describes the final stages of the experience of moving beyond ego to pure unboundedness within as follows:

> Now, infinite [inner] space becomes the object of consciousness, followed by an awareness of objectless infinity, and then by an absorption into a void which has 'nothingness' as its object. Finally . . . there evolves 'neither perception, nor nonperception.'[24] (Austin, 1998, p. 474)

And as Maharishi, within the tradition of Vedanta, puts it,

> When the mind gains this state of chitta [mind without any ripples of activity — or specific objects of awareness]. . . . It holds its individuality in the void — the abstract fullness around it — because there is nothing for it to experience. It remains undisturbed, awake in itself.
>
> The state of the pure . . . individuality of the 'I' [pure ego] . . . [then] directly merges into transcendental Self-consciousness (Maharishi, 1967, p. 312).

where (as we have seen) one

> steps out of the process of experiencing and arrives at the state of . . . unmanifested, absolute, pure consciousness (Maharishi, 1966, p. 52).

---

[23] Compare, for example, Hsu Yun: 'We sentient beings all have the Fundamental Consciousness, or the so-called Eighth Consciousness, which is comparable to the king of all consciousness. This king is surrounded by the Seventh, the Sixth, and all the other five consciousness — seeing, hearing, smelling, tasting, and touching. These are the five outer thieves. The Sixth Consciousness is the mind, the inner thief. The Seventh clings to the cognizant faculty of the Chief, or Eighth, Consciousness as its own great ego' (Chang, 1995b, p. 83).

Exactly the same typology is found in Yoga and Vedanta, along with the notion that ignorance of our true nature is reflected in what they call the intellect's error ('the mistake of the intellect', *pragya aparad*), namely, taking itself, rather than consciousness itself, as one's true nature.

[24] This last move (from surrounding void to pure unmanifestedness) is what I take to be reflected by the famous Zen imperative, 'Step *up* from the hundred foot pole!'

Compare also Tibetan Buddhist accounts of experiences first of 'consciousness . . . left in an absence of appearances . . . as if one's mind has become indivisible with space,' and then of 'the ultimate nature of awareness, free of all conceptual mediation and structuring, transcending even the concepts of existence and non-existence.' (Wallace, this issue, pp. 182, 186.)

Thus, in short, we see what appear to be comparable experiential accounts of moving from awareness of abstract, surrounding voidness (at the level of 'ego') to absolutely pure, unmanifest consciousness, beyond the categories both of perception (for there is no-thing there to be perceived) and of non-perception (for there is a rememberable experience). Zen and Vedanta, of course have significant differences of metaphysics in general, and their interpretations of the significance of the experience in question are, in particular, often extremely difficult to understand. Nevertheless, accounts of the purportedly experienceable 'layers' of mind such as the above, placing 'pure consciousness' at the ground of all of our inner awareness, suggests to the present authors, at least, that the hypothesis that the experience in question may in fact display the 'pure' nature of consciousness itself is worth further investigation.[25]

XI

The Eastern meditation procedures from Zen and Vedanta we have been discussing are all oriented towards the experience of pure, qualityless consciousness. There are, of course, many other types of meditation procedures, both Eastern (in Zen and Vedanta, as well as other traditions) and Western. In particular, there are those that start 'from the top', so to speak, and focus on the systematic deconstruction of the contents of ordinary awareness in the attempt to uncover general principles, dynamics, and/or structures of consciousness as they relate to ordinary awareness. The particular procedures we have been discussing however have traditionally been conceived of as moving in an opposite direction, to the ground of consciousness first, and developing from this ground 'up' to our ordinary awareness on the basis of knowledge of this ground. Our discussion has accordingly emphasized (i) the logic of 'reversing' attention to 'pure' qualityless consciousness, (ii) the nature of the experience of this supposed ground, and (iii) its physiological correlates.[26]

We should also note here that the meditative procedures we have been discussing are ordinarily understood as having very different goals from the intellectual approaches of modern Western cognitive science and phenomenology, namely the bare, purportedly non-cognitive display of deep 'layers' of consciousness, rather than the generation of accounts of semantic, syntactic and other cognitive functions. Nevertheless the relevant Eastern traditions generally also hold that the experiences produced can ultimately prove of use in the intellectual effort of explaining our various cognitive processes. And the aim of the authors of the present paper is, similarly, to examine the use of these procedures and the experiences they produce to see what

---

[25] For a discussion of the relation of this experience to modern Western theories of self, for example, see Shear (1990a), chapter 4, and Shear (1996).

[26] We should also note that the procedures discussed here are reported to produce many experiences in addition to the ones we have been discussing. Most notably, perhaps, among these being the experience of what we can call 'pure positive affect' (pure bliss, joy, happiness, beauty, etc.) independent, like pure consciousness, of all discursive thought and concrete phenomenological content. While we have been talking about meditation procedures only in terms of their usefulness in helping generate objectively evaluable knowledge of consciousness, these procedures have traditionally been valued much more for their reputed role in the development of individuals' consciousness than for their potential role in abstract cognitive projects. Discussion of these topics, however, would take us too far afield (cp. Shear, 1998; Alexander et al., 1990; Shear, 1990b).

they might offer our modern scientifically-oriented investigations of human consciousness.

In this regard, we have seen so far that there is good reason to think that it is in fact possible to gain experience of pure consciousness by itself, independent of all empirical phenomenal content by means of the procedures and experiences we have been analysing. We have also seen that this experience, as gained through traditional meditation procedures, appears to be correlated with a characteristic physiology, as long claimed by meditation traditions throughout the world. These correlations in turn provide grounds for concluding that both the experiences and the associated physiological state are natural, culture-independent products of the relevant meditation procedures, and also for taking the experiential reports at face value as displaying the (empirically contentless) phenomenal nature of the experiences themselves. Finally, we have hopefully at least suggested something of the intelligibility of traditional claims that the pure consciousness experience, rather than being a mere curiosity, displays a fundamental feature, and perhaps even the fundamental nature, of consciousness itself. These sorts of results should by themselves be enough to indicate the value of meditation procedures of the sort we have been discussing for any future science of consciousness.

There are also reasons to suspect that these procedures may in fact have much more to offer scientifically. For if meditation procedures of the kinds discussed actually do enable human consciousness to settle down completely into the alert silence of pure consciousness, as has long been claimed, they may be able to provide a unique platform for the study of the internal phenomena of consciousness. In the physical sciences a typical research strategy for studying a new encountered substance is to obtain a pure sample, examine it as it is in itself, and then interact it with simple inputs to see its intrinsic and relational properties. By analogy, the meditative procedures in question might enable us not only to obtain a 'sample' of 'pure' consciousness and examine its phenomenological nature and physiological correlates, but also to begin to explore how this 'pure' consciousness responds interactively to selected phenomenal inputs, as ancient texts such as the *Yoga Sutras* maintain (Shear, 1990b). Indeed, whether or not such ancient claims have any validity, it does not seem implausible to think that developing the ability to allow the activity of consciousness to settle down into its simplest, non-active, completely silent state might have the effect of decreasing overall internal subjective perceptual and conceptual 'noise', thus making it easier to detect more subtle internal contents and dynamics of consciousness, as also claimed in Eastern meditation traditions. The result, again, would be to provide an enhanced platform for the internal explorations crucial to phenomenology, introspectionism, and, indeed, any fully developed science of consciousness.

Appendix

The physiological research referred to above is important enough for our methodological analysis to warrant reviewing in more depth. The original impetus for these studies was the widespread existence of traditional claims of meditation-related psycho-physiological correlates. As put by C.C. Chang, for example,

> In the higher states of meditation, the circulation of the blood is slowed down almost to cessation, perceptible breathing ceases, and the yogi experiences some degree of illumi-

nation, or 'brightness,' together with the thoughtfree state of mind. Then not only does a change of consciousness occur, but also a change in the physiological functioning of the body. In the body of a fully enlightened being [in whom, among other things, the experience of pure consciousness has become fully established], the breathing, the pulse, the circulatory and nerve systems are quite different from those of ordinary men. Much evidence in support of this fact is available from Hindu, Tibetan, and Chinese sources (Chang, 1959a).

From the modern scientific point of view, such claims have understandably been regarded as at best anecdotal and pre-scientific, and at worst merely fanciful. Their widespread occurrence, however, suggested they might be worth investigating. The earliest scientific studies of physiological correlates and effects of meditation procedures were conducted in conjunction with Zen and Yoga meditators, and later studies have often focused on TM. As discussed above, ancient authors in diverse traditions often emphasized suspension of respiration as a conspicuous correlate of the pure consciousness experience. Research on this correlation in conjunction with the TM technique was discussed at some length above. A brief view of some other physiological studies related to this topic follows:

Early studies of Zen showed decreased respiration rate and oxygen (O_2) consumption (Sugi and Akutsu, 1968). A later study (Akishige, 1977, discussed in Austin, 1998, pp. 94–5) reported that Rinzai Zen monks' ordinary respiration rate while sitting quietly was a very low six breaths per minute (apparently, as Austin points out, a product of their rigorous training in breath control); in meditation, however, this rate increased (perhaps due to the typically strenuous nature of Rinzai procedures), but only to the still very low eight breaths per minute. The same study also reported that the respiration rate of Soto Zen monks (who practise less strenuous procedures) decreased from nineteen to sixteen breaths per minute. Overall, these results and those on TM led Austin to conclude in his review of the physiological research on Eastern meditation techniques that respiration is the single most significant variable for examining 'meditation from the standpoint of its basic physiological mechanisms' (Austin, 1998, p. xx).

There are, however, significant problems in applying meditation-related research on respiration in general to questions about the experience of pure consciousness *per se*. Many of the procedures studied employ direct manipulation of respiration during meditation. Most of the studies examine respiration changes over whole meditation periods, without any attempt to correlate changes in breathing pattern specifically with reports of pure consciousness experiences. Also many of the meditation techniques studied are difficult to practise, often requiring isolation or other special circumstances, with the result that statistically adequate subject pools have often not been available.

The respiration studies on TM meditators were able to avoid these particular problems. The technique is standardized, is learned in a few hours, and does not involve attention to physiological processes. As a result, suitable numbers of experimental subjects have been widely available. Furthermore, and most germane to this paper, the TM studies are, so far as the authors can ascertain, to date the only ones that have specifically examined the correlation between respiration and the pure consciousness experience. Studies examining the relation between respiratory patterns and reports of this experience by meditators practising other techniques thus clearly need to be undertaken. Presumably they will be, as appropriate numbers of experimental subjects become available.

Given the central role of the TM respiration-suspension studies for our present discussion, it is worth noting other studies using TM subjects that are consistent with the results of the respiration-suspension studies and may help make their results more intelligible. In early studies on the TM technique, papers by Wallace (Wallace *et al.,* 1971) reported marked decline of O_2 consumption and CO_2 elimination, without change of respiratory coefficient (RQ), during thirty minute periods of meditation. Decline of O_2 consumption in the absence of change of respiratory coefficient indicates achievement of a state of rest without effort to manipulate respiration. When the availability of 'long-term' (at least five years) meditators increased, more sophisticated studies of respiration were undertaken. Farrow and Hebert (1982), for example, reported 40–50% respiratory decline, as well as the periods of breath stoppage highly correlated with subjective experience of pure consciousness discussed already. The same authors also compared respiration rates in ordinary eyes-closed relaxation and TM meditation, and reported significant decreases during TM, and no significant change during ordinary rest. Wolkove *et al.* (1984) reported similar findings.[27]

The above studies at the level of the whole body were then supplemented by studies at the organ level. Studies of organ blood-flow and metabolism provided more fundamental dependent measures than respiration and whole-body O_2 consumption. Dye-dilution and radioactive clearance measurements (Jevning *et al.,* 1978a) of blood flow showed (i) overall relaxation of blood vessels, and (ii) specific circulatory changes, including decreased liver and kidney blood flow. A later study by the same authors (i) indicated that much of the whole-body decline of O_2 consumption in meditation was due to decreased skeletal muscle metabolism (Jevning *et al.,* 1983a), and also (ii) showed the relaxation of individual tissue directly. And a more recent study (Jevning *et. al.,* 1996) showed that blood flow to the brain increases by 15–20% in frontal and occipital regions.

These studies at the whole-body and organ levels have now been supplemented by in-depth studies at the levels of tissues and cells. One such study (Wilson *et. al.,* 1987) reported cessation of CO_2 generation by forearm skeletal muscle. Another study (Jevning *et. al.,* 1983b) reported decreased red cell metabolism, an effect that implies that circulating chemicals modulating cellular activity are produced during the meditation practice. Thyroid stimulating hormones (TSH) decrease, again indicating less metabolic excitation (Jevning *et al.,* 1987). Blood cortisol, an indicator of stress, declines during long-term meditators' practice (but not for short-term meditators, or during ordinary relaxation [Jevning *et al.,* 1978b]).

While most of the above physiological processes are indicative of decreased activation, central nervous activity appears to *increase*, as evidenced by EEG, sensory-motor response, and brain blood-flow data (Banquet and Sailhan, 1974; Jevning *et al.,* 1987; Lang *et al.,* 1979) and by the subjective reports of pure consciousness as experience of enhanced, rather than diminished, alertness (Jevning, 1988; Jevning *et al.,* 1996), clearly distinguishing the state produced from that of sleep. Indeed, most of the changes of hormone and neurotransmitter concentrations, blood flow, cell and

---

[27] Fenwick *et al.* (1977), however, earlier had reported similar respiratory declines in TM and rest. A possible explanation of the discrepancy is that the study the later studies of Farrow and Hebert and Wolkove used more experienced TM subjects.

organ metabolism, and respiratory function accompanying TM are not found either in sleep or ordinary rest. Some of these measures (respiration, EEG coherence) are directly correlated with reports of experiences of pure consciousness. Others, while not time-sensitive enough to be correlated with the typically reported episodes (up to a minute or so) of pure consciousness, still indicate that this procedure, productive of pure consciousness, generates a characteristic physiology at the levels of cell, tissue, organ, and whole body. In short, taken together, these measures indicate that the body is often in a distinct, unusual physiological condition, both during whole meditation periods associated with reports of pure consciousness experiences, and during reported episodes of these experiences in particular.

The above results directly support the standard traditional cross-cultural reports of physiological correlates of pure consciousness — reduction of pulse, circulation and metabolic rate, and cessation of respiration. It would appear justified, then, to conclude that these physiological measures are in fact cross-cultural, procedure-independent correlates of the pure consciousness experience. This leads the authors to surmise that the more in-depth correlations described above (at the levels of tissues, cells, blood chemistry, etc.), found largely on the basis of research on the TM practice and not noted in the traditional literature, will also be likely to hold for pure consciousness experiences in general, however attained. Nevertheless, as noted, there are significant practical differences between the many meditation procedures designed to produce this experience. Thus full confidence in this general surmise will require future research on pure consciousness experiences as reported both in conjunction with other meditation procedures and independently of any meditation practice.

References

Akishige, Y. (1977), *Psychological Studies on Zen*, vol. 1 (Tokyo: Komazawa University Press).

Alexander, Charles N., Davies, John L., Dixon, Carol A., Dillbeck, Michael C., Druker, Steven M., Oetzel, Roberta M., Muehlman, John M, Orme-Johnson, David W. (1990), 'Growth of higher stages of consciousness: Maharishi's Vedic Psychology of human development,' in *Higher Stages of Human Development*, edited by Charles N. Alexander and Ellen J. Langer (New York: Oxford University Press).

Austin, James H. (1998), *Zen and the Brain* (Cambridge, MA: MIT Press).

Badawi, K.; Wallace, R.; Orme-Johnson, D., *et al.* (1984), 'Electrophysiologic characteristics of respiratory suspension periods occurring during the practice of the transcendental meditation program', *Psychosomatic Medicine*, **46**, pp. 267–76.

Banquet, J.P. and Sailhan, M. (1974), 'EEG analysis of spontaneous and induced states of consciousness', *Rev Electroencephalogr. Neurophysiol. Clin.*, **4**, pp. 445–53.

Chang, Garma C.C. (1959a), 'Yogic commentary', *Tibetan Yoga and Secret Doctrine*, 2nd edition, ed. Evans-Wentz, pp. xli and xlii, reprinted in Chang (1959b), p. 234.

Chang, Garma C.C. (1959b), *The Practice of Zen* (New York: Harper & Row Perennial Library).

Chuangtse [Zuang Zi] (1942), in *The Wisdom of China and India*, translated by Lin Yutang (New York: The Modern Library).

Farrow, J.T. and Hebert, R. (1982), 'Breath suspension during the transcendental meditation technique', *Psychosom. Med.*, **44** (2), pp. 133–53.

Fenwick, P.B.C., Donaldson, S., Gillis, L., Bushman, J., Fenton, G.W., Perry, I., Tilsley, C. and Serafinowicz, H. (1977), 'Metabolic and EEG changes during transcendental meditation', *Biol. Psychol.*, **5**, pp. 101–18.

Forman, Robert (1990), *The Problem of Pure Consciousness* (Oxford: Oxford University Press).

Jevning, R., Smith, W. R., Wilson, A. F. and Morton, M. N. (1978a), 'Redistribution of blood flow in acute hypometabolic behavior', *Am. J. Physiol.*, **235**, R89–R92.

Jevning, R., Wilson, A.F., Davidson, J.M. (1978b), 'Adenocortical activity during meditation', *Horm and Behavior*, **40**, pp. 54–60.

Jevning, R., Wilson A.F., O'Halloran, J.P. and Walsh, R.N. (1983a), 'Forearm blood flow and metabolism during stylized and unstylized states of decreased activation', *Am. J. Physiol.*, **245**, R110–R116.

Jevning, R., Wilson, A.F., Pirkle, H., O'Halloran, J.P. and Walsh, R.N. (1983b), 'Metabolic control in a state of decreased activation: Modulation of red cell metabolism', *Am. J. Physiol.*, **245**, *Cell Physiol.*, **14**, C457–C461.

Jevning, R., Wells, I. and Wilson, A.F. (1987), 'Plasma thyroid hormones, thyroid stimulating hormone, and insulin during acute hypometabolic states in man', *Physiol. and Behav.*, **40**, pp. 603–6.

Jevning, R. (1988), 'Integrated metabolic regulation during states of decreased metabolism, similarity to fasting: A biochemical hypothesis', *Physiol. and Behav.*, **43**, pp. 735–7.

Jevning, R., Anand, R. and Biedebach, M. (1996), 'Effects on regional cerebral blood flow of acute states of decreased metabolism in man', *Physiol. and Behav.*, **59**, pp. 399–402.

Kant, Immanual (1964), 'Transcendental deduction of the pure concepts of understanding', First Edition, *Critique of Pure Reason*, trans. Norman Kemp Smith (London: Macmillan).

Katz, Steven (1978), 'Language, epistemology, and mysticism', in *Mysticism and Philosophical Analysis* (Oxford: Oxford University Press).

Lang, R. Dehof, K., Meurer, K.A. and Kaufman, W. (1979), 'Sympathetic activity and transcendental meditation,' *J. Neural. Transm.*, **44**, pp. 117–35.

Lu K'uan, Yu [Charles Luk] (1961), *Ch'an and Zen Teaching*, Series One and Two, (London: Rider & Co.).

Maharishi, Mahesh Yogi (1966), *The Science of Being and Art of Living* (Stuttgart: International SRM Publications).

Maharishi, Mahesh Yogi (1967/1984), *Bhagavad Gita: A New Translation and Commentary* (Washington, DC: Age of Enlightenment Press).

Patanjali (1977), in Swami Hariharananda Aranya, *The Yoga Philosophy of Patanjali*, trans.P.N. Mukerji (Calcutta: University of Calcutta).

Plato (1973), *Republic*, trans. Paul Shorey in *The Collected Dialogues of Plato*, ed. Edith Hamilton and Huntington Cairns (Princeton: Princeton University Press).

Roth, Robert, (1987), *Transcendental Meditation* (New York: Primus).

Shear, Jonathan (1990a), 'Mystical experience, hermeneutics, and rationality,' *International Philosophical Quarterly*, **30** (4), Issue 120, pp. 391–401.

Shear, Jonathan (1990b), *The Inner Dimension: Philosophy and the Experience of Consciousness* (New York: Peter Lang Publishing).

Shear, Jonathan (1996), 'On a culture-independent core component of self,' in *East-West Encounters in Philosophy and Religion*, ed. Ninian Smart and B. Srinivasa Murthy (Long Beach: Long Beach Publications).

Shear, Jonathan (ed. 1997), *Explaining Consciousness: the Hard Problem*, (Cambridge, MA: MIT Press).

Shear, Jonathan (1999), 'Ethics and the experience of happiness', in *Crossing Boundaries: Ethics, antinomianism and the history of mysticism*, ed. G. William Barnard and Jeffrey J. Kirpal ((New York: SUNY Press).

Sugi, Y. and Akutsu, K. (1968), 'Studies on respiration and energy-metabolism during sitting in Zazen', *Res. J. Phys. Ed.*, **12**, pp.190–206.

Travis, F., and Wallace, R. (1997), 'Autonomic markers during respiratory suspensions; possible markers of transcendental consciousness', *Psychophysiology*, **34**, pp. 39–46.

Wallace, R.K., Benson, H. and Wilson, A.F. (1971), 'A wakeful hypometabolic physiologic state', *Am. J. Physiol.*, **221** (3), pp. 795–9.

Wilson, A.F., Jevning, R. and Guich, S. (1987), 'Marked reduction of forearm carbon dioxide production during states of decreased metabolism', *Physiol. Behav.*, **41**, pp. 347–52.

Wolkove, N., Kreisman, H., Darragh, D., Cohen, C., Frank, H. (1984), 'Effect of transcendental meditation on breathing and respiratory control', *J. Appl. Physiol.: Respirat., Environ. Exercise Physiol.*, **56**, pp. 607–12.

Part 4

Peer Commentary and Responses

Peer Commentary and Responses*

SIX POINTS TO PONDER

James H. Austin, 2445 Moscow Mt. Road, Moscow, ID 83843-9132, USA.

On page 2 of this volume our co-editors set admirable goals. They seek 'methodologies that can provide an open link to objective, empirically based description'. Moreover, they want 'explicit examples of practical knowledge, in case studies'. My comments will address these words and goals. I too prefer the case-method approach, and seek practical ways to access states of consciousness.

Then, at the top of page 4, Professors Varela and Shear define 'nonconscious phenomena' as those the subject is not aware of. In order to comment further on this issue of awareness and non-awareness, I'll first need to pick up on their other key word — 'blindness' — as introduced in their section VII. I'll then redirect it. For surely a central topic to confront is our own self-imposed blindfold. Which subterranean region of consciousness are we most unaware of? What thwarts our efforts to study all of its regions? Our own covert self.

Physical and psychic aspects of the many-sided self

Before starting Zen training, I wore the same blindfold as do most *JCS* readers. I could not have imagined how it would feel to *really* lose the 'self'. Therefore, I was also blind to how much this direct experiential fact of loss could contribute to scholarly attempts to articulate 'models of the self'(Gallagher & Shear, 1997).

However, I then experienced two separate and distinct alternate states of consciousness (Austin, 1998). The first was an episode of deep internal absorption. Its hyper-awareness took hold while I was sitting in meditation. Years later, the second experience flashed in while I was standing quietly. It would plumb levels much more profound: major intuitions, in the category of insight-wisdom. *Comprehensibilities* were revealed. They differed sharply from the sensory and affective changes during the earlier episode of absorption. One conclusion became obvious. *Point 1*: each event had peeled off different layers of my egocentric self.

Which layers were subtracted earlier, during absorption? They represented sensate functions, coded both for my *physical* self and for the envelope of space around it. Later, during the insight experience, other layers also dropped off. Fear vanished. Time vanished. All motivational roots of doing were undermined. These later subtractions were chiefly *psychic* in nature. They shed primal feelings, attitudes and instincts.

What made their loss even more impressive? The fact that I had been so blinded to their existence previously. I had not been aware how powerfully they had influenced all the rest of my conscious mentation and behaviour. By contrast, absorption's expanded field of consciousness was a shallow penetration. It had disclosed none of these psychic, existential issues. *I remained unaware of them.*

In *Peer Commentary and Responses* section, undated references to authors are to this issue of *JCS*.

Journal of Consciousness Studies, **6**, No. 2–3, 1999, pp. 213–311

Consider how, each day, our usual *non*conscious self busily reconstructs reality. Rarely does our conscious self recognize how covert are such methods. Can we begin to peek around this blindfold? One way is to employ a few shorthand words that summarize the dual operations — both physical and psychic — of the many-sided self. A simplified practical model presents this self as a psychological construct, in terms of its three main interactive components:

I, Me and Mine

A few samples illustrate the more unfruitful aspects of this I-Me-Mine complex (Austin, 1998, pp. 43–7). The sovereign I is aware that its physical body exists and acts. But its basic attitude is that of a 'busybody', ready to meddle. Moreover, its psychic blindspots conceal an arrogant assertion: in all its doing, it can do no wrong. In contrast, the Me occupies the tender butt-end of the self. The Me can get kicked around. It is fearful, easily threatened, and suffers accordingly. The Mine is readily captured by its greedy longings to possess other people and material things. Moreover, it owns, and cherishes firm opinions.

True, our I-Me-Mine complex also confers many egocentric benefits. They do help us survive. But the outcome often involves anguish, disruption, wasted energies and impaired performance. Indeed, it takes many years of hands-on practice, and introspection, before the rare person can completely shed those liabilities of selfhood which had so interfered with its assets.

Point 2: Only as part of the lone process of shedding these previously nonconscious liabilities can the person identify which prior, hidden aspects had been subtracted. The blindfold comes off for the first time during the initial reflective moments of insight-wisdom. Finally, an objective form of consciousness stands free from the old subjectivities. What does consciousness fully comprehend in this state of clear, objective vision? 'The way things really are' *a priori*.

This novel consciousness is utterly empirical. It can understand how thoroughly the former self had filtered and spin-doctored all data into its old conventional notions of consciousness.

Consider the case study of Siddhartha. His final liberation from the pejorative self required six years of rigorous effort. *Point 3*: Meditative methods can be one approach to transforming the way the self attends to the present moment. And meditative training (plus insightful awakenings) can also help restructure some basic personality traits, in ways that appear to influence ordinary behaviour. But do any of the shallower adjustments surmount crisis? Endure in an ongoing manner? Not usually, whereas the rare ongoing stage of sage wisdom is *a deep psychic transformation*. It requires both many years of dedicated daily practice within a sound cultural tradition, plus repeated seismic awakenings and many temperings by adversity (Austin, 1998, pp. 636–53).

Can we begin to study such complex processes longitudinally? Andrew Bailey points toward gaps in our 'seams' of consciousness. The suggestion is that we monitor meditators recurrently, during their silent thought-free intervals, when waking consciousness seems to be 'winging it' from one cognitive perch to another. *Point 4*: 'Silent' transitions are dynamic intervals. They can be eloquent.

Claire Peugeot's observations lend further support to another idea. Physiological studies could be especially fruitful when applied to those dynamic interfaces between wakefulness, sleep and reverie. *Point 5*: We badly need to focus on intuition's circadian and ultradian cycles. Coherent studies could clarify how intuition's rhythms, when refined, sometimes flash into insight-wisdom.

Semantic problems. Example: the word 'Being'

Peugeot's valuable contribution also mentions Heidegger, to the effect that intuition, in its most ideal form, can help us understand 'being in general'. Heidegger once illustrated this most advanced form of intuition (Heidegger, 1958, pp. 33–109). He needed only the word, Being. He then placed an X through it. Does this X cancel out the essential 'isness' or 'suchness' of Being? No. Instead, one can interpret it as pointing toward a very advanced category of alternate states of consciousness. For the deep issue here is meta*physiological*, and lies beyond metaphysical word-play.

Sages hint that — within this rare state — the essence of Being coexists with a zero condition of the personal psyche (Austin, 1998, pp. 570–2). No such state is 'easy' to enter, nor to study. Words such as 'Ultimate Pure Being' only hint at the nature of any experiential paradox so profound that form and emptiness both coincide, and equate (Austin, 1998, pp. 627–32). Our semantic problems multiply when any so-called 'ground level' of conscious experience seems to present itself, simultaneously, as an existence of infinite potential coinciding with *groundlessness*.

Alan Wallace nicely outlines a huge arena, summarizing three optional paths of concentrative and receptive meditation available to the meditator. In actual practice, many trainees gravitate toward simpler techniques, easier to keep on line, and those which seem least contrived. Why? One reason is that along the disciplined path that begins with tranquility, and that then moves to and fro from mindfulness toward becoming one-pointed, the practitioner's consciousness is also subject to a series of other intrinsic fluctuations. These physiological events shift spontaneously among: concentrating and letting go, opening up and focusing down, waking/drowsiness/ sleeping . . .

Still, it is relatively easy to arrive at the early moments of thought-free awareness. When these events last longer, a calm intensified awareness observes that the physical self has dropped increasingly out of the mental field. Such silent moments of so-called 'pure consciousness' intrigue the researcher. Studies of their associated suppressed respirations might help point to their more basic mechanisms. Yet, for the most part, the particular 'pure' moments which seem most available for study in a laboratory appear thus far to be either 'rudimentary' (Forman, 1990, p. 8), or 'shallow preludes' to the major deep absorptions (Austin, 1998, p. 99).

Meanwhile, readers should be aware that some absorptions can themselves present alluring impressions of ' "pure" qualityless consciousness'. But, as Shear and Jevning quickly go on to suggest (seven words later in section XI) this 'pure' consciousness could still be only the 'supposed' ground of consciousness.

The reader may observe, in the paper by Wallace, the lack of such terms as 'absorption,' or 'pure consciousness'. On the other hand, Shear and Jevning cite Maharishi as viewing an '. . . unmanifested, absolute, pure consciousness . . . easily experienced . . . as the "state of Being".'

Point 6: Methodologies alone won't suffice. Our different tribal disciplines are not yet using the same 'sign language'. We need to settle on standardized terms to express the different phenomenological levels of consciousness.

References

Austin, J. (1998), *Zen and the Brain; Toward An Understanding of Meditation and Consciousness* (Cambridge, MA: MIT Press).

Forman, R. (ed. 1990), *The Problem of Pure Consciousness* (NewYork: Oxford University Press).

Gallagher, S. and Shear, J. (ed. 1997), *Journal of Consciousness Studies*, **4** (5–6), pp. 399–540, Special Issue on Models of the Self.

Heidegger, M. (1958), *The Question of Being*, tr. W. Kuluboch and J. Wilde (New York: Twayne).

THERE IS ALREADY A FIELD OF SYSTEMATIC PHENOMENOLOGY, AND IT'S CALLED 'PSYCHOLOGY'

Bernard J. Baars, The Wright Institute, Berkeley, California 94704, USA.

I have great respect for efforts by Francisco Varela, Jonathan Shear and company to create a systematic phenomenology. In support of their efforts it should be noted that there is no need to start from scratch. We already have a systematic study of human conscious experience, and it is called 'psychology'. True, many academic psychologists deny this rather obvious fact, but if we look at what they do rather than what they say, we find that they are always studying the things people can report with accuracy. But the things we humans can report accurately are the same things we experience as conscious! Reportability is the generally accepted index of consciousness. In point of fact, therefore, psychologists are always asking people about their conscious experiences.

This was a commonplace truth in the nineteenth century, when the sciences of mind and brain first began. Since Gustav Fechner, early in that century, psychologists have systematically mapped out sensory consciousness in all modalities, discovering some elegant and beautiful laws in the process. Since Fechner there has emerged a thriving field of science, relating conscious experiences to an enormous variety of physical events in the world. Today, most of our knowledge about sensory processes depends on consciousness reports. S.S. Stevens in this century made the remarkable discovery that humans can map any sensory intensity in vision, say, onto a sensory intensity in hearing, in such a way that the relationship between the two is always described by a power law.

The phenomenology of colour has been successfully explored ever since Isaac Newton and Wolfgang Goethe, and we now have a remarkably sophisticated mathematical theory of hue, saturation and brightness, three *subjective* factors that describe all aspects of conscious colour perception. Indeed, the study of sensory perception routinely makes fundamental distinctions between subjective and objective dimensions of stimulation. Thus 'loudness' is officially defined in the psychology of perception as a label for a subjective aspect of auditory experience, and contrasted with 'sound amplitude', which is the corresponding physical dimension. 'Brightness' is a subjective quantity, while 'light intensity' is the corresponding physical dimension. 'Hue' is the subjective correlate of 'light wavelength', with entirely different features. This evidence about consciousness is quite consistent with the known neurophysiology of vision.

In the realm of hearing, Hermann von Helmholtz in the nineteenth century began the scientific study of sound perception with an exquisite sensitivity to phenomenology, taking advantage of centuries of progress in musical invention. The first artificial vocal tract models were produced in the nineteenth century, and the sounds they make sound like the human voice. All these discoveries involve noteworthy advances in phenomenology.

But the psychological mapping of consciousness has gone much further. Inner speech has been extensively studied under the headings of 'working memory', 'short term memory', 'thought monitoring', or 'protocol analysis' (Baars, 1988; 1997; Baddeley, 1992; Ericsson & Simon, 1984; Singer, 1988). This multiplicity of technical terms is unfortunate, because it hides the simple and overwhelming fact that human beings spend most of their lives talking to themselves, far more so than they tend to talk to any other human being. In the last several years we've discovered from brain scans that during silent inner speech, the left hemisphere areas for speech production (Broca's area) and speech perception (Wernicke's area) show intense metabolic activity (Paulesu *et al.*, 1993). This is exactly what we would expect based on purely psychological studies of consciousness in immediate memory.

Likewise for visual imagery. We now know that there is an 'Mind's Eye', a domain of visual imagery that resembles outer visual consciousness in many respects (Kosslyn, 1994). For example, it is easy to prove that the real visual field has the shape of a horizontal oval, and the imagined field of inner visual experience has the same shape. Indeed, we have largely confirmed Aristotle's hypothesis that visual imagery involves a 'pale copy' of the visual stimulus. The brain regions involved are largely the same (Farah, 1985).

Human phenomenology is remarkably accurate. When people are asked to pair similar vowels, for example, they will put /a/ together with /oh/ and /i/ with /e/. Apply the mathematical technique of multidimensional scaling to those paired vowels, and behold! The vowel circle appears (the circle of tongue positions in the mouth that produce the vowel sounds in speaking.) But we have no conscious knowledge of the vowel circle. Such unconscious regularities only emerge from systematic studies of human consciousness.

Today, there is remarkable progress in relating conscious experiences to measures of online brain function, such as PET, fMRI, MEG, EEG, and even single-cell studies (e.g. Baars, 1998). They show how the brain adapts to the world around us, and relates that process to our own conscious experience. Phenomenology is not solipsistic. It lives in continual interaction with the world, and it almost always makes sense in terms of that interaction. It is no accident that our own conscious experiences almost always correspond to known adaptive processes. Thus we have a remarkable body of scientific evidence about human phenomenology, much of which makes a great deal of sense.

The good news for Varela and Shear's quest for a more complete phenomenology is that we have a well-established foundation on which to build. It makes no sense to start from zero when in fact we have such a solid launching platform. Many established psychological techniques can be put to good use in creating a more complete science of consciousness.

In one respect, however, contemporary psychology is ahead of phenomenology — that is in our willingness to postulate unconscious processes to explain conscious experiences. Try mentally multiplying 9 x 9, for example. Chances are that you immediately came up with the answer, 81. Were you conscious of the process of arriving at an answer? Probably not. Yet we routinely postulate a memory retrieval process to explain the fact that you came up with the correct answer quickly and with minimal effort. Such unconscious steps happen in all mental activities; but pheno- menological rules of the game seem to prohibit us from making inferences about them. That puts us conceptually back in 1890, with William James. It makes it difficult to understand anything. The unconscious is as necessary for a complete understanding of the mind as consciousness is.

Is there more to know? Of course! We should investigate centuries of reports in the Vedanta and Buddhist traditions about 'higher' states of consciousness, beginning with 'pure consciousness' — consciousness without content. We need a much better understanding of special states of consciousness such as dreaming, twilight states, absorption, flow and suggestibility. There is a deplorable dearth of evidence about emotional feelings — that sinking feeling of disappointment, that wave of love, the surge of anger, the pang of guilt, all the conscious signals of emotional ups and downs. Then there are 'fringe' states, what William James called 'the vague', as in feelings of familiarity, beauty, rightness, anomaly, and perhaps mystical states (Mangan, 1993). We also need a better understanding of pathological states involved in loss of control, affective suffering, happiness, and dissociative states.

In the last decade we have found that brain studies are generally consistent with conscious experience, proving again that mind and brain live in the same seamless reality. The unity of the sciences is not a myth; different observers are simply looking at the great mountain peak of the universe from different points of view. As we learn more about the world mountain, psychologists meet phenomenologists and physicists on their paths, and philosophers run into their biological peers from across campus. As conscious human beings, all of us should rejoice at the emerging unity of human knowledge.

There is much to do. Let's build on what we already know.[1]

References

Baars, B.J. (1988), *A Cognitive Theory of Consciousness* (New York, Cambridge University Press).

Baars, B.J. (1997), *In the Theater of Consciousness: The Workspace of the Mind* (New York: Oxford University Press).

Baars, B.J. (1998), 'Metaphors of consciousness and attention in the brain', *Trends in Neurosciences*, **21** (2), pp. 58–62.

Baddeley, A. (1992), 'Consciousness and working memory', *Consciousness & Cognition*, **1** (1), pp. 3–6.

Ericsson, K.A. and Simon, H.A. (1984/1993), *Protocol Analysis: Verbal reports as data* (Cambridge, MA, MIT Press).

Farah, M.J. (1985), 'Psychophysical evidence for a shared representational medium for visual images and percepts', *Journal of Experimental Psychology: General*, **114**, pp. 91–103.

Kosslyn, S.M. (1994), *Image and Brain* (Cambridge, MA: MIT Press/ Bradford Books).

Mangan, B. (1993), 'Taking phenomenology seriously: The "fringe" and its implications for cognitive research', *Consciousness and Cognition*, **2** (2), pp. 89–108.

Paulesu, E., Frith, D. and Frackowiak, R.S.J. (1993), 'The neural correlates of the verbal component of working memory', *Nature*, **362**, pp. 325–345.

Singer, J.L. (1988), 'Sampling ongoing consciousness and emotional experience: Implications for health', in *Psychodynamics and Cognition*, ed. M.J. Horowitz (Chicago: University of Chicago Press).

---

[1]   For Varela and Shear's response to Baars, see their 'Editors' rejoinder to the debate' below (p. 307).

MOVING THE CURSOR OF CONSCIOUSNESS: COGNITIVE SCIENCE AND HUMAN WELFARE

Guy Claxton, University of Bristol School of Education
35 Berkeley Square, Bristol BS8 1JA, UK.

In this commentary I want to offer a general response to the papers: one which links together the introspectionist, phenomenological and Buddhist traditions, and suggests a practical relationship between first-person and third-person perspectives.

One of the issues that is not well addressed in the papers is the relationship between science and soteriology. In both the Buddhist and the phenomenological traditions, the attempt to stand back and observe the workings of one's own mind is viewed as existentially important as well as intellectually interesting and experientially challenging. Cultivating a quiet, disinterested vantage point of awareness that can watch the comings and goings of other contents of consciousness — sensations, thoughts, images, memories, feelings and so on — is seen as being a route, in some sense, to liberation, even 'salvation'. Minds pick up beliefs from family and society that unconsciously infuse perception, showing us a world already saturated with enculturated theory. Some of these beliefs are benign and useful: we call them 'accurate' when in realist mood; 'functional' if we are feeling constructivist. Some were accurate/functional once but have become anachronisms. Some were never right, but we bought them nonetheless.

Continuing to perceive the world through glasses that distort relations and priorities, actions are misguided, interpretations are obliged to maintain unwitting fictions, and emotions are inappropriately deployed. (Chickens obliged to wear prismatic lenses always peck to one side of the seed they are aiming for. When grain is plentiful, they nevertheless hit food often enough to survive, and may even, if I may be anthropomorphic, remain 'unaware' that anything is wrong.) Someone who interprets mild breathlessness as life-threatening can turn normal apprehension into a full-blown panic attack. Someone who construes a selfish thought or lustful impulse as evidence of their irredeemable baseness can generate, on the back of that belief, a week-long depression. For Husserl, as for Padmasambhava, we are all chronic, and more-or-less acute, sufferers from varieties of the same complaint. Dispelling illusions — 'cleansing the doors of perception' in Blake's fine phrase — makes experience sharper, values clearer, action more effective, and life less contaminated with unnecessary pain, confusion and negative emotion.

The role of a 'theory of mind', in these traditions, is to encourage exploration and direct attention: to guide the de-bugging process into productive channels and prevent it running aground on the sandbanks of compulsive, endless deconstruction, or veering off into 'deep water' that the adventurer is not yet emotionally resilient enough to cope with. Such route-maps, to be helpful, must be plausible, accessible and fruitful. They must connect well enough with a prevailing cultural discourse to be accepted as 'valid'. They must be 'personal', vernacular enough to throw light on mundane experience. And they must furnish functional 'tools for thought', offering productive ways of understanding the journey from perdition to salvation. Baldly, the trouble with many versions of phenomenology and of Buddhism is that, however profound they may be, they lack some or all of these qualities. Exotic versions of Buddhism attract some but repel many. Likewise the abstruse and elliptical ruminations of Husserl or Heidegger appeal only to a certain kind of intellectual. The rest of us, the poorer though we might be, simply can't be bothered to sign up for the protracted apprenticeship that is required.

In a scientized, and particularly a psychologized, culture such as ours, there is a large market for spiritual Baedekers written in language accessible to audiences who are scientifically literate, and not temperamentally drawn to the supernatural or esoteric. And this might provide a social function for cognitive science: to offer models of mental development that are plausible, accessible and fruitful to the many general readers of Richard Dawkins, Daniel Dennett and Francis Crick, or Richard Gregory, Robert Ornstein and Daniel Goleman. Not that I am championing a full-blown, Churchland-style 'eliminative materialism', in which the chemistry of love is reduced, once and for all, to exactly that; only the utility of scientifically credible stories that enable people to gloss 'phenomenological reduction' or 'vipassana' — the educability of consciousness — in terms that connect with and draw on familiar ways of thinking.

Such a bridge might look, in its rudiments, like this.[2] Human beings (like animals) are made of a kind of meat that responds to certain sorts and ranges of electromagnetic energy. This clever meat is able to extract those recurrent patterns of such energy that are significant in terms of the body's (developing set of) needs and capabilities: environmental conditions that afford opportunities for advancement, protection and control. Brains represent these affordances as changes of weight and connectivity in complex neural networks, so designed that particular conjunctions of opportunity and motivation activate increasingly sophisticated, flexible and appropriate patterns of response. Perception is essentially a process of pattern detection and completion, driven by response desirability and capability. Learning is essentially a developmental process of pattern attunement, driven by the success or failure of predictions. The processes of perception, response and learning are subserved by a smart, unconscious 'biocomputer' that extends to include immunological and endocrinological systems as well as the central nervous system (and which also learns to distribute its intelligence over social and technological webs external to the body).

As experience weaves ever more intricate and interlocking conceptual patterns on the brain's 'enchanted loom', so the process of perception, in any particular instance, may be more or less elaborated. Starting with 'epicentres' of neural activity, corresponding to the most basic environmental patterns detected, activation may ripple out in ever-widening associative circles that recruit additional beliefs, add layers of interpretation and may discover and activate non-obvious links between the originally remote epicentres that coalesce to form a novel 'gestalt'. Where immediate needs are acute and the preliminary activated pattern is unambiguously significant, such elaborative processing does not occur. One 'cuts to the chase'. Where there is greater leisure, ambiguity or complexity, however, elaborative association-finding may profitably be allowed to run, to see how far preexisting knowledge can augment the bare sensory picture. In particular, building up layers of interpretation will prove advanta-

---

[2] I cannot claim that this represents a consensus view, but it is plausibly woven out of research threads each of which is familiar and robust. This is not the place for a fully documented rationale — Claxton (1994) and (1997/1999) offer that — but there are obvious whiffs of Dianne Berry, Patricia and Paul Churchland, Andy Clark, Mihaly Csikszentmihalyi, Daniel Dennett, Pawel Lewicki, Benjamin Libet, Arthur Reber, Nyanaponika Thera, Francisco Varela and Max Velmans.

geous when two conditions obtain: when the preliminary 'diagnosis' does not reveal the presence of any unequivocally relevant threat or resource; and where a person's needs, interests and anxieties have proliferated to the point where any experience may have latent significance which only further processing will bring to light. People with such intricate goal-structures, who do not meet sharp biological threats very often, may come to adopt this extended, elaborating perceptual mode as the default, snapping out of it only in cases of clear emergency.

Fast processing, in which neural activation runs more-or-less directly from sensory into motor channels is tacit. As Arthur Reber says, 'the implicit is primary'. However processing that is protracted or arrested, in which neural activation pools or intensifies in an area of the network, or reverberates around a closed neural loop for a while, generates the curious condition known as 'being consciously aware'. The habit of delaying a final evaluation of each moment as good, bad or indifferent, probing for subtler layers of significance, creates (in ways we do not yet fully understand) the 'conditions of neuronal adequacy' for consciousness. Thus leisured organisms with complex goal-structures will spend more of their time being 'conscious'; and what they are conscious of corresponds to more highly elaborated neural 'representations' of the environment, into which more of their own hopes, fears and expectations have been unwittingly dissolved. They will inhabit a (conscious) world which seems *sui generis* motivationally and morally complex, though much of that complexity will be a function of their own preoccupations, unconsciously stirred in to the perceptual brew at points prior to conscious 'tasting'.

While extended pre-conscious checking of the motivational resonances of an experience is going on, it makes survival-sense to continue priming and preparing the response that seems most advantageous on the basis of the preliminary diagnosis. If further checking fails to turn up anything new, you are ready to go. If elaborative processing discloses (or 'imagines') a hidden cost of the projected action, it can be aborted before it is implemented. The association between vetoing an anticipated course of action, and consciousness of its hidden dangers, explains why Libet, Gregory and others are now of the opinion that we possess free won't rather than free will.

The process of Husserl's 'reduction', Buddhism's 'vipassana' ('insight') or James Hillman's 'psychologizing' is one of moving the 'cursor of consciousness' back towards a more immediate, less highly elaborated, state, whilst (a) allowing the associative neural rippling and intermingling to continue; and (b) still inhibiting any physical response. Learning to do this is what the 'cultivation of mindfulness', 'bracketing' and so on are all about. In this state of sharp awareness of experience at a low level of interpretation, three phenomenal effects occur. First the 'world' seems clearer, cleaner and more objective: less, to use Hermann Hesse's phrase, 'a cloudy mirror of our own desire'. Second, assumptions and projections which have previously been dissolved surreptitiously in perception now become visible in their own right. They operate, if they still continue to do so, 'downstream' of the moment of conscious perception, on the surface, rather than upstream, invisibly. And third, the mingling of cognitive currents that extended processing allows is freed of the narrowing concerns of self-reference: it is less firmly channelled by considerations of personal advantage and disadvantage, and 'creativity' becomes more playful and unbounded.

This science-based 'story' of perception, consciousness and suffering (the Buddhist *dukkha*) enables one to escape from the sterile concern with the epistemological validity of 'introspection'. Awareness is never of independently existing inner processes or representations ('images', 'memories', etc.), but only of the conscious concomitants of more or less highly elaborated, transient states of neural activation. And it also highlights the extent to which protracted perception is an habitual processing mode that is acquired, and which can be altered by practice — with direct, and very often beneficial, results. It enables first-person and third-person perspectives to be brought into conjunction, in the context of a practical concern with human welfare.

References

Claxton, Guy (1994), *Noises from the Darkroom: The Science and Mystery of the Mind* (London: Harper-Collins).

Claxton, Guy (1997/1999), *Hare Brain, Tortoise Mind: Why Intelligence Increases When You Think Less* (London: Fourth Estate; Hopewell, NJ: Ecco Press).

SEPARATING FIRST-PERSONNESS FROM THE OTHER PROBLEMS OF CONSCIOUSNESS
or 'You had to have been there!'

David Galin, Dept. of Psychiatry, School of Medicine, UCSF.
Correspondence to: 5 Mt. Hood Ct., San Rafael, CA 94903-1018, USA.
Email: dgalin@itsa.ucsf.edu

Abstract: The concept of first-personness is well defined in grammar, but it has developed two discrepant senses in common usage and in the psychology and philosophy literatures. First-personness is taken to mean *phenomenal experience* (subjectivity, awareness, consciousness), and also to mean a *person's point of view*. However, since we can nonconsciously perceive, judge and behave, all from a point of view which we must name 'our own', these acts can be called first-person acts even though they are nonconscious. Therefore, I propose that the main idea behind first-personness is the point of view; that it is not a unique property of consciousness; and that consciousness will be easier to understand if it is not freighted with extraneous issues.

This essay explores the concepts underlying *point of view* and *entity*. Entiticity is viewed as a matter of degree and as a matter of convention. It is found most coherent to consider an entity's point of view as the total set of discriminations or interactions made possible by the entity's present state and context. Whether or not an entity is a person or is conscious is irrelevant to its having a point of view referenced to itself. Even inanimate objects can receive input and act only in so far as they are enabled or limited by their points of view. Since humans find it awkward at first to say that non-human or non-biological entities have a first-*person* point of view, it would be best to drop the reference to *person* in this context. C.S. Peirce's term 'firstness', developed in 1891, might do nicely.

This analysis of first-personness applies equally to agents as it does to subjects. Once these terms are clarified, it is easier to see how a superordinate entity reconciles conflict when its relatively autonomous subsystems have points of view discrepant from each other or from the whole. This has application in untangling confusions concerning the duality of the cerebral hemispheres and the results of their disconnection in relation to the popular assumption of personal unity.

First-personness is a central notion in psychology and philosophy of mind. Philosophers as different as Peirce (1935), Nagel (1979; 1986), Flanagan (1992), Searle (1997) and Dennett (1991), and physiologists and psychologists such as William James (1890), Sherrington (1947), Bogen (1969 a,b; 1989), Bisiach (1991) and Kihlstrom (1987; 1991) have written about it at length, sometimes from polar positions (these examples are limited to just the last 100 years). This essay explores the confounding of first-personness as point of view and as consciousness. If successful it may free consciousness from some unnecessary problems and unjustified wonderment; it is not intended to explain (or explain away) consciousness. This effort at clarification has direct application to difficult issues of 'self', such as when a split-brain patient does a task with the left hand, and then says 'It wasn't me that did that' (Galin, 1974).

First-personness in grammar and psychology

The notions of first-personness and third-personness arose in grammar and have made their way into psychology and philosophy of mind. Grammar is concerned with the structure of sentences. Grammatically, the terms first-, second- and third-person designate the speaker ('I'), the one spoken to ('you'), and the one (person or thing) spoken about ('he, she, it'). These terms have nothing directly to do with experience, awareness, subjectivity, consciousness, or agency, which are the concerns of psychology.

In the psychology and philosophy literatures and in common usage, first-personness has developed two discrepant senses. It has become a synonym for the properties of awareness and agency that we associate with a live, human speaker. It is also a synonym for the bias of the speaker, that is, those properties of her knowledge which are special to her point of view. What we call the 'first-person perspective or point of view' is the world as it is currently knowable to the 'speaker' (the 'I', the entity that presents sentences), whether or not she is speaking. First-person knowledge is often held to be unique because of its owner's privileged access, in contrast to third-person knowledge[3] which is held to be 'objective' and public.

Point of view as metaphor: The terms 'point of view' and 'perspective' are metaphors taken from the domain of visual-spatial perception and applied to the more general domain of knowing.[4] These metaphors express the intuition that people operate within a frame of reference or coordinate system (analogous with a spatial coordinate system) made up from their repertoire of concepts. Much of the conceptual repertoire is quite abstract and not visual-spatial or sensory-perceptual at all. For example, we can speak of having a particular political, ethical, or pragmatic point of view. Thus *point of view* applies to domains such as values as well as to domains of spatial perception and action; an event or object is good or beautiful or moral *from my point of view* just as an object is above or below, or on the right or the left *from my point of view*.

Provisional definitions

Does an entity have to have consciousness to have a first-person point of view? Does it have to be alive? These questions turn on several potentially problematic terms, and

---

[3] The present analysis clears the ground for a companion paper that considers first-personness in contrast with third-personness, its equally troublesome sibling, and examines confusions concerning subjectivity and objectivity. Scientific knowledge is widely believed to be third-person knowledge. I suggest that third-personness is misunderstood in relation to the practice of science.

[4] See Lakoff (1987), Lakoff and Johnson (1998) on metaphor as the basis for most abstract concepts. Metaphors are ubiquitous but usually not recognized as such consciously, and the ways in which they regulate and enable thought have only recently been appreciated.

some provisional but explicit definitions are needed. In order to define *point of view* we must back up and first define the underlying concepts *frame of reference, form, entity* and *knowledge*. Although these terms are common enough the concepts are uncommonly difficult. The definitions are intended to be as consistent with ordinary speech as possible, and as generalizable as possible. I propose them heuristically to promote clarity, not for *faux rigor* or to trade on the glamour or credentials of mathematics.

Space and frame of reference: It is usual to say that a set of variables (or dimensions) makes up a *space*. If the variables are abstract like (X,Y,Z) it is an abstract space. If the variables correspond to properties like height–length–width, or red–blue–green, or Buddhist–Christian–Muslim–Hindu–Jewish, it is a property space. The phrase *frame of reference* means the same thing; the 'frame' is actually the dimensions or axes of the space. The term *medium* also means the same; a set of variables in which a form can be arranged.[5]

Form: In my scheme there are no instances of disembodied (Platonic) forms; a form always exists in a frame of reference. A form is a particular distribution (set of values) in a property space (or in a frame of reference). For example, if we made up a space defined by integers, religion and degree of observance, then a possible distribution (i.e. a form) could be 4 devout Muslims, 2 lapsed Buddhists, 1 'occasional' Druid. The properties of a form correspond to its values on the axes or dimensions of its property space, or frame of reference. (For the present purposes, the possible topologies and metrics of the space need not be considered.)

Entity: This is the key concept, whose meaning is almost always mistakenly assumed to be naturally given and intuitively obvious. An entity (a unit, a wholeness) is a kind of *form*. An entity is a group of bits or elements distinguished from those in its environment by 'belonging to each other' in some sense. It is the relationships between the elements that make it an entity, not an edge, shell, skin, or border that separates them from their neighbours. The pattern of relationships among the elements creates an implicit or virtual border. According to the analyses of Simon (1969, pp. 209 ff.) and of Wimsatt (1974; also 1976 pp. 242, 261), we call a set of parts an entity if there is *sufficient inter-relatedness* among them.[6] 'Sufficient' is decided by some criterion *chosen for our purpose*. Functional relations, spatial and temporal relations, social relations, are examples of aspects by which we commonly decide that some distribution is an entity or not. For example, a group of people is an entity we call 'family' if the people have sufficiently close relations; whether or not we set the criterion to include second cousins, adoptees, steps, and pets, or only parents and their natural children depends on our purposes. Thus, *entiticity is a matter of convention as well as a matter of degree*. In general an entity does not have a sharp boundary. It depends on the relative amount of inter-relatedness of its components (nothing in a universe has *no* relation to anything else).

---

[5] For my account of awareness (consciousness) as a *medium*, see Galin (1992), p. 153, and also Galin (1994), p. 375, for a taxonomy of forms that can exist in that medium.

[6] For a penetrating analysis of the differences between entities and aggregates see Wimsatt, (1974), and for an account of parts and wholes, levels of analysis and their components and contexts, see Wimsatt (1976) and Simon (1981). For a delightful excursion into the complexities of entiticity, see *Holes and Other Superficialities* (Casati and Varzi, 1995), a curiously concrete study of whether holes really exist, and if so, what sort of entities they are.

I stress the rather surprising conditionality of entities because properties like a point of view or consciousness belong to a specific entity, and to understand the property we must be clear about just what we think constitutes the entity which hosts it. Many confusions about 'person' and 'self' arise here. Humans seem to have a great passion for entifying. We frequently turn verbs and adjectives into nouns, processes and relations into things. Problems arise when we forget that what we are treating as an entity is only more or less an entity, of limited duration, and only by agreement for the present purposes (e.g. marriage, corporation, Republic of Congo).

Knowledge, to know: The definition of this conceptual cluster has a very long history in philosophy and is currently used in many senses: to perceive directly,[7] to be capable of, to be fixed in memory, to be acquainted or familiar with, to be able to distinguish (Webster's dictionary). Note that none of these usages specifies consciousness; they all make sense for instances of nonconscious as well as for conscious knowings. The sense that best captures the phenomena that concern us here is one of the most general; *to know is to be able to distinguish*.

Know implies a knowing entity, and that which is known. For an entity *to know* something XYZ (to know how to XYZ, or to know that XYZ), is for it to distinguish XYZ from at least some not-XYZ, to act discriminatively toward XYZ. No consciousness is implied. The minimum discrimination is detection; something happened, or didn't; something is, or isn't. Knowledge is the capacity to discriminate, *a potential to use information*.[8]

Point of view: Like knowledge, a point of view belongs to an entity. It is the total set of possible discriminations an entity can make *in its present state and context*. It is critical to note here that we are including only those discriminations made by the entity as such, not by one of its erstwhile parts acting for the time autonomously and without effect at the level of the entity. We are generally interested in dynamic systems (i.e. changing over time), and at any one time some of the knowledge that the entity has may not be available for use. For example, in an enzyme molecule the critical receptor region may be temporarily folded inside, unable to interact. Similarly, different capacities for discrimination may be available to you in the context of a street mob than in the context of your private study. Thus the point of view will vary with the properties of the entity, and with the time, place, and other contexts of the entity.

What sort of entity can have a first-person point of view?

With these provisional definitions in hand we can return to the main questions about point of view.

Nonconscious points of view: The two senses of first-personness, point of view and consciousness, are not merely discrepant but in mortal conflict. Nonconscious as well as conscious processing takes place from a point of view. It seems to me that the main idea behind first-personness is the point of view, not the consciousness.

Consider what goes on as you pick up a pencil. You segment the visual field and see the object against the background. As you reach for the pencil, you spread or close

---

[7] I have never understood what is entailed or excluded by 'direct' in this usage. It seems to mean *im-mediate,* without mediation. As mentioned, I have a problem with disembodied forms.

[8] A form contains unique information in so far as it differs from all other distributions in that frame of reference. How the information is embodied, represented, or encoded in particular cases does not concern us here. See Wheeler (1990).

your fingers depending on the pencil's size, and rotate your wrist depending on whether the pencil is oriented horizontally or vertically. You must make and use judgments about its borders, its distance, the space around it, etc., calculating with respect to *a frame of reference*, based on information about your self. In this case it is a spatial frame of reference. In well-practised behaviours one can make these calculations without being aware of doing so, as shown by the ability of patients with 'blindsight' to reach appropriately for objects in their blind visual field (Weiskrantz, 1986). One can also operate nonconsciously in non-spatial frames of reference, such as value judgments (Kunst-Wilson and Zajonc, 1980; Nisbitt and Wilson, 1977). It seems to me that we will want to call all of these *first-person* judgments, whether they are conscious or not.

Therefore, I propose that consciousness and its other properties are a separate issue from having a point of view. This conclusion strikes some people as odd on first hearing, because they associate this point of view uniquely with the other qualities of human consciousness. The oddness dissipates, however, as one recognizes that *a person* includes nonconscious as well as conscious parts, and that nonconscious discriminations and actions carried out from the person's point of view are ubiquitous.

Inanimate points of view: Whether or not an entity is a person is irrelevant to its having a 'first person' point of view, that is, a point of view referenced in some sense to the entity itself. Even non-verbal devices perceive and act; a simple infra-red motion detector has a literally spatial point of view or perspective, monitoring a region of space 'in front' of it. To have a point of view an entity only needs the capacity to interact differentially with its environment. A corporation, a charged particle, and a computer all can interact differentially, and thus qualify as having points of view. Although complex entities generally have wider repertoires of inputs and responses, complexity *per se* does not seem to be required.

Please note that to say every entity has a point of view is *not* the same as saying that every entity is conscious. This error, arising out of the muddling of the two senses of first-personness, seems to fuel fiery conflict, such as Searle's (1997) attack on Chalmers.

The present argument is completely separate from grammatical or linguistic issues that arise in modern times, now that it is commonplace to have sentences uttered (or written) by inanimate speakers. Sometimes the utterance is not a simple recording of an absent human, but is originated in a context-dependent way by a computer.[9] Recall that in grammar 'I' is the speaker, the entity who presents the sentence; this would grammatically qualify the computer to say, 'I'. But in addition, it would be perfectly sensible psychologically for the computer to claim first-person knowledge and a first-person point of view, once we have separated first-personness from consciousness and biology.

It remains only to deal with the 'person' in first-personness. Many people find it awkward at first to say that a non-human, non-biological entity such as a subatomic particle, or a device, or a social institution has a first-*person* point of view. It would be

---

[9] A recent NY Times Magazine article (Lyons, 1997) detailed the excitement over a new class of software products for shopping on the Internet called 'personal agents'. The program interrogates you about your tastes in various matters and then makes recommendations to you based on products chosen by other customers with a similar taste profile. Over time it learns more about your tastes, recognizes you when you sign on, and spontaneously makes suggestions ('You are buying a ticket to Boston? Then may I suggest several restaurants in Boston that people like you have enjoyed?').

best to drop the reference to *person* in this context. C.S. Peirce's term 'firstness', developed in 1891, might do nicely (see Peirce, 1935, p. 191; space does not permit discussion of Peirce's concepts here).

Applications: understanding multiple points of view

Now that we have clarified the concepts of point of view and entity, many confusions can be untangled. One class of confusions concerns a superordinate entity reconciling conflict when its relatively autonomous subsystems have points of view discrepant from each other or from the whole. Because complex entities tend to be hierarchically organized (Simon, 1981), they are likely to include nested sub-entities with discrepant points of view. The point of view of the superordinate entity is not simply the sum or the union or the intersect of the points of view of its parts. This is a source of confusion in talk about 'to whom' a first-person point of view belongs.

Even our human point of view in three-dimensional space is not as simple as people assume. What we take to be directly in front of us is sometimes determined with respect to our body midline, sometimes with respect to our direction of gaze, and sometimes with respect to the frame of reference given by our head position (tonus in the neck muscles), or by our vestibular apparatus (see Vallar *et al.*, 1993, for extensive references). That is, we have multiple frames of reference for 3D space, which can give conflicting points of view. When we cannot reconcile them, as in motion sickness or the hemi-neglect following a parietal lobe injury, we have trouble (Bisiach, 1991; Galin, 1992). Similarly, we have trouble when we cannot reconcile our multiple frames of reference for values (e.g. different ethical standards in business and in the family).

The superordinate entity (e.g. a person) may be able to usefully combine the multiple points of view of its parts (sub-entities, e.g., the eyes). If the eyes are on the sides of the head as in a rabbit, the two points of view can be added to give a wider field of view. If as in humans, the eyes both face front and the two points of view overlap, then the discrepancy between them can be used for information about depth. But when there is too much conflict all but one may be suppressed (e.g. amblyopia, the loss of vision in one eye in a severely 'cross-eyed' person). Another strategy for conflict resolution is to alternate among points of view (e.g. in multiple personality disorder, or in contextual ethics).

Ordinarily we are good at keeping track of which of our multiple points of view are in control at the moment. It must be very important to our species since infants can do it by age 18 months; they can take another point of view in imaginative play without losing track that the new one (the 'pretend') is nested inside of the usual one (the 'real').[10] However, even adults can lose track of a nested hierarchy of points of view, as when one gets 'carried away' at the theatre or cinema and reacts as if it were real, or in hypnosis, where the subject accepts the hypnotist's point of view as overriding the self-monitors.

Hidden confusions about the normal state are often highlighted in cases of pathology. Thus, the study of 'split-brain' patients (whose cerebral hemispheres have been disconnected by surgery or by disease) has produced dramatic observations, and fed the appetite for apparent paradox. Many have marvelled when a split-brain patient

---

[10] See Leslie (1987) for an excellent account of frame of reference in the pretending and imagination of young children's play.

does a task with the left hand, and then says 'It wasn't me that did that', or when one hand corrects or undoes what the other is doing (Galin, 1974, pp. 573–6). Joseph E. Bogen, neurosurgeon and scholar, has addressed these matters for three decades, with respect to the single, the separated, and the normally connected cerebral hemispheres (Bogen, 1969a,b; 1985; 1989; see also Smith, 1974; Wigan, 1844). Although it is generally recognized that each of the disconnected hemispheres is independently conscious, each with a point of view that all would call a first-person point of view, yet there is no general agreement as to whether we are now dealing with one or two *persons* (Sperry, 1968; Pucetti, 1973; Nagel, 1979). In our culture, personal unity seems to be an assumption.

The confusion clears if we remember that entiticity is a matter of degree, and that we choose a criterion for particular cases based on convention and our purposes (see *family* example, above). Mind is a sub-entity in the larger entity *person*. Bogen (1972) cites and confirms Wigan's neurological observations and conclusions of 150 years ago (1844) that since one hemisphere is enough to sustain a mind, possession of two hemispheres makes possible or even inevitable two minds in one person.[11] The logical and verbal analyses I have presented above complement the neurology: to the degree that each mind and the superordinate person are entities, they each have a first person point of view, and they need not agree.

Coda: so what?

This essay has not been just a quibble about words. I have argued for three broad conceptual points:

1. Entiticity is not absolute; it is a matter of degree and of convention. Finding or creating entities is one of our most basic cognitive processes: we segment each sensory and conceptual field into figure and ground; then we try to manipulate the 'figure'. If in fact there is no intrinsic structure in the field, or if the intrinsic structure is much more complex than the way we have parsed it, then serious errors may occur. We are not usually aware of the conditionality of the entities we create.
2. Point of view is associated with a specific entity; it is defined in terms of the set of discriminations that are possible for that entity under the present circumstance. The simplicity or complexity of the entity's repertoire of discriminations is irrelevant. Any entity, conscious or not, biological or not, has a point of view.
3. First-personness of an entity's point of view is that property that derives from its being that entity and not another. That is all there is to the mysterious 'privileged access'.

What this essay does *not* try to do is clarify what consciousness is, or how it works (Galin, 1992; 1994; 1996). The argument's only implication for consciousness is to free it from some unnecessary problems and unjustified wonderment, which may or may not make the real problems more tractable.

---

[11] Wigan believed that no matter how synchronous the two hemispheres may be most of the time, there must inevitably be some occasion when they are discrepant. Bogen points out, 'What Wigan did not know . . . [in 1844] . . . was that whereas the two hemispheres of a cat or a monkey may sustain two duplicate minds, the lateralization typical of man requires that the two minds must necessarily be discrepant' (1972).

References

Bisiach, E. (1991), 'Understanding consciousness: clues from unilateral neglect and related disorders', in *The neuropsychology of consciousness*, ed. A.D. Milner and M.D. Rugg (London: Academic Press).

Bogen, J.E. (1969a), 'The other side of the brain: I. Dysgraphia and dyscopia following cerebral commissurotomy', *Bulletin of the Los Angeles Neurological Society*, **34**, pp. 73–105.

Bogen, J.E. (1969b), 'The other side of the brain: II. An appositional mind', *Bulletin of the Los Angeles Neurological Society*, **34**, pp. 135–62.

Bogen, J.E. (1972), 'Neowiganism (concluding statement)', in *Drugs and Cerebral Function*, ed. W.L. Smith (Springfield, IL: C.C. Thomas).

Bogen, J.E. (1989), 'Partial hemispheric independence with the neocommissures intact' in *Brain Circuits and Theories of Mind*, ed. C. Trevarthen (London: Cambridge University Press).

Casati, R. and Varzi, A. (1995), *Holes and Other Superficialities* (Cambridge, MA: MIT Press).

Dennett, D.C. (1991), *Consciousness Explained* (Boston, MA: Little, Brown & Co.).

Flanagan, O. (1992), *Consciousness Reconsidered* (Cambridge: MIT Press).

Galin, D. (1974), 'Implications for psychiatry of left and right hemisphere specialization', *Archives of General Psychiatry*, **31**, pp. 572–83.

Galin, D. (1992), 'Theoretical reflection on awareness, monitoring, and self in relation to anosognosia', *Consciousness and Cognition*, **1**, pp. 152–62.

Galin, D. (1994), 'The structure of awareness: Contemporary applications of William James' forgotten concept of "The Fringe" ', *Journal of Mind and Behavior*, **15** (4), pp. 375–400.

Galin, D. (1996), 'What is the difference between a duck?', in *Scientific Approaches to Consciousness: 25th Carnegie Symposium on Cognition*, ed. J. Cohen and J. Schooler (Hillsdale, NJ: Erlbaum).

James, W. (1890, reprinted 1950), *The Principles of Psychology* (New York: Dover).

Kihlstrom, J.F. (1987), 'The cognitive unconscious', *Science*, **237**, pp. 1445–52.

Kihlstrom, J.F. and Tobias, B.A. (1991), 'Anosognosia, consciousness, and self', in *UnAwareness of Deficit after Brain Injury*, ed. G.P. Prigatano and D.S. Schacter (New York: Oxford University Press).

Kunst-Wilson, W.R. and Zajonc, R.B. (1980), 'Affective discrimination of stimuli that cannot be recognized', *Science*, **207**, pp. 557–8.

Lakoff, G. (1987), *Women, Fire, and Dangerous Things* (Chicago: University of Chicago Press).

Lakoff, G. and Johnson, M. (1998), *Philosophy in the Flesh* (Chicago: Chicago University Press) in press.

Leslie, A.M. (1987), 'Pretense and representation: the origins of "theory of mind" ', *Psych. Rev.*, **94**, pp. 412–26.

Lyons, D. (1997), 'The buzz about Firefly', *New York Times Magazine*, (June 29), pp. 37–8.

Nagel, T. (1979), *Mortal Questions* (London: Cambridge University Press).

Nagel, T. (1986), *The View from Nowhere* (New York: Oxford University Press).

Nisbitt, R. and Wilson, T. (1977), 'Telling more than we can know: verbal reports on mental processes', *Psychological Review*, **84**, pp. 231–58.

Peirce, C.S. (1935), *Collected Papers, Vol. 6*, (Cambridge, MA: Harvard University Press).

Pucetti, R. (1973), 'Brain bisection and personal identity', *British Journal of the Philosophy of Science*, **24**, pp. 339–55.

Searle, J.R. (1997), 'Consciousness and the philosophers', *New York Review of Books*, (March 6), pp. 43–50.

Sherrington, C. (1947), *The Integrative Action of the Nervous System* (Cambridge: Cambridge University Press).

Simon, H. (1981), 'The architecture of complexity', in *The Sciences of the Artificial* (Cambridge, MA: MIT Press).

Smith, A. (1974), 'Dominant and nondominant hemispherectomy', in *Hemispheric Disconnection and Cerebral Function*, ed. M. Kinsbourne and W.L. Smith (Springfield, IL: C.C. Thomas).

Sperry, R.W., (1968), 'Mental unity following the surgical disconnections of the cerebral hemispheres', *Amer. Psychologist*, **23**, pp. 723–33.

Vallar, G., Bottini, G., Rusconi, M.L. and Sterzi, R. (1993), 'Exploring somatosensory hemineglect by vestibular stimulation', *Brain*, **116**, pp. 71–86.

Weiskrantz, L. (1986), *Blindsight* (Oxford: Clarendon Press).

Wheeler, J.A. (1990), 'Information, physics, quantum: The search for links', in *Complexity, Entropy, and the Physics of Information*, ed. W.H. Zurek (Redwood City, CA: Addison Wesley).

Wigan, A.L. (1844, reprinted 1985), *The Duality of the Mind* (Malibu: Joseph Simon, Publisher).

Wimsatt, W.C. (1974), 'Complexity and organization', in *Boston Studies in the Philosophy of Science*, vol. 20, ed. K.F. Schaffner and R.S. Cohen [Proc. Philosophy of Science Assoc. 1972] (Dordrecht: Reidel).

Wimsatt, W.C. (1976), 'Reductionism, levels of organization, and the mind-body problem', in *Consciousness and the Brain*, ed. G.G. Globus, G. Maxwell and I. Savodnik (New York: Plenum).

A COGNITIVE WAY TO THE TRANSCENDENTAL REDUCTION

Shaun Gallagher, Department of Philosophy, Canisius College, Buffalo, NY 14208, USA. Email: gallaghr@canisius.edu

Natalie Depraz builds on Iso Kern's distinctions to outline three different motivational pathways to the phenomenological reduction — the Cartesian way, the psychological way, and the way of the life-world. I would like to suggest a fourth one that may appeal to cognitive neuroscientists and neuropsychologists, theorists who, for the most part, are not ordinarily motivated to pursue phenomenological methodologies.

Husserl (1913) set out his notion of phenomenological reduction as a way to discover the 'constitutive' nature of consciousness. One of the things we need to understand is this notion of 'constitution', and we will return to this point. First, however, it is important to note that Husserl's motivation was, in part, his own deep concern about science. For that reason, like many of today's scientists, he was suspicious of explanations developed on pre-scientific grounds. In the first instance we can think of the phenomenological reduction (the 'epochè') as a way to push aside, or to suspend our belief in, pre-scientific explanations. We can think of it, for example, as a way to suspend our judgments about folk psychology, folk physics, and so on. Of course, good scientists know that at any particular time, some of what passes for good scientific theory can turn out to be wrong-headed or even false. The scientist's inclination is to test out these theories with empirical methods, to see what stands up and what doesn't. Taking this one step further, the philosophical phenomenologist points out that empirical methods themselves are open to suspicion, to the extent that they too are justified only on the basis of theory — epistemological theory which in turn may be based on a certain trust in perceptual observation and the communicative practices of scientists. In effect, scientific and epistemological theories are constructed only by conscious individuals. In Husserl's view, if we want to be sure about science we need to understand how consciousness itself works. The phenomenological reduction is intended to take us to that level of transcendental analysis, and to address the question: what must consciousness be like if science is to be possible? Husserl calls this a suspension of the natural attitude, and this includes a suspension of belief in both pre-scientific and scientific theories.

The phenomenological reduction, then, has a more radical dimension that extends beyond suspension of belief in folk explanations in order to push the question back to the level of consciousness itself. Clearly this aspect of phenomenology, which involves a large epistemological project, may not be of real practical interest to cognitive scientists, even if it has genuine theoretical relevance to what they do when they do science.[12] I do want to point out two things, however. First, even in this regard

---

[12] Two things need to be said. First, obviously, the working scientist cannot stop her own research to pursue this epistemological project. Second, the phenomenologist indicates here a method that puts method itself in question. There are two ways to deal with this methodological paradox. The first is to claim that there is something special about the phenomenological method, e.g., that it involves a special way of seeing. Husserl was inclined to do this. The second way is to recognize that there are hermeneutical problems involved here and that no phenomenological reduction can be completely free of this paradox. Heidegger and Merleau-Ponty were more inclined in this direction (see also Shear and Varela's remarks on the hermeneutical objection in the introductory essay).

phenomenology is not in opposition to science; this particular epistemological project is run as a theoretical complement to science. Second, this epistemological project is not all there is to phenomenology, and certain other aspects of the phenomenological approach to consciousness may have a more practical bearing on specific projects in the cognitive sciences.

The phenomenological suspension of the natural attitude sets us up in a different attitude within which we can focus on the way that we are conscious of the world. Husserl is concerned to point out that the epochè does not negate the world; rather it allows the world to appear as it does appear — that is, it allows us to recognize the fact that the only epistemic access that we have to the world is through consciousness. Consciousness *constitutes* our access to the world. It does this whether we realize it or not. The point of phenomenology is to understand how this works. Indeed, the fact that consciousness constitutes our access to the world in the way that it does is precisely what puts us in the natural attitude to begin with, and it is precisely because we find ourselves in the natural attitude that we need to step out of it through the reduction in order to discover the constitutional effect of consciousness. This constitutional effect of consciousness is one of Husserl's main themes. To see what he means by the notion of constitution I suggest that we take a short detour away from the question of phenomenological method and turn our attention to the science of biology.

Actually what we need to consider is a neo-Kantian point that formed the basis of some work done in theoretical biology toward the beginning of the twentieth century. I'm thinking of the work of von Uexkull (1926) and others. They took the basic Kantian idea that the human, rational mind has a certain *a priori* structure, and translated it into biological terms. The human mind has a specific *a priori* structure because it depends on a human body with a certain genetically determined structure. Consider vision. Human vision depends on the anatomical structures and physiological functionings of the human eye and visual cortex. Vision is quite different for the frog. What the frog sees is determined by its own evolutionary adaptation to its environment. The frog's eye and the neurophysiology behind it are designed to spot quick moving black specks (insects) that the frog can easily reach with its tongue. Frogs don't pay much attention to the chevron shape of a gaggle of geese in flight, or to computers, etc. They can't because they don't have the biological equipment to do so. For animals who have obtained the upright posture, however, the environment is full of affordances that frogs have no knowledge of.

Affordances and possibilities, that is, the very way in which the environment appears to us, and therefore the human world (as opposed to the frog world or the bat world), and what it's like to be a conscious human (in contrast to what it's like to be a frog or a bat) — these are all relative to the human body. Our embodied consciousness shapes the world as a human world, a world of human affordances and possibilities.

Neither Husserl nor Kant would endorse this neo-Kantian biologism. Like Kant, Husserl's primary concern was rationality, and humans are rational animals. Besides, we don't have phenomenological access to non-humans, so we can't really know what it's like to be a frog. I think, however, the brief non-Husserlian detour through theoretical biology can give us a sense of what Husserl is after in his concept of constitution. The world as it is phenomenally given to us is given to us through the rational structure of consciousness, a structure that allows us to perceive a human world, and to do science. So when the phenomenologist seeks to understand how con sciousness constitutes the world for us, she is attempting to explicate the conditions that allow us to do what we do as rational humans, and these include the conditions of rational cognition.[13]

This means that the phenomenological reduction leads to a transcendental investigation into the conditions of possibility of our experience. Husserl takes a different approach to this than Kant. He does not arrive by transcendental deduction at a set of *a priori* categories. Despite Husserl's mathematical training, he was much more the empiricist. He wanted to start with first-person experience itself and to discover the structures implicit in that experience which allow for rational cognition. It is just in this respect, where the phenomenologist attempts to explicate the structure of our cognitive acts, that cognitive scientists and students of consciousness should have a practical interest. The specifics of that structure, which involve temporality, spatial perspective, the constitution of meaning, and so forth, are precisely the details that need to be accounted for in scientific explanations of experience and cognition.

Empirical science, of course, seeks causal rather than transcendental conditions. This defines the difference between Husserlian phenomenology and cognitive approaches. Yet, an important component of the cognitive approach is that the subject matter under investigation — cognition, experience, memory, perception, and so on — be clearly described. One task of phenomenology is to do precisely that for the human case.

References

Husserl, E. (1913), *Ideas Pertaining to a Pure Phenomenology and to a Phenomenological Philosophy*, trans. F. Kersten (The Hague: Martinus Nijhoff, 1982).
von Uexkull, J. (1926), *Theoretical Biology* (New York: Harcourt, Brace, Co.).

A NEW MODEL

E.T. Gendlin, Dept. of Psychology, University of Chicago, 5848 South University Avenue, Chicago IL 60637, USA.   TDNMCDINE@aol.com

Varela and Shear invite:

(1) re-examination of the notion of 'consciousness';
(2) attention to change in content;
(3) distinguishing content / process;
(4) systematic first-person methodology;
(5) somatic transformations;
(6) linking first-, second- and third-person.

At home the scientist looks into the eyes of the child, and the child looks back. But the scientist thinks: 'Isn't it sad that you are really just a machine!' This would not happen if one recognized that our science uses a certain approach, the model in which anything studied is cut up into stable, well-defined units, and then reconstructed. We say that we have 'explained' something when we can reconstruct it out of the units. This is the most successful model in history so far, but it is only one model. There are others.

---

[13] I emphasize the rational here, as does Husserl. Husserl recognized that we are also emotional animals, and phenomenology can also be directed to give an account of the emotional aspects of our experience. I ignore here the issue of how rationality and emotion are related.

We now have a successful second model, not replacing but interacting with the first. Ecology takes the opposite view: everything is part of the whole. You cannot know any unit because it plays some part in the whole and you can never fully know the whole, so don't touch these fish. It might change everything.

It is not sad that we seem to disappear when we are reduced, and reconstructed as machines. This is simply an obvious characteristic of the unit model. Neither need we complain that the holistic model evaporates us into the cosmos. To include ourselves, we can add a third model next to these two. The basic terms need not be units nor the whole; the basic terms can be processes.

In the new model, a process does not consist of stable units which are located in unit times that determine the future from the past. Process makes a series of always freshly created new wholes. It puts the holistic model on wheels, so to speak. It makes itself as a string of wholes that cannot be predicted, deduced, or constructed from previous ones because the process makes its own next steps. Its 'contents' are not separate from it; they derive from the process which makes and re-makes them.

Like the other models, this one can be used to study anything. New concepts for a process physics with 'retroactive time' can solve some anomalies (Gendlin & Lemke, 1983; Gendlin, 1997b, IV). Rather than reducing living bodies to the current biology, we can create a new biology to study what the other models miss in every kind of living body (Gendlin, 1997b, V; Matsuno, 1989). *We humans live from bodies which are self-conscious of situations.* Notice the 'odd' phrase 'self-conscious of situations'. 'Consciousness', 'self' and 'situation' are not three objects with separate logical definitions. With current habits the absence of such definitions may seem to make everything arbitrary, but that isn't so. Instead of differentiating units and objects, we can be very precise about different *kinds of processes*, how to enable them to happen, and their different effects. We do not predict the future from the past, but we can say very exactly in what way the steps of each kind of process are not arbitrary.

We must recognize that the same words and phrases have different meanings in different models. 300 years of reductive success have given most words a unit-model meaning. By using words in new ways we can change this.

1. Let us re-examine 'consciousness'

Currently this notion is shaped and cut to fit the unit model. We can see this if we compare it to a pre-modern notion. For example, Aristotle's: 'When we see (colour, shape or motion), we also see *that we see* (colour, shape or motion).' In modern times the perceptions are set up as if they were independent 'objects' that exist alone in advance. The *consciousness-of-red* is split into two components: The 'red object' is taken away and seems to exist independently (red light and brain events as third-person things existing alone over there), leaving consciousness to be the mere 'of', which now adds nothing. We can become perplexed, trying to think about this empty half, this mere left-over, which can no longer make any difference. So let us not accept the project of showing that this consciousness makes a difference, once its contents (which it really makes and re-makes) seem independent. Let us redefine 'consciousness' in a model of process: *consciousness is the self-sentience of making and re-making itself-and-its-environment.* It is an organismic-environmental interaction process.

2. Contents change in process

Let us not fall into the misleading discussion of 'qualia', as if we should find 'stable' contents, internal objects, static entities modelled on third-person 'objects'.

The manner of process determines the contents produced. For example, if one's attitude is welcoming, even long-fixated memories come as part of fresh living forward, rather than as constriction and stoppage. The philosophy of experiencing has long rejected the old assumptions. Experiential content does not lie there, waiting to 'become conscious'. It does not consist of 'objects' that precede attention and are unchanged by it. Just the contrary! Process *should* make and change the 'objects'.

3. Contents arise in bodily process

The third-person unit model makes objects from perceptions, but let us not begin with perception. A more deep-going approach starts with the body. The living body is an interaction with its environment. A plant's body 'knows' light, earth, and water because it makes itself with those. Animals do more; they interact with each other. Human bodies are interactions in language-elaborated situations. *Our bodies sense themselves and thereby their situations.* The next bit of action forms out of that (Sheets-Johnstone, 1998). Let us begin with the body, rather than the five senses. Your body senses what is behind your back right now, without seeing, hearing, or smelling it. You sense not just the things there, but your situation, what would happen if you suddenly turned around, or if you pounded on the wall where your neighbours live.

The body senses the situation more encompassingly than cognition. If an experienced pilot says 'I don't know why, but I'm not comfortable about the weather', don't go.

For example, a researcher pursues 'an idea'. It's not really an idea. It's a pregnant bodily sense acquired in the lab. If it is new, the bodily sense is at first inarticulate. 'It' will be *carried forward* by many odd thoughts and moves in the lab, until 'it' develops into a feasible project. 'It' stays stable only when nothing comes to carry 'it' forward. '*Carrying forward*' is a useful concept, because so many processes are neither predictable from pre-existing units, nor arbitrary. Einstein's autobiography reports that for fifteen years he was 'guided by a feeling for the answer'. Obviously the feeling didn't contain the finished theory. No wise scientist or programmer ignores such a 'sense'. It does not consist of logical units, but new logical units can be derived from it. Every computer program 'crashes' (becomes unworkable) eventually. Then the programmer must 'dip into' an as yet unclear sense, to develop another program (Sterner, 1998). When we think freshly, we pursue an experiential sense that leads to steps of 'carrying forward'. Later we say that this sense '*was*' the experiment we now design, or the theory we write in thirty pages, but earlier we could not explicitly say what we 'meant'. We could think to a certain juncture, and after that we had only '. . .' There is not even a word in the language for such a '. . .', such a 'dot-dot-dot,' which is *our plant-animal-human body's self-sensing of a situation.*

Implicit sensing can never be equated with its eventual verbal explication. The process of explicating is itself a *further* experiencing which develops and changes 'the content'. Explicating is not like representing, not like picture-taking. It always makes more parts and terms than we had before. *We can explicate the process of explicating.* This is only one *kind of process*, but it is of special interest. 'Carrying forward' is one of many concepts that can be made from the process. This philosophy holds that experiencing is '*non-numerical*' and '*multischematic*'. It is an active ordering that can create and respond to many schemes and is more intricate than a scheme. When it functions in relation to logical inferences, it has certain odd but precise 'characteristics,' and performs many indispensable functions in all cognition (Gendlin, 1997a; Levin, 1997).

4. Systematic methodology

We can measure the role of experiencing in certain kinds of processes. As just one example, consider the Experiencing Scale. It describes seven modes of verbal expressions. In studies of psychotherapy it correlates with successful outcome (according to therapist, client, and psychometric measures). Random four-minute segments of tape-recorded therapy hours are rated. The method needed improvement. In each group of raters they were reliable with each other, but another group of raters on the same data might not correlate with the first. Raters must not work in the same room; their comments influence each other. Now, with standard training segments, each trains and rates alone. Only the Scale determines the ratings. The process is now reliably measured by raters anywhere (Klein *et al.*, 1989).

Therapists are said to respond to 'feelings'. They hear anger, sadness, and joy, but when therapy goes well, they hear '. . .' followed by uncategorizable intricacies like those on this transcript:

Silence . . . 'I wish my big energy channel didn't always have to be only sexual . . .'

(Therapist responses after each step, omitted.)

Silence . . . 'Saying this is very hard for me, but that feels like the right place . . .'

Silence . . . 'There's some way that I don't want to let go of it only being sexual . . .'

Silence . . . 'Like . . . maybe then I won't have that big energy at all . . . That's where it is' (begins to cry).

Silence . . . 'It's so important to have a channel at all' (sobs).

Silence . . . 'There's more there . . . What is that? . . . why is that so scary?'

A large step now:

Silence . . . (sobs) 'I could live in relation to that energy *all* the time. I've always been hidden. It's saying, "don't do that anymore. Look! Let your energy be visible, live in it".'

Silence . . . 'That would be such a change in who I am! Be in it in the daylight.'

Silence . . . (big sigh) (crying) 'Take it seriously . . . ' (big sigh, breath, quieter).

Silence . . . (Laughs) . . . 'That old way still wants to pull me down and back into that dark hole, but it's a little more free now. It's moved a little. It's like, "Oh, maybe there is a road".'

5. Somatic transformations

Many little steps of carrying forward lead to a large one. Such a step is both a physical evaluation and a physical relief. (If not, the process continues.) Such steps change how the body carries the situation. They are bits of physical change.

Life-process implies and enacts its own next steps. If its implying cannot be carried forward, the living body continues to imply *some* way forward, until a new step can form. This capacity for new life-forwarding steps is one of the most important and least known facts that the process-methodology has shown so far.

Where does her attention go in the silence between steps? As client (first-person) I attend to the dot-dot-dot, that murky *physically-sensed* edge of what I have been saying. For the rater (third-person) these verbalizations are recognizable as '7' on the Scale. These sentences are linked neither by reasoning nor narrative; they have their well-defined observable characteristics.

From this philosophy a world-wide network has developed to teach this bodily explicating, popularly called 'focusing' (Gendlin, 1981). People locate and *speak from* (carry forward) more of what they are living through, which they physically sense but at first cannot say. New steps and phrases that are more intricate than the usual language 'come' from the murky bodily 'sense'.

More than 60 (small and major) studies have found that the Scale predicts success or failure already at an early stage of therapy, and that focusing instructions can reverse a failure-prediction. Standard measures show whether focusing was learned, or not. Focusing also correlates with measures of health, lack of psychosomatic complaints, better immune system functioning, and other variables (Hendricks, in press).

When people learn to contact this bodily level, they do it for many purposes, for example to reduce tension, to become open for the next task, to discover why something is scary, unpleasant or difficult, to find what's going wrong in a situation, to pursue an 'idea', but especially to live and speak 'from there'.

The process is easier and deeper with a focusing partner who pays attention but puts nothing in. Partners take turns; each is both *a first and a second person*. Our network offers partnerships. Focusing is now used in very diverse settings (e.g. Boukydis, 1990; Grindler, 1984; McMahon, 1993; Perl, 1994).

An industrial chemist comes to learn focusing. We teach him to find the *bodily* sense of the project he is working on. After one round of focusing he runs out on the porch. What is he doing there? He is on his mobile phone to his lab assistants with new instructions! He comes back vastly enthusiastic. Now he'd like to focus on his other project. Again he runs out to call. Since then we are founding a company together to bring focusing to scientists.

All this is just one example of existing knowledge which can be had only in the model of process. This model is needed for knowledge about many other kinds of processes.

6. Third-person procedures can be employed by any model

They can give objectivity to first-person processes. When I came to research as a philosopher, I was told that objective research is impossible on something so 'subjective'. I asked the therapists: 'Do you notice when clients sense something and cannot yet say it?' They all said 'yes'. I said, 'In that case it has observable marks and we can 'operationalize' it.

First- and third-person can both contribute to observable operational procedures. We should doubt all theories, but *procedures and results* have a truth apart from theories (Gendlin, 1995; 1997c). If someone says 'I don't get all this subjective stuff", fine, but these scale-numbers predict those other numbers. Once this is found and many times replicated, people get interested in how you developed this. Suddenly they understand what before they insisted they could not.

I do not agree that validation is always by third-person measures of first-person measures. Validation is needed equally in the other direction. Current theoretical rationales of 'objective' measures are often quite poor. I advise students to test themselves on any measure they use. It is the only way to find out what the measure measures, and whether one's theoretical predictions would apply to it. *First- and third-person calibrate and add to each other.*

What the different models bring is truly different. If they were largely correlated, we would not need more than one model. They will not, and need not correlate except at a few junctures. Neurological engineering can look like 'science' alone, because our other knowledge does not (and should not) easily relate to it. Social policy must not be based on unit-model science standing alone, as if it were the only science about *human bodies*.

Unit-model scientists are redesigning the plants, the animals, and now us. Your great-grandchild may stay alive indefinitely when they take out the genes that cause aging, but who knows what else they will take out? I don't denigrate our wonderful unit-science; I wouldn't write against it on a computer! But bodily human beings are capable of an immense variety of kinds of processes, and thereby also kinds of 'self'. kinds of 'contents', and kinds of observable results. In certain kinds of process we find that the body has a capacity to generate new life-forwarding steps. This must not be lost. Before the unit-model scientists redesign us *without even wanting* to understand how human beings (they) are, let us establish a first-person science *not within but around* third-person science.

References

Boukydis, C.F.Z. (1990), 'Client-centered / experiential practice with parents and infants', in *Client-Centered and Experiential Psychotherapy in the Nineties*, ed. G. Lietar, J. Rombauts R. VanBalen (Leuven: University of Leuven Press).

Corea, G. (1985), *The Mother Machine* (New York: Harper and Row).

Gendlin, E.T. (1981), *Focusing* (New York: Bantam Books). www.focusing.org.

Gendlin, E.T. (1995), 'Crossing and dipping: some terms for approaching the interface between natural understanding and logical formation', *Minds and Machines*, **5** (4), pp. 383–411. www.focusing.org.

Gendlin, E.T. (1997a), *Experiencing and the Creation of Meaning* (New York: Free Press [hbk]; Evanston, IL: Northwestern University Press [pbk]).

Gendlin, E.T. (1997b), *A Process Model* IV, V (http://www.focusing.org, and printed from Focusing Institute, in eight parts).

Gendlin, E.T. (1997c), 'The responsive order: A new empiricism', *Man and World*, **30**, pp. 383–411.

Gendlin, E.T. and Lemke, J. (1983), 'A critique of relativity and localization', *Mathematical Modeling*, **4**, pp. 61–72.

Grindler, D. (1984) 'Focusing with a cancer patient', in *Imagination and Healing*, ed. A.A. Sheikh (New York: Baywood).

Hendricks, M. (in press), 'Research basis of focusing-oriented / experiential psychotherapy', in *Research Bases of Humanistic Psychotherapy*, ed. D. Cian & J. Seeman (Washington, DC: American Psychological Association).

Klein, M.H., Mathieu, P.L., Kiesler, D.J. and Gendlin (1989), *The Experiencing Scale: A Research and Training Manual* (Madison: Bureau of Audio-Visual Instruction, The University of Wisconsin).

Levin, D.M., (ed. 1997), *Language Beyond Postmodernism: Saying and Thinking in Gendlin's Philosophy* (Evanston, IL: Northwestern University Press).

Matsuno, K. (1989), *Protobiology* (Boca Ratan: CRC Press).

McMahon, E.M. (1993), *Beyond the Myth of Dominance* (Kansas City: Sheed & Ward).

Perl, S. (1994), 'A writer's way of knowing', in *Writing and the Domain Beyond the Cognitive*, ed. A. Brand and R. Graves (Portsmouth: Boynton-Cook Press).

Sheets-Johnstone, M. (1998), 'Consciousness: A natural history', *Journal of Consciousness Studies*, **5** (2), pp. 260–94.

Sterner, W. (1997), 'Logical meaning creation', delivered at 'After Postmodernism' Conference (http://www.focusing.org/postmod.htm).

PURE CONSCIOUSNESS AND CULTURAL STUDIES

William S. Haney II, Eastern Mediterranean University, North Cyprus.

First-person methodologies have evolved in the humanities from the romantic intro-spection of a unified self, through a modernist nostalgia for that unity, to the fragmen-tation of the self in poststructuralist and postmodernism, which questions the pheno-menological unity of the self based on commonsense introspection as well as the pos-sibility of an unmediated pure consciousness event. Literary and cultural studies can benefit from the way the *Journal of Consciousness Studies* draws upon Eastern approaches to first-person experience and corresponding western physiological research. Of particular relevance to the unity–fragmentation debate is the chapter by Jonathan Shear and Ronald Jevning, 'Pure consciousness: Scientific explorations of meditation techniques' in this special issue of *JCS*. Shear and Jevning explore pure consciousness as a state emptied of all 'empirical phenomenal content' (pp. 198–9), a void similar to that described in deconstructive postmodernism in terms of the experi-ence of the real as difference. But while Shear and Jevning propose that the experience is culture-independent, poststructuralists hold that it remains a linguistic construct.

In the shift from the romantic to the postmodernist era the self has steadily moved from an inward to an outward focus. The romantic and modernist notions of the self can be said to be unmediated or decontextualist, yet because they are usually described in terms of empirical content they may seem to be pluralistic or culture-dependent. Hence these descriptions become vulnerable to a constructivist critique by poststructuralists like Jacques Derrida. The romantic self possesses a 'deep interior,' a centre 'of passion, eternal love, the communion of souls, deep inspiration, wrenching grief, will, creativity, and true genius' (Gergen, 1991, p. 227). Similarly, the descriptions of the modernist self can be rendered through the metaphor of a machine: 'knowable (through observation), predictable, and subject to training by culture' (Gergen, 1991, p. 227). The move from an inward to an outward experience culminates in a new consciousness: postmodernist. Here a new multiplicity of con-flicting voices replaces the old unity of the self. In literary and cultural studies, how-ever, as in the history of Western psychology, first-person experience is rendered through third-person descriptions that do not adequately convey the ground and structure of that experience.

One problem with the Western approach to subjective experience is that it fails to distinguish between mind and consciousness, a distinction emphasized in Eastern cultures (see Rao, 1998). As Shear and Jevning observe, the empirical qualities ascribed to the self do not belong to consciousness *per se* but to the rational mind characterized by intentional content. In describing their first-person experience of consciousness after the fact via culturally specific third-person representations, romantic and modernist writers such as William Wordsworth and James Joyce seem to belie the possibility of a cross-cultural experience of consciousness, even while pointing to such an experience. Postmodernists in turn question this experience because their epistemology cannot accommodate a subjective state beyond language and the play of difference. Their deconstructive (constructivist) critique can only investigate the empirical qualities of the rational mind. Consciousness itself, as Shear and Jevning observe, is the ground of mental content, 'independent of the variables of culture and belief' (p. 198); 'Thus if consciousness is in fact ubiquitous, as common sense would have it, it must be devoid of all empirical qualities' (p. 202).

In his deconstruction of consciousness and transcendentality, Derrida seems to arrive at a cross-cultural conceptual void similar to that of a pure consciousness event. But in 'A Hindu response to Derrida's view of negative theology', Harold Coward argues that Derrida's description of the real corresponds to an experience of mental content, or what Shankara's Advaita (non-dual) Vedanta calls the lower level of reality, that of *maya* (Coward, 1992, pp. 210–11). From Coward's perspective, Derrida and other poststructuralists are unwilling to 'pole-vault' beyond language as a system of difference into the realm of pure consciousness or Brahman (p. 211).

In his essay 'Edmund Jabès and the Question of the Book', Derrida claims that in Judaism one does not find God or Being intuitively or directly, as through the Book: 'Being never is, never shows *itself*, is never *present* . . . outside difference' (Derrida, 1978, p. 74, original emphasis). One reaches it only in a certain stillness through which God questions us and demands a moral response. But as Coward notes, 'Unlike the perfect stillness of the Greek *logos* or Shankara's intuition of Brahman, Derrida, following Jabès, talks of a God who constantly questions out of silence' (p. 206). For Derrida, an experience not fixed or closed by any phenomenological content (or transcendental signified) can only start from God's silence. Yet this silence is never completely beyond language, for meanings emerge through it from God's desire and questioning. Thus God or the real is described in terms of a quality of dynamism and originary force. As the most inward layer of first-person experience for Derrida, silence still contains the phenomenal properties of speech and hearing, making it a conceptual content and thus culture-dependent. As Shear and Jevning comment, however, when awareness moves from the conceptual content of the mind to the stillness of pure consciousness devoid of empirical qualities, it moves beyond the sensory realm, 'beyond the categories of both perception (for there is no-thing there to be perceived) and of non-perception (for there is a rememberable experience) (pp. 203–4).

The difference between Derrida's deconstructive understanding of silence and Shear's and Jevning's Advaitan (non-dual) understanding can be seen in the distinction Robert Forman makes between 'knowledge-about' or 'knowledge-by-acquaintance' and what he calls 'knowledge-by-identity' (Forman, 1998, pp. 20–1). The former two, which encompass the poststructuralist epistemology, involve sensory processes: they 'are intentional in structure, involving a subject that is aware of some object, be it sensory, thought, or feeling'; knowledge-by-identity transcends the subject–object distinction: 'the subject knows something by virtue of being it' (pp. 20–1). Knowledge-by-acquaintance, as defined by William James, while still involving a separation between knower and object of knowing, is similar to knowledge-by-identity to the extent that neither must be known linguistically — unlike a language-bound deconstructive knowledge.

Knowledge by deconstruction, however, does allow for linguistic gaps, or what seem to be traces of a (incipient) knowledge-by-identity. Shear and Jevning would agree with Derrida on the need for transcending the conceptual oppositions of language to know the real. But in their Advaitan approach they would transcend language (in its manifest form) altogether to reach pure consciousness, while Derrida tries to escape conceptual oppositions from within language by finding a middle path between opposite pairs. Coward notes that in Derrida the real is experienced only 'when the opposites of language are maintained in dynamic tension . . . through a continual deconstruction of first one opposite and then the other' (p. 210). Derrida attempts to undermine the Western logocentric tradition by arguing that we never reach a moment of presence or pure consciousness, but only its trace in the linguistic flickering of presence and absence. Nevertheless, the gaps between the pairs of opposites in the pendulum swing of deconstruction, or the traces of presence, need to be understood in terms of the first-person experience of such moments of presence. In spite of arguing that the silence between the words of God's voice and between the words and letters of writing are pregnant with desire and intentional meaning, Derrida cannot describe these silences in terms of knowledge-by-acquaintance. We can have no knowledge-about them for they remain conceptually ungraspable and irreducible. Furthermore, as Shear and Jevning would argue, if a linguistic gap or silence is by definition empty of empirical phenomenological content, it must also be cross-cultural and ubiquitous and hence accessible only through knowledge-by-identity. In describing their version of the real, postmodernists tend to ignore gaps as an empirical emptiness potentially accessible through knowledge-by-identity and to focus instead on a negative knowledge-about conceptual oppositions. In Shankara's Vedanta, on the other hand, the negative descriptions of *neti, neti* (not this, not this) focus on the positive knowledge-by-identity beyond empirical qualities (Deutsch, 1973, p. 11). If poststructuralists were to focus more on the first-person experience of the gap, they might discover that the real doesn't stop with a negative knowledge-about linguistic difference but extends to the positive affect of knowledge-by-identity.

The experiences of Zen and TM meditators, described by Shear and Jevning, suggest a model that literary and cultural theorists may find useful in testing their knowledge-about experience. The authors report that descriptions of meditative states achieved through different methods in diverse cultures correlate to the same physiological states. These findings 'support the standard traditional cross-cultural reports of physiological correlates of pure consciousness — reduction of pulse, circulation and metabolic rate, and cessation of respiration. It would appear justified, then, to conclude that these physiological measures are in fact cross-cultural, procedure-independent correlates of the pure consciousness experience' (p. 208). One could speculate about the cross-cultural physiological correlates that might emerge if the claims made for knowledge-about experience were to undergo scientific verification. The multiplicity of conflicting voices that supposedly comprise postmodernist consciousness abound with spaces both between these voices and between the resulting social identities. The view from within offered by Shear and Jevning should make it more difficult for literary and cultural theorists to misconstrue the linguistic and other cultural gaps that empty consciousness of its conceptual content.

References

Coward, Harold (1992), 'A Hindu response to Derrida's view of negative theology', in *Derrida and Negative Theology*, ed. Harold Coward and Toby Foshay (New York: SUNY Press).

Derrida, Jacques (1978), 'Edmund Jabès and the Question of the Book', in *Writing and Difference*, trans. Alan Bass (Chicago: University of Chicago Press).

Deutsch, Eliot (1973), *Advaita Vedanta: A Philosophical Reconstruction* (Honolulu: U. of Hawaii Press).

Forman, Robert K.C. (1998), *The Innate Capacity: Mysticism, Psychology, and Philosophy* (New York and Oxford: Oxford University Press).

Gergen, Kenneth J. (1991), *The Saturated Self: Dilemmas of Identity in Contemporary Life*. (New York: BasicBooks).

Rao, K.R. (1998), 'The two faces of consciousness', *Journal of Consciousness Studies*, 5 (3), pp. 309–27.

THEORY AND EXPERIMENT IN PHILOSOPHY

Piet Hut, Institute for Advanced Studies, Princeton, NJ 08540, USA.

When I got my first camera, I noticed something very interesting. After an intensive period of picture taking, the streets of my familiar small town had somehow landed in a different world. I saw everything in a different light. More accurately, I saw the world as light, rather than as matter. My attention had shifted, first rather innocently from seeing a lit-up *building* to seeing a *lit-up* building. Then the shift deepened, from seeing a building that was lit-up by the sunlight to seeing the light itself, that happened to carry the imprint of a lit-up building.

Soon afterwards, still in high school, I experienced a different shift. In Latin class we were given the option to choose a favourite writer. My choice was Seneca, and I started reading the collection of letters he wrote to a student of his, in which he gave him his Stoic advice to drop our usual neurotic engagement with the everyday world. Whenever I would read Seneca's advice to view everything in a more calm and detached way, a strange change in atmosphere would occur. I marvelled at this predictable and reproducible shift. Something seemed to stop. The atmosphere would quickly grow quiet, as soon as I would start reading. It felt as if someone had just switched off a radio that had been playing continuously in the background. And on an almost physical level, it changed my whole sense of embodiment.

Around that time, I began to read a wide variety of other books in philosophy and religion, European as well as non-European. And always this change in atmosphere would be a sign that a book had something real to say, something rooted in a reality that is normally obscured through our frantic absorption with the next moments in time, and the objects nearest to us, in the light trance that we call daily life. I began to realize that the shift did not signal the start of a new form of trance, but rather the dropping away of an old form. The shift coincided with a letting go of an obsession with the trivia of daily life: the preferences and petty goals that pull us through the day. Such a liberating form of shift occurred when I was reading about people like Socrates, Ruysbroeck, Ramakrishna, Dogen, or Thoreau. In each case a wonderful, and more and more familiar form of detachment would set in.

Only much later did I stumble upon Husserl's writing. After I had studied various Asian philosophical and contemplative traditions, and while my career in astrophysics was well underway, I felt the need to search for a form of stepping stone. I wanted to make a connection between the objective scientific approach that I valued so much, and the contemplative introspective methods that seemed no less scientific, even though they embraced a more explicit role for the subject. And it was at the junction between both types of tradition that I felt that Husserl's method of the epochè could play a role. Making philosophy more scientific, by adding a form of experimentation to what often had degenerated into armchair theorizing, Husserl seemed to have found a balance between theory and experiment, in a way that reminded me very much of the methodology of physics.

While first reading Husserl, I felt a sense of home coming. I recognized what type of experience he was trying to point at, in describing the epochè, a systematic method for suspending judgement. Stepping out of the world in order to step more fully into it, this move is ubiquitous in all kinds of contemplative training, in one form of another. And indeed, it is analogous to the role that a laboratory plays in natural science: we step out of the vast complexity of the world, and retreat into a small controlled environment in order to get greater insight — which we can then apply to the world we stepped out of, in order to understand that world better.

What struck me was that Husserl seemed to be far ahead of his time. As a Leonardo da Vinci, drawing a helicopter, he had no clear way in practice to embed the epochè within the programme he envisioned. Indeed, he sometimes complained that even his best students did not seem to understand what he was after. The problem was, I think, that he used a nineteenth-century philosophical writing style to describe what I expect to become a twenty-first-century style of investigation in experimental philosophy.

The notion of an epochè, as an exploration of new degrees of freedom in experience, is a very rich one. The possibilities go far beyond the specific ones that Husserl envisioned. He was a trail-blazer, but as Varela has emphasized repeatedly in his contributions to this volume, we should not limit ourselves to studying his writings. Instead of going into the mode of an historian, the attitude of a physicist is more appropriate, taking past accomplishments as inspiration for finding whole new ways to extend both experiment and theory.

My opening example already presented a different form of 'reduction': to step back from seeing objects 'as' physical objects to seeing them 'as' light. I have found this to be an effective way to introduce students to the epochè, in a way that beckons them beyond a mere theoretical or verbal analysis. Reading about the epochè typically leads a student to contemplate the *concept* of the epochè, rather than really *performing* the epochè (a danger Husserl kept warning about). In contrast, shifting to seeing light where previously one saw matter is likely to have a real impact, in a way that goes beyond intellectualization. Since light is still something external, although mediating between the external and the internal, an initial half-step to a light shift may be easier. Moving on to the epochè proper, by shifting to see objects as given in their conscious-experience aspect, is then less likely to lead to getting stuck in conceptualization.

Let me mention one other way of playing with unsuspected degrees of freedom in our every-day world. It is instructive to take a pen and hold it in front of you, at a comfortable viewing distance. Now move this object closer to you and away from you a few times, and observe what is happening. Notice how the perceived size of the pen is getting smaller and larger. Notice too how the *felt* size of the pen does not change.

Clearly, two different types of seeing are involved. And corresponding to them, two types of pen are 'seen'. There is the apparent pen, shrinking and growing. And there is the 'real' pen, which we feel maintains the same size. And presumably, the 'real' pen is indeed the real, objective pen that other people can agree upon, even though they will see an apparent pen that is different (as an image) in many ways from the apparent pen I perceive. Or is it?

Would it not be more correct to say that we have *three* pens? There is the apparently shrinking pen that you 'see' directly as clearly shrinking, at least in appearance. Then there is the 'real' pen that you can also clearly 'see' as keeping its old size. *And then there is the 'really real' pen*, the one objectively out there, the one you and your friends all agree upon. This is the objective pen, that can be talked about, handed over, borrowed and forgotten-to-be-given-back; the pen that can be analysed physically and chemically and described in scientific equations of various sorts. In contrast, the other two pens are subjective, in the sense of being part of subjective experience, according to our normal interpretation.

But wait, there are more distinctions to be made. Simply closing our eyes is enough to split our notion of the 'real pen that we see in front of us' into two separate branches. With closed eyes we no longer *see* the 'real' pen, but still we *believe* there to be a 'really real' pen. With open eyes we saw both, or more accurately, a package deal of both-in-one: the seen-to-be-there pen and the convinced-to-be-there pen. And so it seems that closing our eyes is a good trick to pull out the 'really real' one. Alternatively, we could have pulled out the 'real' one while suppressing the 'really real' one, by holding up a mirror. While looking at the reflection of the pen in the mirror, we would of course know that the really-real pen was not really behind the mirror. All the same, we could still watch the pen in the mirror as not-really-changing-in-size, when moving to and from us, in the space of the world conjured up behind the mirror.

But were we correct in our identification of the two branches in which our closing-the-eyes had split the object? Surely, the 'real' pen, 'meant' as a constant-size pen in its overlay on top of the apparent pen had disappeared. What we were left with was our conviction that the pen was 'really' still there. But is a conviction the same as an objective object? Clearly not. The conviction was still something that belonged to us, to our realm of experience. In contrast, the objective pen by definition is not something that as such can enter our experience. Conclusion: somehow we have to admit that a *fourth* pen has appeared in our midst!

To sum up: there is the apparent pen, the seen-and-felt-as-real one, the assumed-to-be-there one which remains as a conviction when we close our eyes, and there is the objective pen, that others can agree upon. The third is still part of my subjective experience, and the latter is (posited as) objectively present.

And while we are at it, why not throw in an additional pen, by making a distinction between the objective pen of the every-day world, as a piece of metal and plastic, and the scientific model of the pen, as a congregate of atoms and molecules.

So we have the pen as it appears to us, the pen as we feel it to be, the pen as we think it should be, the pen that others can agree upon as a piece of plastic and metal, the pen the scientist sees as a collection of molecules, and, yes, there are more! The last pen immediately splits *once again* in several varieties. There is the pen of the solid-state physicist, describing its molecular structure. There is the pen of the nuclear physicist, describing the properties of the nuclei and the electrons that are the building blocks of the molecules. There is the pen of the particle physicist, who see the nuclei as made up out of a bunch of quarks and gluons. And so on.

So, which is the real pen? What is reality and what is imagination? Are all of these pens real, but somehow real in a different way? Or are some of them more real than others? Do the 'less real' ones have some degree of imagination mixed into them? Whatever answer we come up with, we simply have to accept the striking differences between the various pens, as soon as our attention has been led to them. And all these differences can play a role in an extension of science which studies not only a world of objects, but which admits subjects to appear in the world as well.

To conclude, I see great potential for the Husserlian notion of epochè, as a tool to make philosophy more scientific, and to make science more philosophical. The present collection of articles, in this special issue, forms one of the steps towards a rekindling of the Husserlian method of 'going back to the things themselves'. It is wonderful to see such a serious attempt at redressing the balance between the study of the object and subject poles of experience. The articles are certainly provocative, in claiming that a whole dimension of investigation has been overlooked in science, by focusing only on third-person knowledge. I hope my brief remarks about the epochè will also help to provoke a reaction, towards the establishment of what Natalie Depraz refers to in her article as a co-empathic community of individuals dedicated to a serious study of the epochè. I plan to present more detail elsewhere (Hut, 1999b; see also Hut & Shepard 1996; Hut, 1999a).

References

Hut, P. (1999a), 'Exploring actuality through experiment and experience', in *Toward a Science of Consciousness III*, ed. S.R. Hameroff *et al.* (Cambridge, MA: MIT Press).

Hut, P. (1999b), 'On the role of the subject in science', in 'Tokyo 99 — Toward a Science of Consciousness: Fundamental Approaches', to be held in Tokyo, May 25–29, 1999.

Hut, P. & Shepard, R. (1996), 'Turning "The Hard Problem" upside down & sideways', *Journal of Consciousness Studies*, **3** (4), pp. 313–29; reprinted in *Explaining Consciousness*, ed. J. Shear (Cambridge, MA: MIT Press).

ON THE METAPHYSICS OF INTROSPECTION

William Lyons, Trinity College, Dublin 2, Republic of Ireland

1. Vermersch's commitment to a two-level account of introspection

In the course of his interesting article on the practice of introspection and its justification, 'Introspection as practice', Pierre Vermersch reveals a commitment to a particular framework or model of the nature of introspection. My comments in this discussion note will be directed towards that model. The following passage from Vermersch's article may serve as a clear account of the model to which I refer:

> Let us try to clarify the framework which might allow us to throw light upon the act of introspection . . . [A]t time t1 the subject carries out a task. He lives through something and this lived experience constitutes an initial point of reference (L1) with reference to what follows. In the context of his research work, the subject, alone or with a mediator, tries to describe his lived experience L1. *In the course of doing this he lives through another lived experience L2, which enables him to gain access to L1 and to describe what he thereby becomes conscious of* (Vermersch, pp. 32–3; emphasis mine).

What concerns me in particular in regard to this model is the last sentence which reveals an unmistakable commitment to a version of a two-level accessing (or scanning or monitoring or inspecting) account of introspection. For this model proposes that there is, first, L1, 'a lived experience' which, I take it, is a phenomenal event or, to use Jamesean terminology for a moment, an episode in the subject's stream of consciousness. It then postulates that there must be a second such episode, L2, 'another lived experience which enables him [the subject] to gain access to L1'. That is to say, L2 is a conscious episode which involves gaining access to L1, the initial or ground-level conscious episode. The picture is of the employment of a second-level conscious or lived experience to enable a subject to gain access to a first-level conscious experience. My concerns about this model, which I first voiced many years ago (in Lyons, 1986), will be set out quite briefly in the following sections.

2. Practical difficulties in splitting consciousness into two levels

Such a model, whereby one conscious lived experience is employed as the means of gaining access to another conscious lived experience, implies that both experiences must survive the accessing procedure as fully alive (or lived) and conscious. If this were not so, the accessing procedure would be deemed a failure, because it would have reduced the target lived experience to a 'dead' nonconscious something which thereby could not be an experience. The essence of an experience is to be conscious. If it ceases to be that, it ceases to be an experience.

In turn this model of one lived experience accessing another, and preserving them both as lived, implies that a particular subject's consciousness is being split into two. In being experiences, they are *ipso facto* conscious. In being conscious, they are *ipso facto* both occurring here and now in the stream of some person's consciousness. In being in the relation of one experience accessing another, they are *ipso facto* in the one single stream of one single person's consciousness. That is to say, to sum up, there must be two tasks to which one is giving conscious attention at one and the same time, namely to the conscious lived experience labelled L1, and to the task of carefully accessing this experience via a second-level conscious lived experience, L2.

Historically and critically such claims about the possibility of splitting consciousness have not fared well. First in the 1950s and then again in the 1970s, there was a good amount of experimental work done on the possibility of splitting consciousness so that one might consciously and attentively engage in two tasks at one and the same time, irrespective of whether the two tasks were or were not in the relation of the one accessing the other. My reading of that work was summed up in Lyons (1986), chapter 1, section 4. The conclusion I came to then was that, while debate was still possible, there was little comfort in those experiments to any view which held that one could split fully attentive consciousness into two, whether that be for the purpose of engaging in two tasks or two experiences both of which required careful attention.

One simple illustration of this conclusion is the extremely difficult parlour game, let us call it 'The Two-Handed Tracing Game', of trying with the right hand to trace continuously, in an anti-clockwise direction, a circle around the top of your head while at the same time, with the left hand, trying to trace in a clockwise direction a square around the perimeter of your stomach. The best one can do is to render one of the operations automatic, that is to say, to withdraw it from the realm of the subject's lived experiences, so that in consequence consciousness is not now split and splintered but directed at any one moment to just one of the tasks. Alternatively one might attempt to oscillate one's attention rapidly from one task to the other in the manner of a professional juggler. This latter move also does not involve splitting attention (splitting consciousness) but oscillating the focus of consciousness, now to one of the tasks, now to the other.

I am inclined to think that, in 'The Two-Handed Tracing Game', the best strategy is to employ the former method. One might be able, if right handed, to begin to trace with the right hand a circle around one's head in an anti-clockwise direction and then gradually to speed up this task till it is performed on automatic pilot. Then, and only then, should one attempt to set in motion the second task of tracing a clockwise square around one's stomach with one's left hand. I admit that I have never been able to employ either method successfully.

Perhaps I have made my point that any model of introspection that involves splitting consciousness into two lived experiences, with one accessing the other, is not a promising account.

3. *Some theoretical problems about a two-level account of introspection*

Even to be tempted into flirting with a two-level model of introspection (of one conscious lived experience accessing another), seems wholly unnecessary. *One can explain introspection perfectly adequately in terms of just one level of conscious experience.*

Let me elaborate on this point. If suddenly I become conscious of a hissing sound in my computer, I can tell you about it immediately. In practice, I do not have to call into play another experience which would, concomitantly, provide the needed access to the conscious lived experience of hearing the hissing sound in my computer, for the simple reason that the latter experience is already a fully conscious experience and so already fully available for being expressed linguistically for the benefit of some second or third person. In theory, it does not even make much sense to invoke such a second-level, accessing experience. By itself, the first or ground-level experience, in being a conscious one, *ipso facto* makes the subject of that experience aware of all that can ever be known about that experience subjectively. Therefore any additional, second-level conscious lived experience, will be both practically and theoretically superfluous.

The principle of parsimony (most often associated with the work of the medieval Franciscan logician, William of Ockham, and so known sometimes as 'Ockham's Razor'), advises that, in fashioning one's theory or model, *one should not multiply the entities or processes,* postulated as part of the theory or model, *beyond the minimum that is required to make sense of the known facts.* So, by a simple application of the principle of parsimony, all that is required for my introspection of my experience of hearing the hissing sound in my computer is

   (i)   *that I experience the hissing sound,*
  (ii) *that I not be distracted,*
 (iii) *and that I have sufficient linguistic skills to tell someone about it.*

I do not need to postulate a second experience which would provide access to the first experience described under (i) above. For the very nature of any conscious lived experience (such as occurs under (i) above) is that *ipso facto* it is accessible to the subject of the experience. With conscious experiential episodes, the reality, the sole reality, is the appearance (the phenomenal presentation in the subject's stream of consciousness).

Let us take the above argument in a little more detail. You might say, 'I know that right now you are listening to that rather alarming hissing sound made by your computer. Now, by way of gathering data for my psychology project, I would like you to introspect and carefully report on that inner experience of your hearing the hissing sound in your computer.' I might reply, 'Of course. I am most willing to oblige. I will introspect my experience of hearing that hissing sound in my computer and report my findings to you.' Grammatically, with the phrase 'introspect my experience', it looks as if I have agreed to add a second conscious experience, the introspecting one, to my first one of hearing the hissing sound. It looks as if I have agreed, for the sake of a psychology project, to direct an inner conscious searchlight, an introspective act, upon my current consciousness of the hissing sound in order the better to be able to report on the details of my hearing of the hissing. But, in fact, all I can do, since I cannot split my consciousness into two workable streams of experiencing-the hissing and experiencing-the-experiencing-of-the-hissing, is *to concentrate on* the hissing sound. But to concentrate is not to inaugurate a second-level conscious process that sits parasitically upon the first and thereby brings the first into clearer view. It is *to obliterate* something. It is to banish distractions, by 'bracketing out' all that is irrelevant. In fact, all that I need do is banish distractions so as to leave untouched, and so in full focus, the hearing of the hissing. Then I need to tell you about it by choosing my words carefully and so on. But to express linguistically my experience of the hissing (even if it is now lodged in short-term memory and so needing to be revived), is no more and no less difficult that my now expressing linguistically the fact that a seagull is now flying or has just a moment ago flown past my window. If, without any need to call upon some second-level process of consciously experiencing one's first-level conscious experience of seeing, I can directly report upon what I am now seeing, then surely I can also directly report upon what I am now hearing or what I have just heard or on a fleeting after-image or on an hallucination or on a queasy feeling in my stomach.

Let me backtrack for a minute. If Vermersch's position is to be interpreted in a slightly different way, then there is still theoretical trouble in store. For if his position is that the first lived experience, L1, is *not fully conscious* and so requires a second lived experience, L2, to make it fully conscious and thereby reportable, then his model would fall victim to an infinite (and so impossible) regress of required events. For to report on one's second experience, L2, which *ex hypothesi* would also not be fully conscious, then the reporting subject would require yet another lived experience, L3, to make it fully conscious and so reportable. And so on *ad infinitum*.

4. Valediction

Perhaps if we gave up talking about introspection and the method of introspection, both of which perpetuate the myth that there is a special, second-level, inner activity for intro-specting (for inner-observing) our stream of consciousness, then we would avoid so many theoretical wrong turnings. Perhaps, instead of talking about introspection, we could talk simply about banishing distractions. If we hankered after a technical term, we could talk about *attendation* (from the Latin *attendere*) and define it as 'the method for carefully attending to and reporting on conscious experiences'.[14]

References

Lyons, William (1986), *The Disappearance of Introspection* (Cambridge, MA: Bradford / MIT).

REPLY TO LYONS

P. Vermersch

My article has a pragmatic orientation. I left aside any discussion on the nature of introspection in order to emphasize its practice, as the title clearly indicates. As in any domain, we can carry out actions here without having a consensus about how it works. Accordingly, whether Lyons and I agree or not about the division of consciousness does not stop introspective observations from being carried out. In fact, one of my points in the article is that the critics of introspection typically stay at the

[14] In producing a final version of this discussion note, I am very grateful for some very perceptive critique from my colleague, Paul O'Grady.

theoretical level and refuse to engage in the work itself, as if this would somehow be a contamination (like Galileo's judging cardinal refusing to look through the telescope). In spite of this caveat let me play the game on Lyons' ground, since obviously doing a practice does not entail ignoring its basis and problems.

My scheme is not a doubling, like two simultaneous activities demanding a hypothetical division to exist. Instead it poses two successive and different kinds of acts (L1 is a perception for instance, while L2 is a remembrance of the perception). So there is no conflict here, since one starts where the other stops. Thus there is no uncertainty in the proposed tasks, since what is at stake is to evoke the lived experience, taken as reference, in order to describe it.

Furthermore, several of the points raised by Lyons have a shaky basis. Let me concentrate on three. The first one is that he takes every experience as being fully conscious. But if it was that simple then there would be no gap between the subject's experience and its description, since one would have full access to it just by the fact that one has experienced it. Now there are two strong factual and theoretical limitations to that stance. Every experience has a pre-reflexive component which occupies a large part of phenomenal 'space'. Thus most of the content of our experience is only *amenable* to, rather than being expressed as, reflexive consciousness. Accordingly there cannot be a detailed verbalization of what has not yet been made conscious. Such a process of bringing into awareness can only be done on the basis of what categories the subject has, and these surely are less diverse that the infinity of segmentations that any experience is open to.

This leads into the second point of disagreement with Lyons. He takes every experience as simple, and thus entirely given just in the fact of living it. In other words, experience of a sound is, he says, simple and straightforward. Describing that experience is an entirely different affair, and a much harder one, because that experience has a complex structure which can be described with many degrees of fine-grained resolution. For instance I can describe focussing on the sound itself (which is what Lyons does exclusively). But I can also focus on *how* I listen, that is, on the act of listening rather than the sound-object, with the inherent finesse all such acts are capable of. Or I can still focus on the attentional modalities that will change over time, as well as a number of other aspects such as the feeling tone, the postural and motor correlation, and so on. I would ask the reader (and Lyons) — actually *try* and describe your experience and you will be surprised.

Thirdly, Lyons thinks that in order to accomplish a cognitive act I must necessarily have a complete reflexiveness, which leads, unnecessarily, to an infinite regress. But accomplishing a cognitive act is, in itself, to a large extent pre-reflexive, since the awareness is concerned with its objectives and main stages, but not with its full constitution. To have an experience of L2, I definitely do not need a full reflexiveness of how I carry out such an act. In order to evoke a sound previously attended to, I do not have to have a full reflexiveness of the act of evocation. The distinction between the act and its object is what cuts the ghost of infinite regress. Obviously, at a different time t3, there can be an evocation of the mental content of evocation that preceded, and which takes as its content a focussing on the manner in which introspection is carried out. But this L3, like any other experience, will not be doubled.

THE FRINGE:
A CASE STUDY IN EXPLANATORY PHENOMENOLOGY

Bruce Mangan, Institute of Cognitive Studies, University of California, Berkeley CA, USA. Email: mangan@cogsci.berkeley.edu

William James' greatest achievement is, arguably, his analysis of the fringe — or, as he sometimes called it, transitive experience.[15] In trying to understand this vague, elusive, often peripheral aspect of consciousness, James broke new ground. But in so doing he also began to lay down the first stratum of a radically new methodology, one that intersects first- and third-person findings in such a way that each is able to interrogate the other, and so further our understanding of both.

James was a trained physician, and he was impressed by the then new understanding of neural processes as both dynamic and (as we now say) massively parallel and distributed. It may even be that it was James' *prior* sense of neural dynamics, learned as a medical student, that gave him the hint for his later and most distinctive phenomenological findings (Mangan, 1991). In any case, James linked neural and phenomenological structure closely in his writings, at times explaining features of our phenomenology as consequences of our underlying neural dynamics.[16] This aspect of James' enterprise I would call 'explanatory' phenomenology.

After lying dormant for most of this century, research has started to return to the method James helped pioneer. One example is Varela's neurophenomenology. It, too, aims to go beyond phenomenological description, and take the next step — to explain to some degree *why* our phenomenology is the way it is. For example, Varela's paper on present-time consciousness in this special issue (see section III, especially) brings out some intriguing ideas about the levels of temporal constraints on neural processing that may condition the time horizon in the fringe. Some of my own work (Mangan, 1991; 1993a, b) is also concerned with explaining fringe phenomenology as conditioned by neural factors, especially overall features of network integration that are conveniently captured by PDP models.

But I think it is important to see that explanatory phenomenology can be completely scientific without *necessarily* having to (1) consider the neural substrate, (2) employ reductive arguments, or (3) operate at the third-person level. If I am right, explanatory phenomenology can be a remarkably plastic member of the set of first-person methodologies for the study of consciousness.

---

[15] In this special issue, Bailey makes a sharp distinction between the terms 'fringe' and 'transitive' experience. On my reading of James, these terms are rough synonyms. There can be no question that for James both terms refer to the same basic phenomenological fact: feelings of relation. It is true that when James wants to emphasize the dynamic and integrative function of feelings of relation, he will often call them transitive experience; and when he wants to consider feelings of relation as context feelings around a single definite image (or 'nucleus' as he sometimes calls it) James will more often use the term fringe. But as Bailey himself notes, James sometimes writes of the fringe as having all the attributes of transitive experience (e.g. 1890, V. 1, p. 253). And Bailey forthrightly notes other difficulties with his own interpretation. I must point out that contrary to Bailey's assertion, the relation between transitive experience and the fringe has been considered in the literature — briefly in Mangan (1993a), and more extensively in Mangan (1991). Bailey cites Galin (1996); but this paper simply recapitulates some of my previous work on the fringe, though this fact is not always clear. Galin does, however, offer some original ideas on alternatives to James' terminology.

[16] See, for instance, James' discussion of the neural/phenomenological linkage using the brilliant analogy of a kaleidoscope (1890, Vol 1, pp. 247–8).

Let me expand slightly on these contentions, and at the same time illustrate them with a concrete example — an analysis of one aspect of fringe phenomenology, in particular its diaphanous, indistinct, unarticulated character. I will do this solely from the first-person stance, but I believe this nevertheless begins to explain the structure of our phenomenology *just as biologists explain many aspects of organic structure*. If we wish, we can go further and integrate the following first-person analysis with additional third-person findings. But even so, this would not entail a third-person reduction, nor otherwise make the first-person stance subservient to the third. My basic point will be that we can identify a conservation principle operating in consciousness: that as something becomes clear, something else must become vague; but throughout a huge number of clear–vague phenomenological transformations, a rough parity in articulation capacity is preserved.

First of all, it is crucial to see that (neo-positivist dogma notwithstanding) some standard methods of explanation in science are not restricted to 'person' — be it first, second *or* third. Science already possesses what I would call 'person-independent' or 'stance-independent' explanatory principles. One of them is to explain a phenomenon by identifying a salient constraint or limitation.

Consider for a moment how explanation via limitation is used in third-person research. Probably the most mathematically precise instance of this is the principle of conservation of energy in physics. And in biology, too, third-person explanations will often rest on identifying the right limitation, i.e., the operative limitation that helps explain the phenomenon in question.

Probably the most successful example of this is Malthus' insight that the environment puts an upper limit on the number of organisms able to survive at any given time. In Darwin's hands, this became the basis of the most powerful explanatory theory in the history of biology, natural selection. But explanations that identify an operative limitation can be very mundane. Why does eating yogurt reduce gastrointestinal disorders? One might think that yogurt somehow attacks harmful bacteria directly. But according to a current theory, yogurt protects us because of 'competitive exclusion'. The area on the surface of the intestine is limited, and the bacteria in yogurt occupy this limited area so completely that little room is left for harmful bacteria. So by recognizing the relevant limitation — there is only so much room in the intestine — we explain why yogurt works to reduce digestive problems.

Now one kind of limitation is a trade-off. A trade-off occurs when an advantage can only be 'bought' by giving up an alternative advantage. The notion of a trade-off is stance-independent, and this is our point of departure for explaining the vague or indefinite phenomenology of fringe experience.

But first a final third-person example showing how a trade-off limitation helps explain the distribution of receptive fields in the human eye. An ideal eye would not have to trade off acuity for sensitivity. But in fact the limited surface area of the retina imposed a trade-off in the size and distribution of the eye's receptive fields. Narrow (acute) receptive fields cluster around the fovea, wide (sensitive) receptive fields are peripheral. Wide receptive fields are inherently less able to resolve details than are narrow receptive fields, and wide receptive fields of necessity yield relatively blurry or fuzzy output. But a wide receptive field, because it covers a larger area, is more sensitive to light, and so gives us *some* visual information when a narrow receptive field is in effect blind. Our night vision would improve if we had more wide receptive fields in the eye, but this would then of necessity reduce the area left for narrow receptive fields, and our ability to see details would suffer. Again, we explain a trade-off by identifying the operative limitation that underlies it — in this case, the limited area of the retina.

Now, in some ways fringe phenomenology is quite like the fuzzy or ill-defined quality of peripheral vision produced by wide receptive fields. But a note of caution. While this analogy is helpful, it should not be pressed too far. The fringe is found in *all* sensory and non-sensory modalities of experience, not just vision. (James' own examples of the fringe are drawn from non-sensory experience.) And even in visual experience, fringe effects can be separated completely from those of peripheral vision (Rock and Gutman, 1981).

A good illustration of the fringe in sensory experience is the cocktail party effect. Two conversations are in earshot, but we cannot clearly attend to both of them at the same time. The best we can do is shift attention back and forth; at any given moment, we can only experience one or the other conversation clearly. For once we shift attention away from the clear conversation, its phenomenology is immediately transformed. What had been a clear conversation is now a vague, hazy background of ill-defined words and voice timbres.

This is a standard example, but I believe we can now extract a new point from it: there is a trade-off strategy at work in consciousness. This is hardly an ideal situation; it would be more efficient if we could experience both conversations clearly at the same time. But for some reason the resources of consciousness are not up to this task. (By contrast, we have very good evidence that this limitation does not apply to non-conscious processing. See Baars, 1988). In general, consciousness represents the unattended or background conversation with very sketchy strokes. And if, for an unstable moment, we do succeed in attending to both conversations simultaneously (and aren't just shifting attention quickly back and forth), we experience the two conversations at an *intermediate* level of clarity. Neither conversation is experienced as clearly as it would be if it were alone in the foreground, but neither is experienced as vaguely as it would be if it were completely in the background. At an intermediate level of clarity, there are more contents in consciousness, but via the trade-off they are less phenomenologically defined than if there were fewer contents.

In general we explain a trade-off by grasping its operative limitation. And so if we can do this in the case of consciousness, we will have begun to explain *in purely first-person terms and using a stance-independent explanatory principle* why consciousness has a fringe.

What, then, is the operative limitation on the trade-offs in consciousness? At this point the answer should be evident: Articulation capacity. *At the deepest level, consciousness IS the limited but infinitely plastic capacity to articulate experience.* This overall capacity is conserved during a huge number of phenomenological transformations. Normally, when something becomes clear, something else becomes vague — the 'sum' of total articulation remains at least roughly constant.

But we can apply the idea of the conservation of consciousness to more extreme cases. At a low articulation level throughout the field of experience, our standard 'amount' of consciousness would be spread out as an extremely diffuse, vague, diaphanous field, and without a clear focus. On the other hand, we would expect that lacking clarity the field of consciousness would have immense extension. At the other extreme, we could experience very high articulation, with a focal object more finely detailed than we usually experience, but at the cost of giving up our background sense of setting, horizon, context relations, etc., that the fringe normally gives us.

From this perspective, the actual structure of consciousness is remarkably lop-sided. At any given moment, most of its resources are devoted to the high articulation of a single object in attention, consisting of only a few clear component features (its 7 ± 2 'chunks'). Again, only the smallest bit of consciousness articulation capacity is reserved for the fringe and transitive experience. Of course this raises a further question. Why does consciousness have the particular ratio of clear/vague articulation we actually find? Perhaps the answer here will take us beyond the limits of first-person analysis, and into third-person biological considerations, perhaps a process of evolutionary tuning for optimum efficiency given the antecedent limitation on the capacity of consciousness to articulate experience.

References

Baars, B.J. (1988), *A Cognitive Theory of Consciousness* (New York, Cambridge University Press).

Mangan, B.B. (1991), *Meaning and the Structure of Consciousness: A Essay in Psychoaesthetics* Doctoral dissertation, University of California, Berkeley.

Mangan, B.B. (1993a), 'Taking phenomenology seriously: the 'fringe' and its implications for cognitive research,' *Consciousness and Cognition* **2** (2), pp. 89–108

Mangan, B.B. (1993b), 'Some philosophical and empirical implications of the fringe,' *Consciousness and Cognition*, **2** (2), pp. 142–54

Rock, I. & Gutman, D. (1981), 'The effect of inattention on form perception', *Journal of Experimental Psychology*, **7** (2), pp. 275–85.

BUILDING MATERIALS FOR THE EXPLANATORY BRIDGE

Eduard Marbach, Institute of Philosophy, University of Bern, Laenggasstra. 49A, CH-3000 Bern 9, Switzerland.

In recent years, David J. Chalmers (1995; 1996; 1997) has forcefully made a point that I consider to be extremely important for the study of consciousness, also from a Husserlian perspective. The point is that conscious experience is 'an explanandum in its own right' (1995, p. 209). In order to make progress in addressing the problem of the *explanatory gap* between physical processes and conscious experience, new approaches are therefore to be explored. As Chalmers has it, 'a mere account of the functions stays on one side of the gap, so the materials for the bridge must be found elsewhere' (1995, p. 203). Now, as I see it, the editors of this Special Issue pursue, precisely, the most promising avenue for adequately studying the problem of consciousness in such an exploratory spirit. For, in their excellent Introduction, they unequivocally propose to *include* first-person, subjective experience as an explicit and active component of a science of consciousness, to be elaborated with appropriate methods by a research community. Jonathan Shear already put it very clearly elsewhere: 'what is needed . . . is not so much new conceptualizations of science or new objective methodologies for exploring relationships of the phenomena of consciousness to physiology and behaviour . . . but new systematic methodologies for the exploration of the subjective phenomena of consciousness' (in Shear, 1997, p. 369). Among such methodologies, the editors now include 'the most important western school of thinking where experience and consciousness is at the very heart: Phenome-nology as inaugurated by Edmund Husserl . . .' (p. 5, this issue).

After all, then, it looks as if Husserl's hope, expressed in the early years of this cen-tury, is getting closer to being fulfilled at the turn of the next one. Consider, for instance, scientific psychology and its failure to take into account the potential bene-fits of working with the first-person methods of phenomenology. Husserl already noted in 1912 that 'the future will probably teach that *evident data* cannot be removed by not looking at them, and someday the psychologists will consider the "instrument" of phenomenological *eidetic theory* to be no less important, indeed at first probably very much more important, than mechanical instruments' (Husserl, 1980, p. 42; my emphasis).[17]

In this short contribution, I will however not be concerned with technicalities of Husserl scholarship, focussing on which would all too readily smack of 'some kind of Husserlian scholastic obsession', rightly discarded in this context by Francisco Varela (see p. 111, this issue). As a consequence, I will not address specific points of what Natalie Depraz and Francisco Varela, in particular, have contributed in their rich and wide-ranging papers. Doing justice to them would go beyond the limits of this contribution anyway. Instead, with tools from a Husserlian first-person methodology, I wish to concentrate directly on 'the need to overcome the "just-take-a-look" attitude in regards to experience' by taking up the editors' 'main question' with regard to carefully examining subjective life: 'how do you actually *do* it? Is there evidence that it *can* be done? If so, with what *results*?' (p. 2). To conclude, I very briefly try to relate some of my observations to Varela's research direction of 'neuro- phenomenology' which I, in principle, find very attractive. With this, I hope usefully to complement the papers of the section dedicated to phenomenology.

To begin with, it will be helpful to draw attention to the following distinction between performing and reflecting on a mental activity. On the one hand, we can speak of *performing* a mental activity, e.g., perceiving something, remembering something, viewing something in a picture, etc. A person's being conscious while performing, say, an activity of remembering something, is tantamount to her *pre-reflectively* knowing or being innerly aware of intentionally referring to something past. Such pre-reflective consciousness, I take it, is involved when Thomas Nagel and others talk of 'what it is like' to be conscious in one way or another: it pre-reflectively or innerly feels different, precisely, to be remembering something rather than to be imagining something. I presume that David Chalmers, too, must be thinking along these lines when he states that 'there is nothing that we know more intimately than conscious experience' (1995, p. 200). However, even if we intimately know in a sense what is essential in our practical life — e.g., to be currently imagining rather than remembering something — it is crucial to notice with Husserl that we know this *only implicitly*. On the other hand, therefore, we must speak of *reflecting* upon a mental activity and *explicitly* elaborating the structure or form of the experience. Reflec-tively uncovering forms of conscious experience can then be seen as providing articu-late answers to the question *why* and *how* it *feels* or is *experienced* distinctly differently to be, for example, perceiving, or remembering, or pictorially represent-ing something, etc. To be sure, this reflective clarification of conscious experience is

---

[17] Marbach (1988) elaborates on Husserl's metaphor of the 'instrument' of phenomenological analysis.

not by itself the much sought after scientific explanation of consciousness. I would want to argue, however, that the explanatory work can be much facilitated if systematic knowledge about *conscious experience as such* is made *explicit* so as to approach the problem to be solved in a way that is as far as possible adequate to the issue at stake. In this way, we overcome the monolithic conception of 'conscious experience' and are led to uncover properties, structures or forms, lawful dependencies etc., pertaining to various *kinds* of conscious experience. In short, we get building material on the 'other side' of the explanatory gap!

Now consider briefly how to proceed in *doing* reflective observations on conscious experience of one kind or another. Speaking quite generally, one can *reflect* properly only upon a mental activity which is not now performed but which one now represents to oneself in order to investigate what constitutes it. For example, instead of actually looking at the red house in the picture over there, I now decide to remember such an activity. Or, even more readily, I decide to imagine that I look at the house in the picture. Now, while one actually only *represents* the activity — instead of actually performing the activity and thereby being interested, aesthetically or otherwise, in the red house — one can think of the red house with an awareness that it is the object of a *represented* (i.e. not simply actually performed) activity of picture viewing. The next move to make is decisive in order to establish the theme of the phenomenological analysis of the conscious experience in question. The idea is, as Husserl has shown, to take the object of the mental activity as the guiding thread for unpacking the multiple constituent parts which will be said to be operative when referring to objects on the basis of an activity of the kind in question. Thus, in our example, focus attention upon the represented red house, and now mentally *shift to* addressing the properly *reflective question* of how the red house is given to (or appears in) the corresponding represented activity of picture viewing. You must then patiently proceed step by step, allowing yourself to be guided by the way of givenness of the object, in order to elaborate the corresponding unified structure of the conscious experience. With the help of this method of reflection, more distinctness will be obtained regarding the property of *being conscious* or of *having conscious experience* that is all too often assumed to be some sort of uniform or unitary phenomenon that is either present or absent, a simple quality of some mental content or a feeling, 'elusive even to acquaintance'.[18]

Addressing the issues of communication, errors regarding the reflectively established phenomenological data, and their correction, Husserl himself pointed out the following in one of his main publications in 1913:

> 'Consciousness of something' is . . . something obviously understandable of itself and, at the same time, highly enigmatic. The labyrinthically false paths into which the first reflections lead, easily generate a skepticism which negates the whole troublesome sphere of problems. . . . If the right attitude has been won, and made secure by *practice*, above all, however, if one has acquired the courage to obey the clear *eidetic data* with a radical lack of prejudice so as to be unencumbered by all current and learned theories, then firm results are directly produced, and the same thing occurs for everyone having the same attitude; there accrue firm possibilities of communicating to others what one has himself seen . . . of making known and weeding out errors by measuring them again

---

[18] The phrase is by Colin McGinn (1982, p. 13), in the context of discussing the notion of *consciousness* as a possible 'criterion of the mental'.

against intuition — errors which are also possible here just as in any sphere of validity (Husserl,1982, § 87; my emphasis).

Here I can only briefly comment on the importance of what Husserl calls 'eidetic data'. Such data are, precisely, crucial for the *scientific status* of the reflective investigations. For in view of the fact of the incessant flow of conscious experience, Husserl very early on realized that he had to aim at studying the subjective phenomena not as *this* or as *that* singular phenomenon in the flow. Much rather, he had to adopt the (eidetic) attitude of determining the fact of this or that phenomenon '*as* the fact of its essence' which 'is determinable only *through* its essence' (Husserl, 1970, § 52, p. 182). In the eidetic attitude, the question is, *what it is* to be perceiving something, *what it is* to be remembering something, *what it is* to be viewing something in a picture, etc., always asked with regard to possible perception, possible remembering, etc., in general. To be sure, in phenomenology too, a factually given conscious experience provides the experiential basis for the elaboration of its form in accordance with its very possibility. But the factually chosen case will be taken as an arbitrary example, a mere starting point for the analysis. The main task of the reflective-eidetic analysis in Husserl's 'science of consciousness' is to establish cognition about that which essentially or invariably, i.e. eidetically, belongs to an experience of this or that kind. His concern as a philosopher was with first analysing the *possibilities* of conscious experience and the system of *possible* modifications of such experience, rather than with the experience as actual matter of fact that is of interest in scientific psychology and neuroscience. But Husserl argued, convincingly, I think,[19] that knowledge about what there *possibly* is in the sphere of conscious experience should be brought to bear in empirical investigations into consciousness.

With these general points of the methodology in mind, consider now some *results* of reflective analysis. Space here does however not allow lengthy discussion, so let me immediately focus on a detail in order to convey a sense of what I take to be a *specifically phenomenological contribution* to the study of conscious experience. Suppose you experience a sensation of vivid red, or any other colour for that matter. Now, as a Husserlian phenomenologist, I am *not* addressing the question of why it is, as David Chalmers puts it, 'that when electromagnetic waveforms impinge on a retina and are discriminated and categorized by a visual system, this discrimination and categorization is experienced as a sensation of vivid red' (1995, p. 203). Instead, the main point a phenomenologist has to elucidate with regard to such an experience is to describe *what it is for my consciousness* to experience the colour when I perceive something *in contrast to*, for example, *what it is for my consciousness* to experience the colour when I view something in a picture, etc. To illustrate, suppose that what I experience as a sensation of vivid red occurs in viewing the house in the picture over there. Now suppose that what I experience as a sensation of vivid red occurs while I am looking at the red patch of colour that is really present on the canvas. Here, I want to argue that my consciously experiencing the one case is pre-reflectively distinctly different from my consciously experiencing the other, even though, considered abstractly, the puzzling fact of experiencing a red sensation at all may be the same. Concretely viewed, however, these two cases of conscious experience are radically distinct from one another. Establishing causes *why this is so*, as a complete science of

---

[19] For more on this claim, see Marbach (1988).

consciousness has to do, would thus seem to have to take into account the phenomenological results relative to the case in point.

Regarding such results, which reflection permits to make explicit, let me just try to sketch how the experience of giving attention to the pictorially appearing red house is very different from an experience of simply perceptually attending to something really present such as a flat shape of the colour red. Is it not clear that the red that I actually see when I look over there has to be attributed to an object that is itself also actually present, providing the location where red actually appears? What else could it be in the given case, if not the picture in its physical presence over there? But then, the red that I see would just be the colour which, in our pre-scientific ways of speaking, the two-dimensionally appearing picture can be said to have. If so, the colour red over there would have to be taken by me to be a constituent part of the flat piece of canvas, such that if I were to take scissors I could cut up the canvas into a bunch of red-coloured clippings. A merely perceptual (visual) presentation would then be required for making this red appear over there, and (all things being equal) this perceptual activity would also be sufficient for this to happen.

By contrast, if I take the red to belong to the house, or if I speak of the red in relation to the house, then it should be clear that the objective identification here involved takes me consciously *beyond* that which I take to be *really perceptually given* over there. For, clearly, I do not believe that there is any house over there in my room where I see the piece of canvas. Thus it is crucial to notice that a merely perceptual activity gets you to the red only as a property of the canvas (or photo-paper, etc.), *not* to the red as a property of the pictorially appearing house. The latter, the iconic red as well as the iconic shape of the pictorially appearing house, must be attributed in one way or another in virtue of a representational attitude towards some really *absent* house. And this amounts to saying that the iconic green and the iconic shape are *not actually perceived* as really being over there. To the extent, then, that the colour red and the given shape are attributed to the pictorially appearing house they are at once also integrated in one way or another in the pictorial relation to the depicted (real or fictional) house.

To conclude, I consider that phenomenological data of this sort concerning the structure of conscious experience, all too briefly discussed, alas,[20] present strong *constraints* for any scientific, and especially neuroscientific study of consciousness. Francisco Varela's 'working hypothesis of neurophenomenology' makes precisely this point, too, arguing convincingly that both domains of phenomena, those of the biological mind and those of the experiential or the conscious mind, relate to each other through reciprocal constraints and have equal status in demanding full attention and respect for their specificity (Varela, 1996, p. 343). In the end, then, it is to be hoped that more and more scientists face up to the fact that conscious experience is an explanandum *in its own right*, indeed, and that they begin to take advantage of well-established results provided by first-person phenomenology.

---

[20] In Marbach (1993) I have presented phenomenological data in more detail, proposing a notation in order to capture structural differences of conscious experience of different kinds in clear-cut ways.

References

Chalmers, D.J. (1995), 'Facing up to the problem of consciousness', *Journal of Consciousness Studies*, **2** (3), pp. 200–19. Reprinted in Shear (1997).

Chalmers, D.J. (1996), *The Conscious Mind. In Search of a Fundamental Theory* (New York: Oxford University Press).

Chalmers, D.J. (1997), 'Moving forward on the problem of consciousness', *Journal of Consciousness Studies*, **4** (1), pp. 3–46. Reprinted in Shear (1997).

Husserl, E. (1970), *The Crisis of the European Sciences and Transcendental Phenomenology: An Introduction to Phenomenological Philosophy*, trans. D. Carr (Evanston, IL: Northwestern University Press).

Husserl, E. (1980), *Ideas Pertaining to a Pure Phenomenology and to a Phenomenological Philosophy. Third Book: Phenomenology and the Foundations of the Sciences*, trans. Ted E. Klein and William E. Pohl (The Hague: Martinus Nijhoff).

Husserl, E. (1982), *Ideas Pertaining to a Pure Phenomenology and to a Phenomenological Philosophy. First Book: Phenomenology and the Foundations of the Sciences*, trans. F. Kersten (The Hague: Martinus Nijhoff).

Marbach, E. (1988), 'How to study consciousness phenomenologically or quite a lot comes to mind', *Journal of the British Society for Phenomenology*, **19** (3).

Marbach, E. (1993), in *Mental Representation and Consciousness: Towards a Phenomenological Theory of Representation and Reference. Contributions to Phenomenology*, volume 14. (Dordrecht: Kluwer Academic Publishers).

McGinn, C. (1982), *The Character of Mind* (Oxford: Oxford University Press).

Shear, J. (ed. 1997), *Explaining Consciousness – The 'Hard Problem'* (Cambridge, MA: MIT Press).

Varela, F.J. (1996), 'Neurophenomenology', *Journal of Consciousness Studies*, **3** (4), pp. 330–49. Reprinted in Shear (1997).

A 'HERMENEUTIC OBJECTION': Language and the Inner View

Gregory Nixon, Prescott College.   Email: nixer@northlink.com
Correspondence: 303 Merritt Avenue D, Prescott, AZ 86301, USA.

> They said, 'You have a blue guitar,
> You do not play things as they are.'
> The man replied, 'Things as they are
> Are changed upon the blue guitar.'
>   Wallace Stevens (1954), 'The Man with the Blue Guitar'

I: The View from 'Without' & 'Within'

In the worlds of philosophy, linguistics and communications theory, a view has developed which understands conscious experience as experience which is 'reflected' back upon itself through language. This indicates that the consciousness we experience is possible only because we have culturally invented language and subsequently evolved to accommodate it. This accords with the conclusions of Daniel Dennett (1991), but the 'hermeneutic objection' would go further and deny that the objective sciences themselves have escaped the hermeneutic circle.

The consciousness we humans experience is developed only within the context of crossing the 'symbolic threshold' (Percy 1975; Deacon, 1997) and one of the earliest and most important symbols we acquire is that of the self, or 'the subject experience'. It is only when we achieve self-awareness that the world, as such, comes to exist for us as an object (which contains categories and sub-categories of objects). Any consciousness imputed to prelinguistic stages of development is based on projection and guesswork, since we can know nothing directly of it. It can be said that any experience which does not separate an inner subject from an outer world is probably a continuum of sensation in which environmental stimulus and instinctive response are experienced as a unity; it may be 'lived experience' but it is experience 'lived' nonconsciously.

Speech requires assertion and by learning to speak we find ourselves asserting, in essence, our *selves* into the world. The narrative form of language allows us to develop life stories, self-knowledge, and, most important, narrative memory coincident with narrative time. All this is made possible by the intersubjective 'net' of language which allows us to know ourselves by first identifying with the viewpoint of others; and, later, this allows us to identify with other minds as we anticipate their reception of our communication. These three, assertion, narrative and intersubjectivity, are the essence of what language is and are the keystones that make culture possible outside of nature.

Outside of language there is nothing to which we can directly refer, since all language is indicative only of itself (Derrida).[21] Thus knowledge outside of language is literally unthinkable. Lacan (1977) makes it clear that, for whatever reason, it is an error of immense proportion to simply assume that there is a world of experience 'out there' or 'in here', previous to or beneath or beyond language, to which we have access. In fact, the world anticipates and forecloses us:

> Symbols . . . envelop the life of man in a network so total that they join together, before he comes into the world, those who are going to engender him 'by flesh and blood'; so total that they bring to his birth . . . the shape of his destiny; so total that they give the words that will make him faithful or renegade, the law of the acts that will follow him right to the very place where he is not yet and even beyond death (p. 68).

We find ourselves created in the net of language and have no sense whatsoever of the creation or the end of the self we 'find' ourselves to be. Birth and death are abstract concepts inconceivable because the self is only experienced between them; yet this self has had its linguistic creation prepared for it before its biological birth and it will leave linguistic echoes after its biological demise.

Lacan deals with the biological substrate with his conception of the 'real', referring, it seems, to raw, instinctive drives. Alan Sheridan, in a translator's note to Lacan's *Ecrits* (1977), explains this important concept this way:

> The 'real' . . . stands for what is neither symbolic nor imaginary, and remains foreclosed from the analytic experience, which is an experience of speech. What is prior to the assumption of the symbolic, the real in its 'raw' state (in the case of the subject, for instance, the organism and its biological needs), may only be supposed, it is an algebraic x (pp. ix–x).

Experience of the 'real', outside language, must therefore certainly exist. But it can lead to no new knowledge. As soon as comprehension is attempted, one is drawn into the inescapable web of the hermeneutic enclosure of language.

----

[21] 'il n'y a pas de hors-texte' (Derrida, 1976, p. 158).

II: The View from Within

What if all this theory's the equivalent of nightmare, its menace
masquerading as philosophy?
. . . wouldn't anything I'd come up with have to be a monstrous mix of
substance and intention?

C.K. Williams (1992), 'The Method'

1. The methodologies

Such a variety of approaches tends to leave a reader feeling somewhat helpless. Psychological introspectionism does appear to share much with philosophic phenomenology. Though both appear in many varied manifestations, both also rely finally on language. Both seek to 'step back' from what is thought to be direct experience and to take positions outside the usual 'stream of consciousness' to observe experience in action, as it were. Such observations can be as mundane as the listing of *all* sensations while one has a just-as-mundane perception, or it can be elaborated into analysis of the psyche, body-image, intuition, or even time-consciousness.

In either case, it is the position of the observer that creates doubt in this commentator's mind. Can one really undertake deeply abstract cognition without, in essence, creating a new version of self who observes the old version of self? It seems likely that such high-level self-abstracting is in fact delving further and further into more minute symbol processing. The position of the observing self is cast further back in the temporal penumbra from the postulated present of actual experience.

Meditation, though often surrounded by all sorts of conceptual games and abstract edifices which eventually appear as religious dogma, at the same time actualizes a very different route. As I understand it, at first the meditator takes the position of an observer 'watching' his or her own experience right down into the basics of breathing and heartbeat. The major difference between the first two methodologies and meditation is that in the latter case this observation is entirely passive and does not seek a 'conceptual grasp'. Eventually, the meditator hopes to do away with the observer, as well, and merely *become* awareness without a content of such awareness. This also is very different from the assumption of (most) introspectionism (going back to Locke) and phenomenology (going back to Brentano) that consciousness must have both content and direction (intentionality) or it is something other than consciousness.

It is difficult to address such divergent methodologies, though they agree on the inner nature of such explorations and the central importance of temporality. It is intriguing that all three methodologies implicitly or explicitly call for further temporal distancing — experience further from the moment of bodily activation than even that provided by linguistic consciousness — as the position from which normal conscious experience is to be analysed, as in the first two methodologies, or undercut for more profound experiences, as in meditation. According to Depraz, Husserl understood his phenomenology to be made possible by observations made from increasingly extended time from the actual events in question. Transcendental subjectivity is essentially memory. Wallace likewise declares that such time-regression is the position taken by the mind as it opens out toward non-content.[22]

If my thesis that we languaged animals — which have built empires and created worlds out of our time-delayed reaction-systems — are prisoners of our own device is

---

[22] Even though the eventual goal is commonly timeless awareness.

taken seriously, then it must be wondered toward what sort of 'devices' the increasing abstractions of the three 'views from within' are leading. If the abstractions are further and further from natural experience and simultaneously further and further time-delayed, then such hyper-methodologies make possible only abstracted 'knowledge' in self-created and virtually isolated worlds of their own, far from the life of natural experience.

Another major concern is the assumption that conscious experience can occur 'within' yet not necessarily require a subject of such experience. In their introduction, Varela and Shear declare right off that it is necessary that the 'process being studied . . . appears as relevant and manifest *for* a "self" or "subject" that can provide an account' (p. 1). This is a very good definition of human conscious experience, especially as it admits the need to 'provide an account'. They agree that *experience* in some sense may occur that is unaccountable, but they insist it cannot be called a methodology without 'public verification and validation according to complex human exchanges' (p. 1). Again the question presents itself as to how we can be so certain that such unaccountable experience can be called conscious when in fact it may be *lived* without any awareness of its being so?

Varela and Shear are aware that experience happens that does not reach consciousness. Since the 'notion of consciousness itself is clearly meant primarily to designate the fact that the subject knows about, is informed about, or in other words is aware of, the phenomenon' (p. 4), it remains confusing to see them concurrently standing by Nagel's 'what it's like to be' definition of consciousness. Nagel himself in the original (1974) article declared that we cannot know whether or not it would be like anything to be a bat. We have no reason to assume that there is a bat-subject which 'knows about, is informed about, or in other words is aware of' any of its experiences. Assuming consciousness without a subject of consciousness is to delve beyond human knowledge into realms of pure speculation. This does not imply that the boundaries of consciousness cannot be expanded or shifted, as the authors intend.

There is an attempt to get around this by the process of expert validation of inner experience. To validate what *seems* to be private inner experiences (whether of phenomenological observation or of contemplation), Varela and Shear call for 'second-person' mediation. They don't just ask for mutual dialogue; they ask for exchange with someone 'steeped in the domain of experiences under examination' (p. 10). This seeking of validation by outside authorities is common in all cultures and helps to determine the value of one's own experiences. This is also the essence of cultural transmission: experiences are made conscious by validating or invalidating them within the web of cultural articulation. Secondly, of course, there is the hermeneutic entanglement which asserts that, since *subjects of experience* are at least partially linguistic creations, then any 'public verification' which takes place will alter the original experience and to some extent self-determine it in the future.

To their credit, Varela and Shear are cognizant of this quandary and do not claim 'privileged access' within any of their methodologies. Simultaneously, however, they deny that any such 'unprivileged access' — i.e. intersubjectively validated access — 'creates nothing but artifacts, or a "deformed" version of the way experience "really" is' (p. 14). But when the depth of how language creates experienced worlds is understood, there simply is no 'really is'. All intersubjectively experienced worlds are created worlds. Inner methodologies in this understanding, important as they are for experiential exploration, cannot claim the status of revealing consciousness as it 'really is'.

2. Introspection

Introspection seems to take one of two forms. Either it is an infinitely boring compendium of internal observations, or it is based in a speculative reverie. Introspection is an essential part of conscious experience; there would be little to being conscious without it. As such an integral part, however, it cannot stand outside of consciousness and — using the language of consciousness — describe what it subjectively experiences *objectively*. Its veracity is forever compromised by its involvement in the hermeneutics of the eternal return: to describe is to change and to be changed is to alter the 'object' being described. It is a nice circular practice, however, and certainly worth the trouble in the name of expanded consciousness. The mistake is to assume that anything universal or of scientific value can emerge from one's self-study.

Introspectionists in this issue of *JCS* wisely suggest that private introspections be compared with introspections of others and ultimately with a mutually agreed upon set of objective standards. This adds something important to the mix but it seems likely that what will be constructed will be another cultural matrix — an exchange of ideas based upon institutionalized ideals and standards. To break these walls, perhaps it may be possible to study also the fabric of such walls: language. Linguist Wallace Chafe (1994) suggests just this: 'When careful and consensual introspective observation can be paired with public observations — and especially with overt evidence from language — the resulting combination may be the most powerful one we have for advancing understanding of the mind' (p. 15).

The illusion that something of scientific value is emerging is unnecessary. Something more important than science may be taking place in such exchanges. The cultural matrices of literary circles are far more interesting, imaginative and, finally, more enlightening than any introspectional methodology. Why not let in emotion and literary language? The arts have done the best so far in revealing what human experience in this world is like — or so it seems to me.

3. Phenomenology

Phenomenology is being recommended as a cautious means of both expanding experience *and* its understanding, a combination which, it is promised, will break new ground in consciousness studies. This is a demanding undertaking and I admire those who are willing to attempt to work their way through it.

Natalie Depraz in this issue gives a compelling portrait of Husserlian phenomenological praxis. Still, just as Husserl himself seems to have done, she runs almost immediately into the problem of the subject. She states the goal of praxis is 'phenomenological scientificity' which is ultimately capable of 'giving rise to a new type of objectification' (p. 97). This is also to say a 'new type of subjectification'. This new subject will concern itself with 'apodictic evidence' and thus escape the net of language, at least, presumably, until scientific explanation is required. The whole notion of 'self-evident evidence' has already been questioned by the editors of this issue and I concur.

Ignoring the power of language over our perceptions and cognitions has been recognized as the major error of all metaphysics, and metaphysics is what we have as soon as we speak of knowledge outside of language. Husserlian phenomenology depends for its reduction and praxis on the ability of language to *express* previously occurring experience (i.e. observations of a transcendental ego) essentially without changing that experience or being implicated in it in the first place. As a source of knowledge, such demands to exceed language may be asking too much.

Derrida has famously contested the idea that philosophy can work its way back to a logic of meaning derived from the immediate data of consciousness itself, *sans* language. There is no beyond of language for Husserl any more than for anyone else, according to Derrida. Husserl's insistence that his language went beyond the indicative to a purely expressive posture was deconstructed by Derrida, according to Norris (1982), to reveal 'that the totality of speech is caught up in an indicative web' (p. 31). The positing of the position of the transcendental ego or the activity of the 'transcendental reduction' were fodder for Derrida (1973) to expose the covert figurative ploys within Husserlian phenomenology. No language expresses pre-existing experiences. All words, sentences, and works are 'indicative': that is, indicative of other words, sentences, and works.

Varela notes early on that 'consciousness does not contain time as a constituted psychological category' (p.113). It could not, in fact, insofar as time is constitutive of such consciousness. The position I have taken is that the same applies to language. Language, subjective consciousness, and time may well be different aspects of the same underlying reality. (And, as I hope I have made clear above, consciousness without a subject of consciousness is inconceivable.)

Varela, however, works hard to portray time — especially the duration of the present in experience — as both preceding and being essential for subjective consciousness. He may well be right but it is not assured through his co-examination of Husserl and of neuronal cell assemblies, i.e. *neurophenomenology*. His test case of neurophenomenology appears highly successful in that he shows how phenomenological philosophy and neuroscience can complement each other in 'bipartisan' research; however, there is no way of confirming that what we think of as time has anything to do with the reality of time, and this applies as much to Varela's 'triple-braided analysis' as to previous linear-point time assumptions. It is widely agreed that time and consciousness are intimately intermingled (e.g. Ricoeur 1984–8; Wood 1989) but less widely accepted that time itself precedes consciousness, though it *may* well be the case. Objective information gives strong evidence of this, as Varela shows, but it is most dubious that subjective experience can do so.

Varela, it should be noted, is not indifferent to the question of language, experience and knowledge. He recognizes that actual memory (as opposed to the penumbral 'presence of the past') depends upon it as does the 'aim' of the 'perceptual horizon' (p. 115). But he brackets the question for the sake of his test case. The question is whether such bracketing is justified when dealing with conscious experience.

The question in point is the 'three scales of duration' from section three. His first durational scale concerns the usual physical conception of time which concerns events at the '1/10' scale. No consciousness and probably no experience of any sort here. The next scale has durational events on the '1' scale. This appears to be equivalent to nonlinguistic or prelinguistic 'consciousness' based in instinctual responses (which correlate with appropriate cell assemblies). Is Varela suggesting non- or primary conscious species/entities *intentionally* 'constitute objects-events'? If so, this is precisely the heart of Derrida's (1973) deconstruction. If not, there is no reason to believe that perceptual events are *consciously* constituted at all[23] or even constituted *for a consciousness*.

Varela recognizes the final durational scale as relating to 'descriptive-narrative assessments' on what he calls the '10' scale. What I wish to note is that there would be no objective understanding of the first level without this third level. Insofar as durational scale two is meant to relate to non-descriptive or non-narrative consciousness — and perhaps non-intentional consciousness, as well — the question remains at least moot that such non-subjective 'consciousness' could ever be experienced by human minds — phenomenologically, introspectively, or otherwise. What I am here suggesting (and I'm not sure Varela would object) is that his three durational scales do not necessarily portray one level arising from the previous one but may, instead, be a subtle circle with the third narrative-descriptive scale 'turning back' and becoming involved in the manifestation of the first two scales.

Indeed, Varela sees the connection between scale three and human narrative identity which is, of course, narrative time. Since human identity is so central to all our conscious experiencing, it must still be wondered what sort of time awareness or indeed consciousness of any sort is imagined to exist before or transcending the 'broad temporal horizons' provided by imagination and remembrance through the symbolizing mind. It seems to this writer more likely that all such imagined pre- or trans-experience is 'always already' deeply ingredienced with language.

Most phenomenological philosophy and certainly Varela's article continue to use figurative language. It is not clear just how completely Varela wishes to keep language out of his picture. He forthrightly calls upon the reflexive act and remembrance to access the flow of time. This application of the linguistic mind seems most reasonable. He calls upon *reflection* and quotes Husserl saying 'Every experience is itself experienced' which surely would be impossible without a conceptual grasp. But at the same time, he notes that experiences themselves 'appear slipping into the past and gradually disappear into the fringes of time' (p. 126). For whom do these appearances appear if not to a conscious experiencer who has the symbolic capacity to understand such experiencing, i.e. experience which is itself experienced? This is to say that even for the best phenomenological methodology, we begin and end with indicative reference — and with a narrative self who remains unable to 'jump over his own shadow' (Heidegger, 1987, p. 199).

4. Meditation

Ah! Meditation — the rose which flourishes above this circular morass of linguistic consciousness. There is no doubt that meditation, in all its multifoliate forms, accomplishes something. The question is: does it live up to its claims to gain knowledge or wisdom in a direct fashion, beyond language and culture? Can it even lead into the hallowed precincts of the 'pure consciousness experience' (PCE)?

From the foregoing, it should be clear that spiritual revelations are based in the conceptual imagination. Furthermore, every single word that is uttered to explain the direct experience brought about through contemplation, chanting, or meditation is self-evidently a culturally constructed phenomenon. As soon as the experience is spoken of, it changes, becoming influenced by the expectations and projections of a cultural matrix.

---

[23] Even human perceptions are seldom 'consciously constituted'.

This is to say that meditation, no matter how enlightening it feels, does not bring new knowledge to the rest of us not so enlightened. Every experience must be interpreted and interpretation is always a linguistic, cultural, and psychological manifestation.

But there is still the experience itself, directly enlightening for the experiencer who will thence be changed by it, is there not? There seems to be, if one accepts the many accounts from different times and places of such experiences. Again, however, the nuanced words used to explain or explore such experiences connote, most often, either spiritual or at least transcendental awakenings. *Why else mediate?* However, there is no need whatsoever to declare or even imply that any *beyond* is 'there', waiting to be experienced. What seems to be much more likely is that the 'pure consciousness experience' (Shear 1990) is related instead to 'pure pre-conscious experience'. That is to say, through prolonged meditation techniques the practitioner undergoes an atavistic return to the energic source of all sensation and perception, but still a source *of* this world.[24]

Shear and Jevning, in this issue, imply not only that the pure consciousness experience occurs and is real, but that it can also be remembered. From experience to memory: here is the crack between the twilight and the dawn! It is quite believable that some have *succumbed* or *abnegated* into an experience of awareness without bounds (without experiencing space, time, or substance). But it must be wrong to say one 'had' such experience. This would be to place oneself beyond or even above such an experience — or, at the very least, to imply that one's self remained present as an observer, distinct from the rest of the unboundedness.

If the PCE is really without any distinctions or attributions then it must be pure experience itself — without an *experiencer.* To claim an experiencer who privately 'possessed' the PCE would to be to set definite limits and indulge in obvious duality. If such an experience is indeed real, it is beyond anything that can be said about it, beyond personal consciousness or memorable attributes, beyond even the qualities which make up the larger, dynamic experience we call life. Memory would become an active possibility only as one returned to daily consciousness, i.e. human consciousness, and would require the return of the subject-who-remembers. Since this subject could not have been present during the experience, it would now be forced to interpret the nature of said experience through the 'impressions' left upon it, like assuming the wind by noting the bending boughs or wondering what animals had previously passed by observing tracks in the snow. What we put back together, i.e. remember, of self-transcendent experiences are the impressions such experiences have made upon the patiently awaiting ego-self (the subject-of-experience). It could be no other way if, as so many commentators have observed, memory and self are so inextricably linked.

To experience is one thing, but it reeks of idealism or the irrational possession of religious belief to claim one's self has experienced self-transcendence. To experience

---

[24] Jonathan Shear has long supported the importance of attaining PCE for understanding consciousness. (E.g. Shear, 1990; Shear & Jevning in this issue); however, though he calls the experience 'pure consciousness', he does not feel it necessarily implies a separation from nature. D.T. Suzuki (1964) agreed, calling the 'new consciousness' arising in Zen, actually the return of paradisal 'old consciousness' (which transcends nothing but ordinary experience). Like Shear, Suzuki considered the experience to be beyond or before language; unlike Shear, he also considered the experience to be one of no-self, in the usual sense, *nonconscious*: 'In Zen, consciousness in its ordinary scientific sense has no use; the whole being must come forward' (p. 179).

so purely must be to experience 'no-self', though this is denied by Shear. To have awareness without content or contexts must surely exclude the personal self since such a self, no matter how it is understood, is at the very least a context for consciousness, if not necessarily a content. But such experience without a subject of experience recrosses the rift into what I (and others) have been calling 'nonconscious experience' or, perhaps, 'pre-conscious experience'. Nothing can be said about experience beyond words.

If it is claimed that consciousness is being brought to what was previously unconscious potential, then this is something else entirely and far beyond anyone's ability to contest rationally without having such experience for themselves. However, for this writer, who has had no such experience, a certain involuntary distaste creeps in upon thinking about it.

There must be some 'potential energy' source which is called forth to become a self-in-the-world through the circumstances I have described and deep meditation may indeed bring meditators in touch with it. But why would one do so? If consciousness is a creative act, as I propose, then to seek it in non-action is sheer abnegation.To atavistically return to an undifferentiated state of contentless awareness smacks strongly of life-denial in the first degree. It opposes evolution, natural and cultural, and puritanically denies those facets of life which are the richest and deepest, if necessarily transient: physical action, passion, and thought itself. Desire and yearning (along with good doses of fear and anxiety) may be the forces which foundation our humanity and wonderful they are when fulfilled. To avoid them, or the frustration of not attaining them, by mantra-chanting into what might well be self-induced trances seems so obviously contrary to what the *Sturm und Drang* of life has to offer that I must question not only the epistemology which surrounds such efforts but even the actual value of the experience itself *for the experiencer* (if there is one).

This is not a humanly conscious experience where selves and worlds interact. Forlorn as it may be to some, I strongly feel that human consciousness begins only with the separation of self and world — with our banishment from the garden of the senses into our virtual, symbolic 'experiencing of experience'. To the extent that deep meditators, too, become 'nonhuman' (and consciousness is understood as a human creation) such meditators have little to offer consciousness studies.

III: Conclusion

Death of the self in a long, tearless night,
All natural shapes blazing unnatural light
Theodore Roethke (1964), 'In a Dark Time'

Existence then, is for us a suspension over the abyss. Consciousness (or higher-order consciousness) has been gained over long periods of time with great effort as the result of the development of speech, narrative and intersubjectivity. Its survival value consists in the 'capture' of our environment, which becomes our world. There is no escape from our lives and our predicament but we may choose to retreat into navel gazing, which, at least, 'feels really good' even though it helps neither our world nor our actual understanding. Norman O. Brown has insisted that our task is so much larger: 'The integration of the psyche is the integration of the human race, and the integration of the world with which we are inseparably connected. Only in one world can we be one' (Brown, 1966, p. 87). Because we are the worldmaking animal, we are the only animals who can save the world.

The idea that we can better understand existence and do more for the world through nonlinguistic exercises seems to this author patently absurd. It is only through the symbolic that we imagine that which might be in the first place. As Gaston Bachelard protested, 'How unjust is the criticism which sees nothing in language but an ossification of internal experience! Just the contrary: language is always somewhat ahead of our thoughts, somewhat more seething than our love. . . . Without this exaggeration, life cannot develop' (1983, p. 30). Abandon hope, all ye who abandon language. To lose language is to lose conscious experience.

To the cries of 'anthropocentric!', I can only respond 'anthropomorphic!' This paper makes no claims that we are at the top of the evolutionary ladder. If life is war, I'd guess we're doing pretty well. On the other hand, we continue to have a disquieting sense that we have 'eaten of the tree of knowledge' and been banished from the 'paradise' of physical impulsion and sensory grandeur. If the life given by nature consists in awakened senses and an overwhelming sense of aliveness, then we will need all our culturally-developed resources and rationality to avoid going mad for, in general, this 'aliveness' escapes us. Within language, and now the rapidly expanding intersubjectivity of the computerized media, we face the move into, at best, a kind of psychic mutuality which might be called 'love' or, at worst, a descent into a final, global insanity. We have become permanent exiles from our origins and, to a large extent, from our own natural processes and have condemned ourselves to live our span within the prison of our own minds — intersubjective minds, yes — but still our own minds.

The passion with which the question of existence and consciousness is argued is testament to the passion for meaning we each have. What are we all really doing reading and writing for the *Journal of Consciousness Studies*? Let me state baldly here that we are doing what we are driven to do: to seek *meaning* in our own exile. Discovering no meaning, we attach our selves to philosophies of consciousness and hope to create life-meaning for ourselves by convincing others of our truth. However, language has the last laugh. Our truths become our prison — *including the 'truths' explicated here*.

Such a stark realization of the hopelessness of perfect communication in the world in which we find ourselves may lead us eventually to yearn for escape from these intolerable conditions. In all brute honesty, it must be considered that we are forced to accept that consciousness holds our experience of reality in a non-actual, time-delayed 'present'. It gives us 'self' and gives us a modicum of power but life itself desiccates as we hold it in the grip of the hermeneutic garrote.

On the other hand, this is all the life we have. The hermeneutic circle need not be a 'vicious circle'. It seems more likely that Bachelard is right, that we need language to give us dreams of 'might be'. Experience outside language does indeed occur; we see it daily. But the only way we *know* of it personally is through those impressions left by its passing on our own re-memorying self. Though indicative language used literally cannot *express* those impressions adequately, non-literal, metaphoric language such as that found in mythopoetics may at least succeed in conveying the *feel* of such things. In fact, all the expressive arts have done so for millennia and will, hopefully, continue to do so.

Perhaps we ask too much of science (including 'inner-science') to express experiences which are trans- or pre- or beyond language. Such expression may be best left to the arts, even though we live in times when the arts in general are seen as peripheral to the mainstream of current technocratic culture. Not that the various 'views from within' in this issue are without value. On the contrary, if consciousness is created reflexively through language and intersubjectivity, then these methods — especially introspection and phenomenology — are most certainly studying consciousness from within it. But isn't that exactly what we are doing here now?[25]

References

Bachelard, Gaston (1983), *On Poetic Imagination and Reverie*, trans. with preface & introduction Colette Gaudin (Dallas: Spring Publications).

Brown, Norman O. (1966), *Love's Body* (Berkeley: University of California Presss).

Chafe, Wallace (1994), *Discourse, Consciousness, and Time: The flow and displacement of conscious experience in speaking and writing* (Chicago & London: University of Chicago Press).

Deacon, Terrence (1997), *The Symbolic Species: The co-evolution of language and the brain* (New York: W.W. Norton).

Dennett, Daniel (1991), *Consciousness Explained* (Boston/Toronto: Little, Brown, & Co).

Derrida, Jacques (1973), *Speech and Phenomena and Other Essays on Husserl's Theory of Signs*, trans. D. Allison (Evanston: Northwestern University Press).

Derrida, Jacques (1976), *Of Grammatology*, trans. G. Spivak (Baltimore: Johns Hopkins University Press).

Heidegger, Martin (1987), *An Introduction to Metaphysics*, trans. R. Manheim (New Haven: Yale University Press). First published in German, 1953.

Lacan, Jacques (1977) *Ecrits: A selection.*, trans. A. Sheridan (New York: Norton).

Nagel, Thomas (1974), 'What is it like to be a bat?' *Philosophical Review* **4**, pp. 435–50.

Norris, Christopher (1982), *Deconstruction: Theory and practice* (London & New York: Routledge).

Percy, Walker (1975), *The Message in the Bottle* (New York: Noonday).

Ricoeur, Paul (1984-88), *Time and Narrative* (3 vols.), trans. K. McLaughlin & D. Pellauer (Chicago: University of Chicago Press).

Roethke, Theodore (1964), *The Collected Poems of Theodore Roethke* (New York: Anchor Books).

Shear, Jonathan (1990), *The Inner Dimension: Philosophy and the experience of consciousness* (New York: Peter Lang).

Stevens, Wallace (1954), *The Collected Poems* (New York: Vintage).

Suzuki, Daisetz T. (1964), 'The awakening of a new consciousness in Zen', in *Man and Transformation: Papers from the Eranos yearbooks*, ed. J. Campbell (Bollingen Series XXX · 5; Princeton: Princeton University Press). First published in *Eranos-Jahrbücher* XXIII, 1954.

Williams, C.K. (1992), *A Dream of Mind: Poems* (New York: Noonday Press).

Wood, David (1989), *The Deconstruction of Time* (Atlantic Highlands, NJ: Humanities Press).

REPLY TO NIXON ON MEDITATION

Jonathan Shear

Nixon's critique of the usefulness of meditation-related empirical research for the study of consciousness raises interesting epistemological questions. But it suffers from its almost exclusively *a priori* orientation, and, most tellingly, it fails to recognize the many places where empirical research is directly relevant to claims he makes. A few examples:

> [E]very single word that is uttered to explain the direct experience brought about through contemplation, chanting, or meditation is self-evidently a culturally constituted phenomenon. As soon as the experience is spoken of it changes, becoming influenced by the expectations and projections of a cultural matrix (pp. 263–4 above).

---

[25] For Varela and Shear's response to Nixon's overall criticisms, see their 'Editors' rejoinder to the debate' below (p. 307).

I suppose that what Nixon intends to claim is that it is our *memories* of experiences (rather than the past experiences themselves) that change when we come to speak of them. Understood in this way, there is a lot of truth in the claim. (The literal way, of course, makes no sense.) The words we use are obviously cultural artifacts, and it is apparent that that memory and conceptualization generally (and perhaps even, as Nixon would have it, always) impose structure and/or content on our memory of past experiences. This general observation by itself however says nothing useful about actual experiences, descriptions and research. What is needed here is to distinguish specifically which, if any, components of particular descriptions are best understood as referring to features of experiences themselves, and which to cultural overlays. Taking this approach Jevning and I examine a particular meditation-related experience (the 'pure consciousness' experience) in terms of (i) commonalties of descriptive content found in different cultures and conflicting conceptual contexts and (ii) specific, culture-invariant physiological correlates, in order (iii) to see what can be inferred about the experience itself. Whether or not the specifics of our analysis are convincing, it is clear that just this sort of empirical approach is what is needed to increase our factual knowledge. Nixon's hermeneutical observations simply miss the point here.

> [T]he nuanced words used to explain or explore such experiences connote, most often, either spiritual or at least transcendental awakenings. *Why else meditate?* (p. 264).

Even a cursory review of research on meditation makes it clear that there are many reasons other than spiritual and metaphysical concerns why people learn to meditate, such as (hoped for) relaxation, improved sleep, normalization of blood pressure, enhancement of athletic performance — and even just to debunk the whole process. Again, the question is an empirical one, not one of armchair theorizing.

> If it is claimed that consciousness is being brought to what was previously unconscious potential, then this is something else entirely and far beyond anyone's ability to contest rationally without having such experience for themselves (p. 265).

Traditionally, of course, exponents of Zen, Yoga, Vedanta, etc. have often claimed that tapping into one's 'previously unconscious potential' is *precisely* what is involved here (cf., for example, Luk, 1961; Maharishi, 1966; Suzuki, 1996). Again, this is a matter not for armchair speculation, but empirical research. Jevning and I did not discuss the question of latent potential. But as it happens even our article reports research indicating that, as traditionally claimed, the 'pure consciousness' experience is correlated with enlivenment of a latent potential to produce the uniquely restful physiological state of respiratory suspension. Numerous other studies directly examine questions of latent psychological potentials (cf. Alexander, 1990; Eppley *et al.*, 1989; Shear, 1990). Evaluating the results of such research rationally by means of standard third-person protocols does not, despite Nixon's pronouncement, require one's having the relevant experiences at all.

> To atavistically return to an undifferentiated state of contentless awareness smacks strongly of life-denial in the first degree. It opposes evolution, natural and cultural, and puritanically denies those facts of life which are richest and deepest, if necessarily transient: physical action, passion and thought itself (p. 265).

This of course is precisely the *opposite* of how the experience traditionally has most often been understood, namely, as the basis for really living life naturally and fully —

whether in everyday acts such as eating, sleeping, cooking and lovemaking, or the rarefied heights of painting, music, martial arts and religious ecstasy (cf. Maharishi, 1966; Suzuki, 1949; 1966). Again, determining the truth or falsity of such claims is a matter for empirical research, not abstract speculation.

In short, hermeneutical and other *a priori* speculations clearly have many valid uses, including, for example, as aids in the design of research protocols. But if we become too attached to them, they can indeed become 'garrotes' (to use Nixon's term), choking off growth of empirical knowledge in the field of consciousness studies, as anywhere else.

References

Alexander, Charles, *et al.* (1990), *Higher Stages of Human Development: Perspectives on Adult Growth* (Oxford: Oxford University Press).

Luk, Charles (1961), *Ch'an and Zen Teaching*, Series Two (London: Rider & Co.).

Maharishi Mahesh Yogi (1966), *The Science of Being and Art of Living* (International SRM Publications).

Eppley *et al.* (1989), 'Differential effects of relaxation techniques on trait anxiety,' *Journal of Clinical Psychology*, **45** (6).

Shear, J. (1990), *The Inner Dimension: Philosophy and the Experience of Consciousness* (New York: Peter Lang).

Suzuki, Daisetz T. (1949), *Essays in Zen Buddhism*, First Series (New York: Harper & Brothers).

Suzuki, Daisetz T. (1996), *Zen and Japanese Culture* (New York: Princeton Univ. Press/MJF Books).

THE HUSSERLIAN PHENOMENOLOGY OF CONSCIOUSNESS AND COGNITIVE SCIENCE: WE CAN SEE THE PATH BUT NOBODY IS ON IT

Ian Owen and Neil Morris, School of Health Sciences, University of Wolverhampton, 62–68 Lichfield Street, Wolverhampton WV1 1DJ, UK.

Abstract: This response chooses as the sole topic for its concern the central question 'how can Husserl's approach to consciousness be used to inform cognitive science?' This paper is a response to the papers on phenomenology, in particular the one by Varela. The response makes brief comments on Husserl's phenomenology and the breadth of cognitive science is alluded to as well as its wide spectrum of phenomena. The authors are agreed that there could be a Husserlian cognitive science, but it would take some compromises from both traditions. In general we find that there is some good neuroscience in Varela's approach, but he mixes the contradictory perspectives of natural science and Husserl's phenomenology without explaining or mentioning the major problems which could be entailed by this.

The authors of this response believe that the three papers on phenomenology (Depraz; Naudin *et al.*; Varela) are not helpful in establishing new empirical methods, nor do they adequately meet the large number of theoretical and empirical questions that the papers raise. Where the phenomenological authors are lacking is that they present condensed accounts of phenomenology which omit the basic overview required to critique and develop cognitive science. Therefore none of the three contributions communicate sufficiently well to inform or attract cognitive scientists to Husserl's work and so miss the opportunity to explain a source of potential help. In order to mend this deficit, a succinct overview of Husserlian pure psychology for cognitive science is required. Please allow the following remarks to set the scene before we try to indicate how to bridge the gap between the ideals of philosophy and the necessary forms of empiricism within cognitive science.

There is a great deal that could be written in trying to define a working version of Husserlian pure psychology, as Husserl intended it to be practised, never mind critiquing or developing its assumptions and method (Husserl, 1977; 1980; 1981; Owen, in press). Furthermore, given sufficient space it would be possible to argue for and against Husserl's position. But it is not possible to make any detailed discussion of this large subject here. It is only possible to refer the reader to some writers who have kept true to the original emphases (Bernet *et al.*, 1993; Marbach, 1993; 1996; Ströker, 1993). There are many writers who have argued for cognitive science to turn to Husserl's themes in order to improve cognitive research (Chalmers, 1996; Natsoulas, 1983).

Husserlian pure psychology asserts that the criteria for the philosophical acceptability of empirically-derived theorizing about consciousness need to attend to fundamental theorizing for the scientific community first of all. It is argued that the concepts that a scientific community requires for its empirical work should arise out of the distinctions within the experiences of consciousness in its social dimension, intersubjectivity, as well as the experience theorists have of their own consciousness and the consciousness of others. These experiences are considered as elements of human consciousness in general. Husserlian pure psychology provides a pre-empirical conceptual grounding for the scientific community by seeing the universal essences of the many distinctions, conditions for phenomena to exist, interrelations and sources of meaning in one's own consciousness. The aim is not to base conceptual distinctions on assumptions or inappropriate metaphors that cannot deliver an accurate understanding of consciousness. Pure psychology should not project an inappropriate conceptualization onto consciousness, before it begins its theorizing, or follow through with inappropriate empirical methods.

On the other hand, cognitive science is a set of empirical practices already. Generally, what is acceptable to it are those practices which have to make an assumption, state it in such a manner that it can be investigated and to test such hypotheses in a variety of ways. It employs measurement of chemical and electrical neurological events. It employs mathematical modelling of various types. Only in the light of its own findings might it alter its theory, conclusions or methods. For instance, in the standard procedure for constructing deontic reasoning tests of the rationality of consciousness, it is assumed that rationality can be investigated through card tests in which a question can be posed and the participants in the experiment are free to give one of eight answers in allegedly controlled conditions. From a phenomenological perspective it is background tacit processes in involuntary out-of-awareness aspects of consciousness that are decisive in the processes of everyday decision-making. Thus what is the norm for the various areas of cognitive science is not the norm for phenomenology. Initially the two traditions are far apart.

Having sketched out pure psychology and cognitive science we now turn to the specific problems of Varela's paper. The main problem is that he fails to provide sufficient details to frame the problem of consciousness correctly within a pure Husserlian approach. It could be argued from either of Husserl's transcendental or pure psychological phenomenological positions that there could be no such thing as a neuro-phenomenology. The order of events that Husserl requested should be in place, namely to attend to consciousness as consciousness, without first trying to model it in some way. For Husserl's pure psychology this would achieve a community of psychologists who would have had personal experiences which informed their theorizing. The main aim of the theorizing is to think in a manner free of the constraints of the immediate assumptions of scientism. Husserl's radical critique of natural science was against explanations which jump between the secondary natural sciences of biology, psychology or neurology. Varela does not state this, nor make any comments that show how or why he has been able to progress from the Husserlian aim of attending to *consciousness as consciousness* and concern himself rather with an attention to meaning (in a wide sense of 'meaning').

The central and most valuable contribution of Husserl to science is to encourage scientists to think in orderly yet creative ways before engaging in empirical work, to enable better theorizing and for new methods to be created and shared. Varela does not state this and moves from a mention of the Necker cube to Husserl's formal and abstract analyses in *On the Phenomenology of the Consciousness of Internal Time* (Husserl, 1966; 1991). Therefore, there is a deeply problematic jumping between foundations right at the beginning of the paper. This is unacceptable to Husserl, for no shared system of pure psychology is current among neuroscientists, never mind among psychologists. Also, the mention of an internal clock in consciousness is not Husserlian. This is particularly incorrect when Husserl clearly rejected the use of inappropriate metaphors, natural science and empirical measuring devices in the *Time* book (Husserl, 1966, pp. 4, 9, 339, 348; Husserl, 1991, pp. 4, 9, 350, 359). Following Husserl, it is much easier to argue that neurology or neuroscience can tell us nothing of first priority about how to create phenomenology, Husserl's own project of creating a perfect science of consciousness that obeyed philosophical rigour for an experiential grounding of its knowledge. All other aims are of lesser importance. In fact natural psychological science often does not turn itself to the task of theorizing and experimenting in ways that have the sole purpose of modelling qualia and meaning as these occur for people in their families and communities.

But we claim that between the positions of (a) the ideal of a philosophy that grounds its concepts in experience and (b) a set of empirical practices that grounds its concepts in empirical falsificationism, there lies the ultimate ground to be covered during the next century for cognitive science. The key question is 'what would a Husserlian-based cognitive science be like?' In order to be true to its Husserlian side, a hybrid phenomenological science of consciousness would need to have initial conceptualizations that mirror the invariant aspects of the processes of consciousness itself. To date there is no such agreement within the many sub-disciplines that comprise cognitive science. Because cognitive science has gone on ahead and produced within its schools many natural scientifically-grounded distinctions, a great many of these stances would have to be altered to make them more Husserlian. A truly Husserlian empirical phenomenology would be like gestalt psychology. In social science, ethnomethodology is probably the closest and most fruitful offspring of Husserl (Garfinkel, 1984). In cognitive science Dennett's 'multiple drafts' metaphor is quite like what Husserl would have termed an interplay between the now, the 'primordial impression' and 'retentional consciousness', short and long term involuntary memory (Dennett, 1991; Husserl, 1966, p. 331; 1991, p. 343). The empirical documentation of various forms of amnesia, aphasia and neurological variance and injury are all material that a Husserlian approach to theorizing would have to take on board. This would also mean that the form of theoretical argument and thought experiments would have to take empirical events and relations to physical entities into account.

In closing, a position that might be a crossover between phenomenology and cognitive science is one that would value a broad view of the key phenomena to be investigated. But there are many experiences which are difficult to be made fully conscious or to describe or to empathize with. Consciousness is hard to describe and hence the great difficulty of a science of consciousness. But after successful empiricism, Husserlian psychology could change its original stance in the light of theoretical or practical findings agreed by the community of colleagues, and yet maintain its ideals of being true to the phenomena as they are experienced. In a longer paper it would be possible to argue for and against the multiple stances that together comprise what is known as cognitive science. But overall, phenomenology is judged to be the way out of the impasse in theorizing and empiricism and the non-collegiate pluralism in cognitive science. Hence, we can see the path but nobody is on it.

References

Bernet, R., Kern, I. & Marbach, E. (1993), *An Introduction to Husserlian Phenomenology* (Evanston, IL: Northwestern University Press).
Chalmers, D.J. (1996), *The Conscious Mind: In search of a fundamental theory* (Oxford: Oxford University Press).
Dennett, D.C. (1991), *Consciousness Explained* (Harmondsworth: Penguin).
Garfinkel, H. (1984), *Studies in Ethnomethodology* (Cambridge: Polity).
Husserl, E. (1966), *Zur phanomenologie der inneren zeitbewusstseins* (Haag: Nijhoff).
Husserl, E. (1977), *Cartesian Meditations*, trans. D. Cairns (Dordrecht: Kluwer).
Husserl, E. (1980), *Phenomenology and the Foundations of the Sciences*, trans. T.E. Klein & W.E. Pohl (Dordrecht: Kluwer).
Husserl, E. (1981), 'Philosophy as rigorous science', in *Husserl: Shorter Works*, ed. and trans. P. McCormack & F.A. Elliston (Notre Dame: University of Notre Dame Press).
Husserl, E. (1991), *On the Phenomenology of the Consciousness of Internal Time (1893–1917)*, trans. J.B. Brough (Dordrecht: Kluwer).
Marbach, E. (1993), *Mental Representation and Consciousness: Towards a phenomenological theory of representational reference* (Norwell: Kluwer).
Marbach, E. (1996), 'Understanding the representational mind: A phenomenological perspective', *Human Studies*, **19**, pp. 137–52.
Natsoulas, T. (1983), 'Concepts of consciousness', *Journal of Mind and Behavior*, 4, pp. 13–59.
Owen, I.R. (in press), 'Using the experience of gender to explain the difference between Husserlian and Heideggerian phenomenology', *Phenomenological Inquiry*.
Ströker, E. (1993), *Husserl's Transcendental Phenomenology*, trans. L. Hardy (Stanford: Stanford University Press).

REPLY TO OWEN AND MORRIS

Francisco Varela

Owen and Morris chide me for not framing 'the problems of consciousness within a pure Husserlian approach', thus betraying Husserl's sustained rejection of any naturalization (i.e. circulation with natural sciences of any kind at all). I entirely agree. My work is *not* concerned with preserving Husserlian orthodoxy, but, as I say, to draw 'inspiration' from its advances (methodological and descriptive) and to go *beyond* its statement and the limitations typical of the early twentieth-century intellectual atmosphere. Perhaps the very notion of neurophenomenology might make the grand old man turn in his grave. But the issue is to pragmatically build the bridges between third- and first-person, not to stay stuck in the repetitions of the same well known difficulties that Owen and Morris continue to hold dear. Keep the essential insights from the founding father and then move on. I know — as well as anybody who has studied Husserl's writings on time — that his main concern is, as they say, to create a science of consciousness with philosophical rigour grounded in experience. But this essential requirement is in no way contradicted by a complementary grounding in empirical, third-person experiences, Owen and Morris notwithstanding (cf. Roy *et al.*, 1999, for an extensive discussion on naturalization).

Paradoxically, in the second part of their comment Owen and Morris seem, with no apparent justification, to flip their position, and affirm that a future phenomenological cognitive science *is* possible after all. But here they choose Dennett's multiple drafts as an example of work that could be linked to the structure of time consciousness! This is plainly contradictory, since it is Dennett himself who, in the same book, has asserted 'that there is no such as phenomenology', and his entire edifice is built on a mild third-person position he terms hetero-phenomenology, i.e. a refined experimental psychology of reporting. His approach is far away from the experiential grounding that is needed in first-person research, as Husserl emphasized and that I used in my own paper on time. In brief, I am left completely in the dark as to what these commentators could possibly mean by their final statement concerning phenomenology as the way out of the 'non-collegiate pluralism in cognitive science'. The fact is that there is a growing body of work being carried toward a phenomenological cognitive science or neurophenomenology, as papers presented in this Special Issue and other articles (cf. Gallagher, 1988; Petitot *et al.*, 1999) have clearly shown. Owen and Morris think they see the path but that there is nobody on it. This is perhaps because they are still looking at the tips of their shoes.

WORDS AND SILENCE

John Pickering, Psychology Department, Warwick University
Coventry, CV4 7AL, UK. Email: j.pickering@warwick.ac.uk

There is a story of a surgeon who experienced a disturbance when working on hands. It seemed that seeing both the hands of his patient and his own at the same time acted as a fundamental and unwelcome reminder that he and his patients were the same thing. This disturbed his usual attitude which, for understandable professional reasons, was to see his patients as meat.

Now in working on consciousness, cognitive scientists too are reminded that they are studying themselves. This encounter with the first person is disturbing since, for understandable historical reasons, cognitive science is concerned to be seen to be following the third-person ethos of natural science. Therefore first-person methods, even though they enrich and complement conventional scientific ones, are treated warily. Accordingly, this issue on first-person methods is to be warmly welcomed even if it produces disturbance which, after all, can be a sign of growth.

And disturbance there is bound to be, since employing these methods will change how scientific culture is transmitted. Good first-person data depend on rigorous training of individual mental skills and possibly on exceptional individuals to teach and learn them. The transmission of research skills thus becomes rather more like the personalized and private chela–guru relationship of Hindu spiritual training than the more open and collective apprenticeship of Western scientific laboratories. What then passes on from generation to generation may be more like indoctrination into an ideology than training in methods of discovery. But it is part of the postmodern critique of science, or, more accurately, of scientism, that something of the same sort is already true of Western research.

The logic of extending scientific practice with first-person methods is overwhelming. A question is: how is this to be integrated with the explosion of research into consciousness over the last two decades? One concrete answer in this issue is Varela's research programme into the subjective experience of time. Here, theories that combine neurobiology, non-linear dynamics and reductive phenomenology are to be developed in the light of a mutual constraint between first- and third- person data. But first-person methods may have domain-specific characteristics that third-person methods do not. Consider the claim, made in different ways by Bergson, Husserl and Heidegger, that the experience of time, primordially a first-person phenomenon, cannot be identified in any systematic way with third-person observations of physical events. Therefore there may be limits to the mutual constraint between first- and third-person data here that may not apply elsewhere.

Accordingly, we might seek a more general benchmark against which to assess the potential contribution of first-person methods. One example might be Neisser's seminal paper on five types of self-knowledge (Neisser, 1988). These five types of knowledge are: ecological, interpersonal, private, remembered and conceptual. This list is ordered by how much direct perceptual experience is involved in each sort of knowledge, the two earlier items having more (Neisser, 1993). It seems clear that first-person methods would apply to all these types but to different effect. The investigation of private, remembered and conceptual knowledge of selfhood patently requires the research methods of what Harré & Gillet (1994) call discursive psychology. Here, then, first-person methods would contribute relatively little that was new. If, by contrast, they were used to investigate the first two items on the list, it would make a more radical contribution. They are a natural complement to research in ecological psychology and together give a more balanced understanding of the perceptual encounter with the cultural world (Pickering, 1998). Such research is beginning to appear, Hunt's innovative integration of cognitive, phenomenological and transpersonal perspectives being an excellent example (Hunt, 1995).

Thus the contribution of first-person methods may vary with the field of inquiry. This special issue also shows that the broader scientific role of first-person methods may not be uniform. For Vermersch, Depraz and Bailey, introspection and phenomenological reduction are an epistemological end in themselves. New objects for scientific investigation are disclosed as well as a new type of objectification which combines individual phenomenological inquiry with intersubjective agreement. This, again, suggests that the impact of first-person methods will not merely be to make new discoveries but to challenge the meta-narrative of science as a privileged methodology based on objectivity. But this challenge is not destructive. With the incorporation of first-person methods, the objects of science are enriched. They are not merely the givens of the material world, but also the recurrent patterns of experience that arise in encountering the world and in the intersubjective flow that binds people together.

By contrast, for Peugeot and Naudin *et al.*, the objectives of first-person methods appear to be more instrumental. Peugeot correctly identifies intuition as a 'blind spot' in the treatment of creativity, whether in science or in other disciplines. While there have been numerous studies of creative intuition, relatively few have inquired into it *qua* experience. Likewise, in using phenomenal reduction to deepen the encounter with psychopathology, Naudin *et al.* are moving psychotherapeutic practice into a deep, perhaps dangerous, arena of interpersonal identification lying beyond mere empathy. It is interesting to note that both papers deal with experience that is highly charged with emotion and human value. These things do not sit easily with detached, neutral third-person engagement with the world. Again, this shows that what is at issue is not only an enlargement of science's methods but also a challenge to its ontological assumptions, its objectives and its implicit value structure.

One of the most exciting issues raised by this collection of work is the incorporation of techniques from prescientific traditions, predominantly meditative ones. But there is a problem here: that of detaching a technique from its cultural background. Any system for discovery is practised within a framework of cultural assumptions, science and meditation being no exceptions. Shear and Varela are well aware of this but even so suggest that we can 'completely put aside' the motivation and values underlying, for example, Buddhist Samatha meditation and simply recruit it into scientific psychology as another methodological resource. Of course, some engagement with meditation practices is possible without any commitment to the beliefs and values of the tradition from which these practices come. It is unlikely, though, that they will have the same power to reveal the mind as they do when employed by someone who practices them in full knowledge of their wider soteriological significance. We might bear in mind Jung's caution that Westerners should not assume that Eastern cultural practices are simply open for inspection and adoption, however empathetically they approach them. To employ Buddhist practices fully may require a deeper engagement with the whole ethos of Buddhism and engaging with them will challenge the value-neutral stance of Western science. But, again, such a challenge is a dialectical disturbance that is bound to be productive.

Methods are hard to separate from metaphysics. Assumptions about what can be known through phenomenological and introspective practices may well influence what is discovered. For example, the idea that the mind cannot divide in order to observe itself is broadly accepted in the West on the grounds of logical necessity. Although the Buddha said similar things, many Buddhist traditions assume that with rigorous training self awareness can develop to far greater levels than those experienced in everyday consciousness. In Vipassana traditions for example, the objective is said to be the observing of the mind's activity without interfering with it or evaluating it. But to assume this is possible may be a necessary precursor to using the method to its full capacity.

Finally, a comment on words and silence. In a book called *Teachings from the Silent Mind*, a renowned teacher describes the objective of Vipassana mediation as, simply, 'being the knowing' (Sumedho, 1984). It illustrates the beautifully simple language in which Eastern techniques and their objectives can be described. By contrast, accounts of reductive phenomenology, and those in this issue are no exception, are often complex, densely worded and hence difficult to follow. They can also give the impression that peeling off layers of perceptual interpretation may be an interminable project. This may be an effect of a contrast that Jung labelled introvert–extrovert: Western epistemological techniques are directed externally while Eastern ones are directed inward. The Eastern project is to silence the mind and observe what then arises. A torrent of words makes this task more difficult.

References

Harré, R. & Gillet, G. (1994), *The Discursive Mind* (London: Sage).

Hunt, H. (1995), *On the Nature of Consciousness: Cognitive, phenomenological and transpersonal perspectives* (New Haven: Yale University Press).

Neisser, U. (1988), 'Five kinds of self-knowledge', *Philosophical Psychology*, **1**, pp. 35–59.

Neisser, U. (ed. 1993), *The Perceived Self: Ecological and interpersonal sources of self-knowledge* (Cambridge: Cambridge University Press).

Pickering, J. (1998), 'On cultural apprenticeship and affordance', in *Advances in Perception-Action Coupling*, ed. by B. Bril, Ledebt, G. Dietrich, & A. Roby-Brami (Paris: Editions EDK).

Sumedho (1984), *Cittaviveka: Teachings from the silent mind* (Hemel Hempstead: Amaravati Publications).

OBJECT, LIMITS AND FUNCTION OF CONSCIOUSNESS

*Jean-François Richard, Dept. of Psychology, University of Paris 8,
Paris, France.   Email: richard@univ-paris8.fr*

The following comments are from a psychologist, involved in the study of complex human information processing such as problem-solving, in which overt behaviour cannot be isolated from the subject's representation, since it is the prototype of goal-directed activity. In that respect perception, i.e. interpretation of the situation, is intrinsically linked to action, i.e. to changing the situation so as to complete the goal. In that field representation cannot be assimilated to consciousness, and it is very important, in my opinion, to understand what makes a representation become conscious and what is changed in behaviour when an implicit representation becomes explicit and reportable; and to develop a precise methodology for obtaining and analysing verbal reports, which are in those situations the only ways of access to the subjective experience of other people.

My bias is probably different from that of the majority of the contributors to the volume, since the model of inner experience which is privileged by the phenomenological approach is perception and mental imagery: it is not an accident that the pioneer works in the field are the books by Merleau-Ponty (1945), *La phénoménologie de la perception*, and Sartre (1939), *L'Imaginaire*, and that the major empirical controversy at the beginning of the century was about the presence of images in mental activities. However intentions and goals are indisputably thought-contents in the same respect as percepts and perhaps the study of consciousness through purposive behaviour may provide another grasp of consciousness. I have three comments: the first is on the object of inner experience as viewed by the majority of the contributors of the volume, the two others concern matters which are marginal or completely over-looked in this volume: the limits of consciousness and its function.

1. The object of inner experience

Two aspects of inner experience are considered in papers, which seem to be quite different and in some respect incompatible. First of all there is a difference in the object aimed at. In the first case the object is the content of a thought process, either provoked by the experimenter (by giving a cognitive task to the subject) or else naturally occurring during the subject's life: this approach is characteristic of introspection. In the second case what is looked for is the experience of conscious activity when it has been cleared out of all specific content, so that the object of inner experience is pure consciousness. This is indisputably the case of meditation techniques and of the phenomenological reduction and probably of the apprehension of the present time, since this apprehension is not tied to any content.

Secondly there are differences in the ways of bearing testimony of this experience. In the first case testimony is provided by a verbal report given during the unfolding of the mental event or afterwards during a recollection of the event, the differences being minor, since the mental event has in any case to be re-lived either immediately or after a while. In the second case, there is no verbal report, because this experience is unreportable, uncommunicable and even ungraspable. As a consequence, the methods used to study both types of awareness are different: interview in the former case, neurophysiological methods in the latter.

Thirdly, there are differences in the ways of access to this experience. In the first case the experience has an immediate character of givenness for the subject, it is characterized by self-evidence. In the second case there is a need for special training: training in the practice of phenomenological reduction or training in the practice of meditation techniques.

A correlated difference is the motivation of the search for experiencing. In the case of introspection there is no special motivation for experiencing itself, since it is assumed that experiencing a thought process is concomitant with producing the thought process. There is a motivation however for reporting the experience, which is communication to a peer in natural settings or communication with an experimenter in an experimental situation. The motivation is quite different in the search for an experience of pure consciousness void of content. There is a strong motivation in this case, which explains why a long training is accepted: it is a metaphysical or a religious need for a quest for personal identity, an investigation of the very nature of subjectivity.

What is the relation between these two types of activities? They have different objects, different goals, different methods and they are dependent of different processes. Introspection is bound to language and to culture: the introspective report is modelled by language, since it uses necessarily the categories established by the cultural environment and the words designating these categories. In the same way as this has been discussed for perception, one may wonder whether the coding itself of this experience is not dependent on language and we cannot tell what this experience would be without the help of words which allow this coding and the semantic properties referred to by the words.

I am convinced that introspection is facilitated in societies which have developed an internal representation of the law, the idea of personal responsibility and personal guilt and the practice of self-examination. The phenomena related to the second approach are probably more universal, because what is searched for through consciousness in this case is the experience of subjectivity, the experience of permanence of the self, which breaks down in pathologies such as schizophrenia, and the quest for personal identity. This is probably more characteristic of mankind and it is for these reasons that, in my opinion, neurophysiological methods provide rather stable characteristics of these mental states, as reported in the present issue. This would probably not be the case for phenomena which are dependent on language and culture.

The question is: are we dealing with the same type of phenomena in both cases and consequently is consciousness the same concept when one moves from introspection to phenomenological reduction or meditation techniques or vice-versa?

2. The limits of consciousness: what is reportable and not reportable?

In a number of cases dissociations have been observed between the thought processes as manifested by actual behaviour and those the subject was aware of and was able to report. A well known case is the phenomenon described as implicit learning. In these situations the subject is confronted with a task, which is governed by a complex rule but he is not informed of that. With practice the performance improves, which proves an adaptation to the constraints of the task. However the subject is not able to report anything relevant to the rule governing the task. This has been shown for different types of tasks and rules (Reber, 1967; Levicki, 1987; Berry and Broadbent, 1984). When the technique of interview is improved, it has been shown that the subject may be conscious of some parts of the rule (Marescaux, 1991) and there is still a debate about the existence of unconscious learning (Perruchet et al., 1990), but the general conclusion seems to hold that the manifestation of a regularity in behaviour precedes conscious awareness of the rule and explicit planning of the action.

The relation between adaptative behaviour and conscious awareness of goals has been more clearly put into evidence in problem-solving situations. For instance a recent study (Kanellaki-Agathos & Richard, 1997) has shown that four-years old children behave almost as efficiently as seven-year olds in familiar complex tasks requiring decomposition of the goal into subgoals, ordering of subgoals, taking account of prerequisites, but there are major differences in the way the action is described. The pattern of development is quite systematic: the youngest children are able to report only the global goal, which is the final goal given in the instructions, then as a function of age the successive steps are observed: expression of the subgoals which are the components of the global goal and expression of the subgoals which are aimed at satisfying the prerequisites of a subgoal of the first type (i.e. I remove this one in order to be able to take this one). It is only at seven that the prerequisites are explicitly reported.

Classically, two phases are distinguished in problem-solving tasks: an exploratory phase, which varies widely among different isomorphic versions of a problem, and a final phase which is constant (Kotovsky and Fallside, 1989). The behaviour in the final phase reflects planning and reports concerning this phase show a relatively explicit understanding of the goals involved. In the exploratory phase on the other hand the behaviour looks erratic and unsystematic and the reports are very poor: subjects state only the actions they are doing. However, using models of problem-solving, which allow simulation of behaviour based possibly on erroneous interpretations of the instructions, and on the idea that the subject's basic behaviour is trying to reduce the distance to the goal, as they conceive it (which may be inappropriate), it has been shown that even in the exploratory phase the behaviour is quite consistent although inadequate. The errors are explained by the fact that subjects have goals which are well defined but inappropriate, because the decomposition of the major goal is inadequate, the ordering is wrong, or the prerequisites are not considered, or because they have an interpretation of the instructions which is understandable, but inappropriate in the context (Richard *et al.*, 1993; Richard, 1994; in press).

It has been possible to compare the goals and the interpretations which are reported by the subject with those which are manifested by his behaviour, those which allow a nearly perfect simulation of his trial by trial behaviour. This comparison allows a first response to the question: what intentions and representations are reportable and what are not? Two uses of goals have to be distinguished: the first use is to plan actions, but it may happen that the goal structure is too poor to allow planning: planning requires an ordering of subgoals and some idea of the prerequisites of an elementary action. In that case the subgoal which has been produced is used to evaluate each possible action as regards this goal: the action chosen is the one which leads to the state which reduces most the distance to the goal. This mechanism may generate impasses which are observed in difficult problems where the appropriate action apparently increases the distance to the goal. It has been observed that goals are conscious when they are used in planning but are practically never reported when they are used to evaluate the distance to the goal. In a similar way, correct interpretations, which are the interpretations which are used in planning at the end of the task, are usually reported but not the erroneous ones which are abandoned during the exploratory phase.

3. What is the function of consciousness, what is its utility?

This question has been approached, it seems to me, in only one paper: that by Carl Ginsburg, who presents himself as a practitioner and gives evidence of improvement in bodily adjustment following practice in becoming aware of sensations involved in motor control.

I think that the function of consciousness for a subject is to communicate with other people but also to communicate with himself: this allows memorization and recollection of past experience. Being conscious of the representation of the situation and of the goals results is increased consistency of behaviour. Theories of social cognition insist on the idea that people tend to reduce the dissonance between what they do and what they think, the result being the adjustment of cognition to behaviour or the reverse. The issue is the same in cognitive processing. Goals are modelling behaviour at an implicit level via the role they play in evaluation and when goals become conscious, they can be taken as objects for reasoning: anticipation becomes possible, so that they may be used to plan behaviour in an explicit way. The idea that consciousness gives consistency to behaviour has been anticipated by writers such as Stendhal, who develops the notion of 'crystallization': this corresponds to becoming aware of some behaviour, attitude, feelings which are suddenly perceived as united and receive an interpretation. From this point things become completely different.

Consciousness increases the consistency of behaviour, but the correlate is that change becomes more difficult. The literature on transfer in problem-solving suggests the idea that the recognition of the analogy between a problem having a known solution and a new problem is more difficult when the solution of the first problem has been taught explicitly than when it has been discovered through errors and impasses (Gick & Mc Garry, 1992). Important semantic changes are probably made more easily on an implicit level than on the explicit level of consciousness. Consciousness is probably characteristic of phases of cognitive functioning that are stable: the subject is not aware of what happens in phases of change, especially of what happens during learning.

Becoming aware is a type of activity and we have to understand what are the conditions for this activity to take place.

References

Berry, D.C., & Broadbent, D.E. (1984), 'On the relationship between task performance and associated verbalisable knowledge', *Quarterly Journal of Experimental Psychology*, **36A**, pp. 209–31.

Gick, M. & McGarry S.J. (1992), 'Learning from mistakes : Inducing analogous solution failures to a source problem produces later successes in analogical transfer', *Journal of Experimental Psychology: Learning, Memory and Cognition*, **18** (3), pp. 623–39.

Kanellaki-Agathos, S. & Richard, J.F. (1997), 'Planification et représetnation de l'action chez l'enfant', *Archives de Psychologie*, **65**, pp. 4–79.

Kotovsky K. & Fallside D. (1989), 'Representation and transfer in problem solving', in *Complex information Processing (What has Simon wrought?)*, 21st Symposium of the Carnegie Mellon Institute, ed. K. Kotovsky (Hillsdale, NJ: Lawrence Erlbaum).

Lewicki, P. (1986), 'Processing information about covariations that cannot be articulated', *Journal of Experimental Psychology: Learning, Memory and Cognition*, **12**, pp. 135–46.

Marescaux, P.J. (1991), *Contribution à l'étude de la distinction entre connaissances implicites et connaissances explicites* (Thèse de Doctorat, Université de Bruxelles).

Merleau-Ponty, M. (1945), *La phénoménologie de la perception* (Paris: Gallimard).

Perruchet, P., Gallego, J. & Savy, I. (1990), 'A critical reappraisal of the evidence for unconscious abstraction of deterministic rules in complex experimental situations', *Cognitive Psychology*, **22**, pp. 493–516.

Reber, A.S. (1967), 'Implicit learning of artificial grammars', *Journal of Verbal Learning and Verbal Behavior*, **6** , pp. 855–63.

Richard, J.F. (in press), 'L'analyse des buts et des représentations de l'individu à partir de ses comportements', *Psychologie Française*.

Richard, J.F. (1994), 'La résolution de problème', in *Traité de Psychologie Expérimentale*, tome 2, ed. M. Richelle, J. Requin and M. Robert (Paris: PUF).

Richard, J.F., Poitrenaud, S. and Tijus, C. (1993), 'Problem-solving restructuration: elimination of implicit constraints', *Cognitive Science*, **17**, pp. 497–529.

Sartre, J.P. (1939), *Esquisse d'une théorie des émotions* (Paris: Hermann).

THE SYMBIOSIS OF SUBJECTIVE AND EXPERIMENTAL APPROACHES TO INTUITION

Jonathan W. Schooler and Sonya Dougal, University of Pittsburgh

We all have had convictions (i.e. a hunch about how to solve a problem, an inkling about the intents of another, or a wariness of a situation) that we were unable to substantiate on a purely logical basis. Such intuitive experiences have intrigued philosophers for centuries, although the construct of intuition as such has generally been given an undeserved cold shoulder by researchers. As Peugeot, in this issue, observes, 'It is therefore very surprising that so few studies have been dedicated to the study of the subjective experience which is associated with it' (p. 43). Peugeot is correct in her observation that modern research has had little to say explicitly about intuition and its subjective concomitants. However, this omission may be as much a matter of terms as it is of fact. Specifically, if we consider the definition of intuition we see that a considerable amount of research that has been called by other names, actually reveals important insights into *both* the cognitive processes that lead to intuition and the subjective experiences associated with it. Moreover, because this research explicitly relates subjective experiences to more objective measures and methodologies, it circumvents a central criticism that can be levelled against the first-person phenomenological methodology used by Peugeot; namely that it may not reflect underlying processes, nor even necessarily the subjective experiences that it purports to measure.

The pertinence of recent research to the understanding of intuition becomes clear when we consider several of its standard definitions. According to Webster's Dictionary (1975) intuition involves 'the power or faculty of attaining direct knowledge or cognition without evident rational thought or inference'. A narrower definition of intuition, involves the 'quick and ready insight' experience that Peugeot and others consider in their analyses of creative illuminations. Although there are some important differences between these two characterizations, they both suggest that intuition involves *meaningful cognition that occurs without consciously mediated deliberation*. From this vantage, demonstrations of intuition require evidence of two distinct claims. First, an intuition must be shown to have transpired *without conscious deliberation*. Since the discernment of conscious deliberation is largely a phenomenological question, resolution of this issue must fundamentally rely on subjective reports. Although central to intuition, the demonstration of cognition in the absence of deliberation is not sufficient to provide a meaningful demonstration of intuition. In order to distinguish intuitive judgements from mere fancy, they must also be shown to be sensitive to some underlying truth or significance. Thus, the second claim is that demonstrations of intuition must provide evidence of *meaningful cognition*.

The above framework allows us to see how many domains of cognitive research, involving both subjective and objective measures, can be reconstrued as illustrating incidents of intuition. For example, consider Marcel's (1983) original demonstration of subliminal perception. Marcel flashed words at a rate at which participants reported no subjective awareness. Participants were then asked to identify which of three words was a synonym of the previously flashed word. Although participants found this task rather peculiar, they nevertheless were well above chance at identifying matching synonyms. This paradigm clearly fits with the above characterizations of demonstrations of intuition. Evidence for *nondeliberative processes* is provided by participants' subjective reports of being unaware when words were flashed. Evidence of *meaningful cognition* is provided by the objective finding of above-chance performance in identifying the appropriate matching word.

Another more recent example of intuition is provided by the research of Dunning and Stern (1994). In their studies, individuals witnessed a staged crime, attempted to identify the perpetrator in a line up, and then subjectively reported how they made the identification. Deliberative processes were indicated by the endorsement of statements such as 'I compared the photos to each other in order to narrow the choices'. Nondeliberative processes (what we would call intuition) were indicated by endorsing statements such as 'His face just popped out at me.' Strikingly, and in support of the meaningfulness of intuitive judgements, Dunning and Stern found that recognition judgements were actually *more* accurate when participants characterized their recognition decisions as relying on nondeliberative processes relative to deliberative processes.

One potential concern with the above characterizations of intuition is that the focus on subjective experience is rather modest. In the Marcel study, subjective reports were limited to a simple acknowledgement of awareness. In the Dunning and Stern study, subjective report was constrained by the specific alternatives that participants were given. On the one hand, such limitations clearly constrain the amount of information that can be derived about the subjective experience of intuition in these cases. On the other hand, it should be noted that even such relatively modest uses of subjective experience represent a departure from a strict positivistic approach and have consequently been viewed with some scepticism (e.g. Holender, 1986). Indeed concern regarding the applicability of subjective reports has some foundation, as without objective verification one cannot be certain whether they accurately reflect the contents of individuals' thoughts. Peugeot tacitly acknowledges the uncertainties surrounding self-report measures, by alluding to techniques such as subjects 'using the present tense' or 'letting go eye contact' for verifying 'if the subject is really reliving an experience' (pp. 46–7). However, no evidence is given for why we should trust such techniques as verifying individual reports. Moreover, recent research suggests that simply attempting to subjectively report on non-verbalizable intuitive experience may disrupt those very experiences.

There is now a growing accumulation of evidence that individuals' ability to employ nonverbal intuitive knowledge may be impaired as a result of self-report procedures (see Schooler *et al.*, 1997 for a review). For example, in one study (Schooler & Engstler-Schooler, 1990), participants viewed a bank robbery and then half described the appearance of the robber while the other half engaged in an unrelated activity. Finally, all participants were asked to identify the robber from a photo line-up. Strikingly, having verbalized the appearance of the robber actually interfered with participants' subsequent ability to recognize him. Since this original demonstration, comparable verbally-induced memory disruptions (termed 'verbal overshadowing') have been observed to occur with memory for: colour (Schooler & Engstler-Schooler, 1990), taste (Melcher & Schooler, 1996), visual forms (e.g. Brandimonte *et al.*, 1997) and audition (Schooler *et al.*, 1996). In addition, similar disruptive effects of verbalization have been found for a variety of other tasks that rely on non-verbalizable (intuitive) knowledge, including: affective decision making (Wilson & Schooler, 1991; Wilson *et al.*, 1993), analogical reasoning (Sieck *et al.*, in press) and (as will be discussed later) insight problem solving (Schooler *et al.*, 1993).

Although verbal overshadowing effects raise serious problems regarding the use of self-reports for articulating intuitive experiences, they at the same time help to reveal the nature of these experiences. Specifically, such effects can be readily understood as occurring because verbalization, by encouraging deliberation, impairs participants' ability to rely on their gut feeling; i.e. their intuitions. Consistent with this view, Schooler & Engstler-Schooler replicated the prior verbalization procedure with one modification; at the time of test half of the participants were forced to respond on the basis of their intuitions by requiring them to make speeded recognition decisions.

As predicted, when participants were forced to rely on their gut intuitions, the disruptive effects of verbalization were attenuated.

More recent research using the 'verbal overshadowing' paradigm (Schooler *et al.*, 1996) has added self-report measures to further document the impact of verbalization on the reliability of deliberative and intuitive judgements. Critically, however, rather than asking individuals to expound on their non-verbalizable experiences, participants were simply asked to indicate whether they had made a 'reason' based judgment (i.e. whether they had some specific reason for choosing the face that they did) or a 'just know' decision (i.e. they were unaware of any specific reason for choosing the face that they did). Cf. Gardiner (1988). In this study, verbalization was found to markedly disrupt recognition decisions classified as having been made on a just know basis, while if anything improving those decisions characterized as having been based on reasons. The fact that verbalization disrupted just know judgments but not reason-based judgments supports the contention that verbalization specifically hampers the use of intuition. It also simultaneously demonstrates that while invasive self-report measures (i.e. describing ones thoughts) are impairing intuitive processes, more modest subjective self-report measures can still reveal whether or not intuition is being employed. More generally, the systematic relationship between objective manipulations of deliberation and subjective reports of intuition illustrates the value of using both approaches in the investigation of intuition.

Intuition as illumination

One especially compelling example of intuition is the experience of illumination in which the solution to a problem seems to come out of the blue. Consistent with our more general characterization of intuition, such experiences are (1) not precipitated by explicit deliberation and (2) often associated with meaningful (indeed even profound) cognition. Contrary to Peugeot's claim in this issue, however, quite a few researchers have amassed retrospective accounts of the subjective stages associated with illumination (e.g. Csikszentmihalyi & Sawyer, 1995; Ghiselin, 1952; Hadamard, 1949; Shrady, 1972; Wallas, 1926). Although some of these investigations were more anecdotal than the approach described by Peugeot, others (at least from the perspective of this reader) were comparably rigorous. For example, Csikszentmihalyi & Sawyer (1995) interviewed nine creative individuals who reported at length their phenomenological experiences of discovery. Some examples of their reported subjective experiences included 'suddenly in the middle of the night while we were going through Kansas, the whole picture became crystal clear, the eureka experience or whatever you like to call it' (p. 351) and 'You have these ideas . . . as you work on them you get new ideas . . . If you don't work on it they hide in there . . . Something has begun to work and you continue it, you feel the singing inside you' (p. 352). Clearly such descriptions, though admittedly not in the present tense, convey much of the same type of observations as those reported by Peugeot.

In addition to deriving similar types of subjective reports, these other analyses also identified four subjective stages of intuition not too dissimilar from those described by Peugeot. These include preparation, incubation, illumination, and verification. Preparation involves the gradual, deliberative accumulation of knowledge as a result of attempting to solve the problem. Incubation refers to a period in which all conscious deliberative mental processing devoted specifically to solving the problem is stopped. Illumination corresponds to the flash or moment of 'aha' in which the problem solution appears in consciousness. Finally, verification denotes the process of determining whether the solution gained through illumination is valid.

Such subjective case analyses have done much to flesh out the phenomenology of illumination, and in particular the suggestion that the hallmark of the illumination experience is the point at which unconscious, non-deliberative processes become conscious. Nevertheless, they are susceptible to the same concerns as the subjective self-report measures described earlier; i.e. they do not necessarily reflect the actual underlying processes involved in the task. Moreover, because such retrospective analyses typically occur well after the fact, they run the additional risk of being biased by memory distortions (e.g. Dunbar, 1995; Ericsson and Simon, 1980). For example, Dunbar sat in on laboratory meetings in which major scientific insights were made. Subsequently he queried participants of the groups regarding their recollections of when particular insights occurred. On several occasions he observed critical disparities between individuals recollections of their insights, and what he had witnessed actually occur (Dunbar, December 1996 personal communication). Finally, as will be described shortly, extensive self-report procedures can actually interfere with the successful implementation of insight processes.

Because of the inherent limitations of retrospective case analyses of real world discoveries, it is important to complement such approaches with more controlled laboratory investigations that combine subjective reports with objective measures. Towards this end, Metcalfe (1986 — all Metcalfe references are to this work) had participants characterize their subjective feeling of warmth (i.e. how close they are to the solution) as they tried to solve 'insight' riddle problems known to induce aha experience. Interestingly, Metcalfe found that in insight problem solving, continuously increasing feeling of warmth (FOW) ratings actually predicted erroneous solutions. However, an abrupt increase in FOW rating just prior to solution predicted correct solution. This finding provides an example of how intuitive hunches can be misleading. At the same time, it validates the phenomenological suddenness of illumination.

Using a somewhat different paradigm, Bowers et al. (1990 — all Bowers references are to this work) provided evidence that hunches prior to the moment of illumination can reflect actual progress towards the solution. Their procedure used a 'remote associate' paradigm (Mednick & Mednick, 1967) in which individuals see a three word triad (e.g. playing, credit, report) and must identify a single word corresponding to all three (e.g. card). In the Bowers paradigm, individuals were simultaneously given two triads, only one of which had a solution. Interestingly, Bowers found that subjects were above chance at guessing which triad had a solution even if they could not solve it. Thus, in contrast to Metcalfe, the Bowers procedure revealed that individuals can possess some intuitions prior to actually seeing the solution.

There are several important implications of the disparities between the Bowers and the Metcalfe findings. From a conceptual perspective, the two approaches highlight differences between two manifestations of intuition. Bowers' research demonstrates intuition in the sense of *possessing a hunch* without being able to rationally substantiate it. Metcalfe's research demonstrates intuition in the sense of *recognizing a solution* without any awareness of the cognition that led to it. Although these two manifestations of intuition are clearly related, the rather different findings of Metcalfe and Bowers also help to illustrate their disparities. From an empirical perspective, the disparity of the Metcalfe and the Bowers results suggest that the way in which intuitive hunches are measured may have important implications for the meaningfulness of the intuitive experience. In Metcalfe's experiments subjects were directly queried about the quality of cognitive processes that clearly were not readily available to consciousness. In contrast, Bowers merely asked participants to make a gut judgement about which of two alternatives was likely to have a solution. It is thus possible that Metcalfe's participants, in their effort to deliberately gaze into their unconscious percolation, may have lost sight of the very intuitions they were seeking.

Research by Schooler et al. (1993) adds credence to the potentially disruptive effects of explicitly focusing on the intuitive processes leading to sudden aha experiences. They found that thinking aloud while trying to solve problems actually disrupted participants' ability to correctly solve insight problems while having little effect on more logical analytical types of problems. (Similar findings were also observed when participants were interrupted in the middle of their solution attempts and asked to retrospectively report on the processes that they were using.) In this study, participants were engaged in first-person self-report very much like that reported by Peugeot; nevertheless, the central finding of this study was that attempting to articulate the contents of inner thought fundamentally disrupted the process of intuition, i.e. participants were markedly less successful at reaching insightful solutions.

Further support for the inherently non-verbalizable quality of the intuitive processes comes from Schooler and Melcher's (1995) in depth analysis of the think aloud protocols generated in the Schooler et al. study. In effect this content analysis mirrors that provided by Peugeot, and is arguably more valid as individuals were reporting thoughts as they occurred rather than trying to reproduce thoughts that happened sometime ago. However, the central finding of Schooler and Melcher's analysis was that subjective first-person protocols revealed very little about the processes that lead to insights. It is not that such protocols are inherently meaningless, since for logical problems there were various elements of individuals' think-aloud protocols (e.g. the use of logical arguments) that were highly predictive of whether or not a participant ultimately solved a problem. In contrast, for insight problems there was very little in individuals' reports that predicted whether or not they were making progress toward a solution. Instead participants were much more likely to comment on the ineffability of their thoughts with observations such as 'there is nothing that's going through my mind that's really in any kind of — that's in a verbal fashion' or 'There is not a whole lot that I can say about this while I am trying to figure it out' or 'I know I am supposed to keep talking but I don't know what I am thinking' (p. 115). When considered together with the fact that thinking aloud interferes with insight problem solutions, such protocols clearly illustrate the limitations of relying exclusively on first-person think aloud techniques for gaining insight into intuition.

The clear limitations of first-person think aloud reports for revealing insight processes illustrates the importance of alternative empirical approaches to document the nature of the intuitive insight processes that are vulnerable to verbalization. For example, using a split visual field priming paradigm Fiore & Schooler (1997) found evidence that insight processes may be specifically associated with the right-hemisphere. Using an individual differences paradigm, Schooler & Melcher (1995) found that the ability to solve insight problems is highly correlated with that of recognizing out-of-focus pictures, suggesting that the intuitive processes associated with insight may be similar to basic perceptual pattern recognition processes (cf. Schooler, Fallshore & Fiore, 1995.) Finally, using the 'just know'/'reason' self-report measure (described earlier), Schooler *et al.* (1996) found that the disruptive effects of verbalization were again exclusively associated with solutions reached on a 'just know' basis. Methodologically, this latter finding illustrates the value of combining objective manipulations of intuition with subjective measures of it. Conceptually, it suggests that intuitions, like faint stars, may vanish if scrutinized too closely.

Conclusion

A complete understanding of intuition will necessarily require both subjective and objective techniques within both naturalistic and laboratory settings. Alone, each of these approaches has significant limitations. Subjective measures may misrepresent the processes contributing to intuition, whereas objective methodologies alone fail to illuminate underlying phenomenology. Naturalistic studies can introduce hindsight biases, whereas laboratory studies must necessarily rely on relatively mundane intuitions. Despite their individual weaknesses, the convergence of techniques holds great promise. Regrettably most researchers have been reluctant to integrate approaches. Researchers studying subjective experience rarely examine how their measures interact with more objective manipulations and measures, while experimental researchers tend to dismiss the importance of subjective experience. In most domains, these alternative tacks have progressed independently, however the inherent properties of intuition require that they be synthesized. Ultimately, intuition must be defined in terms of subjective conscious experience, and indeed, recent research indicates that individuals can report when they are making intuitive 'just know' judgments. At the same time however, the validity of an intuitive judgment depends on the objective assessment of its products. Moreover, the very act of subjective scrutiny can hamper the intuitive processes under investigation. Such reactive effects pose very serious problems for analyses such as Peugeot's that exclusively rely on participants' *attempts* to provide extensive first-person reporting of their intuitive thought processes. Although problematic from the vantage of a purely subjective analysis, the disruptive effects of verbalization on intuition highlight the value of integrating subjective and experimental approaches. Specifically, by encouraging verbal introspection we can manipulate access to intuitive knowledge, and thereby assess the role of such knowledge in cognition. Thus, a fundamental limitation of subjective introspection (i.e. its reactivity) can actually serve as an experimental tool for illuminating the otherwise mysterious qualities of intuition.[26]

References

Bowers, K.S., Regehr, G., Baltazard, C. and Parker, K. (1990), 'Intuition in the context of discovery', *Cognitive Psychology*, **22**, pp. 72–110.

Brandimonte, M.A., Schooler, J.W. & Gabbino, P. (1997), 'Attenuating verbal overshadowing through visual retrieval cues', *Journal of Experimental Psychology: Learning Memory and Cognition*, **23**, pp. 915–31.

Czikszentmihalyi, M. & Sawyer, K. (1995), 'Creative insight: The social dimension of a solitary moment', in *The Nature of Insight*, ed. R.J. Sternberg & J.E. Davidson (London: Bradford).

[26] For Peugeot's replies to this and the next commentary, see p. 290 below — *Editor*

Dunbar, K. (1995), 'How scientists really reason: Scientific reasoning in real-world laboratories', in *The Nature of Insight*, ed. R.J. Sternberg & J.E. Davidson (London: Bradford).

Dunning, D. & Stern, L.B. (1994), 'Distinguishing accurate from inaccurate eyewitness identifications via inquiries about decision processes', *Journal of Personality and Social Psychology*, **67**, pp. 818–35.

Ericsson, K.A. & Simon, H.A. (1980), 'Verbal reports as data', *Psychological Review*, **87**, pp. 215–51.

Fiore, S.M., & Schooler, J.W. (1997), 'Right hemisphere contributions to creative problem solving: Converging evidence for divergent thinking', in *Right Hemisphere Language Comprehension*, ed. M. Beeman and C. Chiarello (Hillsdale, NJ: Lawrence Erlbaum).

Gardiner, J.M. (1988), 'Functional aspects of recollective experience', *Memory and Cognition*, **16**, pp. 309–13.

Ghiselin, B. (1952), *The Creative Process* (New York: Wiley).

Hadamard, J. (1949), *The Psychology of Invention in the Mathematical Field* (Princeton, NJ: Princeton University Press).

Holender, D. (1986), 'Semantic activation without conscious identification in dichotic listening, peripheral vision, and visual masking: A survey and appraisal', *The Behavioral and Brain Sciences*, **9**, pp. 1–66.

Marcel, A.J. (1983), 'Conscious and unconscious perception: Experiments on visual masking and word recognition', *Cognitive Psychology*, **15**, pp. 197–237.

Mednick, S.A. & Mednick, M.T. (1967), *Examiner's Manual: Remote Associates Test* (Boston, MA: Houghton Mifflin).

Melcher, J. & Schooler, J.W. (1996), 'The misremembrance of wines past: Verbal and perceptual expertise differentially mediate verbal overshadowing of taste', *The Journal of Memory and Language*, **35**, pp. 231–45.

Metcalfe, J. (1986), 'Premonitions of insight predict impending error', *Journal of Experimental Psychology: Learning, Memory, and Cognition*, **12**, pp. 623–34.

Schooler, J.W. & Engstler-Schooler, T.Y. (1990), 'Verbal overshadowing of visual memories: Some things are better left unsaid', *Cognitive Psychology*, **22**, pp. 36–71.

Schooler, J., Fallshore, M. and Fiore, S. (1995), 'Epilogue: Putting insight into perspective', in *The Nature of Insight*, ed. R.J. Sternberg and J.E. Davidson (Cambridge, MA: MIT Press).

Schooler, J.W, Fiore, S., Melcher, J. & Ambadar, Z. (1996), 'Verbal overshadowing and the just know/reason distinction', Paper presented at the Annual Meeting of the Psychonomic Society, Chicago, November.

Schooler, J.W., Fiore, S.M. and Brandimonte (1997), 'At a *loss* from words: verbal overshadowing of perceptual memories', in *The Psychology of Learning and Motivation*, ed. D.L. Medin (San Diego, CA: Academic Press).

Schooler, J. & Melcher, J. (1995), 'The ineffability of insight', in *The Creative Cognition Approach*, ed. S.M. Smith, T.B. Ward & R.A. Finke (Cambridge, MA: MIT Press).

Schooler, J.W., Ohlsson, S. & Brooks, K. (1993), 'Thoughts beyond words: When language overshadows insight', *Journal of Experimental Psychology: General*, **122**, pp. 166–83.

Shrady, M. (1972), *Moments of Insight* (New York: Harper & Row).

Sieck, W.R, Quinn, C.N. & Schooler, J.W. (in press), 'Justification effects on the judgment of analogy', *Memory and Cognition*.

Wallas, G. (1926), *The Art of Thought* (New York: Franklin Watts).

Webster New Collegiate Dictionary (Springfield, MA: G. & C. Merriam Co., 1975)

Wilson, T.D. & Schooler, J.W. (1991), 'Thinking too much: Introspection can reduce the quality of preferences and decisions?', *Journal of Personality and Social Psychology*, **60**, pp. 181–92.

Wilson, T.D., Lisle, D.J., Schooler, J.W., Hodges, S.D., Klaaren, K.J. & Lafleur, S.J. (1993), 'Introspecting about reasons can reduce post-choice satisfaction', *Personality and Social Psychology Bulletin*, **19**, pp. 331–9.

DISTINGUISHING INSIGHT FROM INTUITION

Rachel Henley, University of Sussex, Falmer, Brighton
rachelhe@biols.susx.ac.uk.

As Peugeot says, the subjective experience of intuition has received remarkably little attention, so her paper is a valuable start to a systematic study of this important phenomenon. There are a number of possible meanings of 'intuition', for example, authors such as Bowers *et al.* (1990), use it to mean a feeling of being close to solving a problem before the solution is consciously available (similar to tip-of-the-tongue states in memory). Despite referring to the volumes that have been dedicated to the definition of intuition, Peugeot herself does not offer a definition of the phenomenon that she is studying. Before embarking on a detailed exploration of intuition, it is worth identifying the phenomenon in question, so as to provide a framework in which further investigation may meaningfully take place. I would like to suggest that Peugeot uses the term intuition to encompass two distinct phenomena, but that her results describe only one of these. Secondly, I would like to consider the role of intuition in people's lives.

When introducing intuition, Peugeot states that, 'the history of the sciences . . . is full of testimonies of scientists telling about how a new idea came to them in a sudden, unexpected manner, without any discursive activity' (p. 43) and, 'it surges forth with a leap . . . out of our control' (p. 44). These new ideas tend to be the solutions to problems on which the scientists had already worked extensively. The most famous example is Archimedes' discovery of measurement of volume by displacement of water, which was the final part of the solution to the problem of how to determine the purity of a gold crown. This is generally referred to as insight (e.g. Sternberg & Davidson, 1995), and was postulated as a stage in problem solving by Wallas (1926). His four-stage model was (1) Preparation: initial work on the problem. (2) Incubation: a break during which no conscious work is done on the problem. (3) Insight: the solution comes 'out of the blue'. (4) Verification: conscious work is required to confirm the insight is the solution to the problem. The scientists listed by Peugeot are often also listed as providing examples of insight. Indeed, it seems that no introductory text on insight is complete without a quote from Poincaré describing his holiday taken when frustrated at his inability to proceed with his work, during which the solution came to him as he stepped onto a bus. This was followed by verification 'at his leisure', on returning home.

However, there are other features of intuition that Peugeot mentions which are not consistent with equating it with insight. She refers to the 'character of "immediacy" which defines intuitive knowledge. "Immediate" knowledge is . . . direct knowledge, which *cannot* be reached through an intermediary reasoning process' (p. 44; my italics). She also mentions the presence of intuition in the work of several philosophers. Descartes, for example, divides his thoughts into three types, innate, adventitious and invented by himself. Of the first, he gives the following illustration: 'My understanding of what a thing is, what truth is, and what thought is, seems to derive simply from my own nature'. He also attaches considerable weight to clear and distinct perception of ideas, and states that, 'whatever I perceive very clearly and distinctly is true' (Descartes, 1641, Third Meditation). The type of understanding described here is not only arrived at without prior reasoning, but is of its nature not penetrable by reason. Whilst insight is characterized by its unexpected appearance, it would be possible to reach the same conclusions by a process of incremental reasoning. The role of the verification stage in Wallas' model makes it clear that once an insight has occurred, it must be verified by the normal reasoning process. This distinguishes insight, which is an unusual mode of arriving at an ordinary type of understanding, from intuition, which is a direct knowledge of a type different from that arrived at by reasoning or perception.

Insight and intuition may also be different subjective experiences. Insight always occurs suddenly, without warning. This is referred to as the 'Aha' experience, and is taken by some authors to be the defining feature of insight (e.g. Kaplan & Simon, 1990). Whilst intuition may also occur suddenly, Peugeot says, 'instantaneity is not the most common mode of appearance of intuition: it appears most often in a progressive manner'. Furthermore, she discusses a stage preceding intuition; a stage of preparation that makes it more likely that intuition will occur. This is supported by the philosopher's accounts, 'Platonic conversion, Cartesian doubt, phenomenological reduction, etc. . . . liberate an interior space for intuition to spring forth' (pp. 44–5). This kind of preparatory phase does not seem to be part of the experience of insight.

If Peugeot's introduction confuses insight with intuition, which of these phenomena is she studying? All of the experiences she selected to study were about 'knowledge that came about without the intermediary either of a deductive mechanism nor through the habitual senses'. Since this definition focuses on the appearance of the knowledge, rather than its nature, it does not distinguish between insight and intuition. These two phenomena may also differ in the subject matter of their contents. As was mentioned above, insights generally contain the solution to a problem which the subject had previously been working on. Of the twenty-four intuitive experiences listed, four fall into this category. Three were about what to do in a given situation, whilst the majority were what might usually be called ESP; knowledge of a distant or future event, or of another person's state of mind or body. It is possible that Peugeot has studied two (or more) distinct phenomena. Since there were only four experiences which seem likely to have been insight (regarding the solutions to problems), Peugeot's model will probably reflect the rest of the cases — the experiences of intuition.

Looking at the results of Peugeot's investigation, the intuitive experience is described as one in which the subjects use some technique to achieve the intuitive state, then make a connection and 'listen' for an intuition. This preparation is clearly at odds with the suddenness of insight, so the intuitive experience studied by Peugeot cannot be insight. Whilst she refers to the unexpected nature of intuition on a number of occasions, in her concluding remarks she says, 'Even if intuition keeps an unpredictable, capricious character, it is possible to encourage its appearing . . . by a very meticulous interior preparation' (pp. 76–7). It is not clear how these two features are to be reconciled. Is intuition a phenomenon that is usually unpredictable but can also be encouraged by preparation? Or does it just seem to be unexpected, with preparatory stages that can be discerned only by careful introspection of the kind facilitated by Peugeot's interview of explicitation? The latter interpretation is suggested by the testimony of Reik, who reports speaking, 'without the slightest hesitation', during his intuitive experience, but subsequently describes, 'suspense, a waiting for something to come', (p. 53) in the preceding moments.

The view of intuition as involving a preparatory stage of which the subject is unaware fits well with Peugeot's statement that, 'the gestures which prepare and follow the emergence of an intuition belong to that dimension of experience which is not a part of thought-out consciousness' (p. 45). However it does not fit well with the reports of her subjects, which contain phrases such as, 'I . . . visualize my interior landscape', 'I am concentrating', 'I'm going to place my consciousness . . . towards the back of my skull' (p. 48). These are all deliberate, conscious actions. It would seem that the preparatory stages of intuition are largely under conscious control, as reported by some of the subjects, despite Reik's assertion that, 'This process [of connection] has none of the characteristics of conscious activity. It takes place wholly in areas that are not accessible to our thought-efforts and it is almost unthinking' (p. 65). Consistent with this, Peugeot reports that several of her subjects benefited from daily practice, particularly in the first stage, of achieving the intuitive state (p. 59).

Distinguishing intuition from insight, the latter being characterized by its sudden appearance, allows for an investigation of the preparatory stages of intuition unconstrained by the requirement that they must be inaccessible to consciousness. Some of Peugeot's subjects were not only conscious of their preparation, but had developed this skill through practice. This sets the phenomenon of intuition in a new light, not as a widespread occurrence which comes to us unexpectedly (though it may do in some cases), but as something experienced by those who have increased their sensitivity to it by practising meditative techniques.

References

Bowers, K.S., Regehr, G., Balthazard, C. & Parker, K. (1990), 'Intuition in the context of discovery', *Cognitive Psychology*, **22** (1), pp. 72–109.
Descartes, R. (1641/1986), *Meditations on First Philosophy*, Trans. J. Cottingham (Cambridge: Cambridge University Press).
Kaplan, C. & Simon, H.A. (1990), 'In search of insight', *Cognitive Psychology*, **22**, pp. 374–419.
Sternberg, R.J. & Davidson, J.E. (1995), *The Nature of Insight* (Cambridge, MA: The MIT Press).
Wallas, G. (1926), *The Art of Thought* (New York: Harcourt Brace Jovanovich).

REPLIES TO SCHOOLER & DOUGAL AND HENLEY

C. Petitmengin-Peugeot

Schooler and Dougal raise three main questions regarding my work: (1) the supposed distortion of intuitive experience by verbalization; (2) the validity of the kinds of first-person descriptions I utilized; and (3) the complementarity of subjective and objective approaches in the study of intuition.

1. The authors recapitulate a number of studies in order to show that verbalizing perturbs the intuitive process, and draw the conclusion that this process cannot be verbalized and subjected to a description. I do not question the validity of these experimental results, which coincide well with my own phenomenological observations that in the pre-intuitive phase the discursive activity is slowed down. But I do question the soundness of Schooler and Dougal's conclusion, since it is based on a knot of conceptual confusions.

In the example they discussed in some detail, it is shown that the effort of describing a thief's face verbally perturbs the emergence of intuition (recognizing the thief's face). But it is false to conclude from this that intuitive emergence cannot be described. This would amount to confusing the intuitive process itself with the process of *description* of the intuitive process. That the first is perturbed by verbalizations does not mean that it cannot be described (that the second process is impossible). My work shows, on the contrary, that what we have to deal with are non-discursive experiences that can, nevertheless, be described.

As Schooler and Dougal themselves observe, verbalization in itself is not what perturbs the intuitive process (in fact intuition often emerges in a verbal form), but the fact that it 'encourages deliberation' (p. 282). What perturbs is the focalization on the goal ('focusing', 'effort to deliberately gaze into', 'scrutinizing', p. 285), the attitude of tension, of effort. The emergence of intuition requires, on the contrary, an inner movement of letting go in regard to the desired goal, a de-focusing and a redirection of attention, an attitude of receptivity and welcoming. Thus the problem is not words as such, but the fixation attitude which is normally associated with them.

In the light of these remarks, let me turn to Schooler and Dougal's review of the work where the subjects were asked to 'think aloud' while solving a problem. In these kinds of protocols the intuitive process is visibly altered by the verbal descriptions carried out concurrently. The authors deduce, once again, that a description of the intuitive process is impossible. But this is again an unwarranted conclusion: what is true of the intuitive process is *also* true of the process of verbal description. It is not language which is the problem, but the attitude of focusing upon a content. Tracking thoughts as they appear has the inevitable consequence of stopping them, and *a fortiori* of blocking any attempt to describe the way in which the thoughts emerge. Description of intuition requires (just like any specific object of study) a method that is adapted to its characteristics, in other words, a method that mobilizes capacities which are close to the intuitive process itself. Such a process of explicitation is far from straightforward. Schooler and Dougal are simply naive when they think that a subject can directly describe his/her inner processes as they occur by 'thinking out loud' without mediation and without training. The extracts from such self-reports are quite typical of those one gets at the very early stages of the explicitation interview: 'I don't know what I am doing', 'I can't say what am I doing', etc. The paucity of such results, far from illustrating the impossibility of a description, is merely the consequence of the absence of a method pitched at the right level.

2. The second criticism Schooler and Dougal direct against my work is the validation of the descriptions obtained through my interview methodology. How do we know the subjects are expressing the 'true' lived experiences? Schooler and Dougal at this point raise doubts concerning the explicitation session, and proceed to make a caricature of the way the interviewer is able to verify that the person really is re-living a past experience (p. 282). In my article I make a detailed list of such criteria which the reader can refer to. Such caricature is typical of those who have never *tried* these kinds of methods, and somehow still hold that third-person criteria are more 'solid' than first-person. What it is missing here is any taking into proper account of the second-person position: the veracity of such criteria, once one has engaged in a detailed explicitation (as interviewer or interviewee), appears in an entirely different light, since such criteria are solidly anchored in the re-living of a specific experience and carry an intensity that is not arbitrary.

Schooler and Dougal also conveniently forget that in my results there is an *inter-subjective* criterion: the convergence of individual descriptions, the kingpin of any validation, including that of classical science. The fact that different people find very similar detailed descriptions, gestures and internal states — although there is no previous framework for the description — is impressive. The convergence of such hesitant, often convoluted descriptions constitutes a strong argument and a guarantee of the validity of the material we have presented.

My hope is that other researchers will attempt similar descriptions using other methodologies. This would then allow us to compare results and the robustness of various methodologies, and would constitute a true validation (or refutation) of what I have presented. In this regard, the comparison with the result obtained by Csikszentmihalyi and Sawyer shows some striking similarities but also some differences. In fact, their work addressed a different topic from mine: the role of social factors in the process of invention and discovery. Their methods are not 'comparably rigorous' to mine. In the excerpts of nine interviews, a number of commentaries, judgements and beliefs are mixed with what seem to be re-lived descriptions of the experiences. These remain quite imprecise, tainted with implicit assumptions about intuition. This underlines once again the need for a rigorous technique of explicitation to enable the subject to describe his/her experience with a precision beyond that resulting from the simple request to do so. Contrary to what Schooler and Dougal say, my method provides a significant step beyond what has been provided so far.

In any case, any first-person method, including verbal reporting as practised by Schooler and Dougal and many others, necessarily demands such intersubjective validation. And in this regard my experience leads me to think that at each moment of the explicitation session a manifestation, a reality of its own, a re-invention of experience of some sort emerges. Descriptions are a compromise between perfect mirrors of raw experience and mere inventions of no descriptive value. Instead of wanting to escape this 'hermeneutic circle' at any price, a true phenomenological description of the way in which the description arises can lead eventually to new criteria of the 'truth' of experiential descriptions and their validation. In the meantime, it is wise to remind ourselves that all attempts to work at the first-person level are still in their infancy, and it is premature to pretend to regulate the field *a priori* without a respectful and thorough debate.

3. The third point of their commentary concerns the complementarity of third- and first-person approaches to the study of intuition. How can one disagree? But Schooler and Dougal implicitly assume I am one-sidedly for a purely subjective approach, which misinterprets what my wider research orientation is. In any case, in Schooler and Dougal's hands this desirable search for integration risks remaining mere lip service, if we follow their own conclusion that subjective experience has no place in any case (cf. 'the inherently non-verbalizable quality of the intuitive process', p. 285), except for a very peculiar idea that it is enough to 'just know' if the subject has used intuition.

Before speaking of a dreamed integration it is first necessary to break away from the prejudices that still dominate psychology, and truly make space for the description of experience by rigorous methods. Perhaps mine is not ideal, but at least it moves in the right direction. I think Schooler and Dougal grossly under-estimate the difficulty of this task, which is, nevertheless, the sole effective counter-balance for third-person empirical studies such as those that can be carried out with brain imaging.

Henley poses the delicate problem of the initial definition of a phenomenological object. She suggests that I should have better defined the object I wanted to study, and differentiated between intuition and insight. This distinction would have enabled me to avoid a number of what she considers incoherences (such as saying that the emergence of an intuition is unpredictable, while at the same time saying that this emergence can be prepared); it would also have allowed me to avoid a number of *ad hoc* hypotheses to solve such incoherences (for instance assuming that such preparation is necessarily unconscious).

On the contrary, I think that starting from a restrictive definition would be to go directly against the central phenomenological orientation of letting go all preconceptions in order to return to the experience itself. The commentary by Henley illustrates the opposite position well: she works from a number of implicit presuppositions, or more precisely, of implicit equivalences, which are well clarified by a phenomenological analysis.

In fact, the 'sudden' or 'unpredictable' characteristic, attributed to insight, hides several distinct experiential characteristics which are clarified in my study when discussion starts from the 'immediate' character of intuition. I proposed distinguishing very carefully between:

- The preparation: the fact that the emergence of an intuition can be prepared by a set of internal gestures leading to a state conducive to intuition. This capricious character appears in *all* the interviews I have examined.
- The progressive or sudden emergence of intuition: an intuition can appear all of a sudden, complete, or in a progressive. In the latter case knowledge appears as a premonition, an inner direction which acquires shape step by step.

The distinction that Henley introduces, on the one hand between the suddenness and unpredictability of insight, and on the other the progressive nature of intuition ('this preparation is clearly at odds with the suddenness of insight'), is based on a confusion of these different characteristics. As Henley herself reminds us, a number of scientific discoveries considered as insights (for instance the discovery of Fuchsian functions by Poincaré) were preceded by a preparatory phase of 'incubation'. And intuition and insight can be either sudden or progressive. A premonitory intuition can be sudden, and again the history of science is full of insights (in the sense of problem solving) which emerge in progressive manner, as a direction of research.

It is thus not necessary to assume that pre-intuitive gestures are unconscious in order to resolve a supposed contradiction between unpredictability and preparation. Intuition is unpredictable *and* various gestures are possible to favour its unpredictable emergence.

MENTAL FORCE AND THE ADVERTENCE OF BARE ATTENTION

Jeffrey M. Schwartz, UCLA Department of Psychiatry, 760 Westwood Plaza, Room 67-468, Los Angeles, CA 90024-1759, USA.   jmschwar@ucla.edu

I

The working hypothesis of this special issue of *Journal of Consciousness Studies* on 'The View from Within' — that the world of inner experience can be scientifically and systematically explored — represents the re-emergence of a perspective which, while once considered the foundation of all psychological research, has fallen on hard times throughout much of this now concluding century. There are a variety of reasons for this, some of them elegantly reviewed in the contributions to this issue by Varela & Shear and Vermersch, among others. But the predominant explanation for the orchestrated demeaning of first-person investigations during recent decades is rooted in the elevated role that the materialist perspective has ascended to in Western societies.

Among the many societal transformations that have occurred in conjunction with the cultural ascendance of the materialist view, one stands out as particularly compelling — the notion that what is essential to any valid explanation of naturally occurring phenomena is that it be based on data immediately derivable from the five senses. To those committed to the systematic investigation of inner experience this raises the not insignificant problem of validating, within the context of a predominant cultural norm, explanations using data which, while as immediate and as vivid as 'externally based' five sense data, do not neatly fit into the somewhat arbitrarily drawn boundaries that materialist science accepts as 'consensually verifiable'.

One of the great merits of this special issue of *JCS* is that it forthrightly attempts, with considerable success, to meet this difficulty head on and in terms largely drawn from a conceptual framework clearly based within the traditional confines of modern scientific investigation. For example, there is an emphasis throughout the issue on the systematic use of carefully structured intersubjective validation. This is highly laudable, especially insofar as it enhances the observational power and precision of the various investigators as well as their capacity to communicate the results of their studies fully and accurately. But an important question remains: are the power and beauty of enhanced communication of the methods and results of an investigation the primary justification for systematic attempts at consensually validating data? Or is consensual verification of outward impressions, as a *sine qua non* for the highly culturally esteemed title of 'scientific', a criterion so intuitively obvious that its sacred status need not even be subject to justification? Of course, this question leads directly to the massively complex issue of what constitute proper criteria for consensual verification, a subject far beyond my scope here.

The work of the French philosopher Maine de Biran, cited by Vermersch as the first modern psychologist, merits particular attention with regard to these matters. Biran observed, in constructing a response to Hume's scepticism concerning the nature of causation, that one's inner awareness of a causal relationship between the will to movement and bodily motion is so direct, vivid and spontaneous that it transcends the possibility of reasonable doubt. Whether this proposition is consensually verifiable raises issues of great significance, but one must acknowledge that there is a serious sense in which Biran's statement elicits as full and immediate a sense of agreement among honest observers as any statement concerning five-sense experience possibly could.

II

My work as a neuropsychiatrist over the past decade has mainly involved investigating obsessive-compulsive disorder (OCD), a brain related condition characterized by bothersome intrusive thoughts and urges which frequently lead to dysfunctional repetitive behaviours such as excessive hand washing or ritualistic counting and checking. My central research focus has involved brain imaging studies which have demonstrated systematic alterations in cerebral activity in OCD patients successfully treated with drug-free cognitive-behavioural therapy. Essential features of this treatment involve educating patients to regard the intrusion of OCD symptoms into consciousness as the manifestation of a 'false brain message', and training them to willfully select alternative behavioural responses when experiencing these bothersome thoughts and urges. This process of willful behavioural change requires significant training and practice in skillfully learning to refocus one's attention in response to the very bothersome intrusions into consciousness — intrusions which are very probably caused by brain biochemical imbalances. However, this training results in significant symptom relief over a period of ten weeks, accompanied by systematic changes in metabolic activity in brain circuits which have been implicated in OCD symptoms by a substantial amount of data collected over the past decade (Schwartz, 1998a).

'Consciousness is conscious of . . . that which affects it,' says Husserl (in a passage quoted by Varela). The experience of OCD (in contrast to the experience of schizophrenia, the profound complexities of which are intricately explored by the contribution of Naudin *et al.* to this issue) is one in which the 'boundaries of the self' are largely preserved — but they are transgressed, and with profound effects on inner consciousness, by viscerally disturbing thoughts and urges that mechanistically push one's attention towards phenomena which the sufferer finds both discomfiting and bizarre. For example, a typical attack of OCD could involve a person scrupulously inspecting his surroundings in search of minute quantities of possible contaminants, all the while almost entirely aware of the fact that the search concerns nothing of any real significance. In other words, during an attack of OCD, one's consciousness and attentional focus become profoundly affected by phenomena which are cognitively judged to be trivial. The key to successful psychological treatment is to willfully strengthen one's grasp of reality in order to take back control of the focus of one's attention.

To accomplish this requires precise 'management of the affect', by means not entirely dissimilar to those so ably described by Depraz, for the purpose of carefully modulating the relative balance and interpretation given to successive acts of mindfully directed inner and outer attention. The goal is to clearly recognize that the disturbing intrusions affecting one's consciousness are largely the result of faulty brain messages, and then to use that clear insight as a means of gently but forcefully refocusing one's attention on phenomena which are valued as genuinely worthy of conscious examination. The act of so doing on a consistent basis over several weeks has now been demonstrated to systematically alter the function of brain circuits which a large data base suggests are operating in a pathological manner in people with OCD (Schwartz, 1997). Ongoing investigations, being done in collaboration with physicist Henry Stapp (1998), take as a working hypothesis the involvement of a physically operating mental force in the generation of the measurable alterations in cerebral function which occur in conjunction with these willful changes in attentional and behavioural focus (Schwartz, 1999).

III

The traditional practice of Buddhist meditation is based on two broad categories of mental cultivation — Samatha (calmness/tranquillity, or quiescence, as Wallace translates the Sanskrit) and Vipassanā (insight). Both Wallace and Shear & Jevning eloquently discuss the role of developing tranquillity as a means of investigating consciousness. A brief mention of insight, which is specifically assigned the role of *purifying* consciousness in the Theravāda School of Buddhism, may suggest the potential for further developments in consciousness research. The German monk Nyanaponika Thera, a major figure of twentieth-century Buddhist scholarship, coined the term Bare Attention in order to precisely explain to Westerners the type of mental action required for the attainment of Vipassanā. 'Bare Attention is the clear and single-minded awareness of what actually happens *to* us and *in* us, at the successive moments of perception. It is called "bare", because it attends just to the bare facts of a perception as presented either through the five physical senses or through the mind . . . without reacting to them' (Nyanaponika Thera, 1962, p. 30). As a practical matter, it is the mental act of adverting attention in this manner which enables sufferers of OCD to develop the insight necessary for consciously choosing new and more adaptive responses to the intrusive and intensely bothersome thoughts and urges which bombard their consciousness. In this assertive act of the will they systematically alter their own brain chemistry through, as I have recently discussed (Schwartz, 1998b; 1999), the directed application of a specific and potentially measurable force of nature — mental force. These therapeutic acts of OCD sufferers provide paradigmatic examples of, to use Varela's eloquent phrase, 'the bootstrapping effect of action modifying the dynamical landscape' of both consciousness and its cerebral correlates. In this way, and here I use Varela's words not (as he does) metaphorically but literally, 'the walker and the path are intrinsically linked'.

References

Nyanaponika Thera (1962), *The Heart of Buddhist Meditation* (York Beach, ME: Samuel Weiser).

Schwartz, J.M. (1997), 'Cognitive-behavioral self-treatment for obsessive-compulsive disorder systematically alters cerebral metabolism: A mind-brain interaction paradigm for psychotherapists', in *Obsessive-Compulsive Disorders: Diagnosis, Etiology, Treatment*, ed. E. Hollander & D.J. Stein (New York: Marcel Dekker Inc.).

Schwartz, J.M. (1998a), 'Neuroanatomical aspects of cognitive-behavioral therapy response in obsessive-compulsive disorder: An evolving perspective on brain and behavior', *Br. J. Psychiatry*, **173** (suppl. 35), pp. 38–44.

Schwartz, J.M. (1998b), *A Return to Innocence: Philosophical Guidance in an Age of Cynicism* (New York: Harper Collins).

Schwartz, J.M. (1999), 'First steps toward a theory of mental force: PET imaging of systematic cerebral changes after psychological treatment of obsessive-compulsive disorder', in *Toward a Science of Consciousness III: The Third Tucson Discussions and Debates*, ed. S.R. Hameroff, A.W. Kaszniak, D.J. Chalmers (Cambridge, MA: MIT Press, forthcoming).

Stapp, H.P. (1998), Abstract and outline of talk at the Institute for Noetic Sciences, Sausalito, CA October 14, 1998. http://www-physics.lbl.gov/~stapp/abnoetics.txt

DOES PSYCHIATRY NEED THE HUSSERLIAN DETOUR?

Mark Sullivan, Dept. Of Psychiatry, University of Washington, Box 356560, Seattle WA 98915-6560, USA. Email: sullimar@u.washington.edu

Reading the article by Naudin *et al.* on Husserlian reduction in psychiatry prompted me to review a few chapters of my intellectual autobiography. I entered graduate school enamoured with Husserl, believing him a potent and necessary antidote to the hubris of the 'natural attitude' expounded by natural science. But I left graduate school believing that Husserl was too wrapped up in the debate as to whether reality was objective or subjective. Hence I ask in response to Naudin *et al.*: must we take on Husserl's Cartesian baggage only to shed it as we move from trascendental subjectivity to the life world to narrative? The Husserlian apparatus seems a needlessly complicated and convoluted tool for exploring the essentially social deficit of the schizophrenic. Perhaps the most valuable contribution of phenomenology to psychiatry is (as Varela states in his paper) its assiduous cultivation of 'beginner's mind' as it is often spoken of in Zen practice.

Let me begin with a clinical teaching strategy that I use with medical students and psychiatry residents. I will initally send them to see a psychotic patient in the emergency room with no information. Without a chart or diagnosis in hand, they are forced to grapple with the patient as a person. They do not begin by hearing the patient's words as symptoms of their mental illness; they try to have a conversation with the patient. Later, I will send them in to see a patient armed with chart, diagnosis, and clinical history. We will then contrast their approach to the patient when psychopathology is assumed and when it is not. This method does not achieve the presuppositionless state to which Husserl aspires but forces the student to recognize the contrast between professional and cultural presuppositions concerning interpersonal interactions. It allows them to contrast the dialogue typical of most conversation with the professional 'monologue on madness' (as Foucault has described it). This turn to the intrinsically social second-person perspective seems to me a more productive way to overcome the dichotomy between first-person and third-person psychiatric accounts than starting with transcendental subjectivity and then adding in the life world.

How are we to understand the transcendental reduction through which the split between the empirical subject and the transcendental subject is revealed? Does it reveal anything more than the difference between 'me' and 'I'? As we turn again to introspection as a method of inquiry, we would do well to remember the admonition of the natural scientist: thought experiments are not experiments. I wonder if we really can discover anything truly unexpected through Husserl's procedure of imaginative variation. Do we discover the essences of things in themselves or simply clarify the boundaries of our concepts and images? How could a strongly held belief be disconfirmed through such a procedure?

I find value in Jaspers' admonition to suspend explaining in favour of empathy and in Binswanger's critique of the primacy of the experience of the observer over the observed given by psychiatry. But I question whether the perspective of transcendental phenomenology is the best perspective to resolve this tension between the subject and the object? What if the 'whole constitutive structure . . . of the world, of reason, of truth and reality' that breaks down for the schizophrenic is intersubjective and not transcendental? What if the lesion is not a breakdown in constitutive subjectivity but a breakdown in dialogue, a rupture in the process by which the consensus of reality is achieved?

Are the processes of active and passive thematizing revealed by the transcendental reduction fundamentally the actions of individuals? Perhaps the intersubjective comes first with individual subjectivity derived from it. Naudin et al. acknowledge: 'Only a way which passes by way of the lifeworld is capable of taking account of the communitarian dimension of the experience of the reduction.' (p. 162) So we must ask whether the highly individualistic method of the Husserlian reduction is the best method to reveal the fundamentally social lesion of the schizophrenic: bizzare, profoundly isolated, incapable of empathy, with ideas immune to disconfirmation, almost completely cut off from social consensus? Why suspend the social to explore its absence?

Naudin et al. appear to consider this parallelism between the suspension of social reality in the transcendental reduction and in the schizophrenic as a strength, stating that the schizophrenic imposes a 'looking-glass reduction' on the psychiatrist : 'The rules of exchange (and the meaningful 'co-constitution' of situations) which habitually preside in the encounter with others in everyday life have been put in abeyance' (p. 167). It is true that this forces the attentive psychiatrist to doubt presuppositions she holds about competent dialogue. It does fracture the 'natural attitude' we use without thinking. But is this 'looking-glass reduction' anything more than naming the challenge involved in developing empathy with the schizophrenic? When confronted with the bizzare and disturbing, we seek refuge in naturalistic explanation. It is true that this grasping for explanation can interfere with empathy. But I believe Naudin *et al.* overstate their case when they say: 'Only the practice and the knowledge of the transcendental reduction is able to give the psychiatrist the means of interpreting the language, and more generally the behaviour of his patients, in so far as they are the expression of a fundamental disturbance of their experience.' This is only true if the 'fundamental disturbance' is understood in individualistic terms.

In *Madness and Modernism*, Louis Sass (1992) argues that schizophrenic manifests a hyper-subjectivity typical of modern times. So, we ask, why use a radically individualistic method to understand the pathological individualism of the schizophrenic? If we understand empathy to be both the lesion and the task, should we not pursue second-person perspectives and techniques? Empathy is a skill underrated and underdeveloped by a modern psychiatry preoccupied with nosology and biological mechanisms. As such it represents a challenge in psychiatric training.

If we are seeking to understand and restore the capacity for dialogue, isn't a more effective and radical method to give voice to the schizophrenic himself? This might include newsletters by and for schizophrenics, care by the remitted for the afflicted, and other self-help models (cf. Podroll, 1990).

References

Podroll, E.M. (1990), *The Seduction of Madness* (New York: HarperCollins).
Sass, L. (1992), *Madness and Modernism* (New York: Basic Books).

REPLY TO SULLIVAN
J. Naudin

We share Sullivan's opinion when he affirms (with Varela) that the most important contribution of Husserlian phenomenology to psychiatry is the cultivation of the beginner's mind. And we also agree with him that a second-person perspective is essential in order to ground an empathic access to what is proper to schizophrenic experience. Yet he parts company with us in our view that phenomenological reduction can provide such an access. For Sullivan, phenomenology constitutes a useless detour, forever trapped in solipsism, since the eidetic progress would be non-scientific by being irrefutable and constitutionally *ad hoc*. Sullivan appropriately reminds us that 'thought experiments are not experiments'. But we would like to ask back: what is psychiatry if not an uninterrupted succession of 'thought experiments'?

In our paper we merely follow Binswanger when he says that the role of phenomenology in psychiatry is none other than to help the psychiatric practice to have consciousness of itself. What psychiatrists carry out are 'thought experiments' regarding non-corporeal, affective intersubjective life. This is based on imaginary variations which are born from intersubjective encounters. This constitutive intersubjectivity is not limited to dialogue, and the way to comprehend it cannot be reduced to the articulation of an 'I' and 'Thou' in the Buberian sense, or an 'I' and an 'I–me' in a Jamesian sense. Its comprehensive understanding leads us to explore the transcendental foundations of the world within intersubjectivity. As Schutz has already shown, the trans-cendental and eidetic methods are insufficient to give access to this intersubjective dimension that determines both the psychiatrists' experience and the basic psychiatric problem. Thus we do not intend to *apply* Husserlian phenomenology literally. Our interest is to follow in its main 'spirit': we propose that this spirit is naturally invoked when we encounter a 'person with schizophrenia'. Thus we do not so much think of Husserl and his philosophy, but we address the very foundation of the world — the central spirit of this philosophy.

To explore this question demands a momentary and paradoxical suspension — since it is done *a deux* — of social living. This suspension cannot, of course, be sustained for long, and psychiatric experience attests to this impossibility. Since we share with Sullivan the need to anchor the necessary analysis in intersubjectivity, we have tried to find the appropriate words to describe all these phenomena (such as 'transcendental reduction', 'schizophrenic reduction', 'impossibility of maintaining the attitude of reduction in the real world', 'dialogue based on a common horizon') which go along with our actual psychiatric encounters. It may happen that such words appear bigger, more ridiculous or scary than the phenomena themselves, but we have not been able to do better. And they give us the advantage that they are parallel to the pathways of exploration followed by Husserl and his successors. The experiences behind these words can be found in the difficulties that the schizophrenic finds accessing worldly social life, and, conversely, those which find the philosopher and the psychiatrist becoming detached from their ordinary social life in order to describe it, whence the term 'specular epochè'.

In brief, it is vain to invoke a supposed Husserlian solipsism to make us say what we never said. We never affirmed that reduction can replace the contributions of people touched by schizophrenia. On the contrary, we are in favour of 'self-help models', that we find more pertinent for psychiatric practice than Husserlian abstractions. However it is the critical spirit of this philosophy which is sorely needed in modern psychiatry, for it provides a critical perspective for the understanding of the inter-subjective foundations of this science, and it contributes to the validation of such analyses not only by ethical, but also by methodological criteria.

INTERSUBJECTIVE SCIENCE

Max Velmans, Department of Psychology, Goldsmiths, University of London, New Cross, London SE14 6NW, UK. Email: m.velmans@gold.ac.uk

Abstract: The study of consciousness in modern science is hampered by deeply ingrained, dualist presuppositions about the nature of consciousness. In particular, conscious experiences are thought to be private and subjective, contrasting with physical phenomena which are public and objective. In the present article, I argue that *all* observed *phenomena* are, in a sense, private to a given observer, although there are some *events* to which there is public access. Phenomena can be objective in the sense of intersubjective, investigators can be objective in the sense of truthful or dispassionate, and procedures can be objective in being well-specified, but observed phenomena cannot be objective in the sense of being observer-free. Phenomena are only repeatable in the sense that they are judged by a community of observers to be tokens of the same type. Stripped of its dualist trappings the empirical method becomes *if you carry out these procedures you will observe or experience these results —* which applies as much to a science of consciousness as it does to physics.

From the time that Descartes separated the conscious mind (*res cogitans*) from the material world (*res extensa*) consciousness has been thought by many to be beyond science. The problems which need to be addressed by a 'science of consciousness' are of three kinds:

1. Epistemological problems: How can one obtain public, objective knowledge about private, subjective experiences?
2. Methodological problems: Given that one cannot attach measuring instruments directly up to experiences, what methods are appropriate to their study?
3. The relation of the observer to the observed: The more closely-coupled an observer is with an observed, the greater the potential influence of the act of observation on the nature of the observed (observer effects). Given this, how can one develop introspective and phenomenological methods where the observer *is* the observed?

Many established methods for investigating conscious experiences within cognitive science and neuropsychology are reviewed in Velmans (1996a) and Cohen & Schooler (1997). This issue of the *Journal of Consciousness Studies* focuses on the development of new phenomenological methods which attempt to grapple with observer/observed interactions. An extensive treatment of methodological issues is also forthcoming in Velmans (1999a). Given the limits of available space in this article, I will restrict myself to the epistemological problems. Broadly, I will argue that the epistemological problems posed by a 'science of consciousness' are largely artefactual, arising from a misconceived dualism that we have inherited from Descartes. This is clearly shown in the model of perception shown in Figure 1. This 'splits' the world in two ways: (1) the observer (on the right of the diagram) is clearly separated from the observed (the light on the left of the diagram) and (2) public, objective 'physical phenomena' in the external world or in the brain (in the lower part of the diagram) are clearly separated from private, subjective psychological phenomena 'in the mind' (represented by the cloud in the upper part of the diagram).

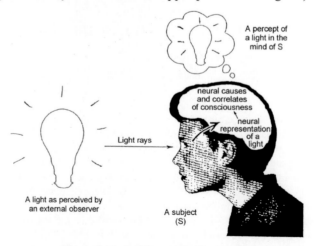

Figure 1. A dualist model of perception.

How we make sense of this in conventional studies of perception

Following usual procedures, a subject (S) is asked to focus on the light and report on or respond to what she experiences, while the experimenter (E) controls the stimulus and tries to observe what is going on in the subject's brain. E has observational access to the stimulus and to S's brain states, but has no access to what S experiences. In principle, other experimenters can also observe the stimulus and S's brain states. Consequently, what E has access to is thought of as 'public' and 'objective.' However, E does not have access to S's experiences, making them 'private' and 'subjective' and a problem for science. This apparently radical difference in the epistemic *status* of the data accessible to E and S is enshrined in the words commonly used to describe what they perceive. That is, E makes *observations*, whereas S merely has *subjective experiences*.

Although this way of looking at things is adequate as a working model for many studies, it actually misdescribes the phenomenology of consciousness, and consequently misconstrues the problems posed by a science of consciousness. An alternative model of the way events in the world are experienced by subjects is shown in the *reflexive* model of perception in Figure 2.

This reflexive model accepts conventional wisdom about the physical and neurophysiological causes of perception — for example, that there really is a physical stimulus in the room that our experience of it *represents*. But it gives a different account of the nature of the resulting experience. According to this nondualist view, when S attends to the light in a room she does not have an experience *of* a light 'in her head or brain', with its attendant problems for science. She just sees a light in a room. Indeed, what the subject experiences is very similar to what the experimenter experiences when he gazes at the light (she just sees the light from a different angle) — in spite of the different terms they use to describe what they perceive (a 'physical stimulus' versus a 'sensation of light'). If so, there can be no actual difference in the 'subjective' versus 'objective' status of the light *phenomenologically* 'experienced' by S and 'observed' by E. I have developed the case for this and analysed its consequences elsewhere (Velmans, 1993, 1996b, 1999b). However, one can easily grasp the essential similarities between S's 'subjective experiences' and E's 'objective observations' from the fact that *the roles of S and E are interchangeable.*

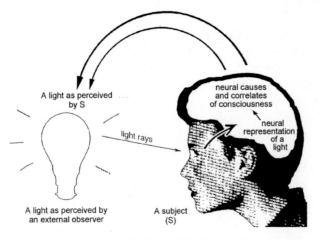

Figure 2. A reflexive model of perception.

A thought experiment: 'changing places'

What makes one human being a 'subject' and another an 'experimenter'? Their different roles are defined largely by *differences in their interests* in the experiment, reflected in differences in what they are required to do. The subject is required to focus only on her *own* experiences (of the light), which she needs to respond to or report on in an appropriate way. The experimenter is interested primarily in the *subject's* experiences, and in how these depend on the light stimulus or brain states that he can observe.

To exchange roles, S and E merely have to turn their heads, so that E focuses exclusively on the light and describes what he experiences, while S focuses her attention not just on the light (which she now thinks of as a 'stimulus') but also on events she can observe in E's brain, and on E's reports of what he experiences. In this situation, E becomes the 'subject' and S becomes the 'experimenter'. Following current conventions, S would now be entitled to think of her observations (of the light and E's brain) as 'public and objective' and to regard E's experiences of the light as 'private and subjective'.

However, this outcome is absurd, as the phenomenology of the light remains the same, viewed from the perspective of either S or E, whether it is *thought of* as an 'observed stimulus' or as an 'experience'. Nothing has changed in the character of the light that E and S can observe other than the focus of their interest. That is, in terms of *phenomenology* there is no difference between 'observed phenomena' and 'experiences'. This raises a fundamental question: If the phenomenology of the light remains the same whether it is thought of a 'physical stimulus' or an 'experience', is the phenomenon *private and subjective* or is it *public and objective*?

All experiences are private and subjective.

I do not have direct access to your experiences and you do not have direct access to mine. For example I cannot experience your pain, your thoughts, your colour qualia, the way your body feels to you, the way the sky looks to you, the way I look to you, and so on. I can only have my own experiences (however well I empathize). The privacy and subjectivity of each individual's experience is well accepted in philosophy of mind. It seems to be a fundamental given of how we are situated in the world.

In dualism, 'experiences' are private and subjective, while 'physical phenomena' are public and objective as noted above. However, according to the reflexive model there is no *phenomenal* difference between physical phenomena and our experiences *of* them. When we turn our attention to the external world, physical phenomena just *are* what we experience. If so, there is a sense in which physical phenomena are 'private and subjective' just like the other things we experience. For example, I cannot experience your phenomenal mountain or your phenomenal tree. I only have access to my own phenomenal mountain and tree. Similarly, I only have access to my own phenomenal light stimulus and my own observations of its physical properties (in terms of meter readings of its intensity, frequency, and so on). That is, we *each live in our own private, phenomenal world*. Few, I suspect, would disagree.

Public access to observed entities and events; public phenomena in the sense of similar, shared, private experiences.

If we each live in our own private, phenomenal world then each 'observation' is, in a sense, private. This was evident to the father of operationalism, the physicist P.W. Bridgman (1936), who concluded that, in the final analysis, 'science is only my private science'. However, this is clearly not the whole story. When an entity or event is placed beyond the body surface (as the entities and events studied by physics usually are) it can be perceived by any member of the public suitably located in space and time. Under these circumstances such entities or events are 'public' in the sense that there is *public access* to the observed entity or event *itself*.

This distinction between the *phenomena* perceived by any given observer and the entity or event *itself* is important. In the reflexive model, perceived phenomena *represent* things-themselves, but are not identical to them. The light perceived by E and S, for example, can be described in terms of its perceived brightness and colour. But, in terms of physics, the stimulus is better described as electromagnetism with a given mix of energies and frequencies. As with all visually observed phenomena, the phenomenal light only *becomes* a phenomenal light once the stimulus interacts with an appropriately structured visual system — and the result of this observed–observer interaction is a light as-experienced which is private to the observer in the way described above. However, if the stimulus itself is beyond the body surface and has an independent existence, it remains there *to be* observed whether it is observed (at a given moment) or not. That is why the stimulus itself is *publicly accessible* in spite of the fact that each observation/experience of it is private to a given observer.

To the extent that observed entities and events are subject to similar perceptual and cognitive processing in different human beings, it is also reasonable to assume a degree of *commonality* in the way such things are experienced. While each experience remains private, it may be a private experience that others share. For example, unless observers are suffering from red/green colour blindness, we normally take it for granted that they perceive electromagnetic stimuli with wavelength of 700 nanometers as red and those of 500 nanometers as green. Given the privacy of light phenomenology there is no way to be certain that others experience 'red' and 'green' as we do ourselves (the classical problem of the inverted spectrum and 'other minds'). But in normal life, and in the practice of science, we adopt the working assumption that the same stimulus, observed by similar observers, will produce similar observations or experiences. Thus, while experienced entities and events (phenomena) remain private to each observer, if their perceptual, cognitive and other observing apparatus is similar, we assume that their experiences (of a given stimulus) are similar. Consequently, experienced phenomena may be 'public' in the special sense that other observers have similar or shared experiences.

Being clear about what is private and what is public

- There is only *private* access to individual observed or experienced *phenomena*.

- There can be *public* access to the entities and events which serve as the stimuli for such phenomena (the entities and events which the phenomena represent). This applies, for example, to the entities and events studied by physics.

- If the perceptual, cognitive and other observing apparatus of different observers are similar, we assume that their experiences (of a given stimulus) are similar. In this special sense, experienced phenomena may be *public* in so far as they are *similar or shared private experiences*.

From subjectivity to intersubjectivity

This re-analysis of private versus public phenomena also provides a natural way to think about the relation between *subjectivity* and *intersubjectivity*. Each (private) observation or experience is necessarily *subjective*, in that it is always the observation or experience of a *given* observer, viewed and described from his or her individual perspective. However, once that experience is shared with another observer it can become *inter*-subjective. That is, through the sharing of a similar experience, subjective views and descriptions of that experience potentially converge, enabling intersubjective agreement about what has been experienced.

How different observers establish intersubjectivity through negotiating agreed descriptions of shared experiences is a complex process that we do not need to examine here. Suffice it to say that it involves far more than shared experience. One also needs a shared language, shared cognitive structures, a shared world-view or scientific paradigm, shared training and expertise and so on. To the extent that an experience or observation can be *generally* shared (by a community of observers), it can form part of the data base of a communal science.

Different meanings of the term 'objective' that are used in science

According to the analysis above, phenomena in science can be 'objective' in the sense of *intersubjective*. Note, however, that intersubjectivity requires the presence of subjectivity rather than its absence. Observation statements (descriptions of observations) can also be 'objective' in the sense of being dispassionate, accurate, truthful, and so on. Scientific method can also be 'objective' in the sense that it follows well-specified, repeatable procedures (perhaps using standard measuring instruments). However, if the above analysis is correct, one cannot make observations without engaging the experiences and cognitions of a conscious subject (unobserved meter readings are not 'observations'). If so, science cannot be 'objective' in the sense of being *observer-free*.

Intra-subjective and inter-subjective repeatability

According to the reflexive model, there is no phenomenal difference between *observations* and *experiences*. Each observation results from an interaction of an observer with an observed. Consequently, each observation is *observer-dependent* and *unique*. This applies even to observations made by the same observer, of the same entity or event, under the same observation conditions, *at different times* — although, under these circumstances, the observer may have no doubt that he/she is making *repeated* observations of the same entity or event.

If the conditions of observation are sufficiently standardized an observation may be *repeatable* within a community of (suitably trained) observers, in which case intersubjectivity can be established by collective *agreement*. Once again, though, it is important to note that different observers cannot have an *identical* experience. Even if they observe the same event, at the same location, at the same time, they each have their own, unique experience. *Inter*subjective repeatability resembles *intra*subjective repeatability in that it merely requires observations to be sufficiently similar to be taken for 'tokens' of the same 'type'. This applies particularly to observations in science, where repeatability typically requires intersubjective agreement amongst scientists observing similar events at *different* times and in *different* geographical locations.

Consequences of the above analysis for a science of consciousness

The above provides an account of the empirical method — i.e. of what scientists actually do when they test their theories, establish *intersubjectivity, repeatability* and so on — which accepts that observed, physical phenomena just *are* the entities and events that scientists experience. Although I have focused on physical events, this analysis applies also to the investigation of events that are usually thought of as 'mental' or 'psychological'. Although the methodologies appropriate to the study of physical and mental phenomena may be very different, the same *epistemic* criteria can be applied to their scientific investigation. Physical phenomena and mental (psychological) phenomena are just different kinds of phenomena which observers experience (whether they are experimenters or subjects). $S_{1 \text{ to } n}$ might, for example, all report that a given increase in light intensity produces a just noticeable difference in brightness, an experience/observation that is intersubjective and repeatable. Alternatively, $S_{1 \text{ to } n}$ might all report that a given anaesthetic removes pain or, if they stare at a red light spot, that a green after-image appears, making such phenomena similarly public, intersubjective, and repeatable.

This epistemic closure of psychological with physical phenomena is self-evident in situations where the same phenomenon can be thought of as either 'physical' or 'psychological' depending on one's interest in it. At first glance, for example, a visual

Figure 3. A visual illusion 'Flying Squirrel', produced by Dr. Kitaoka, available on URL

http://www.akita-u.ac.jp/~kmori/img/kmori@ipc.akita-u.ac.jp

illusion of the kind shown in Figure 3, might seem to present difficulties, for the reason that physical and psychological descriptions of this phenomenon conflict.

Physically, the figure consists entirely of squares, joined in straight lines, while subjectively, most of the central lines in the figure seem to be bent. However, the physical and psychological descriptions result from two different observation procedures. To obtain the physical description, an experimenter E typically places a straight edge against each line, thereby obscuring the cues responsible for the illusion and providing a fixed reference against which the curvature of each line can be judged. To confirm that the lines are actually straight, other experimenters ($E_{1 \text{ to } n}$) can repeat this procedure. In so far as they each observe the line to be straight under these conditions, their observations are public, intersubjective and repeatable.

But, the fact that the lines *appear* to be bent (once the straight edge is removed) is similarly public, intersubjective and repeatable (amongst subjects $S_{1 \text{ to } n}$). Consequently, the illusion can be investigated using relatively conventional scientific procedures, in spite of the fact that the *illusion* is unambiguously *mental*. One can, for example, simply move the straight edge outside the figure making it seem parallel to the bent central lines — thereby obtaining a measure of the angle of the illusion.

The empirical method

In short, once the *empirical method* is stripped of its dualist trappings, it applies as much to the science of consciousness as it does to the science of physics in that it adheres to one, fundamental principle. Stated formally:

> If observers $E_{1 \text{ to } n}$ (or subjects $S_{1 \text{ to } n}$), carry out procedures $P_{1 \text{ to } n}$, under observation conditions $O_{1 \text{ to } n}$, they should observe (or experience) result R

(assuming that $E_{1 \text{ to } n}$ and $S_{1 \text{ to } n}$ have similar perceptual and cognitive systems, that $P_{1 \text{ to } n}$ are the procedures which specify the nature of the experiment or investigation, and that $O_{1 \text{ to } n}$ includes *all* relevant background conditions, including those internal to the observer, such as their attentiveness, the paradigm within which they are trained to make observations and so on).

Put informally, empirical investigation of external or inner events is simply this:

If you carry out these procedures you will observe or experience these results.

References

Bridgman, P.W. (1936), *The Nature of Physical Theory* (Princeton, NJ: Princeton University Press).
Cohen, J.D. and Schooler, J.W. (ed. 1997), *Scientific Approaches to Consiousness* (Hillsdale, NJ: Lawrence Erlbaum).
Velmans, M. (1993), 'A reflexive science of consciousness', in *Experimental and Theoretical Studies of Consciousness. CIBA Foundation Symposium 174* (Chichester: Wiley).
Velmans, M. (ed. 1996a), *The Science of Consciousness: Psychological, Neuropsychological and Clinical Reviews* (London: Routledge).
Velmans, M. (1996b), 'What and where are conscious experiences?', in *The Science of Consciousness: Psychological, Neuropsychological and Clinical Reviews*, ed. M. Velmans (London: Routledge).
Velmans, M. (ed. 1999a), *Investigating Phenomenal Consciousness: New Methodologies and Maps* (Amsterdam: John Benjamins, forthcoming).
Velmans, M. (1999b), *Understanding Consciousness* (London: Routledge, forthcoming).

EDITORS' REJOINDER TO THE DEBATE

Francisco Varela and Jonathan Shear

The numerous commentators to this Special Issue have greatly enhanced its focus and usefulness. We thank them all very sincerely for their efforts. Within the restricted space of this rejoinder we cannot respond in detail to all the issues raised. Instead, we shall concentrate first on some fundamental criticisms. The remaining additions and complementary ideas will only be touched on briefly, merely to see them in perspective.

We shall start with our two main critics of the global enterprise, Baars and Nixon. They both offer arguments that our enterprise is misguided, but their arguments fall on two opposite extremes: empirical and hermeneutical.

Baars: Criticism from the empirical side

Before we proceed, we should point out that some readers might be surprised that Baars figures on the critics roster, given that he is one of the active figures in the resurgence of the study of consciousness. Thus, he is not a critic coming from a position that claims to eliminate any possible participation of first-person research, as several other workers have argued (such as T. Metzinger, D. Dennett, and F. Crick among others). More interestingly, Baars' criticism concerns the necessary ingredients for carrying out a fruitful project for the study of consciousness. Thus his remarks come from a view concerned with the first-person perspective, and are therefore all the more interesting. He criticizes us for two main points: (1) lack of continuity with previous work, (2) unnecessary complication, since first-person methods have been used already as straightforward reporting of experiences — and that's all we need.

Baars takes our endeavour as standing somehow outside or disjointed from modern cognitive neuroscience and its historical sources in experimental psychology, classical sensory physiology, and cognitive neuroscience, which together he succinctly refers to as 'psychology'. To be sure, as Baars says, one can read a number of papers in psychology from the angle of what they actually do, and not what they say they do. Baars brings up work ranging from sensory measurements to higher mental contents (memory, imagery). He urges us 'not to start from scratch'. But this bears no relation to our intention, as plainly stated in the Introduction, where first-person approaches are naturally seen as *complementary* to what we have learned from third-person approaches, including all of 'psychology'. The real challenge, as we see it, is to build the necessary *circulation* between first- and third-person, a proper neurophenomenology. This salutary stance, which we share with Baars, is, however, a far cry from the actual traditions of 'psychology' that have sorely neglected the methods required for a significant first-person access. So we are not about starting from scratch; we are instead demanding the necessary complement for what is *missing*.

That there is a lot missing is also conceded by Baars, but he assumes that the required explorations will simply happen as 'psychology' continues to advance, by some sort of inevitable continuity if not plain luck. The fact is, however, that apart from the early days of the twentieth century (James and Husserl), and the introspectionist schools who tried to construct a first-person discipline, psychology and neuroscience have done precious little to study the structure of subjective experience

beyond what can be gleamed from verbal questioning and behavioural measurements. Baars considers this a very good basis, but this remains only a hopeful claim.
Our point is that such studies can be useful *only* if we extend, cultivate, and expand
first-person methods beyond the current techniques of questioning. This is where we
differ: to say that what psychologists often do is already first-person study misses the
point. Modern research remains mostly silent about first-person data because it is
data we still hardly know how to collect and frame. Thus Baars' 'reportability'
becomes the default strategy. But we insist that recourse to this default strategy is the
result of our current lack of sophistication in the face of the complexity implicit in
human experience, as the material presented in the Special Issue precisely attests.

Does this mean that good old neural mechanisms are not useful for first-person
approaches? Of course they are, as Varela for example shows explicitly in his study of
the experience of present time. But the relation between the third-person and a full
fledged analysis of experience is not simply a given: it requires hard work and
improved methods. Baars thinks current practices will suffice, but offers no direct
arguments. Why should one think that, even with all it has to offer, that 'psychology'
is all we need? It systematically misled research into the long period of the rigid
dogma of behaviourism, and later on to cognitivism, whose methodology reflects
reliance on mere verbal reports. In fact, little in 'psychology' is of *direct* help for what
we are considering here.

Baars also points out that the judgements of human subjects about their experience
can be accurate. This is of course true to some extent. But again this is missing the
point: the need for a first-person methodology arises because that kind of reporting is
not *enough* to exhaust what is accessible to humans in their daily experience, as the
article by Peugeot makes clear in this Special Issue. The peripheral and pre-reflexive
will remain unknown unless they are actively included in our scientific study of consciousness, and no miracle will make this happen by itself. Yes, the Editors know as
well as everybody else that modern neuroscience and brain imaging can be in good
coherence with certain aspects of subjective experience. But in order for this to be
more than a mere rough correspondence, more refined levels of description of human
experience have to be developed and utilized. Yet there is not one published study
with fMRI, PET or EEG/MEG where the 'subjective' is anything other than more or
less sophisticated report-forms. Verbal reporting following a questionnaire is one
thing, learning to discern less-than-obvious subjective experience is quite another.
Clearly both approaches will be essential components of a mature science that
includes first-person methods.

To remain at the current level of analysis would mean that we assimilate subjective
experience to the mere description of what appears for the casual untrained subject
when questioned. But it is one thing to take a minimalist stance where one submits a
subject to contrasting conditions, and quite another when we are concerned with a
complete, open description of the structure of experience. If we are to build on what is
known, this is precisely where we need to learn from the lessons gathered by Husserl
and phenomenological psychology and from traditions of meditation. Baars, too,
notes such a need, but only, it seems, as an afterthought. We, on the other hand,
emphasize its importance explicitly as the major, generally missing component in the
scientific practice of 'psychology'. Why neglect these parallel traditions that mark so
clearly a missing dimension from 'psychology'? We have everything to gain from

incorporating the experience and methods that make such extensions possible, instead of relying on a rain check for 'psychology'. Although it would be much easier to rely on this tradition alone, one cannot but be sceptical here of a scientific field that has long been marked by a scientism that has often led it to too-limited notions of what is to be taken as 'scientifically correct'.

The good news, then, is that we can build on what we know in order to approach what we don't. But let's not continue blindly on the same track without acknowledging that subjective experience is much richer than psychology (apart from the rare witness of a James or a Husserl) has tried to make us believe. This is not a very productive strategy. We need to move from a cavalier attitude to human experience to a methodological one whose rigour matches its complexity.

Nixon: Criticism from the hermeneutical side

Nixon confronts the entire enterprise of this special issue with what he calls the 'hermeneutical garrote'. He passionately argues that nothing we call 'experience' escapes the gridlock of language, and that beyond language there is nothing we can refer to. Whence his main criticism that the enterprise of examining 'experience as such' is misguided, that it is a 'monumental mistake'.

As we gladly admitted in the Introduction, this hermeneutic objection cannot be simply shrugged off. It can only be lived with. The question that is left open is whether Nixon's radical stance is the only space in which we can live, or whether there is not an appropriate, more open-ended tolerance for the complexity of the question and its possible transformations. Language is a central dimension of our being as human beings, this much is quite clear. But this is not the same as claiming that language is the only frame for human experience. Is nothing consciously apprehended apart from a linguistic web? It is one thing to acknowledge the importance of language, it is another to give it an absolute role.

Our attitude was to take a *pragmatic* approach, and continue to carry out the inquiry and let the role of language be clarified in action rather than an *a priori* conclusion. Stated in other terms, to the hermeneutical circle we offer in contrast the 'experiential circle': even if experience has, already and always, a linguistic ground, what in experience does this linguistic activity work upon? This is never made clear by Nixon, and we still have no reason to refrain from a pragmatic, hands-on approach as favoured in this Special Issue.

This can be made even more apparent if we focus on Nixon's sharp distinction between (reflectively) conscious (accessible to language) and nonconscious (inaccessible to language and therefore unknowable). In a telling sentence he says: 'It can be said that any experience which does not separate an inner subject from an outer world is probably a continuum of sensation in which environmental stimulus and instinctive response are experienced as a unity; it may be "lived experience" but it is experience "lived" non-consciously' (p. 258). What is ignored here, of course, is the very concrete possibility that there is a pre-reflective, pre-noetic consciousness. This is not a mere *a priori* or logical question. It really is a matter of examination of experience, as done in phenomenology and empirical studies. Even if what we can provide as evidence does not amount to an airtight proof for the manifestation of pre-reflective consciousness, the evidence and arguments are quite substantial. It allows us to begin to consider the intermediate possibility beyond the hermeneutical garrote that there is such as thing as experience which is not reflectively expressed (thus in language), and yet it is not unconscious.

Further comments and additions

A number of contributors provided various supporting remarks to the overall enterprise. Thus Austin touches on what seem to him six important problems in the way of the study of consciousness, based both on his life-long career in neurology and in Zen practice, as recently developed in a major work, *Zen and the Brain*. Austin's testimony highlights, more than anything, the need for a sustained, disciplined training in order to be able to enter into explorations that are otherwise unthinkable. Claxton addresses the issue of the relation between the scientific and the traditional version of the human capacity for transformation, and pleads for an increased role of scientific narratives to escape 'tribal' expressions. Haney offers an extended discussion on how the kind of comparative approach proposed by Shear and Jevning constitutes a challenge to the traditional Derridian criticism of the notion of pure experience. As Haney points out, the experiences of Zen and TM meditators described by Shear and Jevning suggest a model that literary and cultural theorists may find useful in testing their knowledge-about experience. Hut provides a lucid account of the way in which third- and first-person views co-exist in the midst of every-day life with mirrors and writings pens. His call for an extended community of observers engaged in 'communal reduction' is well taken, and one of the hopes of this special issue as a whole. Pickering offers a number of comments on the various fields where first- and third-person methods can circulate. As he points out, this circulation is highly contextual to the kind of human experience under study, and he particular raises doubts about the extent to which contemplative practices such as *shamatha* can be detached from their soteriological embedding. Schwartz takes the overall enterprise of the Special Issue approvingly and frames a number of interesting questions on the basis of his clinical work on obsessive-compulsive disorder (OCD). This allows him to put his finger on the crucial two-way circulation between the experiential and the neurochemical, as a two-way street wherein change is possible both in clinical practice and in meditative training.

A few authors contribute what can be called an opening and extensions beyond what has been introduced in the articles of this special issue.

Galin invites a careful examination of the problem of entiticity, that is, the entity whose point of view is being considered. Entiticity is problematic because division into entities (subject/object) is problematic. It is, he holds, always a fiction, a matter of degree, a matter of convention and a matter of heuristic. If one calls a human being an entity and does not identify all of these conditionalities, this invites much of the confusion and the apparent paradoxes that have surrounded this topic. This confusion is exemplified when one considers the perspective of consciousness (or the conscious entity, however defined) to be co-extensive with the perspective of 'the human being'. Galin proposes that there are several further dimensions of sub-entiticity in what one may call a 'human being'. In each case, interpreting the phenomenal data depends on identifying the entity that should be said to host it (the person? its left hemisphere? the unconscious?). This links very clearly to our discussion with Baars: awareness (first-person data) is not homogeneous. One question it is obvious to ask is this: when considering the human/consciousness entity, what is there about *its* first-personness that is special to it — that is different from the first-personness of entities such as a bat, a brick or a computer?

Gendlin brings in a broad theoretical re-formulation of consciousness and bodies, and more importantly, a number of years of pioneering work in first-person approach expressed in his technique of *focussing*, an explicit pragmatics of a 'bodily explicating' in which subjects learn to articulate more of what they are living through by attending to what they physically sense, especially in moments of silence, but are not yet able to articulate. We are grateful to Gendlin for his commentary, since his work must surely count as one of the pioneering steps towards a third-first-person science. In this issue, the interviewing technique used by Peugeot and Ginsburg's directly physical-interactive method both display kinship with Gendlin's process-oriented 'focusing' methodology. Together they point to the potential value of working with second-person approaches in a sustained and rigorous manner. Of additional significance for this Special Issue is Gendlin's decision to frame his work within a phenomenological context. One cannot but see the usefulness of cultivating a dialogue between first-person, phenomenological, and objective third-person approaches that goes beyond the traditional stereotype of continental versus Anglo-American opposition.

Velmans adds a much-needed discussion of the epistemological status of first-person methods and the perennial question of the 'inaccessible' nature of lived experience. Our emphasis is on the pragmatics of the first-person data, and Velmans' extension gives a theoretical basis to the methodology essential for future progress. Indeed, as is becoming more and more clear, this supposed inaccessibility is but a paper tiger, an illusion that only good work will remove, but will do so rather quickly. This, again, is the spirit of this Special Issue. As Velmans points out: 'In terms of phenomenology there is no difference between "observed phenomena" and "experiences"' (p. 302). This initially surprising statement becomes almost obvious once we properly take into account the inextricably social nature of science. Time and good work, we surmise, will soon make it apparent that the received sharp boundary between private-subjective and public-objective is as misleading as the sharp boundary between 'dead' and 'living' matter once was.

Mangan introduces in his comment a point which amounts to an overlooked strength implicit in first-person investigation. That is the fact 'that explanatory phenomenology can be completely scientific without *necessarily* having to (1) consider the neural substrate, (2) employ reductive arguments, or (3) operate at the third-person level' (p. 249; original emphasis). If, as Mangan forcefully argues, this is true, then the force and resources of first-person investigations are enhanced a good bit. To this end Mangan offers his own work on the exploration of fringe consciousness, and arrives at the plausible conclusions that a fundamental property of consciousness is that: '*At the deepest level, consciousness IS the limited but infinitely plastic capacity to articulate experience*' (p. 251; original emphasis). This structural description, based on resource allocation in a dynamics setting, is stance-independent. Such a conclusion comes solely from first-person data, but heavily constrains the kinds of (third-person) neural bases that can give rise to it. The mutual constraint loop proper to neurophenomenological analysis is thus productively enhanced.

INDEX

ABOUT AUTHORS

Andrew Bailey received his PhD in philosophy in 1998 from the University of Calgary, where is currently a sessional instructor. His dissertation focused on the problem of reconciling phenomenal consciousness with physicalism. He also has strong interests in William James and metaphysics and has published a dozen philosophical papers in addition to commentaries and reviews.

Natalie Depraz is based at CREA, Ecole Polytechnique, in Paris. Her publications include *Transcendance et incarnation, le statut de l'intersubjectivité comme altérité à soi chez Edmund Husserl* (1995).

Carl Ginsburg received his PhD in chemistry from Ohio University in Athens, Ohio, in 1964. After a career in teaching at Syracuse University he undertook training by Dr Moshe Feldenkrais, who emphasizes the development of human awareness through movement and action. Carl Ginsburg currently directs professional training in the Feldenkrais method in Heidelberg, Germany, in Lewes, UK, and in Atlanta, GA.

Jean Naudin, PhD, MD, is at Laboratoire de Neuropsychologie et Neurophysiologie, Faculté de Médecine de la Timone, in Marseille, France. Recent publications include *Phénoménologie et psychiatrie. Les voix et la chose* (1997).

Claire Petitmengin-Peugeot, DEA in philosophy and DESS in computer science, is associate professor of information systems design and knowledge representation at the Institut National des Télécommunications in Paris. She has recently completed a doctoral thesis in cognitive science on the subject of intuitive experience.

Jonathan Shear, managing editor of *JCS*, teaches philosophy at Virginia Commonwealth University. He has a PhD from UC Berkeley, was a Fulbright Scholar in philosophy of science at the London School of Economics, and has complemented his analytical work with the practice of Eastern experiential procedures for over thirty years. Publications include books and articles in philosophy, psychology and religion.

Francisco Varela holds a PhD in biological science from Harvard University. His interests lie at the crossroads of cognitive neuroscience, philosophy of mind and mathematics, areas where his contribution has became well known through numerous publications including (with E. Thompson and E. Rosch) *The Embodied Mind*. He is now Senior Researcher with the National Centre for Scientific Research in Paris.

Pierre Vermersch trained as a psychologist at the University of Aix en Provence before joining CNRS in Paris. His doctorate is in cognitive psychology. Since 1988 he has developed an interviewing technique designed to produce a detailed verbalization of a specific lived experience. He is examining the foundations of modern psychology with a view to laying the foundations of first- and second-person methodology.

Alan Wallace trained for ten years in Buddhist monasteries in India and Switzerland and has taught Buddhist theory and practice in Europe and America since 1976. He has served as interpreter for numerous Tibetan scholars, including H.H. the Dalai Lama. He earned a doctorate in religious studies at Stanford University and currently teaches that subject at the University of California, Santa Barbara.

Journal of Consciousness Studies

Tenth Anniversary Volume (2003)

Journal of Consciousness Studies

Volume 11, No.6-7

controversies in science and the humanities

Trusting
the Subject?
Part 2

Journal of Consciousness Studies

controversies in science & the humanities

Volume 10, No.1 (2003)

The double life of B.F. Skinner

'With *JCS*, consciousness studies has arrived'
Susan Greenfield, *Times Higher Education Supplement*

The Cognitive Approach to Conscious Machines

Pentti O. Haikonen

Could a machine have an immaterial mind? The author argues that true conscious machines can be built, but rejects artificial intelligence and classical neural networks in favour of the emulation of the cognitive processes of the brain—the flow of inner speech, inner imagery and emotions. This results in a non-numeric meaning-processing machine with distributed information representation and system reactions. It is argued that this machine would be conscious; it would be aware of its own existence and its mental content and perceive this as immaterial. Novel views on consciousness and the mind–body problem are presented. This book is a must for anyone interested in consciousness research and the latest ideas in the forthcoming technology of mind.

The author is Principal Scientist, Cognitive Technology, Nokia Research

300 pages   £14.95/$24.95   0907845_428 (pbk.)

Trusting the Subject?

Anthony Jack and Andreas Roepstorff (eds.)

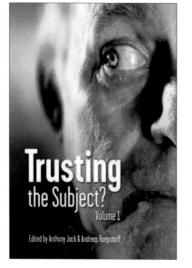

Introspective evidence is still treated with great suspicion in cognitive science. This book is designed to encourage cognitive scientists to take more account of the subject's unique perspective. Confirmed contributors include Bernard Baars, Rodney Cotterill, Richard Cytowic, Patrick Haggard, Chris Frith, Uta Frith, Shaun Gallagher, Russell Hurlburt, Oliver Kauffmann, Donald Laming, David Leopold, Nikos Logothetis, Anthony Marcel, Josef Parnas Jonathan Schooler and Dan Zahavi

250 pages   £14.95/$24.95   0907845_568 (pbk.)

Psi Wars:
Getting to grips with the paranormal

ed. James Alcock, Jean Burns & Anthony Freeman

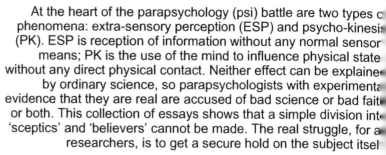

At the heart of the parapsychology (psi) battle are two types of phenomena: extra-sensory perception (ESP) and psycho-kinesis (PK). ESP is reception of information without any normal sensory means; PK is the use of the mind to influence physical state without any direct physical contact. Neither effect can be explained by ordinary science, so parapsychologists with experimental evidence that they are real are accused of bad science or bad faith or both. This collection of essays shows that a simple division into 'sceptics' and 'believers' cannot be made. The real struggle, for all researchers, is to get a secure hold on the subject itself.

"Authoritative and accessible review of the state of scientific research into paranormal phenomena . . . Anyone seeking something more sophisticated than the usual mud-slinging should buy this book.
Robert Matthews, *New Scientist*

250 pages   £14.95/$24.95   0907845_487 (pbk)

The Volitional Brain: Towards a neuroscience of free will

Benjamin Libet *et al.* (eds.)

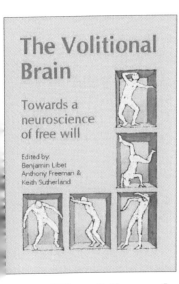

It is widely accepted in science that the universe is a closed deterministic system in which everything can, ultimately, be explained by purely physical causation. And yet we all experience ourselves as having the freedom to choose between alternatives presented to us— 'we' are in the driving seat. The authors, including Guy Claxton, Chris Frith, Gilberto Gomes, David Hodgson, David Ingvar, Jaron Lanier, E.J. Lowe, John McCrone, Wolfgang Schultz, Jeffrey Schwartz, Sean Spence, Henry Stapp and David Wilson, address this puzzling issue.

'The collection is wide-ranging in its scope and reports some fascinating empirical work on the brain activity that underlies volition.' **TLS**
'A timely compilation of essays.' **Contemporary Psychology**

320 pages   £14.95/$24.95   0907845_118 (pbk.)

The View from Within: First-person approaches to the study of consciousness

Francisco J. Varela & Jonathan Shear (eds.)

The study of conscious experience *per se* has not kept pace with the dramatic advances in brain-scanning technologies. If anything, the standard approaches to examining the 'view from within' involve little more than cataloguing its readily accessible components. Thus the study of lived subjective experience is still at the level of Aristotelian science, leading to a widespread scepticism over the possibility of a truly scientific study of conscious experience. Drawing on a wide range of approaches—from phenomenology to meditation—*The View from Within* examines the possibility of a disciplined, practical approach to the study of subjective states.

'The publication is very timely indeed. It is a splendid initiative.' **TLS**

320 pages   £15.00/$25.00   0907845_258 (pbk.)

Between Ourselves: Second-person issues in the study of consciousness

Evan Thompson (ed.)

Second-person 'I–You' relations are central to human life yet have been neglected in consciousness research. This book puts that right utilising a wide-range of approaches—including phenomenology, meditation, studies of empathy and autism, the physiology of mirror neurons and the ethology of animal 'person-to-person' interactions. Contributors include Jonathan Cole, Shaun Gallagher, Vittorio Gallese, Eduard Marbach, Barbara Smuts, Sue Savage-Rumbaugh and Francisco Varela.

'I highly recommend the collection . . . should be looked at by anyone who wants to think about what form a phenomenological contribution to some of the problems of cognitive science might take.' **Human Nature Review**

314 pages   £14.95/$24.95   0907845_142 (pbk.)

The Varieties of Religious Experience: Centenary Essays

Michel Ferrari (ed.)

The Varieties of Religious Experience: Centenary Essays

Edited by Michel Ferrari

William James published his classic work on the psychology of religion, *The Varieties of Religious Experience*, in 1902. To mark the centenary, leading contemporary scholars reflect on changes in our understanding of the questions James addressed—changes due in no small part to research that was stimulated by the book itself. Contributors include Eugene Taylor, Eleanor Rosch, G. William Barnard, Jens Brockmeier, Keith Oatley, Maja Djikic and Martin E. Marty. Editor Michel Ferrari teaches in the Department of Human Development at Toronto Univ.

'I couldn't put it down'. **Nicholas Humphrey**

160 pages   £14.95/$24.95   0907845_266 (pbk.)

Cognitive Models and Spiritual Maps

Jensine Andresen & Robert K.C. Forman (eds.)

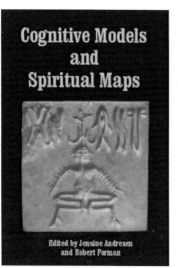

This book throws down a challenge to the field of religious studies, offering a multidisciplinary approach—including developmental psychology, neuropsychology, philosophy of mind and anthropology. Contents: **Jensine Andresen**, *Experimental research on meditation*; **Arthur Deikman**, *A functional approach to mysticism*; **Stanley Krippner**, *Shamanic states*; **Phillip Wiebe**, *Christic visions;* **Ken Wilber**, *Waves, streams, states and self*; **Christian de Quincey**, *The promise of integralism*; **Brian Lancaster**, *Cognitive models and spiritual maps*; **James Austin**, *Consciousness evolves when self dissolves*; **Andrew Newberg and Eugene d'Aquili**, *The neuropsychology of religious experience*; **Robert Sharf**, *The rhetoric of experience.*

'A thoroughly gripping read .' **Human Nature Review**

288 pages   £14.95/$24.95   0907845_134 (pbk.)

Evolutionary Origins of Morality

Leonard D. Katz (ed.)

Four principal papers and a total of 43 peer commentaries on the evolutionary origins of morality. (1) Jessica Flack and Frans de Waal ask if human morality is the outcome of a continuous development from social behaviour found in nonhuman animals. (2) Christopher Boehm synthesizes social science and biological evidence to support his theory of how our hominid ancestors became moral. (3) Elliott Sober and David Sloan Wilson argue that an evolutionary understanding of human nature allows sacrifice for others. (4) Brian Skyrms argues that game theory based on adaptive dynamics must join the social scientist's use of rational choice and classical game theory to explain cooperation.

'The papers are without exception excellent.' **Biology and Philosophy**
'Psychologists will find much to enjoy in this meaty volume.' **APA Rev.Bks**
'Provides a wonderfully rich range of viewpoints.' **J. Moral Education**

368 pages   £14.95/$24.95   0907845_07X (pbk.)